Terms of Exclusion

Terms of Exclusion

Rightful Citizenship Claims and the
Construction of LGBT Political Identity

ZEIN MURIB

OXFORD
UNIVERSITY PRESS

OXFORD
UNIVERSITY PRESS

Oxford University Press is a department of the University of Oxford. It furthers
the University's objective of excellence in research, scholarship, and education
by publishing worldwide. Oxford is a registered trade mark of Oxford University
Press in the UK and certain other countries.

Published in the United States of America by Oxford University Press
198 Madison Avenue, New York, NY 10016, United States of America.

Library of Congress Cataloging-in-Publication Data
Names: Murib, Zein, author.
Title: Terms of exclusion : rightful citizenship claims and
the construction of LGBT political identity / Zein Murib.
Description: New York, NY : Oxford University Press, 2023. |
Includes bibliographical references and index.
Identifiers: LCCN 2023017318 (print) | LCCN 2023017319 (ebook) |
ISBN 9780197671504 (paperback) | ISBN 9780197671498 (hardback) |
ISBN 9780197671528 (epub)
Subjects: LCSH: Sexual minorities—Political activity—United States. |
Sexual minorities—Civil rights—United States.
Classification: LCC HQ73.73.U6 M87 2023 (print) | LCC HQ73.73.U6 (ebook) |
DDC 306.760973—dc23/eng/20230516
LC record available at https://lccn.loc.gov/2023017318
LC ebook record available at https://lccn.loc.gov/2023017319

DOI: 10.1093/oso/9780197671498.001.0001

Paperback printed by Marquis Book Printing, Canada
Hardback printed by Bridgeport National Bindery, Inc., United States of America

For my mother, Zeina Mikati, with love.

Contents

Acknowledgments

I began research for this project on sexuality, gender, race, and belonging in 2012, the same year that a group of LGBTQ political scientists and their allies boycotted the American Political Science Association meeting scheduled to take place in New Orleans. At that time, Louisiana had some of the harshest penalties for LGBTQ people simply existing in public space as well as the largest population of incarcerated people per capita in the world. Although the conference was ultimately cancelled by Hurricane Isaac—and not APSA—many of my colleagues who study sexuality, race, and politics have not forgotten the discipline's unwillingness to stand in solidarity with those cast to the margins of social and political life. I lay out that brief history to underscore that beginning this research at that time was a challenge and could not have happened without the creativity, mentorship, and support from everybody who helped me to develop this project. I want to acknowledge the valuable direction on framing, archives, and methods from Ron Aminzade, Terri Caraway, Kathleen Hull, Daniel Kelliher, Regina Kunzel, August Nimtz, Katherine Pearson, Joan Tronto, and David Samuels. Huge thanks to my small circle of early readers and mentors at the University of Minnesota: Andrew Karch, Kevin Murphy, Joe Soss, and Dara Strolovitch. I owe Dara thanks for a great many things, not least of which is sharing early on that there are aspects of her published work she would change. That valuable bit of wisdom taught me that writing is never done (even if it means I write 11 drafts of a research proposal), and freed me from the voice that so often gets in the way of making progress on the page.

Friends at the University of Minnesota made starting the research that became this book more fun and provided opportunities to practice describing the "So what?" of this work. In political science, I want to thank Pelin Azer Binnet, Phil Chen, Charmaine Chua, Brooke Coe, Adam Dahl, Elena Gambino, Matt Hindman, Chase Hobbs Morgan, Mark Hoffman, Anthony Pahnke, Maron Sorenson, David Temin, and Magic Wade. I owe thanks to Diane Detournay in GWSS for the initial spark of recognition in 2012 that helped set this project in motion. I wouldn't have made it through Minnesota's long winters without Hilarie and Caitlin Conboy's friendship, dog walks, Common Roots/Wilson Library writing dates, and countless home-cooked dinners; thank you with all my heart for being family.

I benefited from the expertise of several archivists as I conducted this research. Thanks to Brenda Marston at Cornell University's Human Sexuality Collection, Patricia Delara at the San Francisco GLBT Historical Society, and the crew of librarians at the New York Public Library who assisted me with the Stephen Donaldson Collection. Finally, I want to express my heartfelt appreciation for the many individuals who had the foresight to preserve and digitize the primary sources that are a key part of this book, including Perry Brass for *Come Out!*, Dallas Denny for *AEGIS*, Urvashi Vaid for the extensive documentation of the National Policy Roundtables, and Steven Donaldson's personal archive on bisexuality.

Various fellowships and grants provided the financial resources necessary to complete the archival research for this book, including a University of Minnesota Doctoral Dissertation Fellowship and Political Science Doctoral Completion Fellowship, the Cornell University Zwickler Memorial Research Grant for the Human Sexuality Collection, and a Fordham Faculty Research Grant. Thanks, too, to my mom and dad for extending a financial safety net when I needed it so I could pursue a career that is uncertain and far from lucrative.

Fordham University has been my academic home while I finished this book. Many thanks to Christina Greer for enthusiastically and generously cheering me on and answering any and all questions about book writing, academia, and teaching. Anjali Dayal rescued me one summer afternoon by sharing her "writing journal" practice, which is a document where I deposited all the writing I was too anxious to delete. Nothing happens at FCLC without Annmarie O'Connor, and I want to give her a heartfelt shoutout for the countless ways she makes my professional life easier. Ida Bastiaens, Bob Hume, Sarah Lockhart, Annika Marten, Monika McDermott, Olena Nikoyanko, and Nick Tampio all offered useful advice as I began this book project. FCLC is a wonderfully interdisciplinary environment, and I want to thank those who invite me along as they make space for those dialogues: Shonni Enelow, Anne Fernald, Laurie Lambert, Yuko Miki, and Dennis Tyler. A group of students took every class I offered between 2016 and 2020. I want to acknowledge their help in shaping the development of many of the ideas in this book through our classroom discussions and thank them for the excitement, support, and friendship they extended to me as I finished it: Yunuen Cho, Aniqa Chowdhury, Rushaid Mithani, Steven Thomas, and Alyana Vera.

Connections with colleagues working in the sub-subfield of sexuality and politics are the highlight of doing this work. I am tremendously grateful to interlocutors at the American Political Science Association and Western Political Science Association meetings for incisive feedback and fostering such fruitful shared spaces for thinking about how to study and do queer politics: Phil Ayoub, Cynthia Burack, Susan Burgess, Courtenay Daum, Heath Fogg Davis, Andrew Flores, Alison Gash, Cyril Ghosh, Isabel Felix Gonzales, Ed Kammerer, Ravi Perry, Erin Mayo-Adam, Samantha Majic, Melissa Michaelson, Julie Novkov, Ken Sherrill, Tony Smith, Jami Taylor, Jerry Queer Thomas, Tiffany Willoughby Herard, Joanna Wuest, and last but certainly not least, my conference spouse, Lisa Beard. Thanks to my gender and politics people for the opportunities to think together on various strands of thought that make up this book: Cristina Beltrán, Jocelyn Boryczka, Nadia Brown, Liza Taylor, Erica Townsend Bell, and Denise Walsh.

Many thanks to Angela Chnapko at Oxford University Press for being excited about this project and asking important questions about how the arguments can be forecast to contemporary politics. I am also sincerely indebted to the two anonymous reviewers whose comments helped me to refine the framework and interventions.

I like to joke that moving to New York City taught me that I made all the friends I would ever have. I am thankful to Sam Majic and John Rasmussen, Ilana Savdie, and Jesse Willis for proving me wrong. I'm especially grateful to Ilana for the use of her artwork, "The Enablers," on this cover. Her brightly-colored (i.e., aggressively queer) abstraction of people attempting to breach walls calls into question who belongs on the inside as well as what it means to have a body, and I am excited that our work is in conversation in this way.

My brother Shad Murib and his wife, Kerry Donovan, actually do the hard work of politics. I want to thank them for their political hot takes, steadfast support, air sign levity, reassuring pep talks, high-intensity (and high-altitude) workouts, and title suggestions. (Unfortunately "Harry Potter and Wizard Rights" didn't . . . fly.)

In the final stages, Maura Finkelstein read this book several times and with painstaking care. She urged me to bring my voice to the arguments and was instrumental in helping me meet my goal of "making things a little weird." There are innumerable reasons to thank her, but the stakes of being succinct are incredibly high so I'll borrow from Whitney Houston, who said all the important things best: my dearest Maura, thanks for taking a chance on a love that burns hot enough to last.

Writing is an isolating activity under normal circumstances, and was even more so in the context of the pandemic that occurred while I was finalizing this book. My one true love forever, Oscar, snored beside me through all the iterations of this book for over a decade and was always up for a walk to help me break through writer's block, jusqu'à la fin. I'm not sure how to express the extent of gratitude I have for my therapist, Charlotte Curtis, except to say that I have found myself on the other end of a challenging time—and for the better—because of the work we did together and her unwavering care. I am deeply grateful to Lyndsey Augé for bringing so much lightness and effervescence to my COVID bubble. Thank you to Alicia Simoni for the many years of meandering late-night talks that touched on everything and nothing all at once and welcoming me to her home in Northampton with Quinn, Liam, and Kellan when I needed a retreat from New York. To my queer chosen family of the CSV, Rebecca Trinité (and Sam and Lucy) and Alyza Jehangir (and Jack and Poppy, who generously hosted me during research trips to the Bay Area): I am sorry I never did the homework for the weekly discussions that truly sustained me during the time I was writing this book, but I hope that you'll understand why when you read it. Thank you for the unconditional love, support, and secure attachment.

Finally: my mom, Zeina Mikati. She brought her Virgo powers of critique to all matters at hand and especially delighted in tearing politicians and political events to shreds (imagine a tiny Lebanese Bernie Sanders). I learned to think and talk about politics from her, and my goal in writing this book was to produce scholarship that she and others like her who find themselves students of power and politics due to the volatility of war and migration might understand and enjoy. Beyond these lofty aspirations, there's not a day that goes by that I don't think about something sharp she said to make me laugh or some loving bit of wisdom she shared, and in these ways her memory infuses every word and thought here. This book is for her.

Introduction

A Seat at the Table

> Initially, I was embraced by the stakeholders of the mainstream
> LGBT movement. I quickly noticed that despite the unifying ac-
> ronym, the people at the table often did not reflect me or my com-
> munity. These spaces and the conversations were dominated by
> men, specifically upper-middle-class white cis gay men. Women,
> people of color, trans folks, and especially folks who carried multiple
> identities were all but absent. I was grateful for the invitation but un-
> fulfilled by the company. This was my political awakening.
>
> —Janet Mock, Redefining Realness, 2014

In June 2015, an undocumented transgender activist named Jennicet
Gutiérrez staged a protest during President Obama's opening of LGBT Pride
festivities at the White House.[1] The event convened many prominent lesbian,
gay, bisexual, and transgender activists and political leaders to celebrate what
was expected to be a positive outcome in the Supreme Court case regarding
the legal status of same-sex marriages. Gutiérrez seized the spotlight of that
highly publicized gathering and interrupted Obama's speech, in which he
praised the progress made by the LGBT group in pursuit of civil rights, by
loudly calling for the end of the Immigration and Customs Enforcement
(ICE) policy of housing detainees by sex. Her protests alternated between
two messages: demanding the end of incarcerating migrants at the border
and underscoring the stakes of this practice by highlighting the disproportionate incidences of transgender women sexually assaulted—and dying—
while in ICE detention.[2]

Although staging loud, disruptive protests has been a hallmark tactic used
by lesbian, gay, bisexual, and transgender people since the 1960s, and while
this was a gathering of political actors well versed in that history, the other

Terms of Exclusion. Zein Murib, Oxford University Press. © Oxford University Press 2023.
DOI: 10.1093/oso/9780197671498.003.0001

attendees at the White House Pride event did not join Gutiérrez's protest in a show of unity and solidarity or maintain respectful silence as she articulated her demands. They instead met her calls to abolish ICE and end deportations with loud booing and shouts to drown out her voice. Perhaps most vocally, one participant near Gutiérrez repeatedly attempted to silence her by explaining, "This is not for you. This is for all of us."[3] The question of who, exactly, comprises the "us" to whom the speaker referred was answered when the booing and jeering quickly changed into clapping and cheers as Gutiérrez was ultimately ejected from the room by the Secret Service. Obama rode the wave of applause by joking to the crowd, "As a general rule, I'm fine with a few hecklers, but not when I'm up in the House." He then went on to observe, "You know, my attitude is if you're eating the hors d'oeuvres and drinking the booze," pausing dramatically before continuing, "Anyway, where was I?"[4]

Some readers might be surprised by Obama's derisive response. After all, he built his presidency around being a community organizer with professed sympathies for those cast to the margins of political life. And he made strides to recast the White House as "the People's House" during his time in office.[5] What at first blush appears to be a contradiction, however, gains some clarity with the knowledge that the Department of Homeland Security under his administration boasted of conducting 462,463 "removals and returns" of undocumented migrants in 2015, which earned him the nickname "deporter in chief" among immigration activists.[6] Obama's joke at the event reflected this legacy as it played off the xenophobic trope of migrants as parasites who feed off the wealth of the United States. In making these comments, he revealed the limits around who constitutes "us," with implications for who belongs in the literal "House" or the figurative nation. Similarly, those in the room who laughed at his dismissive joke revealed how the extension of certain rights to gay men and lesbians was acceptable, if not also expected. However, those rights were certainly not to be extended to an undocumented transgender woman from Mexico who was drawing attention to the harms perpetrated by a federal agency against the most precarious members of the LGBT group at the border.

Public discourse in LGBT and mainstream media acknowledged the urgency of the immigration issues articulated by Gutiérrez while also debating the tactics she used. Those in favor of Gutiérrez's disruption cited the historic importance of a 1992 protest staged by ACT-UP (the Aids Coalition to Unleash Power), during which activists scattered ashes of people who died of AIDS on the White House lawn to urge the attention of the federal government to the epidemic.[7] Other commentators passionately advocated for less "rude" approaches, which they explained should focus on gaining rights through traditional channels such as litigation and lobbying.[8] These ongoing disputes over strategies and goals played out against the backdrop of the Supreme Court's decision in *Obergefell v. Hodges*, issued the following day, in which Justice Anthony Kennedy's majority opinion cited the Equal Protection and Due Process clauses of the Fourteenth Amendment to legally authorize marriages between same-sex couples across the United States. The attention Gutiérrez brought to the issues facing undocumented transgender women proved fleeting, as many of the political actors who attended the White House ceremony seized what they perceived to be a historic moment to celebrate the importance of achieving rights and equality. James Obergefell, the plaintiff in the case, marked the win by taking to the steps of the Supreme Court to explain the pain caused by Ohio's refusal to recognize his marriage even though he lived, worked, and paid taxes in the state for the duration of his marriage to his husband, John Arthur. After solemnly observing that "no American should have to endure that indignity," Obergefell triumphantly announced to the roars of the crowd, "Now, our love is equal!"[9] Beth Shipp, executive director of LPAC (Lesbian Political Action Committee), echoed this appeal to rights wrongfully denied. She said in an interview, "We seem to be at an incredible point in our LGBT history, on the precipice of full equality," before going on to explain that enduring patterns of discrimination experienced by lesbian and queer women threaten "political equality and our personal freedoms" and that she hoped settling the marriage question would allow more attention to be directed to these concerns regarding women's political and social status.[10] Vice President Joe Biden also joined the celebration, issuing a statement saying that the Court's decision marked a victory for "[p]eople of absolute courage who risked their lives, jobs, and reputations to come forward in pursuit of the basic right recognized today, but at a time when neither the country nor the courts would protect or defend them."[11] From all corners of political and social life and within just 24 hours, the urgency of addressing transgender women in ICE detention was eclipsed by a chorus of voices celebrating the positive effects of making appeals to rights and achieving equality as citizens.

These events in June 2015 succinctly capture the persistent tensions that define the history of lesbian, gay, bisexual, and transgender politics in the United States, namely the questions of who comprises these identity-based groups and which political objectives ought to be advanced on their behalf.

The chapters in this book examine the production of lesbian, gay, bisexual, transgender, and LGBT political identities, focusing on how, why, and to what effect struggles over inclusion shaped what comes to be known of those identity-based groups and their political agendas. I argue that erasures like the one Gutiérrez confronted that day at the White House are to be expected, and that they are put into motion by what I term throughout this book as "rightful citizenship claims." More specifically, when political actors articulate grievances and proposals for resolving them based on the presumption that the state is deliberately denying certain rights to which claimants are entitled to as citizens, they explicitly assert their status as normative citizens who, but for their difference, would be folded into the rights and protections guaranteed by the state. Claims to rights and citizenship function in this way because, as feminist studies scholar Amy Brandzel argues, the denial or extension of citizenship to certain groups is an anti-intersectional epistemology employed by the state, "whereby the categories of race, Indigeneity, gender, and sexuality are segregated and set in opposition to each other . . . *to safeguard normative citizenship.*"[12] Political actors representing nondominant and marginalized groups implicitly recognize these lessons about rights and citizenship when they make demands on the state that articulate a group's proximity to normative citizenship with claims such as "Our love is equal" or "We are Americans entitled to rights" and ignore that not all members of the group are citizens or that there are varying degrees of citizenship rights shaped by race, class, gender, indigeneity, disability, and religion. Stating how a group's members are like the prototypical normative citizen consequently comes at the cost of shedding differences that are perceived as potentially imperiling the group's opportunity for recognition and inclusion as citizens. I argue throughout this book that it is the erasure of these differences that give rhetorical weight to the relatively advantaged subgroup's assertion that they are entitled to wrongfully denied citizenship rights. As a result, within-group marginalization and exclusions under the banner of rightful citizenship claims define and reinforce the boundaries of the group in the mold of the prototypical rights bearing citizen: White, heterosexual, middle class, gender normative, able-bodied, and male.[13] These patterns of within-group marginalization endure in contemporary politics even as gay men, lesbians, bisexuals, and transgender people have been ostensibly unified as a political identity group that journalists, academics, politicians, and the members themselves refer to as "LGBT," or what legal scholar Dean Spade revealingly calls "LGB . . . fake T" and others mock by explaining that "the B is silent."[14]

Put another way, and returning to the events that open this book, at perpetual issue are two intertwined questions: Who constitutes the "us" of the LGBT group? Which issues on the LGBT political agenda are prioritized as a result?

Consider, for example, the contested narrative of who set in motion the resistance to a routine police raid of a small gay bar in New York City called The Stonewall Inn on June 28, 1969. Widely hailed as the turning point that inaugurated modern gay politics, the instigation of the riots has been given several origin stories. Some cite two transgender women of color, Sylvia Rivera and Marsha P. Johnson, as starting the protests. Others attribute the uprising to Stormé DeLarverie, a Black butch lesbian who was named the "mother of the Stonewall riots" in her *Washington Post* obituary. Or, in the most recent popular retelling by filmmaker Roland Emmerich, a White gay man from Indiana in an Oxford shirt and boat shoes named Danny throws the first brick.[15] The competing versions of this story and the vehemence with which proponents advance them suggests that claiming who started the riots that night is about much more than a desire for historical accuracy; it is a dispute over who belongs in the group as well as which goals should define the group's political objectives and strategies after Stonewall. Would political concerns advanced by gay-identified people be an extension of the political uprisings at the time, including Black Power, feminism, and the antiwar movement? Or would goals advanced under the banner of "gay politics" be focused on seeking social and political inclusion for gay-identified people? And what is the place of transgender people, especially trans people of color, within "the movement"? Although historians are generally in agreement that the political mobilizations immediately after Stonewall were radical in nature, the contemporary uptake of the Stonewall narrative by scholars, politicians, and pundits also refers to it as the germinal moment for some of the more visible political struggles made in the name of lesbian, gay, bisexual, and transgender people over the intervening years. These include gains that might be considered less radical and more geared toward assimilation and inclusion, such as hate crimes protections, same-sex marriage, and the opportunity for gay men and lesbians to serve openly in the military. Over time, these competing understandings of the Stonewall narrative have been woven together into a teleological account of radical goals naturally giving way to more "viable" and "realistic" demands, most notably claims to rights, and that these achievements are what lesbians, gay men, bisexuals, and transgender people are celebrating each June during Pride.

To some degree, this turn to rights is a logical and strategically sound move in the context of U.S. politics, where the perceived successes of the Black civil rights movement serve as a useful frame for nondominant groups to adopt as they contest institutionalized oppressions. Thanks to the prominence of this narrative, social movement activists and interest group advocates alike prioritize rights claims, which have the benefit of coming with time-proven modes of political action. These include seeking rights through the courts, agitating for legislative interventions, targeting voters with sympathetic pleas in referendum drives, and, as Alison Gash puts it, pursuing rights "below the radar" so as to not attract backlash.[16] The Supreme Court, in particular, has played a key role in these battles as it is widely viewed as legitimizing and ameliorating political grievances that include drawing attention to the injustices of Black people being denied opportunities to exercise the right to vote, women being foreclosed access to reproductive technologies such as birth control and abortions, and bans on marriages for gay men and lesbians. Although conventional wisdom about rights won through the Court holds that these gains are durable over time, recent developments suggest that this tendency might be shifting. In a major blow to the victories won by the Black civil rights movement, the Court's 2013 decision in *Shelby v. Holder* hollowed out Section 5 of the Voting Rights Act. That ruling eliminated the requirement that any changes to voting laws be precleared and consequently paved the way for discriminatory voting laws to disenfranchise Black, Asian, Latine, Native, young, and unhoused voters.[17] And in 2022, the Court repealed *Roe v. Wade* with their decision in *Dobbs v. Jackson Women's Health Organization*, which scholars argue will create a tiered system of abortion access: wealthy people in some states will be able to access abortions, while others will be forced to carry pregnancies to term, even if it costs them their lives.[18]

This book draws on feminist and queer theory to put forward a new interpretation of rights claims as a political strategy for marginalized groups that anticipates the instability of rights gains for nondominant groups. The historical analysis of the construction of lesbian, gay, bisexual, transgender, and, ultimately, "LGBT" political identities in the following chapters shows that the dominant account of rights claims as the most effective and successful way to address political marginalization obscures that not all segments of what has come to called the "LGBT community" have benefited from these gains and that some groups might, in fact, be even more socially and politically precarious than they were before the Stonewall riots in 1969.[19] For instance, the 50th anniversary of Stonewall in 2019 marked a year when 26 transgender women of color were murdered, LGBTQ-identified youth of color were overrepresented in the criminal justice system, and lesbian, gay, bisexual, and transgender people seeking asylum at the border were regularly incarcerated and deported. Although 2020 was a historic year that saw the election of more lesbian, gay, bisexual, and/or transgender representatives to political office at all levels of government than ever before, it was also a year that saw the beginning of successful efforts to enshrine into law discrimination against transgender people, especially transgender youth.[20] In 2022 alone, hundreds of bills were introduced and many were passed in state legislatures to ban transgender youth from participating in sports or accessing lifesaving medical care.[21]

The historical analysis that I present in the following chapters focuses on the discourse of lesbian, gay, bisexual, transgender, and LGBT political identity construction and political agenda development for answers to the questions raised by these contradictory developments. Examining two sets of documents that comprise my archive of evidence—lesbian, gay, bisexual, and transgender publications alongside interest group and social movement internal documents that include speeches by leaders, lobbying notes, and accounts of internal debates over strategy—reveals that political actors working in the name of these identity-based groups from the moment right after the Stonewall riots in 1969 and through the introduction and adoption of "LGBT" by interest groups in 2001 engaged in countless decisions to deploy rightful citizenship claims, which, in turn, elevated the interests of those members who are considered more proximate to normative citizenship. Focusing on discursive struggles over agenda development allows me to show how these choices were made despite objections raised by LGBT people of color, lesbians, transgender people, and bisexuals who continuously articulated concerns that the emphasis on rightful citizenship claims would cast them to the margins of the evolving LGBT group and erase their unique political interests. I underscore these debates and fissures in this historical analysis of lesbian, gay, bisexual, transgender, and LGBT political organizing to highlight that political leaders crafting the strategy of rightful citizenship claims did so with full knowledge that certain members would be closed out of potential political successes. The speeches, articles, internal organization notes, and transcripts of meetings analyzed in this book show that they persisted despite these objections due to the belief that pursuing rights is the only politically viable approach and would consequently be the most expedient route to political gains and shifting negative stigmas.

Placing the negotiations over inclusion front and center in this book intervenes in debates among scholars, political leaders, and pundits of LGBTQ politics about the benefits and costs of assimilation contra radical political objectives, which tends to hold the proponents of these approaches apart or set them in opposition to each other.[22] "Assimilation" is used in these conversations to refer to political praxis that seeks inclusion and recognition in existing systems, and "radical" is used to describe political praxis that advocates for upending institutions and laws that structure and maintain social and political hierarchies. I introduce "rightful citizenship claims" to enter these discussions and disrupt this binary framework. Focusing on the discursive effects of rightful citizenship claims—specifically the exclusions enacted as a result of their deployment—shows that it is not simply the case that radical political goals gave way to assimilation. Instead, my analysis reveals that political actors who are typically glossed as assimilationist or radical with the benefit of hindsight were actually all participating in overlapping political organizations and engaged in protracted negotiations with each other over the boundaries of group identities and the agendas that would be advocated.[23] I argue that what is assumed to distinguish nominally assimilationist and radical approaches to lesbian, gay, bisexual, transgender, and LGBT political identities and political agendas were in practice competing views over who ought to be included in political mobilizations, and the question was often settled by considering which members would be most conducive to advancing successful rightful citizenship claims. Political theorist Sina Kramer terms the deliberate shedding of differences that result from such strategic maneuvers "constitutive exclusions," whereby "exclusion secures the fantasy of a fully intelligible political agency on the 'inside'" that relies upon casting those excluded as mad, wild, or criminal.[24] In other words, what we have come to think of as discrete assimilationist and radical movements were in fact produced through efforts by some political actors to secure normative status, which relied on the designation of a radical "other" to be excluded. I build on Kramer's thinking here to argue that what we have come to know as unique political identities and political interests are not extensions of essential traits or even logical outgrowths of fervent beliefs about political praxis. The analysis in this book shows that these differences are produced by political actors themselves, as they engaged in ongoing and dynamic processes of identity construction that included some individuals as members and relegated those invested in more radical objectives and tactics as deviant, illogical, and politically unsophisticated. In this view, the evolution of an "LGBT movement" increasingly focused on rights for White gay men (and some lesbians) is not the product of a teleological advancement toward a more logical political strategy but rather one marked by a series of ruptures and discontinuities that continue to inform and give shape to inequalities to this day.

The construction of a dominant lesbian, gay, bisexual, transgender, or LGBT subject is consequently the production of two sets of identities: those that are folded into the fabric of normative citizenship and those that that are deliberately foreclosed from membership in the polity to abet the former's entry. Take, for example, the emergence of "queer" as a political identity category and political agenda in the 1990s and early 2000s. I show in the chapter on LGBT political identity construction that "queer" was developed as an alternative identification by those who saw themselves outside the boundaries of the increasingly rights-focused LGBT group. This includes political actors who advocated for goals that might be considered tailored to individuals at the intersection of many different axes of identity beyond sexuality, such as prison abolition, immigration battles, or the decriminalization of sex work.[25] Over time and as a result of the departure of these newly identified queer-identified people from LGBT organizations, what it meant to be a member of the LGBT group solidified as a professed affinity for rights claims and an interest in electoral gains. LGBT political identity further secured its legibility in contrast with queer as anticategorical and thus a critical orientation to power. These meanings associated with queer identity and political praxis, in turn, achieved salience by forcing an explicit break with "LGBT politics," which queer-identified political actors accused of propping up harmful ideologies such as heteronormativity and White supremacy that allowed institutions such as mass incarceration, capitalism, and militarized policing of the border to endure and contribute to the vulnerability and death of queer people understood intersectionally.

In highlighting these dynamic, recursive, and perpetual processes of identity construction and agenda development, this book joins political science scholarship that draws on intersectionality to explore the development of political identities, such as Christina Beltrán's 2007 work on Latino political identity construction and Cathy Cohen's 1999 study of Black political identity.[26] Like Beltrán and Cohen, the analysis I conduct in this book uses intersectionality as a lens to critically examine the ways that structural and ideological factors create the conditions for the elevation of certain members of the group and erasure or minimization of others. As Kimberlé Williams

Crenshaw argues in her 1989 article that introduced "intersectionality" to the academic lexicon, the theory draws attention to the unique experiences of harm produced within liberal frameworks that name specific axes of identity in legal protections and simultaneously erase or occlude consideration for individuals located at the intersection of several axes of identity. In one of Crenshaw's examples, the case of employment discrimination brought by Black women in *Degraffenreid v. General Motors* is not decided in their favor because the judge reasoned that under the last-one-in-first-one-out policy of General Motors, Black men were not fired at the same time as Black women, nor were White women, and thus no racial or gender discrimination occurred. Without the benefit of intersectionality, this decision seems rational. But taking an intersectional view, Crenshaw explains, reveals that Black women were fired first due to a company policy of not hiring Black women until 1964, long after policies denying Black men and White women employment were reversed. Crenshaw concludes, "Because the intersectional experience is greater than the sum of racism and sexism, any analysis that does not take intersectionality into account cannot sufficiently address the particular manner in which Black women are subordinated."[27] Following Crenshaw, in this book I focus on the possibilities and perils of rightful citizenship claims and logic in shaping what comes to be known of groups, asking which members of the group are highlighted as representative when rightful citizenship claims are made, which members are organized out as a result, and to what effect.

Asking questions informed by intersectionality as a theory and approach to understanding marginalization also puts this book in conversation with social science research on political representation, specifically Dara Strolovitch's study of interest group advocacy that empirically demonstrates the persistent and pervasive ways that relatively disadvantaged members are left out of interest group representation. Like Strolovitch, I am concerned with who is excluded from political mobilizations and to what effect, and I build on her findings by focusing on the discourse of political actors at the helm of interest groups and social movements, as well as the members themselves, to show how certain members are constructed outside the boundaries of a political identity group and thus denied representation. Approaching identities as dependent variables, or political outcomes to explain, thus constitutes a significant break from the dominant paradigm of studying identity that is popular in quantitative scholarship, which tends to view identities as static, binary, and mutually exclusive. Theorizing the effects of rightful citizenship claims and discursive processes of identity construction opens up this line of inquiry to shed light on the processes through which a wide range of identity-based groups take shape, especially those comprised of heterogeneous membership and characterized by contests over who will be included and which interests will be advanced. These possibilities for generalizability include political movements for people with disabilities, mobilizations by undocumented migrants, and Black Lives Matter.

Finally, this book directly engages a growing body of scholarship by political scientists interested in exploring the promise and peril of rights claims made by marginalized groups and, with them, bids for inclusion and recognition. Courtenay Daum argues that efforts to have transgender people protected by nondiscrimination laws would do little to alter the structural and ideological sources of anti-transgender bias that intersectionally marginalized transgender people would face.[28] Conversely, Erin Mayo-Adam argues that what she terms "rights episodes"—when the rights that groups enjoy or are entitled to come under fire—serve the valuable purpose of facilitating movement coalitions.[29] These coordinated mobilizations, however, tend not to survive past winning the rights targeted, which means that activists who are left behind by rights wins ultimately fail to see their interests met. Daum and Mayo-Adam are concerned about what happens after rights claims are won. If, as these scholars suggest, winning rights inevitably leaves some groups behind or fails to enact enduring change for the most precarious members, then it is imperative to investigate the political processes and strategies through which these occlusions take shape. My arguments intervene in and build on this important research to draw attention to yet another facet of rights: the work that rightful citizenship claims do to determine from the outset who is considered part of the group and will benefit from movement victories as a result. The chapters in this book take a bird's-eye view on rightful citizenship claims to identify the political strategies and circumstances that make bids for rights successful for some and elusive for others.

A final note on the stakes of these interventions before I turn to situating this book in broader scholarship and developing my arguments in the next chapter. A question that I often get asked when I talk about this research focuses on the historical usefulness of rights and citizenship. Although these questioners say they are compelled by the evidence I present showing that rights claims almost always result in the elevation of White gay men and their political interests, I am frequently urged to offer my take on which political priorities ought to replace rights. These questions are framed against the historically accepted narrative that achieving rights has been meaningful to groups unjustly relegated to second-class citizenship, specifically Black people in the United States. In response, I cite research that describes the uneven social, political, and economic gains in the wake of key rights wins for Black people. When this answer falls short of explaining why rights should be reconsidered, I respond that my goal as a scholar is to build on and extend conversations in research on the perils of rights, which are already well established across disciplines.[30] At some point in the back and forth, somebody usually becomes exasperated at my stubborn refusal to concede the utility of rights, presses harder, and says something to the effect of "But don't rights just *work*?" And it is with this persistent attachment to rights in mind that I want to make one final note about the goals of this book: intersectional thinkers—namely Black feminist theorists and queer activists—tell academics, political actors, and pundits exactly what is to be done to confront the failure of rights to enact meaningful changes for those who need them the most. Across the board, these thinkers exhort activists and advocates to reframe political praxis to focus on grassroots approaches to agenda development.[31] This means asking people who are most politically and socially aggrieved about their political claims and using those statements to develop political agendas.[32] It means fostering sincere conversations on coalition formation across groups and developing a shared orientation to dominant power structures that seeks to critically engage them, not merely extend the terms of inclusion ever outward, only to leave systems of oppression in place, but for fewer people.[33] It means loosening the grip on rights claims to let other political interests, such as abolishing the militarized policing of national borders or chipping away at incarceration, take center stage.[34] It means abandoning the fallacy that social and political struggles are teleological in nature, and that winning rights represents a logical and most desirable endpoint for political action.[35] It means holding open the possibilities for queer world building focused on the never-ending projects of kinship, empathy, contact, anger, and joy.[36] These recommendations take seriously the goal of effecting change for the widest swath of individuals possible and avoiding the pitfalls of agendas organized exclusively around rights claims, which all too often leave too many behind. In the epigraph to this chapter, I highlighted Janet Mock's observation about her participation in a prominent rights-oriented LGBT interest group:

Initially, I was embraced by the stakeholders of the mainstream movement. I quickly noticed that despite the unifying acronym, the people at the table often did not reflect me or my community. These spaces and the conversations were dominated by men, specifically upper-middle-class white cis gay men. Women, people of color, trans folks, and especially folks who carried multiple identities were all but absent. I was grateful for the invitation but unfulfilled by the company. *This was my political awakening.*[37]

The following chapters will show that Mock is not alone. Her observations reveal the stakes of Jennicet Gutiérrez being booed out of an LGBT event and resonates with the words of activists and advocates in this book who contest the terms of their exclusion. Focusing on these ruptures highlights alternatives to rightful citizenship claims, which have proven to be less all-encompassing and durable than proponents of rights claims had hoped. It also underscores liberation, abolition, and mutual aid as modes of political action that stand to benefit the greatest number of people who confront rollbacks in rights previously presumed untouchable, growing economic inequality, and increasingly diminished opportunities for genuine democratic discourse through formal political channels.

Chapter Overview

The empirical analysis in this book traces the development of gay, lesbian, bisexual, and transgender identities individually before shifting attention to the efforts by political actors to construct a nominally inclusive LGBT political identity and agenda in the final chapter. Chapter 1 situates this argument in interdisciplinary scholarship on collective identity, citizenship, rights, interest groups, and social movements. It also outlines my methodological approach and archive.

Chapter 2 explores the nascent years of political activism, 1968 to 1972, often referred to as the Gay Liberation Era. It shows how conflicts over coalitions, particularly with the Black Panthers, ultimately directed political actors to two diverging (and yet overlapping) constructions of gay identity: radical and assimilationist. The former would seek alliances with Black and Third World movements in the pursuit of broad social changes aimed at ending inequality and oppression for all marginalized groups. The latter would be understood as implicitly White, as political actors made explicit efforts to break alliances with Black and Third World movements and advance political goals that follow the logic of rightful citizenship claims. These political commitments, captured as assimilationist or radical politics, resonate throughout subsequent political organizing in the name of sexuality and gender identity, particularly as political actors representing each of these commitments to political praxis engaged in conflicts with each other to define the boundaries of identity groups and their associated political agendas.

Chapter 3 examines efforts to establish and assert the coherence of lesbian identity on three fronts during the 1970s: with mainstream liberal White feminists, who rejected lesbian-identified women from membership on the basis that their sexual deviancy would imperil feminism's reach and appeal to Middle America; as distinct from White gay men, who denied them access to scarce resources, such as space for events or funding for political mobilizations; and against transgender-identified women, who sought membership amongst predominantly White lesbian feminist groups and were met with violent rejection based on the presumption that they were not raised as women and therefore lacked the experiences that were thought to inform feminist action and solidarity. This chapter details these multifocal struggles to establish a lesbian identity that would advance a unique set of interests premised on rightful citizenship logic, specifically the right to self-determination and the right to be free from patriarchal dominance. It shows how the result of this discourse was a "woman-identified woman" for whom, in the words of radical feminist Ti Grace Atkinson, "feminism is the theory, lesbianism is the practice." After laying out these epistemic foundations, the second part of the chapter foregrounds the writings and speeches of Black lesbian feminists who actively resisted the biological determinism at the core of this new lesbian identity. In contesting the narrow construction of lesbian identity emerging in White feminist discourse, Black lesbian feminists put forward a vision of political praxis focused on identifying power asymmetries as the basis of political coalitions and actively eschewed rights discourse.

Chapter 4 analyzes bisexual periodicals and organization minutes from 1970 through 2001 to put forward an analysis of bisexuality as it evolved from being perceived as radical sexuality practiced by celebrities, married couples, and free-love activists, to a relatively marginal political identity on the eve of same-sex marriage struggles in the 1990s and early 2000s. Focusing on why bisexuals were unable to gain political traction, the analysis in this chapter shows that the perception of bisexuality as a "radical" sexual orientation, which challenged binary gender the organizing logic of gender for gay men and lesbians, motivated gay and lesbian political actors to silence bisexual voices in their midst for fear that they would disrupt efforts to make rightful citizenship claims. As with the construction of gay and lesbian identities examined in the first two chapters, this analysis of bisexual political identity construction shows that these cleavages were largely along lines of racial and class differences, with bisexual identification serving as a home for all those cast to the margins of gay and lesbian identification understood as gender-normative and White.

Chapter 5 traces the emergence and construction of transgender as a political identity during the 1990s. It shows how political leaders engaged in stigma transformation to construct transgender identity as an umbrella category to contain and represent all variations of gender expression: butches, queens, genderqueers, drag queens, and intersex people. Over time, however, this broad and inclusive identity category was slowly narrowed as choices about how to represent transgender people in politics, particularly as citizens, were made by political actors and activists. This chapter demonstrates that while the introduction of transgender nominally asserted a broad and inclusive identity, the choices made by political actors to use rightful citizenship claims in their representation of the transgender political identity group to lawmakers relied upon the exclusion of the most precarious members of the group, especially those who are gender-nonconforming, transgender people who are poor or homeless, and transgender people of color.

Chapter 6 examines the period between 1996 and 2001, when lesbian, gay, bisexual, and transgender political actors began to work in concert to develop a unified interest group presence in national politics. Through a detailed exploration of the conflicts that took place over these negotiations regarding what they variously described as coalition formation or identity construction, this chapter traces the ongoing emphasis on rightful citizenship claims from some political actors and the objections raised by those who repeatedly explained that such a political strategy would leave them behind. Over time, this latter group used "queer" to describe not only their sexuality and/or gender identities but also their views on political praxis. This chapter shows how the departure of queer-identified people and proponents of queer politics from the increasingly rights-based mobilizations of LGBT interest groups, such as the Human Rights Campaign, resulted in the construction of two interlinked identity groups and political agendas: LGBT and queer.

Chapter 7, the conclusion, forecasts the lessons drawn from the historical analysis of how rightful citizenship claims shape lesbian, gay, bisexual, transgender, and LGBT political identity construction on the present moment. I present three case studies that show the persistent exclusionary effects of rightful citizenship claims on who is considered a member of the group and which interests should be advanced on their behalf. The first explores the social and economic meanings of Pride flags, specifically the 2017 introduction of black and brown stripes to the rainbow Pride flag to represent the contributions of Black and Brown people to the LGBT movement. The second case study turns to popular culture and representations of LGBT life in Taylor Swift's 2019 music video for the song "You Need to Calm Down." In this case study, I am particularly interested in exploring the ways that rightful citizenship logic has infiltrated everyday understandings of political action and who, exactly, is a member of the LGBT group. The third case study returns to the realm of formal politics and analyzes the 2022 Supreme Court decision in *Dobbs v. Mississippi Women's Health Center*. I think about this Court ruling alongside the corresponding uptick in political attacks against transgender people, especially by antigender feminists, who claim that attention to transgender issues is why abortion was rolled back. I analyze how rightful citizenship claims abet—and even require—assertions that transgender women are not women in order to secure reproductive rights for nontrans women. I use these case studies to offer three recommendations for scholars and practitioners to consider as they develop political agendas that do not draw on the framework of rightful citizenship claims.

The seven chapters in this book underscore the narrowing effects of rightful citizenship claims on who is considered a member of the lesbian, gay, bisexual, transgender, and LGBT groups. They also provide roadmaps for alternative political strategies, which were repeatedly articulated by those who explained that centering rightful citizenship claims would leave them behind. Paying close attention to these conflicts and discursive framings has the potential to move toward political praxis that is not only more inclusive but also reaches beyond identity to effect change for all members of the polity who find themselves left behind.

1

Current Scholarship, Main Arguments, and Approach

Interest group and social movement scholars have been attuned to the tendency of political organizations to universalize the interests of relatively more politically and economically powerful members at the expense of others since E. E. Schattscheider's observation that the "problem with the pluralist heaven is that the heavenly chorus sings with a distinctly upper-class accent."[1] More recent scholarship by political scientists drawing on Black feminist theory radically rethinks this dyadic relationship between power and resources and draws on intersectionality to posit that power functions multifocally. This approach to power alerts scholars to the possibility that actors within nondominant groups can also enact within-group marginalization of their most precarious members, in what Cathy Cohen refers to as "secondary marginalization" and Dara Strolovitch, following Kimberlé Williams Crenshaw, terms "intersectional marginalization." The resulting hierarchies of membership determine whose political claims are heard or ignored.[2] Scholars of American political development also shed light on the normative implications of within-group marginalization, arguing that differing levels of political attention exercises significant influence on constructions of who is considered part of a group, the meanings associated with a group, and state recognition of group demands.[3]

This chapter weaves these strands of scholarship together to develop the analytic framework for examining the construction of the gay, lesbian, bisexual, transgender, and LGBT political identity groups. I begin by reviewing how social scientists approached the question of identity over time and the importance of these questions for understanding contemporary politics. I then discuss the scholarship on citizenship and rights discourse. These bodies of scholarship are brought together in my theory of the effects of rightful citizenship claims on political identity construction, within-group marginalization, and political agenda development. I build this case by working through three major themes in the literature on citizenship: the broader meanings

Terms of Exclusion. Zein Murib, Oxford University Press. © Oxford University Press 2023.
DOI: 10.1093/oso/9780197671498.003.0002

associated with citizenship, specifically a sense of belonging to the nation; citizenship as a raced, gendered, and sexualized formation; and immigration and border control as productive of what it means to be a citizen. Following this, I turn to research examining how social movements and interest groups contest designation as partial or "second-class" citizens. Key to these efforts has been the deployment of rights discourse. Although groups claiming rights have made many notable gains—perhaps none more celebrated than the passage of the Voting Rights and Civil Rights Acts—scholars still debate the effects of rights claims. Some proponents advocate for the power of rights discourse to inject important discussions about marginalization into the public sphere, while others voice concern over the paradoxical effects of rights claims, which they argue inadvertently reproduce and retrench the boundaries around marginalized groups.[4] I work across these two views of rights discourse and return to the scholarship on citizenship to discuss another dimension: the implicitly shared assumption that those articulating demands for rights are citizens who are denied the rights and responsibilities of citizenship. As a result, the articulation of what I call "rightful citizenship claims" reproduces the belief that all members of marginalized groups are citizens entitled to certain rights. Since citizenship relies on drawing and policing borders around who constitutes "us" and "them," often along raced, classed, sexed, and religious lines, this logic abets harmful ideologies that include White supremacy, heterosexism, ableism, Christian normativity, and binary gender as well as capitalism, xenophobia, fascism, and ethnonationalism.[5] I conclude this review with a brief discussion of political science research that examines how political organizations such as social movements and interest groups teach members what it means to be political and how to be political, with emphasis on how these organizations tend to reproduce the very terms of exclusion they seek to upend through the articulation of rightful citizenship claims.

Collective Identity: Movements and Framing

At the core of this book is a set of questions central to the study of politics and the social sciences: how, why, and to what effect identity-based groups develop, become politically active, and are represented by political organizations. Social psychologists approach these questions at the individual level, introducing social identity theory to focus on the interplay of in-group feelings of belonging that are achieved through explicit contrast to out-groups.[6] Sociologists build on these assumptions to analyze collective identity construction by devoting attention to how social movements—as organizations—educate members about political grievances and modes of political action. The main theories of social movement development— resource mobilization and political process theories—attend to the question of the conditions needed for movements to take action, looking at the ways that structural shifts such as political opportunities and material conditions predict movement mobilization and success. Studies of what scholars call "identity work" in social movements take a different approach that examines cultural and social factors to better understand why they organize.[7] Proponents of identity work argue that better understandings of the role that identification plays in social movement activity provides more robust analyses of the political strategies used by movements than resource mobilization or political process theories.[8] They contend that this is because resource mobilization and political process theories of social movement development focus on case studies of the American civil rights movement, which, like social identity theory, assumes collective identities organize along a single axis—in this case, racial identity—to make explicitly strategic demands upon the state for recognition and inclusion.[9] In contrast, what scholars refer to as new social movement theories of identity work posit that people are not only rational or means-oriented but are also motivated by identifications and related issues that are often complex, dynamic, and pertain more to one's identity as it is shaped by the social and political milieux.[10] According to this scholarship, identification with a group can be a strategy of protest, a particular outlook on political praxis, or shaped by the state through legal categories.

If collective identities can take many different forms and are essential for movement mobilization, then a question that arises in the scholarship concerns the factors that amplify individual-level identification and, in turn, motivate movement participation.[11] Framing research is concerned with meaning work—the conflicts over the construction of ideas and meanings that mobilize movements, or what Irving Goffman refers to as "schemata of interpretation" that allow actors to understand, identify, and label occurrences in their lives.[12] Particularly important for the research on framing is the assumption that it is an ongoing process, which sociologists Robert Benford and David Snow describe as a "processual phenomenon that implies agency and contention at the level of reality construction."[13]

In this way, frames are instrumental in directing political mobilizations as they lower the costs for movement participation through affective appeals to belonging, solidarity, kinship, indignation, and rage.[14] These affective attachments foster a sense of collective identity that scholars theorize lower the costs of movement involvement. Verta Taylor and Nancy Whittier's study of lesbian feminist collective identity in the 1970s shows how these meanings are developed through discursive processes of drawing boundaries to contain members, raising consciousness, and negotiating the terms of inclusion to arrive at a sense of collective identity shared by a group.[15] Identities, in this view, are not primordial or essential but rather produced through social and political processes of discursively amplifying certain meanings for members.[16] For instance, Joshua Gamson's 1995 study of queer identity in San Francisco found that queer identification was asserted by some as a protest against what they perceived to be assimilationist goals of lesbian- and gay-identified people.[17] Queer identity is much more than a way to label sexuality in Gamson's study; it is also a way for a group of people who identify as queer to conduct what sociologists Mary Bernstein and Kristin Olsen describe as identification to "critique to confront dominant values," or the focus on assimilation by lesbians and gay men in the Bay Area.[18] Gamson argues that considering the many different possible expressions of collective identity within a group, in conjunction with movements, helps researchers to understand how interests emerge and change over time, rather than taking them as a given and associated with static and presumably essential qualities.

This book borrows from these insights on the constructed nature of political identities and adds to this research by introducing the role of rightful citizenship claims as mechanisms of political identity construction. The subsequent chapters show how rightful citizenship claims set in motion the shedding of differences that produce within-group marginalization in processes of identity group construction generally and, more specifically, ongoing political, social, and epistemic erasure for those cast to the margins of the evolving group.

Identification as Political Processes

Political science scholarship on political identity takes the boundaries drawn to contain and frame identity-based groups from sociology as empirical and theoretical starting points. Political theorists conceptualize identity as contingent and thus produced through various actions taken by leaders members to unite people into groups that seek political change or membership in the polity. Underscoring this contingency, political theorists use words such as "identification" (rather than "identity"), "performance" (instead of "category"), and "groupness" (as opposed to "group") to substitute for theorizations of identity as static and immutable. The focus on processes that give rise to boundaries and the divisions to designate similarity for group members means that identity is understood by political theorists as a paradox: assertions of belonging and membership require the simultaneous articulation of boundaries to exclude outsiders that give the group's identification and groupness meaning.[19] In the words of William Connolly, "Identity requires difference in order to be, and it converts difference into otherness in order to secure its own self-certainty."[20] Studies of identity in political science draw on these theorizations for critical explorations of state-recognized identifications, including nation, race, and ethnicity. Rogers Brubaker and Frederick Cooper outline the steps through which identities are made meaningful: "We should seek to explain the processes and mechanisms through which what has been called the 'political fiction' of the 'nation'—or of the 'ethnic group,' 'race,' or other putative 'identity'—can crystallize, at certain moments, as a powerful, compelling reality. But we should avoid unintentionally *reproducing* or *reinforcing* such reification by uncritically adopting categories of practice as categories of analysis."[21] Denaturalizing identities by examining the processes and mechanisms that give them meaning holds identities like nation, ethnicity, and race open to social science inquiry. Political identity groups are not analytic categories that explain outcomes, in other words, but are outcomes to be continuously subject to scholarly inquiry.[22]

Taking identity groups as social and political outcomes to explain directs political scientists to examine the political effects of the processes and mechanisms that shape identities. These questions about the broader social, political, and economic impacts of identity construction are seen as particularly pressing given the paradox of identity outlined above. If identities are constructed by political actors and members as a way to claim belonging, as political theorist Anne Norton explains it does, then how do we reconcile that these acts of identity construction and associated claims of belonging require the simultaneous designation of an outsider, or other, who is excluded and potentially discriminated against?[23] Iris Marion Young takes up this question about the effects of identity at the site of the state. She argues that while some might claim that the state should be neutral with respect to identity and difference in the name of equality, it is in fact the state's obligation to not only recognize groups but to also engage in redistributive practices that address the discrimination and marginalization that these groups face.[24] The stakes of theorizing and examining the effects of identity construction are highlighted by Nancy Fraser's critique of Young, who she argues engages in the same erasure of difference as the state when she asserts that marginalized groups are unified by shared goals and, by implication, internally homogeneous.[25] Although Fraser stops short of advocating an explicitly intersectional approach to identity, her call for a "differentiated politics of difference" highlights the multifocal, contingent, and heterogeneous nature of political and social groups.

Intersectionality and Identity

Wrestling with the assumed internal homogeneity of groups has directed political scientists and theorists to acknowledge that there are, in fact, variations within groups that shape the representation of their memberships, interests, and political strategies. Political scientists drawing on feminist and critical race theories demonstrate the many ways that the internal heterogeneity of groups is minimized in efforts to present a cohesive and united front and explain that this is because the prevailing political context of liberalism rewards issues that are presented in unitary and discrete ways. For example, Cathy Cohen's 1999 study of Black political identity and political action shows how cross-cutting issues, such as activism and political responses to HIV/AIDS and sexuality, were minimized by political actors to project the boundaries of Black identity and group as assimilating with dominant White supremacist norms of monogamy, heterosexuality, and binary gender. Cohen explains, "By exaggerating out-group differences and minimizing in-group variation, many African Americans use racial group interest as a proxy for self-interest. The progress of the group, therefore, is understood as an appropriate, accurate, and accessible evaluative measure of one's individual success."[26] The need to minimize in-group variation and silence issues such as HIV/AIDS to project Black prosperity, Cohen argues, can be understood only against the backdrop of a long history of social policies (and associated social science) that pathologize Black sexuality and families to maintain racial difference and perpetuate marginalization.[27] Black political identity is consequently shaped by political actors within the group as well as in response to broader political and social contexts as they work to combat these stigmas.[28]

Similarly, Cristina Beltrán traces the processes through which political actors constructed group and identity boundaries to bring together Cubans, Mexicans, and Puerto Ricans—among many other groups—under the signifier of "Latino" at the sites of social movement activism and later interest group advocacy.[29] Beltrán approaches "Latino" as a category that requires denaturalizing—as feminist theorists have posited for the category "woman"—to show how the unique political demands of each of these groups are erased in the construction of a unified and cohesive Latino group. Exploring how sexuality and gender are understood and discussed by political actors working to construct Latino political identity allows Beltrán to show that it is not solely the unique demands of each nation-based group that are elevated or silenced within "Latino" depending on strategic considerations, but also the discrete and pressing issues held by women and lesbian-, gay-, bisexual-, and transgender-identified members and the interests they hold within the categories of "Cuban," "Mexican," and "Puerto Rican."

Cohen's and Beltrán's in-depth case studies of marginalization within identity-based groups reveal varying degrees of silencing and erasure for members who have relatively less power and are seen as imperiling the constructions of Black or Latino identity as unified and assimilating to dominant social and political norms. Each of these studies describes how leaders justify delaying political priorities for some members as a necessary feature of social movement activism and interest group advocacy, which is seen as more successful when unified groups with cohesive demands articulate strategic and feasible claims to the state. Dara Strolovitch's 2007 study of interest groups further reorients understandings of marginalization and erasure within groups. Her analysis of interest group representation shows that while leaders in interest groups claim to represent the needs of all group members, interest groups often do not in practice advocate on behalf of the political interests that affect relatively disadvantaged members.[30] There is rather an expectation expressed by leaders that their advocacy work will implicitly support efforts of other interest groups and eventually "trickle down" to benefit intersectionally disadvantaged members. One of the problems with this assumption, as Strolovitch points out, is that it fails to see how other organizations are also structuring their advocacy and political work in ways that benefits the most advantaged members. This has the cumulative effect of perpetuating neglect for those who are most in need of interest group advocacy, both within the interest group system itself as well as the broader polity. The implications of these findings are particularly pressing given that interest groups and social movements play influential roles in mediating identities and interests for members, projecting the concerns and political issues that then come to be representative of the group in broader politics as well as culturally. As Strolovitch explains, the constructions of group identities along a single axis reinforces—and is indeed premised upon—the exclusion of large portions of the membership outside of the group, specifically those who are intersectionally disadvantaged. This general trend is especially concerning due to the pluralistic assumption that interest groups will represent a variety of political issues that are not addressed in the context of a system of government dominated by two parties.[31] By devoting resources only to their relatively more advantaged members, interest groups claiming to represent marginalized members are instead complicit in perpetuating the effects of marginalization they seek to remedy.

These important studies of groups and identity-based politics in the United States demonstrate the ways that feminist and critical race theories can be used by researchers to open identity-based groups to further inquiry, revealing how marginalization occurs not only between groups—as the predominant theories of identity and groups in social psychology, sociology, and political science hold—but also *within* groups. Intersectionality, specifically the critical insight that race, gender, sexuality, class, nation, religion, and ability are not unitary and mutually exclusive but rather always relationally defined, furnishes the theoretical framework that makes these examinations of within-group marginalization possible. Of further importance, drawing on intersectional thinking, these studies show that the implication of within-group marginalization is not only the ordering of political priorities but also the construction of a normative and representative member of that identity-based group. As a consequence, the needs of the most precarious members of these groups are left unaddressed and those members are effectively erased from projections of identity-based groups, both in politics and more broadly. The marginalization of certain members of identity-based groups that are struggling for standing and membership in the polity thus presents a political problem that is important for social scientists to theorize and investigate as they develop more robust understandings of inequality, marginalization, struggles for standing, and identity in groups. This book joins these conversations by introducing rightful citizenship claims as the discursive mechanism that determines how and to what extent the interests of some members are elevated as representative of the group while others are deprioritized. The following sections build my argument regarding the effects of rightful citizenship claims on within-group marginalization.

Citizenship and Rights

Much of the scholarship on citizenship builds on T. H. Marshall's early theorization of citizenship beyond a binary legal status to consider its social, political, and civic dimensions.[32] This approach opens up possibilities for scholars to investigate how one might be considered a legal citizen and still be denied rights or responsibilities in other realms, which renders one a "second-class citizen," in the discourse of movement mobilization, or a "partial citizen," in the language of scholars.[33] For these thinkers, differential experiences of citizenship are woven into the fabric of national identity— or Americanness—from the founding of the nation, when citizenship was exclusively granted to landholding White men. As the scholarship on political identity shows, implicit and explicit exclusions shape what comes to be known of identities, including the citizen. Patricia Hill Collins describes the hierarchies constructed among White settlers, people of African descent, and Native people as the template for U.S. citizenship, whereby the designation of enslaved people of African origin outside the realm of citizenship and the terms of humanity—through the three-fifths compromise to appease White enslavers—worked alongside Native dispossession to secure whiteness and masculinity as defining features of a "fundamentally racialized American citizenship."[34] Judith Shklar comments on these contradictions at the moment of the nation's founding, stating forcefully that "The equality of political rights, which is the first mark of American citizenship, was proclaimed in the accepted presence of its absolute denial."[35] Others underscore this tension as a paradox in that the promise of rights offered by citizenship, in the words of Collins, "pivots on multiple contradictions, namely, those of the citizenship rights promised to US citizens juxtaposed to differential group discrimination."[36] For Collins and others who share this view, citizenship gains its meanings through those who have been systematically denied its promise over time, including women, African Americans, Native people, unwelcome migrants, people who are not Christian, gay men and lesbians, and, in more recent political machinations, transgender people.[37]

Further probing these exclusions reveals citizenship to be a raced, gendered, and sexualized formation, whereby the prototypical American citizen is one who can "shed their racial and ethnic identities to stand in for the generalized national citizen."[38] Scholars point to the ways that incremental shifts to fold certain groups into legal citizenship entails further designating those who are foreclosed from it. As a result, what it means to be a citizen does not expand to account for a more diverse citizenry, but rather those who are permitted to cross the threshold barring them from legal citizenship status do so at the cost of casting off aspects of their identity that would otherwise mark them as different from the prototypical White male citizen. In some cases, individuals are compelled to make this choice for survival. This is shown most starkly in the 1887 Dawes Act stipulation that Native people could be granted citizenship on condition that they disavow their Nativeness and embrace White, Eurocentric norms of landownership, dress, and (re)productive heterosexual family formations.[39] In other instances, the state's administration of citizenship operates far more insidiously, in what Lisa Lowe refers to as a "technology" of racialization and gendering that reproduces White masculinity.[40] The Page Act of 1875, for instance, permitted the emigration of Chinese men to the United States but barred Chinese women. The resulting concentration of Chinese men in certain labor sectors, such as laundries, rendered them "feminine" prior to 1943, when the Magnuson Act—passed in conjunction with China becoming a U.S. ally against Japan in World War II—permitted Chinese men to be naturalized. "Whereas the 'masculinity' of the citizen was first inseparable from his 'whiteness,'" Lowe explains, "as the state extended citizenship to nonwhite male persons, it formally designated those subjects as 'male' as well."[41] In so doing, these administrative moves also designated those who are constructed outside of citizenship and the polity, as the simultaneous history of incarcerating Japanese citizens and stripping them of rights during World War II illustrates.

The myth of the ideal-type American family—one in which heterosexually partnered White parents nurture children who will assume the responsibilities and rights of citizenship—naturalizes the race and class hierarchies embedded in the presumably neutral language of legal citizenship. Scholars point to the ways that the regulation of sexuality in the name of preserving this particular family type also knits reproductive heterosexuality into the fabric of citizenship. This regulation takes many forms, not least of which is the conferral of legal marriages on certain pairings or designing immigration policies to determine which families are permitted entry.[42] Eithne Luibheid observes, with respect to the latter, that U.S. immigration law serves as a "blueprint" for regulating sexuality in ways that manage prevailing concerns about gender, race, ethnicity, and class.[43] Siobhan Somerville elaborates on these anxieties, describing how the introduction of "homosexuals" and "adulterers" as excludable in the immigration reforms that took place after World War II was just one piece of a larger effort to encourage the formation of nuclear family units that would be the building blocks of the postwar economy.[44] Reconfiguring the porousness of the border in these ways worked hand-in-hand with the extension of GI Bill benefits to White veterans in one of the largest redistributions of wealth in U.S. history, which was denied to Black veterans as well as those veterans who received "Blue Discharges" and deemed "homosexual" for the first time in federal law.[45] These processes of reconfiguring the border and the polity illustrate how the regulation of sexuality through the administrative arms of the state reaches backward in time to elevate those conceived of as the original citizens—White men and their families—and projects that ideal type onto the screen of the present moment in ways that erase all those who cannot, or refuse to, conform.

Perhaps the most visible social movement to contest the paradoxical nature of legal citizenship status and the systematic denial of the benefits and rights is the Black civil rights mobilizations in the 1950s and 1960s. The articulation of rights claims served as a useful frame to challenge the legal segregation Black Americans faced in the Jim Crow South specifically and around the country more generally. However, the passage of the Civil Rights and Voting Rights Acts in 1964 and 1965 eliminated institutionalized racial hierarchy in the form of legal segregation while leaving in place the more insidious features of structural racism and sexism. Chief among these are capitalism and various antidemocratic institutions such as the Electoral College and the U.S. Senate.[46] Although the unique circumstances of legal discrimination justified the demand for rights by the Black civil rights movement, scholars have pointed out that in asking the state to guarantee rights, social movements and political organizations foreclose critiques of the ways that the state's investment in market capitalism reproduces the very conditions of inequality that these movements seek to disrupt.[47] As a result, the significant reforms to voting and civil rights ushered in by the Voting Rights Act and Civil Rights Act function as bandages that alleviate one aspect of disenfranchisement while leaving in place the economic system that at its core requires the maintenance of hierarchies to enable to exploitation of the working class, especially Black workers.[48]

These contradictory effects of rights claims are debated rigorously by scholars. Proponents of rights claims advocate for recuperating rights discourse, despite these drawbacks, due to the possibilities to reconstitute selves and identities through the practice of democratic discourse.[49] These thinkers hold that the conversations instigated during the processes of claiming rights help political actors to further refine what it means to be members of the polity, which they often specify at the level of citizens. Erin Mayo-Adam, for example, discusses "rights episodes" as moments when "intersectional translators" have rare opportunities to highlight the reasons for forging coalitions across groups and issues that might not otherwise be aligned.[50] And yet Joseph Mello explains how the "rights revolution" that followed the success of the civil rights movement led to framing almost all political issues in the language of individual rights at the cost of thinking about social and political problems as collective concerns.[51] As a result, rights discourse elevates the individual as a political unit and reinscribes the categories of marginalization, even when—or perhaps especially when—rights are won.[52] Part of what makes these debates so complicated and high stakes is that they take place in the context of liberalism, which creates a bind for political actors. Even critics of rights language can recognize that, within this space of liberalism, political claims are made more salient when attached to rights. Perhaps most famous among these critiques is Gayatri Spivak's oft-cited observation that "rights are that which we cannot not want," which is often misread as an endorsement of rights and not, as Spivak intended, an urgent call for scholars and activists to inhabit the paradoxes of rights to target how dominant ideologies—namely liberalism, with its focus on laws and individual entitlements—shape our social worlds in ways that foreclose membership for the majority of people.[53]

Although these views are seemingly in opposition, the thread that unites the thinkers in these debates is the presumed citizenship status of those making use of rights discourse.[54] Leaving aside the question of the benefits or harms, I argue that rights discourse relies upon citizens—understood as both a legal status and as belonging to the nation—to serve as reference points for rights claims, and in so doing retrenches beliefs about who, exactly, can and should claim rights at a higher level of analysis than that approached by scholars. In other words, it is not simply that rights discourse erects walls around what it is to be a woman when making a rights claim, as thinkers such as Wendy Brown and Judith Butler posit, but that considerations of rights claims in a more general sense operate under the assumption that those making them are, in fact, citizens.[55] Here I borrow from Hannah Arendt's theorization of "the right to have rights," which uses the example of refugees fleeing genocide and consequently lacking a nation where they can make rights claims. Her observations about the futility of rights for those who are stateless underscores how the conditions of membership shape who possesses rights.[56] In this view, if rights discourse is an opportunity for political actors to negotiate the boundaries of political identities and subjectivities, as proponents of rights discourse such as Drucilla Cornell and Karen Zivi contend, then we must hold open the possibility that one of the potential effects of rights discourse is suturing rights to citizenship by way of the unquestioned assumption that those claiming rights are citizens.[57] Following these overarching assumptions and the relative lack of attention paid to the citizenship side of rights claims, in this book I focus on what happens when rights discourse is approached from the perspective of a blend of intersectionality and queer methodology, both of which take critical aim at binaries—rights and rightlessness, citizen and noncitizen—to examine the ways that they shape how we think about social and political problems.[58]

Political Organizations, Rightful Citizenship Claims, and Identities

Although political language such as rights discourse exerts a significant influence on how political problems and identities are understood, they are only one part of the equation; political organizations also play a key role in shaping what comes to be known of identities and political demands, such as rightful citizenship claims. Scholars of political identity, social movement mobilization, and interest group representation posit that individuals join political movements and organizations to learn how to be political, what it means to be part of a group, and translate grievances into political demands.[59] These theories suggest that the state or prevailing ideologies, such as liberalism, are not the only influences on how people understand citizenship status and rights. This work invites scholars to consider the extent to which political organizations also influence the ways members understand their status as citizens and the political claims they make. Matthew Hindman's historical investigation of gay and lesbian interest group development answers this question, showing how these organizations cultivated members into "interested citizens" who learned over time to align their sexual identities, conduct, and political participation with neoliberal norms of individualism and personal responsibility and use financial contributions to drive political change.[60] That only certain people are recruited into interested citizenship based on access to social, political, and financial resources indicates that political movements might also reiterate and retrench the narrow boundaries of citizenship afforded by the state, especially when the demands made on their behalf are framed through the discourse of rights and citizenship.

The analysis in this book builds on this scholarship by directing analytic attention to the members of the lesbian, gay, bisexual, transgender, and LGBT groups who are invoked in rightful citizenship claims and to what effect. In each chapter, I draw attention to the voices of those resisting the deployment of rights discourse in their name, not due to disagreements about political praxis—radical or assimilatory—but out of deep concern that advancing rightful citizenship claims would require leaving behind those members of the group who were not situated in close proximity to the template of the prototypical citizen. My examination of this discourse reveals that the construction of lesbian, gay, bisexual, transgender, and LGBT groups as White, middle-class, gender-normative, and, in most cases, associated with men and masculinity was produced by advancing rights claims that succeeded precisely because they went hand-in-hand with altering stigmas of same-sex sexuality and gender identity. These transformations were achieved through the assertion that gay men, lesbians, and certain transgender people are citizens—or Americans—entitled to rights.[61] I argue that the discursive and strategic uses of rightful citizenship claims by political actors speaking on behalf of organizations representing LGBT people requires silencing members who, by virtue of being Black, Latine, Asian, Native, women, incarcerated, disabled, bisexual, transgender, nonbinary, and/or a migrant, complicate claims that members of the group would be included in institutions of citizenship, such as marriage and the military, were it not for their sexuality or gender identities. This approach highlights the exclusionary and epistemic effects of rightful citizenship claims on designating an insider citizen who belongs and an outsider partial-citizen who serves as a foil.

Centering marginalized groups consequently reorients scholarship on LGBT politics as well as LGBT political praxis by showing that the lack of attention paid to them is not an inadvertent consequence of an incremental approach associated with mobilizations for rights, but instead a constitutive feature of strategies that foreground rights and citizenship as a basis for political claim making. Throughout the analysis in the chapters that follow, I draw attention to who is left behind in mobilizations that foreground rights, citizenship, recognition, and inclusion. I also highlight the words of political actors who articulate the many negative economic, political, and epistemic consequences that these groups face when they are erased from mobilizations made in the name of the LGBT group through rightful citizenship claims. In taking this perspective, this book shows that the efforts to achieve rights, equality, and standing for LGBT people through rightful citizenship claims creates conditions of vulnerability for those members cast to the margins of the group. This is because seeking recognition and inclusion in existing systems—the very systems that created the precarious conditions in the first place—not only leaves those institutions, laws, and ideologies intact, but it also extends them by earning insider status for those who can compellingly claim proximity to the prototypical normative citizen. These selective inclusions legitimize the state's imposition of hierarchies upon populations. They also manufacture the illusion that the state is responsive to minority interests. As a result, political actors speaking on behalf of lesbians, gay men, bisexuals, and transgender people paradoxically retrench the dynamics of marginalization that they seek to upend when they use rightful citizenship claims.

Analytic Approach

Key to the theory of the effects of rightful citizenship claims on identity construction that I advance in this book are the stories that political actors tell about a group to mobilize members, target political venues, effect change, and disseminate information to the broader public and policymakers about the group's shared identity and struggles. While seemingly benign on the surface, these stories have a significant impact on the degree to which a group can achieve political successes and which members will benefit from those developments. Using intersectionality as an analytic lens to examine the discourse of rightful citizenship claims as stories political actors tell about a group and their political objectives reveals these stakes. Two assumptions that undergird intersectionality make it an especially powerful approach for examining identity construction. The first that no group is homogeneous; rather, as Ange-Marie Hancock explains, "each category of difference has within-group diversity that sheds light on the way we think about groups as political actors in politics."[62] Probing these internal variations and the factors that shape them sheds light on power relations within a group and allows researchers to pinpoint moments of rupture or agreement that shape what comes to be known of a group. The second assumption is that subject positions are contingent and shaped by political and social factors, such as interactions with institutions, the law, and activism. Theorizing subjectivity as "differently and differentially constituted through relations of privilege and penalty, with real material effects,"[63] Rita Kuar Dhamoon explains that intersectionality breaks with the predominant approach to identity and groups in the social sciences by attending to dynamics between *and* within groups that give rise to social and political inequality. Marginalization, in other words, is not solely predicted by factors such as race and gender; those are rather the starting points for analysis that illustrate the ways in which subject positions are influenced by ideological structures, such as sexism, racism, heteronormativity, and classism.[64] In these ways, intersectionality furnishes a powerful theoretical and analytic lens for a study of within-group marginalization that takes place through the discourse of identity group construction. Kimberlé Williams Crenshaw says of these narratives that, "when identity politics fail us, as they frequently do, it is not primarily because those politics take as natural certain categories that are socially constructed but rather that the descriptive content of those categories and the narratives on which they are based have privileged some experiences and excluded others."[65] Crenshaw's observation invites scholars of identity to view it beyond the simple binary that is currently favored by quantitative approaches to consider how political actors and individuals describe themselves and their identifications, and how these elaborations endure or change over time.

Discursive Framework and Approach

I extend these insights from intersectionality to develop a new analytic framework for examining how deploying rightful citizenship claims elevates the political interests of those members who are most proximate to normative citizenship while minimizing others. This three-part framework directs attention to sites and instances of political actors and group members talking about identity, with a focus on revealing within-group marginalization and its effects.

The first discursive site I focus on is the conflicts that take place among political actors and members regarding the people and issues that should be prioritized in the name of the identity group taking shape. These debates are frequent occurrences during political mobilizations and are valuable sites for analysis due to the insight they provide into how political actors describe the boundaries of the group as well as the characteristics associated with it, or what Crenshaw terms the "descriptive content." Perhaps most important, devoting attention to conflicts also directs analysis to the arguments made by those who are excluded by different discursive and political strategies, specifically rightful citizenship claims. Michel Foucault describes an approach focused on these types of conflicts as one in which the researcher "uses this resistance as a chemical catalyst so as to bring to light power relations."[66] Foucault's observation suggests that in order to learn about one social issue— sanity, in his example—it is useful to examine how insanity is understood. In this study, identifying and examining conflicts over who, exactly, will be folded into political claims through the deployment of rightful citizenship claims is articulated most clearly by those political actors who spoke in passionate terms about the ways they would be left behind by such a strategy.

The second discursive site I focus on takes inspiration from the framing literature, specifically what sociologist Mitch Berbrier calls "stigma transformation," or deliberate efforts by political actors to revise negative connotations and stereotypes associated with the group and replace them with positive messages.[67] The rallying call of the Black Power movement's "Black Is Beautiful," Gay Liberation's "Gay Is Good," and even the adoption of "queer" as an identity marker show how political actors create opportunities to shift meanings associated with the group. In this study, rightful citizenship claims are one of ways that movements engage in stigma transformation. This is because the processes of altering stigmas relies on transforming negative associations with the group that are typically used to justify their designation and status as partial citizens. Respectability politics—or the deliberate adoption and projections of characteristics associated with normative citizenship, such as financial solvency and stable family units headed by heterosexually partnered parents—is a feature of stigma transformation that highlights the proximity of the marginalized group to normative citizenship and the injustice of denying them the rights and responsibility associated with that status.[68] As a result, embedded within stigma transformation is the logic of exclusion, whereby all those who imperil this deliberate construction of normativity are relegated to the fringes of the identity-based group and their political demands.

The third component of the framework is representation. I explore representation as a factor that shapes group identity by considering how political actors describe groups in a process that political theorist Melissa Williams terms "representation as mediation."[69] Representation, in this view, functions in two ways to shape group identity. In the first, representation plays a constitutive role, by which I mean political actors actively influence how group members understand their own identities and shape how the broader public perceives the group.[70] In the second, representing groups through the discourse of rightful citizenship claims elevates those members of the group who can assert that they would be afforded the rights and responsibility of citizenship were it not for their sexual or gender identity. This elides those members of the group who have intersecting identities and effectively organizes them out of group membership. As the following chapters will show, examining the discursive content of how a group is represented goes some way in accounting for how the group is consequently perceived, with major implications for the presumed Whiteness of the LGBT group.

Although the elements of this three-part framework are outlined here separately, the political world is complicated and messy, and I want to note that these three processes often occur simultaneously, in response to each other, or in feedback loops to shape political outcomes. For the purposes of advancing this framework to demonstrate its analytic potential, however, each process is taken separately in the analyses that follow to show how each operates to determine the inclusions and exclusions that define groups, even while it will be abundantly clear throughout this analysis that these three processes—conflict, stigma transformation, and representation—all act in concert to shape what comes to be known of group identity. Focusing on these three discursive sites of identity construction and agenda development reveals that it is not simply that some members enjoy less attention and receive fewer benefits due to relative lack of political power (i.e., fewer members) or are disadvantaged because of a dearth of material and economic resources. Rather, as the chapters in this book illustrate at length, within-group marginalization is produced by countless decisions made by political actors to employ discursive strategies, such as rightful citizenship claims, that elevate some members and qualities while simultaneously (and consequently) marginalizing or completely silencing other members and characteristics.

Critical Discourse Analysis

Much has been written about bridging the unique ontological assumptions of intersectionality with an appropriate method for empirical research.[71] I use critical discourse analysis (CDA) as a method to analyze how political actors discursively render identity groups unified and cohesive—and at what costs.[72] Whereas positivist methods such as content analysis examine discourse to identify the frequency a word or phrase is uttered in political discourse and draw inferences from that quantitative data, more interpretive approaches like CDA examine meanings and power relations constituted through language, as political actors articulate what it means to be part of a group and which political interests comprise their political grievances.[73] Using CDA to analyze political speech and writings attunes the researcher to the contingency of the object of study—in this case, identity—by focusing on how these meanings shift or remain static over time.

More specifically, in this study I draw on CDA as a way of knowing to theorize, identify, and examine two main discursive modes that political actors use to construct identities and agendas.[74] The first is the use of analogies, which are common discursive strategies deployed by political actors to highlight the legitimacy of their political claims by locating them in relation to well-known political struggles. On the political Left, the most common reference point for these analogies is the Black civil rights struggle, which is invoked to frame political grievances as recognizably unjust.[75] For example, the formulation "Gays and lesbians, like African Americans . . ." occurs frequently in the movement discourse I analyze. This is because the comparison conveys that gays and lesbians ought to be considered a bounded and legible minority group that is struggling for rights in the context of a long history of oppression, much like Black people in the United States. The effectiveness of analogies for pointing to the definition of groups and their associated agendas, however, comes at the cost of portraying each of the compared groups as separate and not overlapping. Consequently, the analogy of gays and lesbians *like* African Americans poses each of these groups as discrete and bounded entities and implies that gays and lesbians are *not* African Americans. Analogies, when used by political actors, play a significant role in conveying particular meanings about groups and interests through their persistent repetition, or what scholars of performativity refer to as "sedimentation" that takes place through iterated utterances over time.[76] In this book, I probe a wide variety of analogies to reveal the construction of groups as bounded and separate rather than overlapping entities.

The second way political actors construct the boundaries and interests associated with an identity group is discursive linkages. For example, although contemporary audiences may take phrases such as "gay *and* lesbian" for granted, this linkage was a novel innovation in the context of the 1980s, when it was used by political actors to introduce and maintain a new unified group to confront the AIDS epidemic. The same is true of repeated efforts to link gay men and lesbians with sexuality, to the exclusion of other characteristics such as gender identity or class struggles. In this study, I am primarily attuned to instances of political actors linking various groups to citizenship and rights. Examining how political actors use these linkages to define what a group is, and more important, to foreclose other associations and implicitly convey what it is not, reveals how identity boundaries are constructed and maintained in political discourse, and how these meanings change or stay static over time to include more (or fewer) members.

The key assumption driving CDA is that analyzing discourse for meaning is important because the repetition of certain analogies or linkages plays a significant role in shaping what is considered sayable, knowable, and legible in politics over time.[77] Norms of group identity, in other words, are constructed and naturalized through discourse in the repetition of certain characteristics, meanings, and boundaries, which are conveyed by these analogies and linkages. This is how discourse consolidates power. As the following chapters will show, political discourse exerts a regulatory force on identities by defining what a group *is* and, importantly, what it is *not*.

Archives

I conducted extensive archival research to assemble the materials analyzed in this study. These include issues of lesbian, gay, bisexual, transgender, and LGBT publications; political speeches and writing from key political actors; and internal organization documents, which include transcripts of meetings, lobbying notes, and communications among social movement and interest group leaders. I specify where and how I identified the primary source materials for this study in each chapter. A bulk of my materials were collected at Cornell University's Human Sexuality Collection, the San Francisco GLBT Historical Society, the New York Public Library Stephen Donaldson Collection, and the University of Minnesota Tretter Collection. Online archives were also tapped and, when appropriate, the website www. waybackmachine.com was used to access the archived websites of the various organizations examined in this study. Finally, several edited volumes containing important writings from lesbian, gay, bisexual, and transgender political thinkers were utilized, such Robert B. Ridinger's *Speaking for Our Lives* and Naomi Tucker's comprehensive *Bisexual Politics: Theories, Visions, and Visions.*

Conducting CDA

The breadth of materials collected for this study required an elaborate organizational strategy. I used Atlas.ti, a Qualitative Data Analysis software package that allows researchers to aggregate archival materials into document groups. After creating document groups for my 483 documents—each comprising between 10 and 250 pages—organized by each chapter's theme (e.g., gay political identity), I performed several readings of each document within the groups and used the software's "code" function to tag relevant "quotes." In this first level of analysis, I focused on identifying quotes that correspond to my analytic framework: Analogy, Linkages, Conflict, Stigma Transformation, Representation, and Rightful Citizenship Claims. The 1,436 quotes identified in this first reading serve as the unit of analysis for the second stage of the research, which proceeded in a more grounded fashion to link the superordinate codes with subthemes that I identified. For example, underneath the Analogy tag were a number of subtags, such as Analogy-BisexualGay (comparing bisexuals to gay people) or Analogy-Race (i.e., comparing LGBT identities to racial identities). Similarly, under Rightful Citizenship Claims, I identified what I tagged as RCC-AmericanValues, RCC-Belonging, RCC-Citizens, RCC-Rights, RCC-RoleofGov, RCC-SecondClassCitizen, and RCC-Voting.[78] In the third stage of analysis, I used Atlas.ti's Query Tool to get a bird's-eye view on how the first- and second-level codes connected quotes to each other within each document group. This allowed me to identify prevalent themes that emerged in the archive. I then analyzed these connections within their respective contexts.

The following chapters bring this blend of methodical approaches to my archive of evidence, which I use to examine each political identity and associated agenda in their unique historical moments. I show how time and time again, the deployment of rightful citizenship claims by political actors results in the elevation of those members who can compellingly claim they would be afforded the rights in question were it not for their sexual identity. My focus on discourse also reveals moments of rupture, when those left behind contested their exclusion and articulated the consequences of doing so.

2

Come Out!

The Mobilization of Gay Identity

The now famous riots at the Stonewall Inn, which occurred in New York City
late on the night of June 28, 1969, are widely viewed as the moment when
gay identity changed from a hidden and private personal label to a public
and political identification.[1] Less typically associated with this significant
shift in gay visibility is a meeting that took place a few weeks later, on July
16. That night, a homophile organization called the Mattachine Society held
an open meeting for members and activists to discuss how the organization
could exploit the energy generated by Stonewall. Dick Leitsch, the president of Mattachine, favored a slow, cautious route, and proposed a candle-
light vigil in a park to the 200 men and women in attendance. His suggestion
was interrupted by Jim Fouratt, one of the founders of the anarchist, public-
protest-oriented Youth International Party, who decried what he viewed to
be Leitsch's conservative approach and shouted, "We don't want acceptance,
goddamn it! We want respect! Demand it!"[2]

With these words, Fouratt articulated an important shift in the approach
to politics that motivated the Stonewall riots in the summer of 1969. Rather
than fiercely guarding the privacy around same-sex desire that was fostered
by the post–World War II homophile organizations,[3] many of the people
who protested at Stonewall took cues from the ongoing movement for Black
Power, which asserted "Black Is Beautiful" to make political demands. They
echoed this approach by openly declaring their lesbian and gay identities and
asserting the centrality of these identifications to their politics. The public
embrace of gay and lesbian identity advocated by activists and epitomized
in Fouratt's disruption at the Mattachine meeting thus marks an important
juncture in the evolution of what would come to be known of gay political
identity and political interests.[4] Whereas the homophile organizations established in the period after World War II focused energy on providing social connections for men and women interested in same-sex relationships
and put in place many different measures to ensure privacy for members,

Terms of Exclusion. Zein Murib, Oxford University Press. © Oxford University Press 2023.
DOI: 10.1093/oso/9780197671498.003.0003

including discouraging political action,[5] young gay-identified activists in the late 1960s saw themselves as part of a larger social movement of global youth working to address the systemic oppression of all marginalized people. [6] Many had been involved in various radical political groups active at the time and wanted to draw on revolutionary tactics to advance their standing as gay-identified people both within radical politics and in society more broadly.[7] With the assertion "No revolution without us!," gay activists sought their place in the radical political movements of the time.[8] Those present at the brainstorming session that took place after that Mattachine meeting formed a new organization, the Gay Liberation Front, and a new phase in gay politics began: Gay Liberation.

This chapter explores this juncture in the development of gay identity, when political actors worked to construct it as openly articulated and politically active. Although there were similar movements taking place on the West Coast, some of which predated Stonewall, the Stonewall riots were significant because the organizations that sprang up in their aftermath were relatively more successful at institutionalizing subsequent Gay Pride events to mark the anniversary.[9] I focus on New York City organizing in light of this history, with attention to the influence that two new organizations had on shaping what was coming to be known about gay identity and politics in the years after the Stonewall riots in 1969.

The first is the Gay Liberation Front (GLF), founded in 1969 to mobilize gay people to combat their exclusion from radical activism and to cultivate a shared understanding of why and how gay-identified people should be politically involved. I examine GLF's newsletter, *Come Out!*, which ran from 1969 to 1971, to show how GLF members fostered this discursive shift and associated identity construction by linking gay people with the Black Panther, antiwar, Women's Liberation, and Communist movements. They made these connections by arguing that personal identities were secondary to experiences of shared oppression, which stemmed from the intertwined ideologies of sexism, racism, capitalism, and imperialism that required radical social, economic, and political changes to confront. GLF was instrumental in drawing visibility to gay identity and engaging in stigma transformation to shift meanings associated with same-sex sexuality as a result. Moreover, GLF members and leaders reconfigured understandings of political action by introducing solidarity as gay political praxis.

The second organization is the Gay Activists Alliance (GAA), which formed in 1969 when a group of GLF members split off due to public conflict over solidarity work with the Black Panther Party. The racialized nature of this conflict had a direct influence on how gay identity was understood by GAA members and leaders. Unlike GLF, which was devoted to combating oppressive ideologies, embracing diverse membership, and engaging in solidarity work with political groups seeking revolution, GAA members used rightful citizenship claims to advance gay rights as the ultimate political goal. My reading of GAA's founding documents, publications, and speeches by leaders shows how the elevation of gay people as citizens who were denied rights solely on the basis of their sexuality posed gay identity as not including intersecting identities. As a result, the version of gay identity represented by GAA was epitomized by gay, White, middle-class men living in New York City, Los Angeles, San Francisco, and other urban centers. This construction of gay identity created exclusive politics on two levels: first, it left out gay- and lesbian-identified people who were Black, Latine, Asian, Native, transgender, bisexual, and/or women; second, those who were omitted were then also relegated to the borders of gay identity and used as a foil to underscore the claim that White gay men were natural claimants for rights.

Examining these two groups—one that viewed oppressions as intersectional and interlinked and one that made claims to rights on the basis of gay identity along a singular axis of sexuality—alongside each other sets the stage for analyzing the effects of rightful citizenship claims on identity construction and illustrates the main arguments of this book. Throughout this chapter and the ones that follow, I cite the voices of those excluded from this narrow and dominant construction of gay identity to underscore the epistemic, social, and political effects of the tendency to engage in within-group marginalization during the processes of identity group construction and agenda development.

Challenging Exclusion through Stigma Transformation: GLF and New Left Politics

GLF's founding and the approaches to politics different from those espoused by homophile organizations such as the Mattachine Society and Daughters of Bilitis, were strongly influenced by what scholars refer to as "the New Left." This included political groups that advanced radical political goals during the 1960s.[10] The interest of GLF members in mirroring the revolutionary momentum of radical groups such as the Black Panthers and the

Students for a Democratic Society is reflected in the words of one of the founding members, who asserted that GLF would "fill the void" left by the Mattachine Society's lack of a "lively" response to the Stonewall riots.[11] Martha Shelly, another founding member of GLF, explained, "In Mattachine and [Daughters of Bilitis] we couldn't openly state that we were against the Vietnam War because they believed that getting mixed up in other struggles was a bad strategy. . . . But those of us in GLF felt that the struggles should be united: the black civil rights movement, the struggle against the Vietnam War, the women's movement, feminist politics, socialist politics. And of course, the gay cause."[12] Members of homophile organizations avoided what were perceived to be pressing political questions like the war in Vietnam for fear of imperiling their tightly guarded privacy or diluting their efforts at assimilation into the mainstream. The GLF, as Shelly's statement conveys, instead saw themselves as aligned with movements that sought the radical transformation of societal structures, referred to by movement activists as "the Establishment," which maintained White supremacy, patriarchy, imperialism, and capitalism.[13] Prioritizing the contestation of oppression for all marginalized groups and across political issues signaled the evolution in gay and lesbian identities and interests fostered by the GLF and across the Gay Liberation movement more generally.[14] Gay identity was not related to unique political objectives pertaining specifically to same-sex sexuality or gay and lesbian identification. Rather, in GLF discourse, gay and lesbian identities and interests evolved from the belief that they were aligned with all nondominant groups in the effort to challenge the institutions that structure and maintain oppression that affects all members of the polity in varying ways.

Despite their revolutionary momentum, openly identified gay people often met with intense opposition to their attempts to be active in New Left movements. Historian Terrance Kissack notes that this resistance stemmed from anxieties among the men in New Left leadership, who were frequently derided by opponents as "long-haired hippies," which equated them with femininity and political powerlessness.[15] There were some, however, who contested these exclusions, such as Black Panther founder Huey P. Newton who wrote in an open letter: "We should be careful about using those terms that might turn our friends off. The terms 'faggot' and 'punk' should be deleted from our vocabulary, and especially we should not attach names normally designed for homosexuals to men who are enemies of the people, such as [President Richard] Nixon or [Attorney General John]

Mitchell. Homosexuals are not enemies of the people."[16] Newton's perceived need to comment on using "faggot" indicates the degree to which gay men were closed out of New Left political movements and articulated that doing so is a misuse of energy for the larger struggle. Although Newton's 1970 letter circulated widely and ushered in a fruitful era of cooperation between Gay Liberation groups and the Black Panthers, gay-identified people remained shut out of opportunities to openly participate in other New Left movements.

Gay Liberation and GLF speeches and writings published during this period show that the denial of membership in New Left politics and the stigmatization that gay men and lesbians faced helped to mobilize and crystallize gay political identity and political praxis. Rightful citizenship claims were not used during this time, which accounts for the relatively more flexible understanding of identity taking shape. Two themes emerge in this discourse of identity construction and movement mobilization. First, the perception of being shut out of radical politics created the conditions for gay people to contest their exclusion by articulating Gay Liberationist thinking and political praxis that viewed the fight against militarism, police violence, racism, and sexism as interlinked and key to achieving sexual freedom, which would benefit all people.[17] This new orientation to politics represented a shift away from the silence that defined the homophile period and ushered in an era of radical, public, and vocal activism on behalf of gay-identified people understood as fighting shoulder to shoulder with other nondominant groups. Second, the context of omission from the New Left and society more generally provided the motivation for some political actors to (re)frame gay and lesbian identities through stigma transformation. These new constructions emphasized same-sex sexuality as positive, nonpathological, and aligned with all marginalized groups seeking to improve their lives through radical political action. Gay Liberation activists drew on these two themes and reformulated understanding of gay identity to propose a new model of political praxis based on solidarity, in which gay people would work within and alongside radical groups to seek the end of oppression and revolutionary social change.

For example, in 1969, members of the North American Conference of Homophile Organizations (NACHO) Youth Committee, which had strong affiliations with GLF, articulated the exclusions gay people experienced in relation to New Left activism and put forth an understanding of lesbian and gay identities as invested in the struggles waged by marginalized groups. The

Chairman of NACHO, Bob Martin, outlined the group's vision for political action in one of the first issues of *Come Out!*:

> The NACHO Youth Committee has unanimously declared its support for the struggles of the black, the feminist, the Spanish-American, the Indian, the hippie, the young, the student, the worker and other victims of oppression and prejudice. We must note with sadness, however, that many in these oppressed groups have swallowed whole the Establishment's propaganda and have joined in its oppression of those of us who are homosexual or bisexual. We offer our support to you, and so often receive by calumny, ridicule, ostracism, degradation in return. Too many radicals are so uptight about their heterosexual public images that they cannot tolerate us in their midst.[18]

According to Martin, concerns over the public image of various New Left movements motivated some of those leaders to foreclose gay-identified people from membership. Martin challenged their expulsion by highlighting their unequivocal support of all New Left causes and thus claiming space and belonging within those movements, which was radical for the late 1960s and early 1970s for a number of reasons. First, and perhaps most significant, Martin's public recognition of homosexuals and bisexuals, in his words, was a marked departure from the tendency toward silence that earlier organizations such as the Mattachine Society and Daughters of Bilitus practiced by omitting words such as "homosexual," "gay," and "lesbian" from the names of their organizations. Although Martin did not explicitly name gay identity, the NACHO statement set the stage for reconfiguring the boundaries of gay identity by posing it alongside recognized groups engaged in political struggles and arguing that gay-identified people were already mobilizing to make political demands. As I will show in later chapters, this early assertion that gay people have always been involved in activism on behalf of marginalized groups would resonate throughout subsequent organizing as lesbians, bisexuals, and transgender people made efforts to seize space in politics, gain recognition for their respective identities, and articulate political demands. Second, and in relation to this assertion of group identity, Martin challenged the exclusion of homosexuals from radical politics with the argument that doing so only furthered the oppressive norms that New Left movements and adherents to radical politics purported to oppose. By explaining that the rejection of alliances with gay people stemmed from what could be understood as a false consciousness (e.g., "swallowed whole the Establishment's propaganda"), Martin and the NACHO statement asserted the natural fit of homosexuals and bisexuals in New Left politics.

Having laid the foundation for engaging in stigma transformation, Martin went on to say, "Our message to our heterosexual brethren, then, is this: re-examine your attitudes, your actions, and eliminate anti-homosexual bigotry from them; treat your gay brothers and sisters as the valuable and dignified human beings they are; support our cause as we support yours."[19] Here, the discourse shifts from homosexuality to identifying "gay brothers and sisters" as heterosexuals' "brethren." Martin closes the gap between straight activists and gay and lesbian activists, linking them as family members—as human beings—in the same struggle. Furthermore, emphasizing the value and dignity of gay people locates sexuality as a facet of humanity, and human diversity, that should be taken as natural. This directly contradicted excluding gay men and lesbians from social and political groups, and in so doing, asserted "gay" as an identity, not a set of behaviors to be stigmatized. Formulations such as this worked to sever the association between same-sex sexuality and the prevailing attitude that homosexuality was pathological and evidence of illness. Martin's concluding offer to exchange support reveals yet another layer of gay identity he aims to project here, specifically its political orientation and necessary place in radical political movements. To be gay is not only to project a certain understanding of one's sexuality but is also a commitment to solidarity as political praxis.

These two themes endured to become key features of how gay identity was understood in Gay Liberation rhetoric, which is captured in the three-year run of GLF's newsletter, Come Out!. Although Come Out! served as a newsletter for the organization and its members involved in New York City politics, letters that were published at the beginning of each issue indicate that it circulated beyond the borders of New York, with readers from Iowa, Chicago, and as far away as Cuba and Australia writing in to express excitement in response to what they read in the publication. Articles by a dedicated slate of GLF members updating readers about current events and political issues were featured alongside thought pieces from other Gay Liberation organizations as well as gay-identified people around the country. By virtue of its broad circulation and plurality of voices, Come Out! was a hub—not unlike contemporary social media networks—where like-minded authors and readers engaged in conversations about what it meant to be gay, what issues gay people should take up, and how to be political.

Internal Debates over Gay Identity and Political Praxis

One of the most notable features of *Come Out!* is the amount of space devoted to clarifying the nature of political activism, gay identity, and the place
of gay-identified people within broader liberation struggles. The first issue
summarized GLF's orientation toward radical politics in its editorial mission statement: "Through mutual respect, action, and education, *Come Out*
hopes to unify both the homosexual community and other oppressed groups
into a cohesive body of people who do not find [an] enemy in each other."[20]
Key to this editorial statement of purpose is the role of "other oppressed
groups." Lesbian and gay people would fight alongside these groups to direct their protests toward the power-holders in society, who they viewed as
perpetuating the war in Vietnam and maintaining structures of oppression
that fostered racism and sexism in the United States. Early GLF discourse
promoted a representation of gay men and lesbians as joined in struggle with
other radical or identity-based groups to fight against marginalization in
all forms.

These views were clarified in the first article in the third issue of *Come
Out!*, which featured an extensive discussion among three GLF members on
the topic "Homosexuals in the Movement." Printing the conversation in its
entirety and close to the beginning of the issue underscored the importance
of the topic for readers. Moreover, the direct transcription and the ways that
the four participants, identified as Kay, Pat, Bernard, and Bob, made space for
each other's voices in the conversation lend an intimate feeling to the piece,
in which one is encouraged to offer one's own answer to the questions the
four participants posed to each other. Take, for example, this exchange between Bernard and Bob halfway through the article, where Bernard reflects
on his experience in radical politics:

> I see the Gay Liberation Movement as a process which will help liberate
> gay people by making them fully part of the whole liberation movement.
> The movement for change in the system that will eventually annihilate
> any form of oppression. Before GLF I was active in these movements,
> but anonymously—nobody was conscious of the fact that I was homo-
> sexual. I think the only way we can gain respect for ourselves and any of
> the help that we need from everyone else in overcoming our oppression is
> by showing that we participate even though they don't understand why we

participate. I think even among a lot of our own people we have to fight for the right to participate as homosexuals.[21]

The enduring problem of exclusion from New Left movements is identified by Bernard as the circumstances defining political possibilities for gay people. In this case, the way to take part fully is to engage in stigma transformation to locate gay people alongside all others in the effort to challenge the oppression, even though their motivations might be unclear. Bernard suggests that prefiguring the acceptance that gay people wish to see from "everyone else" will also benefit gay people by fostering a sense of entitlement to political action, which positions gay people within gay movements while also holding them separate from other struggles.

Bob's immediate response, however, foreshadows the ways that these narrow understandings of gay identity would begin to shift to be more expansive in order to keep it in line with radical goals: "Gay Liberation to me is seeing 35 or 40 homosexuals marching as homosexuals in a vigil to free political prisoners. We have been political prisoners, and we will be political prisoners. Homosexuals are beginning to see themselves as an oppressed minority. I don't think that homosexuality is a magic tie that binds us all but in a sense there is something. It's being proud of ourselves. And I think that's what liberation will help us find—a pride that we can just stand up and be proud of ourselves as human beings."[22] Bob expands on the theme of stigma transformation that Bernard initiated by highlighting the need to confront exclusion with pride. Like Bernard, Bob poses gay people alongside an oppressed group—political prisoners—but then goes one step further to expand that group to embed gay people within it. His compelling description of gay people in liberation movements does not separate out interlocking ideologies as the roots of marginalization, but instead reframes gay people as oppressed by decisions made by those in power to maintain pernicious hierarchies that impact all groups seeking liberation. The reader of Bob's response to Bernard is not assumed to be White or privileged but an individual who has an interest in mobilizing to contest oppression more broadly. Describing gay identity in these terms shifted understandings away from behavioral definitions favored by homophiles and positioned it as an effect of politics and thus necessarily oriented toward political action.

This theme resonated in subsequent discussions of gay identity and political action that took place in the pages of Come Out!, especially as descriptions of gay identity as analogous to other oppressed groups gave way to an emphasis on targeting the institutions, laws, and individuals in power that maintain the status quo. Sexism, in particular, was identified as the primary force that gives shape to and defines experiences of oppression for all marginalized groups. The development of sexism as the target for liberation movements was reflected by authors regardless of their position within Gay Liberation or GLF. For example, Ellen Broidy, who was one of the organizers of the first Gay Pride marches in New York City, wrote on behalf of New York University's chapter of Gay Student Liberation in *Come Out!* to explain that although everybody has different motivations and objectives when they participate in protests, "the base upon which any action rests must be a revolutionary ideal, a new way. This kind of commitment would bring along a much needed sense of community—knowing that . . . the enemy is common to all, whether in the guise of imperialism, racism, or sexism."[23] This orientation of politics against the shared enemies of imperialism, racism, and sexism echoes the mission statements of *Come Out!* and GLF and is noteworthy for the ways that it poses gays and lesbians as a unified community alongside and within radical activist movements. That is, rather than prioritizing political interests along a single dimension of identity—gay or lesbian identification—Broidy and others active in GLF during this period saw lesbians and gay men as a natural fit in radical politics. This positioning prioritized comprehensive changes to the institutions and ideologies that structured and maintained linked oppressions that affected all politically, socially, and economically marginalized groups. Across these examples of GLF discourse, gay and lesbian collective identity was understood as a balance of identity and solidarity as gay political praxis, with the latter receiving more weight. Gay people, in other words, were just one of many radical groups that fought shoulder to shoulder for liberation. Perhaps most important, the goal for Gay Liberationists was not the pursuit of rights; the goal was revolutionary social change understood entirely outside the framework of rightful citizenship claims.

Representing Gay Liberation

The last issue of *Come Out!* was published in 1972 and reflected these shifts, particularly as authors crystallized Gay Liberation understandings of gay identity as multiracial and revolutionary against the first rumblings of what

would come to known as gay liberalism, which would be marked by an exclusive focus on rights, electoral politics, assimilation, and reform. These
comments on liberalism's perceived perils were new to the pages of *Come
Out!*, and their appearance in the final issue suggests that GLF anticipated
the imminent shuttering of the organization with some warnings for future political action. Under the heading "On Liberalism," for example, the
Ad Hoc Gay Men's Committee explained, "In the struggle for liberation, it is
necessary to distinguish between liberalism and radicalism. Liberalism has
always been the ideology of the hetero-sexist oppressor, attempting to keep
oppressed groups appeased with token concessions, all while wearing a false
mask of benevolence."[24] These anti-assimilationist sentiments were echoed
in another section of the newsletter that detailed hearings for an amendment that would have added sexual orientation to New York City's Human
Rights law. Authors identified as the Gay Switchboard criticized these efforts
at inclusion and took aim at liberalism itself, explaining, "It [the New York
City Human Rights Law] will help a Gay doctor, for example. . . . It might
help teachers. But as Ralph Hall says in *Faggot*,[25] 'we'll now have queer cops
and queer firemen.' In other words, we'll be legalizing our own deviancy."[26]
Reading these two excerpts alongside each other indicates the degree to
which Gay Liberation thinking had evolved in a short period of time to emphasize radical social changes to upend sexism, racism, and imperialism.
These views were widely held. For example, in the same issue, Steven Gavin,
a prominent Black gay activist, described dehumanization as the feature
shared by racism and sexism and urged readers to see that "[t]he oppressor
tries to convince his victims they are subhuman by their very existence. He
creates a society whose very foundation incorporates this dehumanization
and then compels his victims to function in this diabolical creation." Gavin
went on to outline the Gay Liberation response: "It remains for all of us to
develop a joint consciousness, to be able to transcend our own oppression
to reach a common group with our sisters and brothers in all true liberation
Collectivity and Consciousness Raising."[27]

The focus on joint consciousness articulated by Gavin in the final issue of
the newsletter captures the evolution of gay identity that took place in the
pages of *Come Out!* during its brief run. Understanding gay identity as intimately bound up with antiracist, antisexist, anticapitalist, and anti-imperial
struggles marked a significant departure from earlier Gay Liberation discourse that viewed gay identity as analogous, and thus separate from, race,
gender, nationality, and class (see Figure 2.1). For Gay Liberationists and

Figure 2.1 "Coming Out for Good," cartoon, *Come Out!* 2, no. 7b (Spring–Summer 1971): n.p.

the gay Left, to identify as gay was to not only make a statement about one's sexuality but to also commit to a form of political praxis in solidarity with all oppressed people. Although GLF shuttered after this issue of *Come Out!*, the political ethos cultivated in Gay Liberation discourse did not entirely give way to other approaches to gay political action, namely gay liberalism. Rather, Gay Liberationists directed their attention to socialist struggles in Central America that were gaining steam in the 1970s and 1980s and sought opportunities to work with women of color feminists to advance radical social changes domestically.[28] As I will show in the following chapters, proponents of Gay Liberation's vision for political identity and praxis worked continuously to combat the dominance of efforts toward assimilation, rights, and inclusion by highlighting those who were left out of those agendas.

Conflict: Ruptures in Gay Liberation and What It Means to Be Gay

Internal conflicts over the question of solidarity as gay political praxis resulted in a series of dramatic ruptures in GLF, in which some members argued that the strategy ought to be abandoned and energy focused on mobilizing political issues pertaining solely to the unique marginalization experienced by gay people. Others asserted that GLF was no longer necessary given that the goal was radical change, and they advocated for establishing separatist communities where people could live in a manner that reflected their revolutionary ideals. These conflicts over appropriate political strategies and goals illustrate the ever-shifting constructions of gay political identity going into the early 1970s. Whereas early GLF activism focused on constructing gay identity as another facet of human diversity and working alongside and within radical social movement struggles for revolution, the political organizations that split off from GLF in the early 1970s concentrated efforts on constructing gay people as a discrete minority group that would be legible in electoral politics as a valuable voting bloc. These new organizations used rightful citizenship claims to represent what they perceived to be the unique political interests of gay people and channeled resources into constructing gay people as a minority group that would be visible and powerful in law and politics.

The most consequential conflict over the definition of gay political identity, strategies, and agenda ended with some members leaving GLF to form a new organization, the Gay Activists Alliance. GLF solidarity with the Black Panthers was the focus of the dispute. The pages of *Come Out!* reflect that GLF often worked in partnership with the Black Panthers to support and mobilize protest actions in New York City and was considered so embedded within those efforts that representatives from GLF were also invited to participate in the 1970 Black Panther Revolutionary People's Constitutional Convention. The year before, in 1969, the Black Panthers requested the assistance of various radical organizations to post bail for the Panther 21, a group of Black Panthers who were arrested and accused of planning coordinated attacks on New York City police officers.[29] Although the GLF conducted meetings without any sort of hierarchy, it did adhere to the notion that participation should be democratic and strive for consensus, and therefore put the question of contributing to the Panther 21 bail fund to a vote by all members. The debates over spending a portion of the GLF's small treasury for the Panther 21 were divisive, with many arguing that the GLF simply did not have enough money to justify the contribution.[30] Although the majority of GLF members ultimately voted to support the Panther 21 fund, there remained a strong contingent in opposition. The vote and the associated dispute caused a rift in GLF; those against the allocation of funds were led by the treasurer, Jim Owles, who promptly resigned from the organization and formed the GAA as an alternative Gay Liberation group.

The vision for the organization as a powerful one that would have chapters across the country is reflected in the circulation of "The GAA Alternative" in 1971, which specified how chapters should run and how members ought to understand gay identity. Immediately apparent is the emphasis that the GAA founders placed on establishing the organization as concerned solely with issues pertaining to gay people and the focus on rightful citizenship claims as the vehicle for advancing those issues in politics. These statements of purpose and the emphasis on rights contrasted sharply with GLF's mission, which advocated creating a space where different groups could engage in dialogue to find common ground and band together to fight oppression. For example, "The GAA Alternative" opened with the assertion "The gay liberation movement is a movement for the right to be different, the right to be free."[31] This emphasis on rights is also reflected in the Preamble, in which the authors state, "Before the public conscience, we demand an immediate end to all oppression of homosexuals and the immediate unconditional recognition of these basic rights" to introduce a litany of rights claims that span topics ranging from emotions to bodily integrity.[32]

These founding documents as well as speeches by GAA leadership reveal two themes that indicate the extent to which GAA founders used GLF understandings of political identity and political praxis as a foil for developing alternative ways of thinking about gay identity and politics. The first dominant theme was the vision of GAA as a single-issue organization to cultivate "gay solidarity" as a new form of political praxis, in which gay-identified people exclusively sought each other out to mobilize politically. This represented a significant shift away from GLF's understanding of solidarity, which cut across difference to work alongside and within movements to advance radical social, political, and economic changes. Foregrounding rightful citizenship claims is the second theme. Whereas discussions of rights rarely appeared in GLF discourse, many of the GAA's founding documents and subsequent political actions highlighted rights as the primary political objective sought by the group. Deploying rightful citizenship claims as a political strategy contributed to constructions of identity along a single axis—sexuality—to the exclusion of intersecting identifications that include race, gender, and class, among many others.

I read GAA's founding documents as examples of conflicts among political actors and members over how to understand gay political action and identity. In this instance, viewing the break with the Black Panthers as the motivating impetus behind the founding of GAA indicates how the emphasis on gay identity was racialized, specifically as leaders in GAA took issue with working in solidarity with Black activists on issues pertaining directly to systemic racism, mass incarceration, and the overpolicing of Black, Asian, and Latine activists. GAA leaders were aware of this criticism, however, and portrayed the policy of precluding coalitions as a way to avoid the disagreements that were seen to characterize the sometimes slow-moving politics of GLF, which were rife with prolonged discussions about how to best direct political resources and manage competing alliances. Alluding to the often-stymied political proceedings of GLF, Owles defended the GAA policy against coalitions as an instrumental tactic, explaining, "No alliances with other oppressed minorities could be argued over, for none were to be sought."[33]

Concern over time spent debating political agendas was not the only worry that led to the GAA policy against solidarity, understood broadly. "The GAA Alternative" explained to members, "A one-issue commitment in a gay organization builds an intense sense of common gay identity in its members."[34] That is, rather than identifying radical social change as the principal political objective pursued or cultivating identities as activists, as expressed by GLF and other radical groups, the GAA directed its political efforts internally to the task of constructing a "common gay identity," which would be achieved by urging the elevation of gay identity above all other identifications. The resulting construction of gay identity as a discrete identity category along a single dimension—sexuality—was seen by leaders to be more amenable to representation across political venues due to its power for projecting a different kind of unity. As opposed to seeking coalitions across oppressed groups and cultivating a sense of politically linked fate, or solidarity, based on those alliances, as was the strategy of GLF, the GAA put forth a construction of common gay identity to bind together all gay-identified people and *only* gay-identified people. The cohesion of gay political identity around sexuality offered the benefit of a unified identity to represent in politics but required the subordination of other identifications, most especially race, class, and, as I will show in the following chapters, gender—for both lesbians and transgender people.

Organizational structure was viewed as a key way to ensure a single-issue focus on gay rights, with GLF's nonhierarchical and loosely organized collective as the example GAA leaders worked against. Key among these structural features was reliance on a written constitution and the use of parliamentary procedure in meetings to develop an agenda of interests to advocate. While the authors of these founding documents celebrated these structural features as efficient and in the interest of promoting open dialogue, reading these documents against the history of the GLF and GAA split suggests that GAA founders were primarily interested in creating an organization that would advocate issues affecting White gay men. In a section of "The GAA Alternative" titled "A One Issue Organization," for example, the GAA founders describe the organization this way: "Restricted constitutionally to the issue of gay liberation, GAA is better able to focus and use the energy of its members." Later they explain how this focus will be useful: "Rather than being reduced to a mere clearing house which directs gays into support for other non-gay issues, GAA draws its members into the active work of gay liberation towards concrete actions that can make noticeable changes in their lives as *gays*."[35] Although these documents fail to define what constitutes a gay issue beyond the circular observation "A gay issue is one that immediately affects gay people as gays,"[36] further discussion of the reasoning behind the single-issue focus indicates that the goal is to construct a cohesive gay identity by elevating sexuality above other motivations for becoming involved in political action, most notably an interest in mobilizing against racism and sexism. The authors explain, "A one-issue commitment in a gay organization builds an intense sense of common gay identity in its members. Unlike the members of many multi-issue gay organizations, we do not come to think of ourselves as primarily men or women, blacks or whites; we come to think of ourselves primarily as gays. Although involved with other issues outside the organization, when we come together in GAA we experience a heightened feeling of ourselves as brothers and sisters with positive personal character-istics that derive from our being gay."[37] These policies on membership are designed to constitute the organization as well as gay identity. More specif-ically, to be a member of GAA is to commit an explicitly anti-intersectional understanding of one's identity, in which racial and gender identities must be situationally severed from sexuality for the sake of political action with GAA. Despite the authors speculating at various points throughout "The GAA Alternative" that these policies are not meant to preclude members from taking part in other movements, the consistent use of the word "other" reflects the presumption that political issues and identities are discrete and do not have points of overlap. Naturalizing movements and identities as sep-arate consequently paved the way for those individuals who do not need to engage in the complex negotiation of sloughing off one's raced or gendered experiences to participate in political action with GAA: White gay men. In this view, the repeated assurance that the organization is open to all members rings false when made in conjunction with the requirement to commit to the single-issue focus on gay issues, which explicitly pushes people with mul-tiple marginalized identities out of GAA activism. Although political actors in GAA worked to minimize the effects of these anti-intersectional moves, the subsequent formation of lesbian, bisexual, and transgender political or-ganizations against the ascendancy of GAA and rightful citizenship claims that I detail in the following chapters suggests that such claims rang hollow for all those cast to the edges of the narrow version of gay identity promoted in GAA discourse.

Gay Rights and Stigma Transformation

In addition to narrowing the boundaries of sexuality and gender iden-tity captured by the term "gay," repeated analogies to the Black civil rights struggle constructed gay identity as separate from racial identity. GAA

founder Marty Robinson articulated the model that informed GAA's political objectives and identity construction: "[L]esbians and male homosexuals
striving to define their identities and life-style are much like the Blacks and
other minorities who have found that throughout history they have allowed
themselves to be defined by others."[38] In order to wrest control over the defining characteristics of gay identity, GAA should engage in what Robinson
referred to as "image reversal": "The awakening of Black pride provided a
lesson to gays who had many of the same problems as Blacks: a poor self-
image and a poor public image in an endless feedback loop. The concept of
'Gay Pride' and 'Gay is Good' closely parallels the Black efforts for a more
positive identity."[39] GAA would thus provide representation of gay identity
as a minority group with unique interests similar to political organizations
representing Black people. However, in a noteworthy departure from GLF
rhetoric, which made similar efforts at stigma transformation and imagined
its politics as in solidarity with Black politics, Robinson and other leaders in
GAA argued that gay identity was analogous to, or to use Robinson's word,
"parallel" to Black identity and, by extension, Black politics. The rhetorical
power of this analogy stems from the comparison to a movement that had
been successful in advancing rightful citizenship claims attached to voting
and political standing, particularly in the context of the early 1970s, when
these victories loomed large in the political imaginations of activists. And
yet, posing gay identity and Black identity as analogous in GAA discourse
relied on the conception of these two groups as discrete and operating in relative isolation from each other. The requirement to elevate sexuality above all
other identities in order to participate in GAA activism indicates that only
White gay men would be invited into political action, and that their rights
would be foregrounded.

This separation of gay identity, racial identity, and gender (especially with
respect to women but also including transgender women and men) explicitly poses each as discrete identity categories that can be prioritized, or not,
at will. The political importance of this distinction lies in what is lost in the
assertion that one aspect of identity can be emphasized over another. Such a
framing necessarily forecloses conceptualizing gay identity as shaped by race
and gender.[40] Equally important, it sacrifices an understanding of sexuality
that achieves its very meaning from racialized and gendered assumptions
about the proper roles of women and men, gender norms, and the heterosexual nuclear family, all of which combine to erase differences and consequently naturalize White male sexuality.[41] The rhetorical elevation of "gay" as

a discrete identity thus projected it as a narrowly defined group with White, gay men (who are gender-normative) as the central referent.

The elevation of gay White men served an instrumental purpose as GAA began to gain momentum in advancing rightful citizenship claims. Whereas GLF promoted solidarity as political praxis to build critical mass and inject concerns of gay- and lesbian-identified people into radical politics with the hopes of effecting broader social and political changes, the GAA political strategy focused on drawing the attention of elected officials to issues related to discrimination against gay-identified people, narrowly defined. The GAA policy for political action prescribed a strategy of "militant tactics" to draw attention to discrimination to combat silence from elected officials on issues pertaining to sexuality.[42] An example of a militant tactic that the GAA used to draw attention to issues related to gay-identified people was "the zap," during which a group of GAA members would disrupt a political event. These interruptions often took the form of glitter or a pie being thrown into a politician's face during a press conference, or the monopolization of a question-and-answer session during a town hall event.[43] A key architect of the GAA constitution, Arthur Evans, saw the GAA zaps as a way to tell politicians and elected officials that "they are going to become responsible to other people": "We will make them responsible to us—or we will stop the conduct of the business of government!"[44] The zaps, in other words, would be employed as a strategy to urge attention to rightful citizenship claims made in the name of concerns pertaining to sexuality. That gay White men were best positioned to engage in zaps without severe consequences, such as incarceration or assassination by police, as was the case for Black and Latine activists during this time, underscores the ways that rightful citizenship claims implicitly foreground Whiteness as a precondition for political action.

Zaps were used as a site for identity construction by GAA, in which members of the GAA would call into being a very particular (i.e., White and masculine) understanding of gay identity and demand its representation in formal politics. Robinson shows how the GAA desire to portray gay-identified people as a sizable voting bloc had taken hold when he explains the logic of the zap as necessary because "gays comprise one of the largest minorities in America. They are capable of getting the representation they need, but can only do so, it seems, by public confrontations that *make* politicians face and respond to issues they otherwise avoid."[45] Whereas GLF discourse saw gay men and lesbian women as a small segment of a larger minority community with which they sought solidarity to fight oppression,

GAA rhetoric posed gay-identified people as one of the largest minority groups in the United States and deserving of political representation and civil rights on their own terms. This perception of gay people as a sizable, yet disconnected, population was used to justify fashioning GAA as an interest group concerned with providing political advocacy on their behalf, with rightful citizenship claims—such as representation through voting—constituting the primary focus for the new organization.

In addition to constitutionally mandating a single-issue focus and the use of militant tactics, the founding documents stipulate that all meetings and decisions would be conducted using formal parliamentary procedure, or *Robert's Rules of Order*. This approach to decision-making represented a significant shift away from GLF structure, which promoted consciousness-raising and consensus-building tactics drawn from feminist organizing and nonhierarchical approaches to decision-making that aimed to give voice to as many people as possible. When asked about this way of running meetings, Owles explained in a 1972 interview, "There was to be room in GAA for gay people of every political hue, as long as they were willing to work in a structured organization with parliamentary procedure and work militantly, though non-violently, for gay liberation."[46] Owles and other leaders of GAA saw parliamentary procedure as an important departure from other Gay Liberation and radical movement organizations of the time, which they perceived to be stymied by excessive discussions regarding how to allocate resources to reflect the Gay Liberation ideal of solidarity as political praxis. Like the constitutionally mandated single-issue focus, the assumption that people were free to join GAA on the condition that they prioritize gay liberation above all other political objectives forced people of color to choose between interwoven aspects of their identity, such as race, ethnicity, gender, class, and being gay or lesbian. The open break with feminist and nonhierarchical modes of decision-making also emphasized, however implicitly, that feminist tactics and, by association, feminists themselves would not be welcome in GAA mobilizations.

Although Owles and other leaders imagined that a strong constitution and parliamentary procedure would help to ensure a voice for all members and aid in the projection of GAA as a serious political organization, there were many instances of members expressing how the reliance on a rigid organizational structure silenced their voices. Especially affected were gay- and lesbian-identified Black, Third World, and/or working-class members. Arthur Bell, another of the GAA's founders, publicly announced his departure from the organization in 1971 for this very reason: "Many liberationists are not into hard core politics. Many Blacks [sic], transvestites, transexuals [sic], street people, women, plain people and fancy people found they wanted to relate, yet the gifts they had to give were not accepted. Understandably, they deserted us. This fact had to be obvious to the people at the top of the family totem pole. But they set up GAA as a political reformist organization 'according to the constitution.' Period."[47] Bell's critique explicitly states the effects of the single-issue focus mandated in the GAA constitution and the privileged position of White gay men within the organization: exclusion of a variety of voices. Most important, his departure letter describes how the single-issue focus and "hard core politics," that is, rightful citizenship claims advanced in formal politics, led to the quick departure of Black members, women, transgender people, and all those who did not share the upper- and middle-class status of members who remained in the organization. As might be imagined, Bell was not alone in voicing these concerns. In one of the last issues of *Come Out!* before GLF folded due to financial troubles, a piece titled simply "An Article" by eben clark elaborated the joy of being an out gay-identified person active in the political work of GLF and GAA, but expressed strong reservations about the ways that the various rules of GAA organized minority voices out of meeting proceedings.[48] clark explained, "i watched parliamentary procedure destroy minorities within the group. minorities that did not know how to use parliamentary procedure for them and so had it used against them."[49] Whereas Owles outlined the vision of broad inclusion to be achieved through parliamentary procedure, clark's experience was that it silenced, and was even used to "destroy," the voices of minorities within the group. These contradictory observations call into question *whose* voices were to be heard in GAA organizing. clark offered an answer: "i soon discovered that while i was talking gay liberation those in control were talking gay power. while i was talking freedom they were talking politics. while i was talking honesty-to-self they were talking success."[50] The litany of binaries that clark put forward underscored how GAA's political agenda of rightful citizenship claims contradicted Gay Liberation's strong emphasis on personal authenticity, liberation, solidarity, and radical politics. Furthermore, clark's critique articulated how the turn toward rightful citizenship claims entailed the loss of some of Gay Liberation's founding principles, especially the understanding that marginalization stems from oppressive ideologies that impacted many groups, regardless of identity. In the context of GAA activism, sexuality—understood as same-sex desire—was the defining characteristic of gay and lesbian identities, and not shared experiences of marginalization alongside many identity-based groups, as GLF rhetoric asserted. Foregrounding rightful citizenship claims in GAA's political agenda paved the way for this shift, requiring as it did the elevation of gay White men who were best poised to receive those benefits. Put differently, the marginalization of race, gender, and class from gay identity enabled the construction of it as solely associated with sexuality, which, in turn, collapsed sexuality with Whiteness and masculinity.

Representation: Coming Out as a Political Rite

One of the enduring contributions of the Gay Liberation period on gay political identity construction and agenda development was the introduction of "coming out," or the act of publicly proclaiming gay identification, to be performed as a mark of personal authenticity and commitment to gay political praxis. To come out was to seize power over the perception of gay people and was understood as an act of representation, in which the person coming out would work to shape understandings of gay people, gay identity, and relevant political concerns. The title of GLF's newsletter, *Come Out!*, underscores the importance placed on this act by Gay Liberationists, who valued it for its power to combat stigmas imposed on same-sex desire and relationships. To come out was to seize the power of representation to model self-acceptance and urge positive social, political, and economic changes.

In the first step of coming out prescribed by Gay Liberation discourse, one articulates one's gay identification to family, friends, and coworkers. Embracing gay identity was viewed as naturally leading to the second step of coming out as political action, in which one pursued broader social acceptance to mirror one's own self-acceptance.[51] Steve Dansky, one of the founding members of GLF, summarized this dynamic and the motivation behind advocating for people to come out: "[L]iberationists understood that 'coming out' had the capacity to be transformative because it turned personal action into political statement."[52] Coming out, in other words, was considered political for its potential to align personal identity with the efforts to change the political standing and visibility of all gay people. Visibility would thus take on political importance—an action to represent and shape what would be known of gay identity. By emphasizing individual self-knowledge and authenticity as linked to political action, Gay Liberationists sought to portray coming out as a grassroots political act with the potential to incite broader social change and acceptance for gays and lesbians.

The importance of coming out as a grassroots political act to promote positive representations and challenge stigmas was highlighted in many of the personal narratives featured in *Come Out!*. These personal narratives—filled with triumph over disapproving family members or coworkers—provided examples of strategies for readers to use when coming out. They also helped to pose coming out as a rite for attaining membership in the growing politically active gay community. In one such interview in the first issue of *Come Out!*, a woman identified only as Kay captures the significance of the self-recognition associated with coming out: "I see half of gay liberation as a sort of attempt to try to change other people outside of ourselves—to try to make them stop oppressing us. But the half that interests me most now, at the beginning of my gay liberation, is self liberation."[53] In addition to coming out as a political act to contest the stigmas typically associated with gay identity, coming out, according to Kay, is initially an opportunity to reconcile personal discomfort with same-sex desire. One not only comes out to family and friends, but one also comes out to oneself, and is thus liberated from internalized oppression and better positioned to more effectively participate in radical politics as a result. GLF discourse on coming out promoted it as a necessary first step toward political mobilization and shaped the understanding of gay identity as authentic, visible and public, constitutive of group membership, and radical, all of which aimed to combat the broader social and political environment of stigmas against same-sex sexuality by representing gay life as political and offering more robust ways to live.

The twin themes of gay identity as political and the key to living authentically resonate throughout Gay Liberation discourse. An article in the first issue of *Come Out!* by Leo Louis Martello, one of GLF's founders, articulates this relationship more explicitly: "It works like this: If I secretly think of myself as shit then anyone who is involved with me, or who is like me, must be shit too. This is the brainwashed role that all minorities have been forced into: The blacks, Chicanos, poor whites, homosexuals, etc. In order not to be alone join the GAY LIBERATION FRONT. Learn about yourself and others, and more importantly, learn to like yourself."[54] Martello takes aim at the prevailing view of homosexuality as mental illness. Like Kay, coming out for Martello is an act of self-recognition that overcomes internalized discomfort, or learning to "like yourself," with the knowledge that those feelings stem from oppressive ideologies that brainwash all marginalized groups. Coming out and publicly embracing gay identification was consequently both a political act and one that would enhance social and political life by bringing one into conversation and connection with others who shared similar feelings.

Coming out was also valued for its power to inject positive representations of gay people into the mainstream, and the pages of *Come Out!* are filled with reports from gay men and lesbians laying claim to the transformative power of coming out for shifting negative associations. In the very first issue, GLF members organized as the Gay Commandos reported attending a New York City mayoral candidate forum held at Temple Torah in Queens, where they faced resistance and outright hostility from the politicians on the stage. Although the candidates failed to provide satisfactory responses to questions about the status of gay people in New York City raised by GLF members, the authors of the article proclaimed the event a success due to the sympathy and acceptance they received from nongay people in the audience. The article concluded, "We had come out. In this temple people talked to us, met us, and many were astounded. In America, there are a few, token, public, known homosexuals. No wonder people think that we are weird. They never see us. That night they did. Twisted characterizations of what it meant to be homosexual gave way to the sight of real people, determined self-respecting homosexuals. Hello, world! Dig us. No apologies. We have come out. Now world, we want our share, now we want our share."[55] These celebratory words from the Gay Commandos capture the significance Gay Liberationists assigned to coming out. The final line of the article, in which the authors lay claim to "our share," reflects how coming out was understood to be a fundamentally political action that was focused not on claiming rights but on asserting positive associations with gay identity and creating chances to gain social and political standing. Engaging in simple activities, such as having conversations with others in places where gay people were mistakenly perceived to be absent—America, candidate forums, Jewish temples, and the entire borough of Queens—was promoted in GLF discourse as an opportunity to alter perceptions of gay people and knit them into the fabric of those spaces. In addition to altering stigmas, coming out was celebrated as an act of representation that reflected the ethos of solidarity as gay political praxis.

GAA discourse also placed heavy emphasis on coming out; however, in contrast to GLF's focus on coming out as a path toward personal authenticity in which one prefigures the acceptance and social change one wants to see, GAA discourse reflected the focus on sexuality as the central characteristic of gay political identity, to the exclusion of racial, gender, and class identities. This focus on rightful citizenship claims in conjunction with coming out contributed to this narrowed understanding of gay identity. "The GAA Alternative" explained, "Most of the gay population is still in the closet. Because gay issues have never been dealt with openly in the past, the gay population has tended to be apathetic and apolitical, rightly feeling that it made little difference in terms of gay rights which candidate or party came to power. Only by making gays visible and gay issues public can the gay vote be made into a credible threat."[56] According to the GAA vision for coming out, gay people were to be united through the process of coming out and proudly asserting gay identification, which would in turn constitute them as a powerful voting bloc. Also noteworthy is the presumed interest in rights. Unlike GLF rhetoric about coming out that sought presence in space alongside people involved in radical and grassroots politics, GAA political actors viewed coming out as a process of becoming politically involved in electoral politics and in the pursuit of power, rights, and recognition. This formulation foreshadowed the introduction of Coming Out Day, held annually on October 11, as a voter registration event by interest groups in the 1990s.

This view of coming out as a necessary step to take on the path of joining a political field defined by voting and electoral politics set the stage for privileging gay identity and politics above other identifications, especially racial identities. Writing in the early 1990s and reflecting the legacy of this narrow understanding of gay political identity, Isaac Julien and Kobena Mercer describe feeling compelled to come out as gay men as a necessary step to being considered politically active: "Sometimes we cannot afford to live without the support of our brothers and sisters, mothers and fathers, yet we also need to challenge the homophobic attitudes we encounter in our communities. But white gays have passed all this by because race is not an issue for them. Instead, the horizon of their political consciousness has been dominated by concerns with individualized sexuality."[57] This passage illustrates the consequences of coming-out rhetoric that promotes the elevation of sexuality over all other facets of identity. For Julien and Mercer, coming out in such a way entails steep costs: the potential loss of one's Black community and family. But living as gay men does not necessarily mean foreclosing political activity. Rather than elevating gay identity or "individualized sexuality" as White gay-identified people have done, Julien and Mercer imagine possibilities for challenging the discomfort of their families and altering stigmas from positions of safety within the Black community. This multifaceted and intersectional understanding of identity and political praxis is not a form of political action that would be legible in the model of coming out or gay identity introduced by GAA proponents, which emphasized sexuality as the exclusive basis for social and political action. And yet, Cathy Cohen observes, "[t]he acceptance of this conditional black membership is not irrational when we consider the threat of racism faced by many black lesbians and gay men outside of black communities."[58] When read through Cohen, Julien and Mercer's hesitation to come out as a first step toward political action underscores the consequences of such a narrow view of gay identity. While White gay men and lesbian women seemed to enjoy unprecedented visibility for their political concerns by coming out and mobilizing rightful citizenship claims to win what they perceived to be theirs, Black gay people were increasingly rendered invisible within GAA and, by extension, gay identity and gay politics.

Conclusions: Gay Identity for Whom?

This chapter has shown how the construction of gay identity that came to dominate popular understandings not only excluded gay- and lesbian-identified people who were Black, Latine, Asian, Native, transgender, bisexual, and/or women, but also cast them to the borders of gay identity as a foil to underscore the claim that White gay men were natural claimants for rights. Using rightful citizenship claims in movement discourse shaped this construction of gay political identity along a single axis. This is illustrated most starkly in the diverging views of gay identity put forward by GLF and GAA, which had overlapping memberships but different understandings of gay identity and political agendas that varied with respect to the emphasis placed on rights claims and political tactics. Those who identified themselves within and alongside radical movements fostered open discourse about sexuality and targeted oppressive ideologies like sexism, racism, capitalism, and imperialism with actions designed to build critical mass, cultivate solidarity among oppressed people, and pursue revolutionary change. Others argued that gay people faced unique social and political challenges that stemmed from their sexuality, and foregrounded claims to recognition and rights as citizens.

Initially, it is easy to see how these two views on identity and political action have been framed in opposition to each other under the banner of "radical" versus "assimilationist" politics that differ solely with respect to ideas about political strategy and goals. However, this chapter underscores how gay identity was shaped by conflicts over who, exactly, constitutes the proper membership of the group, with race and gender determining where one fits. The founding of GAA in response to anger over partnerships with the Black Panthers illustrates the racialized undercurrents of these splits rather starkly, with GLF members breaking away from the organization and establishing a parallel one to advocate gay people understood anti-intersectionally. These splits took on new significance after GLF folded. Would naming oneself as gay connote a shared understanding of power and opposition to the oppressive and divisive status quo, regardless of who one desires? Or would "gay" be understood as a personal identity defined exclusively by difference from heterosexual norms and same-sex desire? This analysis of gay identity's nascent moments reveals how the deployment of rightful citizenship claims implicitly and explicitly shape understandings of who belongs within the group and who will be cast to the margins.

This chapter also shows how the use of rightful citizenship claims function anti-intersectionally by elevating those members of the group who can state that they would not experience marginalization but for their sexual identity: White gay men and some White lesbians. These boundaries of group identity were enforced through the logic of coming out, which could be safely performed only by White people in positions to force rifts with their families, friends, and social circles. As a result, Black, Asian, and Latine gay men and lesbians, women, transgender people, and poor people, among many others, were organized out of political mobilizations in the name of "gay politics." The raced and gendered dynamics of exclusion enacted through the elevation of rightful citizenship claims in the late 1960s and early 1970s set the stage for the negotiations over lesbian, bisexual, transgender, and LGBT identities in the following chapters.

Finally, the evolution of these different meanings indexed as "gay" highlights that political identities are not static, essential, or based on shared traits but are instead products of rhetorical maneuverings that occur during processes of stigma transformation, conflicts over meanings and agendas, and representation across political venues. That two different political organizations can use "gay" to connote diverging memberships should give scholars pause when they use such terms to refer to a presumably homogeneous identity category. Throughout this chapter and the ones that follow, I cite the voices of those excluded from this narrow and dominant construction of gay identity to underscore the epistemic, social, and political effects of the tendency to engage in within-group marginalization during the processes of identity group construction and agenda development.

3

Feminism Is the Theory, Lesbianism Is the Practice

Jean O'Leary, whose life of lesbian and gay activism spanned the founding of several organizations and the creation of an annual National Coming Out Day, which is still celebrated each year on October 11, offered the following reflection on lesbians in Gay Liberation organizations: "We were trying to establish our identity and, wherever we could, gain visibility. Just as gay people have had to become visible in society, lesbians had to become visible with the gay community, as well as in the larger society. Up until that time, whenever people thought about gays, they thought only about gay men."[1] The writings and speeches examined in this chapter illustrate how the introduction of lesbian identity to the political realm that O'Leary speaks of here was premised on the need to render lesbians visible in a political context dominated not only by gay men, but also by feminists in the mainstream women's movement who demanded that lesbians remain silent about their sexuality as a condition for participation in feminist politics.[2] It is against this backdrop of dual erasure that lesbian activists formulated lesbian identification as a legible and explicitly political—or feminist—approach to political subjectivity.

One construction of lesbian identity that emerged during the 1970s drew upon biological difference—sex, in their terms—to distinguish lesbians from gay men and align them with burgeoning women's movements. These self-proclaimed radical lesbian feminists portrayed lesbians as the vanguard of feminism due to their rejection of relationships with men, who were understood as agents of patriarchy who maintained the monopoly on rights, political standing, and access to social and public space. In response, these new lesbian feminists prioritized a revolution that would abolish patriarchy and male domination, or at the very least withdraw from the patriarchal social order to establish lesbian separatist communities where only women would be welcome and enjoy unmitigated rights. Central to the construction of the radical lesbian feminist, then, was the idea that being assigned female at

Terms of Exclusion. Zein Murib, Oxford University Press. © Oxford University Press 2023.
DOI: 10.1093/oso/9780197671498.003.0004

birth set one up for a lifetime of experiences shaped by sexism, and that these negative experiences informed the grievances that radical lesbian feminists were mobilizing to contest. The emphasis on biological difference worked in tandem with rightful citizenship logic to collapse lesbian identity along a single axis: the newly designated "woman-identified woman," defined with baffling circular logic that used "woman" as both adjective and subject to close the new subject off from difference, would be afforded all the rights and privileges of social, political, and economic standing were it not for the prevailing ideology of patriarchy or the ruling social, economic, and political orders helmed by men.

Elevating the presumably universal experiences of women under patriarchy helped to maintain movement coherence and build critical mass but also required policing the boundaries of lesbian identity and the woman-identified woman to mobilize rightful citizenship claims. My analysis of lesbian feminist rhetoric from this period of rapid change shows that the construction of the radical lesbian feminist, or the prototypical woman-identified woman, was maintained by vehemently denying the ways that race, class, and gender identity also shaped experiences of marginalization, not just for women but for all people. These exclusions were enacted through rightful citizenship claims that foregrounded the entitlement of lesbians and woman-identified women to freedom from patriarchal domination. Emphasizing biological similarity—understood anti-intersectionally—grounded these new political demands while also paving the way for lesbians to position themselves as vanguards of feminism due to the perception that they represented the ultimate resistance to patriarchal domination: refusing intimacy with men. While this within-group marginalization solidified the borders of lesbian identity by attaching it to the purportedly universal experiences of women, it did so at the cost of creating an unwelcoming and at times hostile environment for Black and Third World lesbians, whose political interests they failed to recognize and in some cases actively refused. Additionally, butch and femme lesbians as well as transgender women were excluded due to the perceived threats they posed to the biological logic that grounded the construction of lesbian feminist identity.[3]

Although the radical lesbian feminist as woman-identified woman would come to dominate mainstream perceptions of lesbians and, to some degree, feminists in general during this time, there were simultaneous movements by those who took what Ange-Marie Hancock refers to as a much more "intersectional-like" approach to identity and political action active within women's movements.[4] Black and Third World lesbian feminists during this same period organized, made art, gave speeches, and published essays that theorized ways to integrate sex/gender, sexuality, race, nation, and indigeneity in both lesbian identity and political praxis. These approaches resisted rightful citizenship logic and made explicit breaks with biology as the basis for identity, particularly in the refusal to abandon political partnerships with Black and Third World men who were also engaged in antiracist and anticolonial struggles. Focusing instead on the effects of gender, race, and class in shaping experiences of marginalization, these political actors and thinkers highlighted the interlocking nature of dominant ideologies beyond patriarchy, locating the roots of oppression in White supremacy, heteropatriarchy, capitalism, and imperialism. Black and Third World lesbian feminists built on this multifocal approach to power and advocated for grassroots political praxis that would center their political and social grievances to enact revolutionary change with the idea that doing so stood to benefit all marginalized people, not just lesbians. Whereas radical lesbian feminists and woman-identified women prioritized achieving movement coherence through the rejection of difference to shore up the boundaries of lesbian identity, Black and Third World lesbian feminists theorized difference as a resource that would propel radical changes when tapped. This process of relating across difference was not assumed to be an easy task; it was soberly assessed as challenging and even painful, but worth the investment of energy to ensure that all voices were heard when formulating political goals.

Thus what emerged as the 1970s came to a close were competing understandings of lesbian identity: one that prioritized rightful citizenship claims for lesbians as woman-identified women and another that foreshadowed the introduction of "intersectionality" as a political analytic as well as "queer" as a more expansive approach to normativity and power.[5] As with my examination of Gay Liberation rhetoric, which sought continuities and meaningful divisions in the different constructions of gay identity advanced by political actors and members in GLF and GAA, the analysis in this chapter probes these variations to highlight the contingency of identity and the role of discourse in constructing what came to be known of lesbian identity. What emerges is a picture of lesbian political identity and activism that was hotly contested by political actors and lesbians themselves, as they negotiated the meanings associated with lesbian identity and who, exactly, could call themselves lesbians. I highlight moments of exclusion and rupture in these debates to underscore the role of rightful citizenship claims in producing narrow versions of identity—in this case, what would come to be known of lesbian identity.

In this chapter, I first introduce the conflicts that lesbians involved in Gay Liberation engaged in to create a political identity that was understood as distinct from gay identity. The result of these ruptures was the introduction of the radical lesbian feminist and the woman-identified woman, and I examine how this particular focus on the woman-identified woman closed off lesbian identification to difference, most notably race and ethnicity but also gender differences such as butches, femmes, and transgender women. I then turn to Black and Third World lesbian feminist thinking to examine the ways that their construction of lesbian identity maintained some similarities with radical lesbian thought, namely the attachment to a political agenda organized in relation to people assigned female at birth and self-identified as women, but presented alternative, intersectional understandings of lesbian identity and politics that would ultimately prove to be a more nuanced approach to contesting dominant ideologies. Examining these two constructions alongside each other in this chapter underscores the role played by discourse during conflict, stigma transformation, and representation in constructing what comes to be known of identities. The contrast between the two understandings of lesbian identity that emerged out of the 1970s, as well as their legacies, illustrate my argument that rightful citizenship claims require collapsing identities along a single axis and promote within-group marginalization that ultimately defines what comes to be known about a political identity and political agendas.

Making Lesbian Identity: Conflicts with GLF and GAA

The previous chapter introduced how the construction of gay identity that was closely associated with gay White men during the Gay Liberation period attracted criticism from those who were pushed to the margins, specifically women, bisexuals, transgender individuals, and Black and Latine people. Lesbians were particularly focused on how social events and political agendas were dominated by gay men. Some of the men in positions of leadership were aware of these dynamics. Steve Dansky, one of the founders of GLF, explained to his colleagues in a *Come Out!* article that "lesbianism in practice is exclusive of men," going on to observe, "That is why women, from GLF, from the women's bars, or the women's movement, don't come to our male dominated GLF dances."[6] Some GAA members were similarly self-reflexive; Dennis Altman observed in a *Come Out!* piece, "[I]t is impossible to ignore the extent to which GAA is male-dominated, and I do not see any easy solution to this."[7]

Although these individuals expressed awareness of the increasingly marginalized position of women within Gay Liberation organizations, leaders of GLF and GAA did not take up the question of differentiating or prioritizing lesbian issues and interests, largely due to the assumption that lesbians belonged in those organizations given the centrality of sexuality and same-sex desire to the understanding of gay identity that took shape in Gay Liberation discourse. And yet, in both GLF and lesbian magazines, lesbian-identified members of GLF and GAA expressed disappointment in the lack of attention to their unique political interests—such as combating sexism, parental issues, and reproductive justice—in the name of advancing interests held by gay men, especially GAA's turn to rightful citizenship claims focused on gaining the attention of elected officials and agitating for rights and recognition. In response, some lesbian-identified members and allies of GLF and GAA staged public departures from these organizations for the mainstream women's movement, which cohered around political interests such as equal rights, contesting patriarchal domination, and paving the way for White women to enter the workforce. Reading these ruptures as conflicts through which the boundaries of lesbian identity was imagined and negotiated reveals the various meanings attached to "lesbian" as a political identity, with implications for who is considered members of the group and the political agendas to be advanced under the banner of lesbian politics.

These conflicts and subsequent departures were documented in widely circulated publications, speeches, and essays in which authors encouraged lesbians to form their own political movements by highlighting sex as the primary factor that distinguishes lesbians from gay men and the justification for joining the women's movement. Key among these texts was *The Ladder*, a newsletter circulated among members of a homophile social club for lesbians named the Daughters of Bilitis (DOB). From its inception in 1956 until 1970, *The Ladder* functioned primarily as a literary review focused on women's literature. The perceived subordinated status of lesbians in homophile and Gay Liberation movements and the need to leave those organizations began to take up more space in the pages of *The Ladder* beginning in 1970, when a split among DOB's leadership resulted in a change in the newsletter's editorial staff and a more explicit political focus as a result. These changes in *The*

Ladder, from a newsletter with a focus on lesbian and woman-produced art and literature to a space where political issues could be imaged and debated, reflect the changes taking place among lesbians as they reconfigured the boundaries of lesbian identity in relation to political action outside of Gay Liberation organizations or lesbian social clubs.

One of the most vocal proponents of leaving organizations dominated by gay men to establish a unique lesbian political agenda was Del Martin, whose essay "If That's All There Is" was featured in *The Ladder* and several other Gay Liberation and homophile publications between 1970 and 1971.[8] Martin's large audience for this essay is likely due to her role as one of the founders of DOB and a consistent presence within the pages of *The Ladder*. With the benefit of this wide influence, Martin's essay shaped what would come to be known of lesbian identity and political agendas, particularly in contrast to gay identity and Gay Liberation. Martin's essay began with her announcement, "After fifteen years of working for the homophile movement— of mediating, counseling, appeasing, of working for coalition and unity—I am facing a very real identity crisis. . . . I have . . . been forced to the realization that I have no brothers in the homophile movement."[9] From this opening revelation, Martin listed her experiences of marginalization within homophile organizations, including the minimization of lesbian voices in publications and the silencing of lesbian concerns in the articulations of political objectives. Martin's response that she consequently has "no brothers in the homophile movement" reads as an incisive departure from gay men due to the denial of their status as a coherent "chosen family," which is how some gay- and lesbian-identified people referred to the support networks that replaced estranged family members upon coming out. According to Martin, they must pursue a dramatic break to transition from outsiders to their own, separate group. The marginalization of women in Gay Liberation discourse on politics and gay identity, in other words, presaged Martin's introduction of "lesbian" as an alternative political and social identification.

The GLF and GAA were caught in Martin's sights as well. After announcing "Goodbye to Gay Liberation, too," Martin continued, "There is reason for the splits within their own movement, why there is a women's caucus in GLF in New York and why there is a Gay Women's Liberation in the San Francisco Bay Area. Like the tired old men they berate they have not come to grips with the gut issues. Until they do, *their* revolution cannot be ours. Their liberation would only further enslave us."[10] Referencing the "splits" in Gay Liberation alludes to the prioritization of a specifically gay identity by other Gay

Liberation organizations, especially the GAA, which saw sexuality—defined as same-sex desire—as the shared trait drawing all gay people together as they mobilized to win rights and recognition. This rhetorical elevation of sexuality functioned anti-intersectionally to minimize lesbian, race, class, and gender identification. As might be expected, then, the perceived lack of attention to issues affecting women was consequently used as justification by Martin and others to leave Gay Liberation organizations and instead join the mainstream women's movement, with many lesbians asserting, "We're angry, not gay!"[11] These conflicts over the meanings associated with gay identity—with women abandoning it in favor of lesbian identity—had the further effect of posing men and women in opposition to each other rather than as united. The subsequent departures of women from Gay Liberation organizations set the stage for reconfiguring the boundaries of lesbian identity in two key ways. First and foremost, "lesbian" was introduced as an alternative identification collapsed with being assigned female at birth and identifying as a woman. Additionally, the tight association between "lesbian" and "woman" shaped the political agendas advanced, with lesbians taking issue with gay White men advancing rightful citizenship claims framed as the denial of rights to which they were presumably entitled as citizens, but more important, as men: political standing, unencumbered access to public space, and representation of their political and economic interests. Early lesbian activists made the argument that their political agendas were different because women have never enjoyed the same rights as men. The political agendas advanced in the name of the newly formulated lesbian would focus on rightful citizenship claims to equality with men as well as freedom from patriarchal oppression and institutions. Martin's conclusion to her essay made clear that she viewed the mainstream women's movement as the best alternative home for lesbian politics: "It is a revelation to find acceptance, equality, love and friendship—everything we sought in the homophile community—not there, but in the women's movement."[12]

Stigma Transformation: Lesbians as the Vanguard of Feminism

Martin was not alone in thinking that women's movements might be a better suited home for lesbian politics; however, it was also well known that the mainstream women's movement, specifically its institutionalization in the National Organization for Women (NOW), was not hospitable to openly identified lesbians. In the first issue of *Come Out!*, Martha Shelley discussed the more abstract roots of the resistance to lesbians in the mainstream women's movement politics while describing a protest of the 1968 Miss America Pageant organized by various women's liberation groups. Her retelling of the events that took place during that protest action shows just one of the ways that lesbian identity was linked to feminist identity and, by extension, sought to alter meanings associated with the mainstream women's movement. She recalled how lesbians and straight women were united in their opposition to the pageant until counterprotesters began to use "lesbian" pejoratively to harass the protesters. Shelley noted that many of the straight women burst into tears upon hearing "lesbian" used against them as a slur, and she speculated on the stigmatization of lesbians by straight women, "Society has taught most lesbians to believe that they are sick and has taught most straight women to despise and fear the lesbian as a perverted, diseased creature."[13] Shelley contested the stigmatization of lesbians by recasting them as feminists, regardless of sexuality, writing at the end of her essay, "I have met many, many feminists who were not lesbians—but I have never met a lesbian who was not a feminist."[14] Shelley's logic implies that lesbians are prototypical feminists because they refuse intimacy with men. Deploying this rhetoric to absorb lesbian identity into feminist identity reframed lesbian identity as a central aspect of feminist identity in the face of growing resistance to out lesbians from members of various women's movement organizations across the country.

Subsequent activism worked to strengthen the association between lesbian identity and feminism, with efforts to discursively and conceptually link lesbian identity and women's movements evolving as one of the predominant themes in constructions of lesbian identity put forth by political actors during this time. NOW was the most visible target for this activism, particularly the president of NOW, Betty Freidan, who was a vocal critic of open participation by lesbians in the organization's actions and leadership. In a 1973 *New York Times* interview, she described the presence of lesbian-identified women at a meeting of feminists as a "lavender menace" and worried more generally that lesbians should "stay in the movement's closet" for fear of their "turning off Middle America women,"[15] who she implied were the proper members of the women's movement. The exclusion and hostility experienced by lesbians in those mobilizations gained in intensity as more women who had previously hidden their lesbian identity began to claim it publicly under the aegis of Gay Liberation and the prefigurative promise of coming out.[16]

To maintain the consistency of the straight-only public image that Freidan articulated in the *New York Times* interview and other places, she and other leaders at NOW initiated a purge of leadership positions to ensure that a particular image of the mainstream women's movement—palatable to "Middle America women"—would be projected.

In direct response to NOW dismissing openly identified lesbians from the organization, a group of GLF members from the Radicalesbian cell prepared to use protest tactics to combat Freidan's discriminatory rhetoric and assert their place within the mainstream women's movement. They chose an annual event that gathered all the local NOW chapters and allied organizations, the Second Conference to Unite Women, as the site for their protest action. Appropriating Freidan's pejorative phrase as their own proper noun, the Radicalesbians printed "The Lavender Menace" on T-shirts and banners and composed a ten-page lesbian feminist manifesto titled "The Woman-Identified Woman" to distribute to conference participants. In what was to become the most successful GLF protest action in the history of the organization, the Radicalesbians made a dramatic entrance to the plenary session by turning off all the lights and plunging the attendees in darkness.[17] When the lights were turned on again, the Radicalesbians were on stage brandishing "Lavender Menace" banners and had seized the microphone to initiate a conversation about the place of lesbians in the mainstream women's movement.

The Radicalesbian protest action at the Second Congress to Unite Women illustrates the role of stigma transformation and conflict over meanings in the evolving construction of lesbian identity. At the most basic level, the appropriation of the exact words used to stigmatize them as a rallying call demonstrates the ways in which response to enduring exclusion and opprobrium creates conditions that shape what comes to be known of identity boundaries. For the lesbians seeking membership in NOW specifically, and women's movements more broadly, claiming the mantle of the Lavender Menace became a source of pride and identification to combat being shut out of feminist politics. Furthermore, the role of conflict over meanings to be associated with a group cannot be understated. By using a public protest to reclaim "the lavender menace" as a positive and political identity, the activists staging the Radicalesbian protest used conflicts over meanings to reframe— and reclaim—the construction of lesbian identity as political, public, powerful, and proud.

Beyond these shifts, some also took issue with the elevation of sexuality as central to gay and, by association, lesbian identity. Calling once again on sex as the key factor that should motivate political action by women, these political actors and thinkers distanced lesbian identity from behavior and desire in their rhetoric, and in exchange emphasized general opposition to patriarchal oppression as the defining trait for lesbian identity.[18] These ruptures rearticulated biology and sex difference as the main reason to split off from gay men and pursue work within women's movements with two goals in mind. The first was to effectively establish a rupture with GAA and the centrality of White gay male experience to gay identity. The second was to articulate biological sameness as the reason for a united and cohesive political front to advance rightful citizenship claims.

These two goals were pursued by political actors through protest actions and widely circulated publications, especially *The Ladder*. For example, a key aspect of the Radicalesbian protest at the Second Conference to Unite Women was the circulation of the essay "The Woman-Identified Woman" to all participants, which was also featured in the Fall 1970 issue of *The Ladder*. In it, Rita Mae Brown, whose well-known memoir, *Rubyfruit Jungle*, introduced readers to the struggles of lesbians, outlined the terms of resistance to the backlash lesbians faced from mainstream women's movement politics with what would come to be the famous opening provocation: "A lesbian is the rage of all women condensed to the point of explosion."[19] In an effort to situate lesbians as natural members of women's movements, the authors of the essay redefined "lesbian" to sever the link with any connotations of sexuality and emphasize lesbian identity as the authentic embodiment of "woman." The reformulation of "lesbian" and "woman" was achieved discursively in a variety of ways, namely through staging conflicts over the issues that ought to be prioritized by women's movement politics. Rather than indulging in internecine conflicts between lesbians and straight women, the essay opened by explaining that the focus should be on opposing patriarchy: "It should first be understood that lesbianism, like male homosexuality, is a category of behavior possible only in a sexist society characterized by rigid sex roles and dominated by male supremacy."[20] Brown and the Radicalesbians viewed the institutionalization of sexism that constructs and maintains difference between women and men, or "sexist society," as the location for political struggle. By logical extension, then, defining "lesbian" as a set of behaviors, rather than a politicized identity category, worked to complicate the categories of "woman" and "lesbian" by minimizing the particularity of same-sex sexuality and desire typically associated with lesbian identity. For the Radicalesbians and other lesbian activists, "lesbian" was meaningful as an identity only in the context of patriarchal oppression, which they asserted ought to be challenged by a critical mass of women brought together on the basis of their sex/gender similarity, regardless of sexuality. These assertions echoed the logic of rightful citizenship claims by positing that lesbians and straight women *would* be folded into the fabric of political and social life were it not for the entrenched force of male supremacy, or patriarchy. Whereas rightful citizenship claims advanced in Gay Liberation discourse sought the inclusion of gay people as full citizens, radical lesbian feminist rhetoric advocated for upending the social order to abolish patriarchal dominance and create the conditions to secure more equal status for women in social, political, and economic life. As a result, arguing that lesbian identity is produced by a sexist society allowed lesbian political actors to contend that denying the participation of out lesbians in the women's movement merely replicated the very same oppressions that the women's movement sought to overcome.

Furthermore, by minimizing the close association of same-sex behavior with "lesbian," the reframing of lesbian identity promulgated by Brown and the Radicalesbians also produced conflicts with GLF and GAA conceptualizations of gay identity, which saw same-sex desire as the key distinction between gay and straight and the logical core of gay political identity. Sociologists Verta Taylor and Nancy Whittier explain in their study of radical and lesbian feminists that these activists sought to shift lesbian consciousness away from pathology, which was the target of Gay Liberation struggles against the American Psychiatric Association to declassify homosexuality as a mental illness, and toward an explicit political orientation that would be found in feminist thinking.[21] Being assigned female at birth and identifying as a woman evolved as a precondition for membership due to the emphasis on rights denied to women on the basis of sex. These changes were reflected in discursive strategies employed by activists, with many lesbian-feminists using "woman" or "womyn" as a synonym for "lesbian" in political writings.[22] Whereas the initial exclusion of lesbians from NOW and the other women's movement organizations was advanced on the grounds of stigmatization of same-sex sexuality, Brown and the Radicalesbians used these linguistic strategies to reframe lesbian identity as based entirely on the assumption that women shared immutable experiences of sexism by virtue of being assigned female sex at birth.[23] "Woman," or the many variations deployed to capture both biological and socially constructed similarities, would thus be the proper object of feminist politics, and consequently preclude efforts to exclude any nontrans woman—even if she engaged in same-sex relationships—from membership in the mainstream women's movement.[24]

Much like the GAA discourse, which argued for the elevation of sexuality above all other identifications, the introduction of "lesbian" as synonymous with "woman" collapsed identity along a single axis, which constructed the evolving understanding of lesbian identity in narrow racial, biological, and classed terms. According to Brown and the Radicalesbians, "It is the primacy of women relating to women, or women creating a new consciousness of and with each other, which is at the heart of women's liberation, and the basis for cultural revolution."[25] This cultural revolution, emanating from the construction of the woman-identified women, was oriented toward a purportedly radical approach to politics. These thinkers argued that rather than seeking admission to mainstream political institutions and working to achieve representation in politics, as did the male-dominated GAA and liberal feminists seeking formal inclusion in politics, the newly constructed radical lesbian feminist, or "political lesbian" (i.e., a woman who removes herself from all male-dominated institutions and personal relationships), should unite with radical straight feminists to advance a unique, woman-oriented political agenda that would strive to uproot patriarchal dominance.[26] Rightful citizenship claims were central to these mobilizations against patriarchy, as lesbians argued for the right to live free of oppression from men. They pursued this broad goal through specific projects, such as advocating for state-funded childcare and opposing negative or objectifying representations of women in the media.[27]

The woman-oriented political agenda advocated by radical lesbian feminists hoped to meet its potential in the creation of lesbian separatist communities, which sought to establish matriarchal, non-monogamous lesbian spaces that excluded men because, in their view, monogamy and male domination were social systems produced by patriarchy to oppress women. Radical lesbian separatist communities would therefore aim to provide communities of liberation from patriarchy, where one could make economic, social, and political decisions that prioritized identification as women. One could visit a woman mechanic, raise children exclusively with women, and engage in open relationships with female friends and lovers. All of these activities were understood to be rights long denied to woman-identified women. Although becoming a part of a lesbian separatist community required that one be assigned female at birth as a precondition for membership, it did *not* require that one identify as a lesbian in terms of same-sex desire. In fact, the "political lesbian," a woman who privileged love for women (but did not express it sexually) and identified sexist society as the target for political activism, comprised the majority in these enclaves.[28]

As the construction of the radical lesbian feminist and "political lesbian" suggests, the impact of lesbian separatism on understandings of feminism and women's liberation were important, specifically for the ways that it contributed to narrow understandings of the "woman" to comprise feminist politics. These narrow boundaries, in turn, informed how people adopting the label "lesbian" understood their identity. In her ethnography of lesbian separatist communities in San Francisco, anthropologist Deborah Goleman Wolf describes the ways that lesbians viewed themselves in relation to women's movements and feminism: "As lesbians began to separate from both gay men and heterosexual women a rather curious phenomenon took place. Many heterosexual feminists began to define lesbians as 'the vanguard of the movement'—the purest form of feminism—since lesbians did not cohabit with the enemy and already had to be self-sufficient and self-defining women."[29] Sentiments such as these were famously echoed by lesbian feminist activist Ti-Grace Atkinson, who proclaimed that while "feminism is the theory, lesbianism is the practice." Thus it was from the space of these separatist commitments that radical lesbian feminists advanced a counternarrative of feminism that located the redefined "lesbian" as the authentic practice of feminism. From this vantage point as the self-proclaimed vanguard of the movement, lesbian feminists, much like their peers in the GAA, argued for the elevation of "woman," defined in strict biological terms, above all other identifications, often with similar results for the construction of group identity. As sociologist Alice Echols explains of the mainstream women's movement organizing during this time, the elevation of woman as the defining characteristic of feminist identity was seen by some as a way to absorb the differences—particularly class, race, and gender identity differences—that were perceived as potentially distracting from the stated goal of feminism to subvert patriarchal dominance.[30] "Woman," in other words, served the same purpose in the women's movement as the exclusive focus on "gay" did for Gay Liberation, especially for GAA.

As might be expected, given the parallels to GAA and the priority on single-axis understandings of identity, the elevation of "woman" as the predominant feature of radical lesbian feminist identity functioned anti-intersectionally. This understanding of lesbian identity along a single axis was shaped through an emphasis on rightful citizenship claims conceptualized as zero-sum gains, which pitted (White) women against movements active at the same time, such as the Black civil rights movement. For instance, an essay in the 1969–70 issue of *The Ladder* by Leslie Springvine, "Out from under the Rocks—With Guns!," focused on encouraging lesbians to prioritize their identity as women to join women's movements, specifically NOW. Springvine made this call to political action to her lesbian audience as women and at the expense of all other identifications, even sexuality, and especially race: "Lest I be suspected of masochistically discriminating against my own, let me add that I was also concerned about NOW's formal alliance with the Civil Rights Movement as a whole. I think race should be incidental to a clear-cut fight for women's rights. The rights of any and all Negro women, for instance, should be the concern of NOW, but only because they are women and not because they are Negroes."[31] Statements such as these, in one of the most widely circulated lesbian magazines of the time, suggested that the pathway to political activity could be undertaken only by those who would agree to prioritize their identity as women, deliberately leaving aside the question of which experiences, and by which women, would be drawn on to inform these mobilizations. Rights—specifically whose rights and how they should be advanced—played a significant role in shaping what came to be known of lesbian identity, with Springvine explicitly calling for Black women to abandon their racial identity and political commitments, such as the civil rights struggle, in order to join the Women's Movement.

Others echoed this logic to argue that the exclusive focus on political action as women would help to shift stigmas associated with same-sex sexuality. In the same issue as Springvine's piece, an essay titled "Lesbianism and Feminism" by Wilda Chase educated readers on the potential benefits of becoming politically active: "Not only does participation in the Movement advance the interests of lesbians as *women*, but also a mutually profitable liaison—and this is very important!—with groups of women who are not lesbians is a very good means of gaining acceptance of the lesbian as a citizen of the community, and of achieving recognition of lesbianism as a valid life style."[32] The turn to inclusion as citizens in this essay, coupled with Springvine's aggressive denial of race as a facet of political identity, illustrate the ways that these lesbian-identified political actors evacuated the category "woman" of all difference for the purposes of advancing a supposedly unified political movement of women, with rightful citizenship logic once again influencing this construction. Furthermore, the emphasis on "woman" by Cather and others was cited as a way to combat and, importantly, alter the stigmas associated with lesbian identity. Many of the proponents of this universalizing approach cited critical mass as their main motivation for glossing differences and emphasizing shared experiences as women, even while this logic implicitly and paradoxically recognized the racial, ethnic, and class heterogeneity of "woman" as a category. The discursive choice to link "lesbian" to woman, feminism, and women's movements relied upon the production of all those identities and political mobilizations as related to those who are biologically female, typically middle class, and, as the next section illustrates, implicitly White and gender-normative.

Representing the Woman-Identified Woman

The ways in which race, class, and notions about biology shaped the exclusive boundaries of "woman" and, by association, lesbian identity, are further illustrated in the activism by lesbian and self-identified radical feminists in the predominantly White mainstream women's movement during this period. As the new discourse of radical lesbian feminists began to gain traction and disseminate across activist spaces, so, too, did narrow definitions of what it means to be a woman and participate in mainstream women's movement mobilizations.

To address the growing divides between liberal feminism, which pursued recognition and inclusion, and radical lesbian feminism, which tended toward separatism, self-identified lesbian feminist Robin Morgan delivered a famous keynote address at the West Coast Lesbian Feminist Conference held on the UCLA campus in 1973. Her speech, titled "Lesbianism and Feminism: Synonyms or Contradictions?," attempted to heal some of the rifts of the "lesbian-feminist split" by emphasizing unity in the face of the challenges that the two movements confronted. Chief among the similarities across lesbian and feminist political groups, Morgan argued, was the threat of patriarchy as it was embodied in men—straight and gay—defined in strictly biological terms as those who were assigned male at birth.[33] In a marked departure from similar arguments made by the Radicalesbians, who tended to focus on patriarchy as an ideological force, Morgan argued that most insidious was the persistence of "male transvestites" in feminist and lesbian organizations, some of whom were also attending the conference.[34] After comparing the presence of a transsexual woman[35] at the conference as equivalent to rape, Morgan speculated, "*We know what's at work when whites wear blackface; the same thing that is at work when men wear drag.*"[36] That this claim was printed in italics to emphasize the statement suggests that

Morgan delivered it as a crescendo in her speech to shock the audience with the comparison to blackface. One has to imagine that this formulation would be rhetorically impactful, as the parallel between blackface in minstrel shows and the daily lives of transsexual women would mark those women as offensive to anybody who took the goals of progressive or radical politics seriously. The parallels drawn by Morgan also relied upon the well-worn trope of transsexual women in the realm of fiction or farce, as opposed to authenticity and lived experience, which would haunt antitrans movements for decades after Morgan's speech. Since feminism, for Morgan and her audience, was occupied with the goals of social justice, the analogy to blackface served as a way of drawing boundaries between the "us" of feminists and the "them" of patriarchy and males, with transsexual women serving as an easy rhetorical device to mark the difference. Most significant, Morgan's pernicious use of blackface in her analogy posed both feminist and transsexual identities as closed off to race.[37]

Morgan's narrow construction linking feminists and lesbians as White and biologically female reached its crescendo when she asserted that "where The Man is concerned, we must not be separate fingers but one fist."[38] Rhetorical maneuvers such as this metaphor attempted to heal the rifts between the divided feminist camps and draw the two movements together along a single axis of identity: sex. Locating the definition of woman in immutable biological traits such as two X chromosomes or sexed genitals at birth sought to further hermetically seal off lesbian feminist and feminist identities by posing women in opposition to a knowable other: those assigned male at birth, or men. Thus, to repair the lesbian-feminist rift forged in marginalization and oppression, woman-identified women should not be split by men, but instead stitched together by biological (i.e., female) sameness. Extending beyond a simple metaphor, the united fist advocated by Morgan to confront "The Man" staged feminist activism as a reductive two-person match, with all those who did not conform to the gendered norms of White, lesbian women relegated to positions on the margins, including many self-identified lesbians. Among them were butch-identified lesbians (and often their femme-identified partners), who were accused of imitating heterosexual norms as a symptom of their false consciousness.[39] Transsexual-identified lesbian women were also targeted for exclusion and were often subject to vitriol that would come to shape some strands of trans-exclusive feminist thinking for the subsequent four decades.[40] Furthermore, the combined emphasis on biological essentialism and the persistent use of analogies to the Black civil rights movement and Black experiences to legitimize the goals of lesbian separatists effectively made coalitions with Black feminist movements taking place during this same period impossible by foregrounding the rights of White lesbians and pitting them against Black activists. These theoretical and conceptual moves, in total, represented radical lesbian feminist political identity as implicitly White, explicitly biologically female, and androgynous, or resisting gendered norms of femininity.

Morgan was not alone in promulgating this narrow construction of lesbian identity during this period. Over time, she and others like her were joined by self-identified radical feminists from many fields, including academia, the arts, and activism.[41] Mary Daly, Janice Raymond, and Monique Wittig would all take up the discourse of sex (and later, gender) defined in strictly biological terms. Much like Morgan, these self-identified radical feminist thinkers invested considerable resources in establishing the theoretical foundation for lesbian separatism and feminism, which they defined contra patriarchy and in explicitly biological ways—a distinction they achieved by casting women in opposition to transsexual and transgender women, and closing women off to difference, notably race. Their status as scholars gave this reductive, raced, and gendered version of lesbian and feminist identities academic clout. Most significant, these rhetorical constructions of radical lesbian feminist identity universalized White women's experience as representative of all women at the expense of a multifaceted approach to identity and, by association, political agendas. White women were consequently organized into lesbian and feminist identities through the construction, articulation, and deployment of gendered and racialized logic that excluded transgender women and men; Black, Asian, Latine people; and butch- and femme-identified lesbians. Rightful citizenship claims, or the argument that lesbians and women would be afforded rights were it not for being subjected to patriarchal dominance, played a key role in these evolving identity constructions.

In sum, the exclusion of lesbian women from organizations dominated by gay men, and the marginalization of Black and transgender people from the lesbian political and social organizations formed in response, illustrates to what effect identities are constructed in politics. In the case of lesbian identity, political actors working on behalf of groups like the Radicalesbians—and radical feminists more generally—responded to exclusion and marginalization by attempting to seal off lesbian identity from those on the margins. Political actors like Morgan and other radical feminists sought to position lesbians above scrutiny or stigmatization. They achieved this by policing the boundaries of lesbian identity, which they defined as biologically female. Explicitly casting transgender women out of lesbian feminist circles and implicitly organizing women of color out of separatism and mainstream women's movement politics thus served the purpose of shoring up the boundaries of a particular lesbian identity, one that was gender-normative, biologically female, and also White. This is illustrated most forcefully by the fact that butches, femmes, transgender men, and people of color were also implicitly excluded from the representations of lesbians put forth during this time. These within-group omissions, abetted by rightful citizenship claims, were constitutive of what came to be known of lesbian identity in politics.

What Is a Lesbian?

As discourse of narrowly defined lesbian and feminist identities circulated, so too did more popular understandings of what it meant to be a lesbian and a feminist. Looking to publications from this time gives some insight into how both political actors and members of the lesbian and feminist groups themselves represented their identity across social and political venues. Although *The Ladder* folded in 1973, when DOB officially shuttered, another magazine tailored to lesbian readers, *Sinister Wisdom,* was founded in 1976 by Harriet Desmoines and Catherine Nicholson, who identified themselves in the first issue as White, working-class lesbians living in the South.[42] In addition to serving as a place where contributors and readers were encouraged to engage in intellectual debates and create and consume creative works, the editors described their intention for the magazine as a broader political force. They explained their vision alongside a call for contributions: "We believe that writing of a certain consciousness has greater impact when it's collected, when several voices give weight, harmony, and countermelody to the individual message. The consciousness we want *Sinister Wisdom* to express is—briefly—that of the lesbian or lunatic who embraces her boundary/criminal status, with the aim of creating a new species in a new time/space. We're using the remnants of our class and race privilege to construct a force that we hope will help ultimately destroy privilege."[43] With each issue consisting of 100 pages on average, *Sinister Wisdom* set out to collect a wide array of voices and artwork with the intention of giving shape to lesbian life and identity. The contributions submitted to the magazine reflect this orientation, with essays from a wide array of well-known feminist thinkers, such as Audre Lorde and Adrienne Rich, featured alongside writings from the general readership. Examining the conversations that took place across these essays and works of art provides a unique insight into the ongoing construction of lesbian identity, particularly with respect to negotiations over the boundaries of both lesbian and feminist identities. Looking at conversations among political leaders at the helm of the magazine and the membership also provides insight into how lesbian-identified people themselves perceived their identity and also helped to shape them.

Desmoines and Nicholson approached the task of creating this "new species" as a grassroots effort, and in the third issue invited readers to respond to a series of questions under the heading "What Is a Lesbian?" The prompts for discussion spanned the basic definition of "lesbian," including "[D]oes it mean more than a 'homosexual woman?'"; the scope of feminism: "Some people define 'feminism' as 'humanism applied to women.' Are feminist lesbians really humanists?"; whether or not readers perceived that lesbians might in fact constitute a "new species"; and their thoughts on the relationship between patriarchy and lesbian-identified women. Readers were invited to submit their responses to any or all of the questions with the promise that they would be published in subsequent issues.

The conversation was initiated by a number of well-known figures in lesbian social and political circles, including *The Joy of Lesbian Sex* author Bertha Harris, lesbian feminist poet Mia Albright, DOB founder Barbara Grier, and Martha Shelley, who was one of the founders of GLF. All the answers put forward by these prominent lesbian thinkers and political actors, with the exception of Shelley, reflect continuity with constructions of lesbian identity as emerging in opposition to patriarchy, which was secured by what was becoming the familiar trope of biological sameness located in the experiences that were presumed to cohere in universal woman. For example, Albright's answer to what constitutes lesbian identity was "[L]esbianism, even technically sexually, is not 'homosexual' it is gynosexual."[44] Here, the association with homosexuality is severed and replaced by qualifying sexuality with the prefix "gyno" to connote an exclusive interest in women. This rupture with homosexuality, understood as gay men, was reflected in other answers that specified, as Grier did, that "homosexual is not, as is so often misconstrued, the love of a man for a man but the love of one of the same sex for another of the same sex, but a Lesbian is a Lesbian." "Homosexual" functioned as a descriptor for Grier, regardless of sex, but "Lesbian" was a proper noun, circularly defined as both subject and referent, and explicitly did not share similarity with gay men.

The significance of the break with men, masculinity, and patriarchy for lesbian identity is specified by the final sentence of Albright's definition, in which she explained that "being a womon-identified womon [*sic*], a lesbian, is: opposing the male sex and everything it represents, realistically, and opposing masculinization of the female sex."[45] To be a lesbian is to identify oneself in contrast to biological difference, or male sex, such that even the spelling of "woman" is altered to disrupt the link with "man." In addition to rejecting butch identity expression, Albright emphasized the biological logic at play in her definition of lesbianism, stating, "I prefer 'male sex' to 'patriarchy' because it prevents confusion. The malist regimes, malized societies, are not just rule by father, but rule by son, brother, anything and everything male."[46] Like Morgan, who attempted to bridge the gap between liberal and radical feminism by staging feminist struggles as a two-person match comprised of all women on one side and all men on the other, Albright's meditation on lesbian identity drew on the logic of essential and static sexed difference to define what it means to be a lesbian. This elaboration reflects not only the extent to which lesbian identity was linked to woman, and thus sex, but also the degree to which the emphasis on biological similarity was accepted as standing in for a presumably universal female experience of oppression in male-dominated social, political, and economic spheres, where men hold all rights and women suffer as a result.

Although all the authors in the discussion of defining what it is to be a lesbian agreed upon the uniqueness of lesbian identity contra gay men, homosexuality, and patriarchy, there was some dissent regarding the question of lesbians as a distinct species, which was used to connote woman as the basis for a separatist social, political, and economic matriarchy. While most respondents side-stepped this question or offered fantastic answers to it that playfully defined lesbians as witches or Amazons, Shelley, the founder of GLF, refused the terms of the question for the following reasons: "I think this question is dangerous. Once we start regarding ourselves as a separate species, a new 'uber-mensch'—superior to males and heterosexual women—we are no better politically than the Nazi party or the Ku Klux Klan."[47] Although Shelley agreed that a lesbian is a "woman whose primary sexual and emotional needs are focused on women," her answer suggests that her attachment to woman was not rooted in the prevailing appeal to sex as biological difference, but rather held open the definition of woman in an attempt to subvert the tendency to stage power relations dichotomously. The costs of referring to biology as a totalizing basis for difference, and thus politics and identity, are underscored by the analogies Shelley used to make her point: to do so is to be on equal footing with Nazis and the KKK, which were, and still are, the paradigmatic examples of the social, political, and epistemic violence that can be waged by reliance on biology, let alone "us versus them" logic.

Shelley's attempts to disrupt the conflation of lesbian identity with sex and biology posed in contrast to men and patriarchy was not reflected in subsequent discussions that featured readers' voices. There were, however, efforts to describe in greater detail how it looked for individuals to oppose patriarchy as lesbians. One reader, identified as Judy Antonelli, spent a fair amount of her essay by describing being a lesbian as having a loving orientation to the world that focuses primarily on women but does not apply opposing force (i.e., hate) to men. Antonelli instead advocated for indifference: "Separatism does NOT (as Adrienne Rich says) 'proceed first out of hatred and rejection of others.' Our motive is love of women. Nor does separatism imply hatred of straight women; it is withdrawal from MEN."[48] Love is to be reserved for women and benign apathy applied to interactions with men. The by now well-rehearsed reasons for separating from men and male-dominated spaces were cited by Antonelli alongside the new observation regarding biological sex difference: "The male imperative towards dominance and power over women stems from his insecurity as an incomplete female, his need to compensate (what Karen Horney so perceptively labeled 'womb envy')."[49] Men—understood here as White and nontrans individuals with the power to exercise dominance—are acting from a place of anxiety that stems from the biological inability to create and foster new life, which is a capacity that only women—defined in strictly biological terms as those with a womb, or a uterus—possess. To be incapable of bearing children is thus understood to have the opposite effect: subverting life opportunities for all others to maintain dominance, understood here to be a monopoly on rights and political standing. Although Antonelli's main focus was the negative effect of men on the lives of women, her final line indicated concern with broader forms of oppression: "Racism also has psychological roots in patriarchy's fear of blackness/darkness."[50] Antonelli rested her description of lesbian identity on this final line, suggesting that although her focus had been on men, broadly understood, the true contrast against which lesbian identity took shape was White men who are wracked with anxiety over their inability to create life as well as a prevailing fear of Blackness.

Antonelli's response is unique among the few essays submitted by readers for its mention of race and racism. Put differently, all the readers who responded directly to the question of what it means to be a lesbian explicitly identified themselves as women and lesbians, sometimes including other aspects of identity such as class or political affiliation, but left their racial identity unmarked, implicitly indicating that they were White. For example, one reader named Peggy Kornegger offered the following relatively expansive understanding of what it means to be a lesbian: "The choice of lesbianism (and the opening to womanvision) is a wholistic, integrated choice: the blending of politics, poetics, sexuality, spirituality, philosophy, etc. that transcends opposites, heals schism, and affirms a multi-dimensional reality. To move in the direction of this multi-dimensionality is to choose revolution in the deepest, most transforming sense of the word—(for me) lesbian-feminist-anarchist revolution."[51] The utopian multidimensionality presented by Kronegger indicts binary and reductive understandings of identity while also articulating an understanding of lesbian identity that coalesces around her identity as a woman, which informs an epistemology she refers to as "womanvision." While this nominally inclusive perspective highlights a variety of approaches to social and political problems to put forth a radical vision of revolution—or lesbian political praxis—it does so by defining "lesbian" as a political identity along a single axis of sex commonality, which is achieved through femaleness to the exclusion of race, gender identity, and class as potential influences that give shape to lesbian experiences.

Highlighting the Whiteness of those who responded to the question of what makes a lesbian is not to suggest that Black and Third World women were not reading or writing for the magazine. Lorde, who was a prominent Black lesbian poet, was a consistent contributor, as was Anita Cromwell, a Black lesbian author whose writings were featured in *Sinister Wisdom* and *The Ladder*. It is therefore all the more notable that although there were certainly Black and Third World readers of and contributors to the magazine, none chose to weigh in on the question of what it means to be a lesbian even while these conversations were taken up in other venues and publications at the time. This conspicuous gap in the archive suggests that the construction of "lesbian" as coterminous with "woman," defined in strictly biological and single-axis terms, did not invite those whose identities were shaped by the imbrication of sexuality and race into conversations about what it means to be a lesbian and a feminist. As the 1970s came to a close, however, Black and Third World lesbians and feminists cited the narrow construction of lesbian identity as their reason to engage in sustained debates over what it meant to be both a feminist and a lesbian.

Women's Rights, for Whom?

Black and Third World feminists writing during this period compellingly argued that the presumed biological sameness of women (and difference from men) as a basis for political identity and associated political agendas relied upon and produced the marginalization of women of color in mainstream women's movement and understandings of lesbian identity. In addition to erecting rigid and essentialist boundaries around what was coming to be known of both lesbian and feminist identities, these writers posited that the elevation of biological femaleness as a precondition for membership created a false choice between mobilizing one's identity as a woman *or* mobilizing one's racial identity. These political actors vehemently contested the suggestion by White feminists in mainstream women's movements that one could be a feminist and organize around issues specific to a very particular definition of woman, or one could be active in antiracist struggles alongside men. In so doing, they offered visions of lesbian and feminist politics that utilized difference as a resource for mobilizing political demands, which they celebrated for the opportunities to develop more nuanced understandings of power and how to combat its pernicious effects.

The construction of an intersectional-like understanding of lesbian and feminist identity was ultimately more attentive to difference, demanding as it did a focus on the interlocking sources of oppression, such as sexism linked with racism linked with heteropatriarchy. Key texts by Black and Third World feminists from this period show that these interventions also maintained the attachment to "woman" even while they pushed back against the raced and classed boundaries imposed by White lesbian feminists. Even so, the approach to power and marginalization they introduced functioned as a much nimbler analytic framework that could account for multifaceted identities and multifocal political struggles despite retaining a focus on woman. It also invited White feminists to reflect on their role in fostering White supremacist logics that created vulnerability and marginalization for Black and Third World feminists.[52] This more expansive focus is largely due to the deliberate decision to avoid making rightful citizenship claims. Referring to the identity and political praxis taking shape in their conversations as "Black" and/ or "Third World lesbian feminism" underscores the contingency of identity by illustrating how discursive shifts—such as qualifying "lesbian" and "feminist" to account for race and ethnicity—change what comes to be known of a group, political agendas, and political action.

Perhaps one of the best-known articulations of this approach to identity and politics by Black and Third World lesbians and feminists from this period is the Combahee River Collective Statement (CRCS), which was circulated in 1977 by a contingent of activists that broke from the National Black Feminist Organization—a Black women's organization focused on achieving equality—to pursue more radical approaches to combating racism by focusing on its connections with sexism, classicism, and heteronormativity. Unlike the National Black Feminist Organization, members of the Combahee River Collective would refuse the terms of inclusion and rightful citizenship claims to advance feminism as an analysis of power and domination, not exclusions on the basis of sex or in the interest of equality with men. Writing on the 30th anniversary of the CRCS in 2017, Keeanga-Yamahtta Taylor contextualizes the founding of the Combahee River Collective in relation to women's and Black liberation movements:

> The inability or unwillingness of most white feminist organizations to fully engage with antiracist issues affecting Black women, like campaigning against sterilization and sexual assault or for low-wage labor and workplace rights, alienated Black women and other women of color from becoming active in those organizations. The same was true within the Black liberation movement that was overwhelmingly dominated by Black men. Indeed, it was not unusual for Black male organizations to oppose abortion rights for Black women on the basis that abortion was genocide for Black people. Thus, the narrow agendas of white liberal feminist organizations and some purported Black radical organizations cut them off from a cadre of radical Black women who had been politically trained through their participation in the civil rights movement and the urban-based Black insurgency during most of the 1960s.[53]

It was against this backdrop that the Collective staged its critical interventions to assert the political demands of Black women who were too often invited into grassroots activism without substantive representation for their unique interests. The conditional nature of their inclusion was summarized in the opening section of the CRCS statement, titled, "The Genesis of Contemporary Black Feminism," in which they detailed the nature of their exclusion from both the mainstream women's movement and male-dominated liberation movements that Taylor references. The authors began with the observation, "Black, other Third World, and working women have been involved in the feminist movement from its start, but both outside reactionary forces and racism and elitism within the movement itself have served to obscure our participation."[54] The authors then explained their experiences of disappointment and frustration with male-dominated radical liberation movements, describing how they were relegated to the boundaries of both Black liberation and the White male Left by virtue of being women and the patriarchal assumption that they should be subordinate to men. Summarizing the objectives of contemporary Black feminism in relation to the erasures enacted by the single-axis political orientations of these movements, which prioritized White women on the one hand and Black men on the other, the opening statement concluded by asserting that the Collective was mobilized by the pressing need to "develop a politics that was antiracist, unlike those of the White women, and antisexist, unlike those of Black and White men."[55]

Having established their interest in combating the simultaneous effects of racism and sexism, the authors staged a number of epistemological breaks with the dominant radical movements of the time. These ruptures were made with the intention of centering the experiences of Black women and can be read as instances of reframing that are similar to stigma transformation, in which political actors work to alter meanings associated with the group. For the mainstream women's movement dominated by White women, this meant contesting the priority placed upon the presumed biological similarity of women as the exclusive basis for political organizing. The CRCS authors explain, "As Black women we find any type of biological determinism a particularly dangerous and reactionary basis upon which to build a politic. We must also question whether Lesbian separatism is an adequate and progressive political analysis and strategy, even for those who practice it, since it so completely denies any but the sexual sources of women's oppression, negating the facts of class and race."[56] As the authors indicate, the rhetorical elevation of "woman," or motivating politics solely from "the sexual sources of women's oppression," denied the ways that race and class exert significant and interconnected influence on the lives of Black women. At issue for the authors of the CRCS was not the fact of sexism or its effects, but rather the exclusive focus on sexism at the cost of taking into consideration all the factors that shape social, economic, and political hierarchies, namely race and class, and including colonialism, citizenship status, disability, and sexuality. To focus merely on lesbian separatism, the authors suggest, is to attend to only a very narrow swath of affected subgroups: White, lesbian-identified women who could afford to cut ties due to their relative class privilege and the absence of racism as a force shaping their life experiences.

Describing oppression in other parts of the CRCS as the product of "interlocking" ideologies, this formulation foreshadowed the introduction of intersectionality. It did so by contesting the erasure of Black women produced by single-axis approaches to identity and political agendas, which foregrounded either sexism (defined in relation to White women) or racism (defined in relation to the experiences of Black men). Whereas dominant constructions of feminist and lesbian political identities advanced by White feminists portrayed all men as responsible for patriarchal oppression, regardless of race, the intersectional-like approach to lesbian and feminist identities in the CRCS created opportunities for partnerships with Black men:[57] "Although we are feminists and Lesbians, we feel solidarity with progressive Black men and do not advocate the fractionalization that white women who are separatists demand. Our situation as Black people necessitates that we have solidarity around the fact of race, which white women of course do not need to have with white men, unless it is their negative solidarity as racial oppressors. We struggle together with Black men against racism, while we also struggle with Black men about sexism."[58] Black and Third World feminist and lesbian politics, in other words, should look to be organized in relation to multiple sources of oppressions rather than solely in opposition to men, as White lesbian separatists and radical lesbian feminists often stipulated. The choice of "demand" to describe how lesbian separatists policed the borders of lesbian feminist identity reveals how within-group marginalization functions to deliberately produce meanings associated with groups. In this case, the CRCS made clear that the processes of centering sex/gender at the expense of racial identity conflated lesbians and feminists with the interests of White women, who willfully denied the force of race on their lives unless it was in the interest of maintaining White supremacy with White men, "in their negative solidarity as racial oppressors."[59] The CRCS made clear that the construction of lesbian and feminist identities with Whiteness was not an accident that could be traced back to White women simply outnumbering Black and Third World women in feminist movements. It was instead produced through concerted efforts to patrol the boundaries that upheld biological femaleness as the defining condition that informed lesbian and feminist identities and political praxis. Their attention to these features of the mainstream women's movement exposed how single-axis logic constructed White women as the proper objects of lesbian and feminist identity, which in turn foreclosed membership for Black and Third World women.

The authors of the CRCS accompanied these critiques of lesbian and feminist identities constructed by White feminists with the introduction of political praxis developed to center Black women and attend to the simultaneous effects of race, class, and gender, which they argued had the greatest potential for uprooting systems of oppression. Even while they celebrated the potential power of this approach to political action, the authors of the CRCS recognized that advancing these political goals was not a simple endeavor, particularly against the backdrop of other movements that enjoyed relatively more power and access. In a section titled "Problems in Organizing Black Feminists," the authors explain, "The major source of difficulty in our political work is that we are not just trying to fight oppression on one front or even two, but instead to address a whole range of oppressions."[60] The multifocal struggle Black feminists waged, then, was conducted without the advantage of power that comes from being oppressed along a single axis of identity, as might be the case for some White women. To this point, the authors observed "We do not have the racial, sexual, heterosexual or class privilege to reply upon, nor do we even have the minimal access to resources and power that groups who possess any one of these types of privilege have."[61] Here, the authors named the ways that they were closed out of rightful citizenship claims because they could not claim marginalization along just one dimension. And yet, the multiple and interlocking roots of oppression that Black women faced, according to the authors of the CRCS, positioned them best to enact change that would benefit a wide variety of nondominant groups: "We might use our position at the bottom, however, to make a clear leap into revolutionary action. If Black women were free, it would mean that everyone else would have to be free since our freedom would necessitate the destruction of all the systems of oppression."[62] Whereas the preoccupation with patriarchal dominance demonstrated in White lesbian feminist discourse was productive of further marginalization and exclusion, particularly with respect to organizing Black, Third World, and transgender women out of mainstream lesbian and feminist identities, the political praxis put forward by the authors of the CRCS foregrounded a grassroots approach to political problems and thus advanced a potentially more equitable outlook on social, political, and economic transformation. These goals were heralded by the authors of the CRCS for their power to bring the widest array of people together in political action, not regardless of race, ethnicity, gender identity, and/or class, but due to experiences shaped by race, ethnicity, gender identity, and class.

The CRCS statement concluded with specific projects and steps that Black feminists could undertake to advance this new vision of oppression and political praxis, which required a final note on their relationship to White feminists and lesbians in the Women's Movement. The authors directly addressed them:

One issue that is of major concern to us and that we have begun to publicly address is racism in the white women's movement. As Black feminists we are made constantly and painfully aware of how little effort white women have made to understand and combat their racism, which requires among other things that they have a more than superficial comprehension of race, color, and Black history and culture. Eliminating racism in the white women's movement is by definition work for white women to do, but we will continue to speak to and demand accountability on this issue.[63]

The vision for Black lesbian and feminist identities put forward was not a response to White feminists, as the dominant "wave narrative" of feminism suggests, but rather part of an ongoing dialogue that was perceived to be a political project unto itself. Committing to antiracist work while also refusing responsibility for racism within the mainstream women's movement reflects the grassroots approach to politics advocated throughout the CRCS and foreshadowed the development of a tenet in Black feminist praxis grounded in critique as an act of care for outcomes, even if the process is messy and difficult.[64]

Refusing the terms of separatism laid out by White feminists was an effort by the authors of the CRCS to prefigure the revolution they worked toward. The goal of reframing Black Third World lesbian feminists as the true vanguards of the revolution was made clear at the end of the CRCS when the authors highlighted one of the mainstream women's movement's most vocal proponents, Robin Morgan. The authors quoted her introduction to *Sisterhood Is Global*, in which she opined, "I haven't the faintest notion what possible revolutionary role white heterosexual men could fulfill, since they are the very embodiment of reactionary-vested-interest-power,"[65] which reads as a bit of a non sequitur in a section describing the objectives and nonviolent tactics that Black feminists should use, especially given Morgan's implicit reliance on racist, colonial, and—as my reading of her 1973 speech illustrated—antitrans logic to mobilize women against patriarchy. The final lines of the CRCS, however, make clear the authors' reasons for citing Morgan: "As Black feminists and lesbians we know that we have a very definite revolutionary task to perform and we are ready for the lifetime of work and struggle before us."[66] Here, the authors used Morgan's negative construction of a revolutionary—who could not possibly be a White, straight man—to put forward their vision for the custodians of the revolution. They agreed with Morgan that White men could not lead the revolution, but they asserted that neither could White women. Rather, the true vanguard was Black women, who were prepared for a lifetime of work and struggle against a multiplicity of oppressive ideologies and forces. While effectively disputing any possibilities for a single-axis approach to be viewed as potentially revolutionary, statements such as these preserved the unique role that women play in radical politics. In other words, although quoting Morgan at the end of the CRCS was leveraged to underscore the unique role to be played by Black and Third World women, it did so without contesting the logic of binary sex that structured so many White lesbian and feminist claims about domination and power. All the same, the multifocal and intersectional-like thinking that runs throughout the CRCS set the stage for a much more adaptive approach to power and oppression than that advocated by White lesbians and feminists.

Against Biology: Intersectional Representations

The Combahee River Collective was not alone in advocating approaches to political action that embraced more intersectional perspectives on identity and utilized difference as a political resource. Political actors and feminist thinkers working alongside and within the Collective echoed disappointment with the mainstream women's movement's construction of the normative lesbian feminist subject, which universalized the experiences of White women at the expense of attending to the political problems that Black, Third World, transgender, butch, femme, and gender-nonconforming people face. Organizations and publications designed as sites where Black and Third World lesbians and feminists were invited to share perspectives on identity, politics, love, and art proliferated during this period as a result. The following examination of two of these outlets—*Azalea: A Magazine by Third World Lesbians* and the 1981 publication of *This Bridge Called My Back*—identifies two themes that consistently appeared in the articulation of Black and Third World lesbian feminist identity.

The first prominent theme was a grassroots approach to identity construction and political action that prioritized drawing together voices that had previously been silenced or excluded from lesbian feminist identity and politics. The editorial statement in one of the first issues of *Azalea* in 1978, for example, explains the policy of welcoming all submissions from readers: "*Azalea* was created partially but not totally because we feel that alot of feminist and/or lesbian publications build walls around themselves in the same way establishment publications do and it has been our experience that whenever standards are set in this country the people who most often set and judge them are white and thusly have not sought to include third world people."[67] Although the walls erected by the unnamed lesbian and/or feminist publications were not explicitly identified in the editorial statement, the reader was meant to understand that they were put in place and maintained by White feminists who tended to act in the interest of contesting sexism while also maintaining white supremacy. *Azalea's* editorial policy of publishing all work submitted to the magazine thus reads as an effort to create a sustained space of dialogue, where authors and readers were encouraged to reformulate the boundaries of lesbian feminist identities in ways that reflected their experiences and political objectives as Black and Third World people.

The second theme that emerges in these publications is the continuation of an intersectional-like approach to Black Third World lesbian feminist identity as well as political action more broadly. Writing on the occasion of *This Bridge Called My Back's* 35th anniversary, Cherríe Moraga, one of the original editors alongside Gloria Anzaldúa, describes the voices collected in the volume as an act of creation that would serve as "an account of US women of color coming to late 20th century social consciousness through conflict—familial and institutional—and arriving at a politic, a 'theory in the flesh,' that makes sense of the seeming paradoxes of our lives; that complex confluence of identities—race, class, gender, sexuality—systemic to women of color oppression *and* liberation."[68] In this view, the metaphor of the bridge in the title of the book describes the efforts to cease feeling compelled to choose between identities and instead reach across them to find productive purpose, just as a bridge spans a body of water to facilitate the flow of people. Whereas lesbian and feminist identities put forward by White lesbians and feminist thinkers prioritized biological similarity and shared experiences that presumably stem from being assigned female at birth, the construction of Black Third World lesbian feminist identity would be characterized by finding ways to heal the rifts imposed by white supremacy, heteropatriarchy, and capitalism through a new political praxis focused on grassroots political action.

These themes were reflected in many of the essays and artworks submitted by contributors to *This Bridge Called My Back,* many of which articulated the emerging construction of Third World lesbian feminist identity as a way to resist being forced to choose between one's identity as a woman and one's racial and/or ethnic identities. The predominantly White radical lesbian feminist movement functioned as a foil against which many of these conflicts to reshape the boundaries of identity took place. Mitsuye Yamada, an Asian Pacific activist writing during this time, cited the predominance of separatism as the reason that many Asian Pacific women were not leaders in the mainstream women's movement, choosing instead to focus their political energies in Asian Pacific politics: "This doesn't mean that we have placed our loyalties on the side of ethnicity over womanhood. The two are not at war with each other; we shouldn't have to sign a 'loyalty oath' favoring one over the other. However women of color are often made to feel that we must make a choice between the two."[69] Echoing the Combahee River Collective's assertion that feminist identities are shaped at the intersections with race and class, Yamada continued, "I have thought of myself as a feminist first, but my ethnicity cannot be separated from my feminism."[70] It was for these reasons, Yamada explained, that she was marginalized within separatist politics and the mainstream women's movement. Furthermore, much like the CRCS's description of separatism as a "demand" to prioritize one's identity as a woman, Yamada's sense of being made to articulate a "loyalty oath" demonstrates the ways in which the construction of a narrow identity group also exerts a regulatory and coercive influence on identification. One can be *either* a feminist *or* an Asian Pacific activist, according to the dominant rhetoric of the woman-identified woman by radical lesbian feminists, but one cannot be both. The sense that one is coerced to decide among identities reflects how within-group marginalization and rightful citizenship claims work hand-in-hand to construct what is known of the group by collapsing identities along a single axis. In this case, lesbian identity was understood as White and concerned primarily with issues impacting White women whose experiences were constructed as universal.

These choices and their regulatory effects extended beyond race and ethnicity. Those who did not conform to the radical lesbian feminist separatist tenet of androgyny, in which the trappings of femininity such as clothing and makeup were rejected alongside patriarchal dominance, also expressed feeling organized out of the women's movement and denied both feminist and lesbian identification.[71] Chrystos, a Native American feminist, who did not use gender pronouns or punctuation in their[72] writing, explained at length the ways in which the rigid boundaries and requirements of separatism resulted in their exclusion: "I have felt less understanding between difference races and from many lesbian women than I do from straight people At least their heterosexual indifference allows me more freedom to be myself I felt so much stricture and censorship from lesbians *I was supposed to be a carpenter to prove I was a real dyke* My differences were sloughed over None of them came to a pow wow or an AIM [American Indian Movement] fundraiser to see about me."[73] Like Yamada, Chrystos's reference to the need to "prove I was a real dyke" demonstrates the ways in which the narrow boundaries in radical lesbian feminist rhetoric constrained expressions of identity, especially when Chrystos conveyed that they are made to feel as though the refusal to engage in typical separatist activities, such as carpentry or androgynous dress, disqualified them from membership in the lesbian community and the mainstream Women's Movement. The reader was meant to understand that the boundaries of Women's Movement and lesbian identity were enforced in ways that both generated normative expressions of lesbian and feminist identity and required the erasure of all those who refused to conform. Moreover, Chrystos elaborated the connection between identity and political praxis when they described the failure of Women's Movement members to show up for the American Indian Movement. One gets the sense that the walls built around lesbian identity in radical lesbian feminist discourse not only kept people out but also functioned to keep people in and isolated from other movements. As a result, Black and Third World lesbian feminists expressed disappointment over willful neglect by those in mainstream women's movements who failed to show up—either in solidarity or coalition—with their Black and Third World members.

These dynamics of White women leaving Black and Third World women behind in their feminist praxis were captured throughout *This Bridge Called My Back*. In the preface to the 1981 first edition, Moraga described riding the T in Boston and witnessing a plainclothes police officer throw a young Black man up against the train wall before handcuffing and dragging him off the train. In the next paragraph, she demanded of readers, "I hear there are some women in this town plotting a *lesbian* revolution. What does this mean about the boy shot in the head is what I want to know. I am a lesbian. I want a movement that helps me make sense of the trip from Watertown to Roxbury, from white to Black. I love women the entire way, without a doubt."[74] Moraga's self-identification as a lesbian bookended her call for a political movement to assert her belonging in lesbian spaces. Her emphasis on the lesbian revolution that did not attend to her experiences as a Chicana woman moving between White (Watertown) and Black (Roxbury) spaces thus reads as an indictment of the disconnect between a lesbian identity that was presumably open to all woman-identified women and yet failed to provide an analytic framework for understanding political and social problems beyond a single axis of oppression to include experiences shaped by race and class, as with the young Black man arrested on the train. Moraga clearly articulated associated costs: the inability to address violence that stems from White supremacy and capitalism, which cannot be separated from patriarchy, and the absence of White lesbian feminists from these spaces as a result. In this view, one way of reading *This Bridge Called My Back* is as a collection of essays that both demanded and put forward a theory of Black and Third World lesbian feminist identity and praxis that attends to difference. As the essays by Chrystos and Moraga indicate, the favored approach was grassroots political action in which people did the hard work of showing up and sharing space to engage in productive dialogues across various social and political positions and experiences. Difference could be tapped in political praxis as a resource rather than something to be minimized or erased entirely, as in mainstream women's movement discourse.

Essays in *Azalea* reflected this desire for grassroots political action and showing up to effect political change across difference by highlighting the negative effects associated with the absence of Black and Third World women in lesbian feminist spaces dominated by White women. One such example appeared in the very first issue of the magazine and was submitted by members of the Salsa Soul Sisters (a Third World gay women's organization) and the Jemima Writers' Collective (a Black lesbian writers' workshop), who described conflict associated with a 1978 New York City art exhibit called A Lesbian Show. Their statement reads as evidence of who, exactly, was invited into radical lesbian feminist spaces and identification and, by extension, who was considered a lesbian. After observing that the stated intent of the show was to bring the "lesbian community" together, the authors underscored in all capital letters that no Third World women were included. The authors continued, "The organizers have admittedly stated that the show was pulled together using 'the buddy system.' They stated that the show got off the ground by contacting their friends and asking whether they wished to exhibit."[75] The artists featured in A Lesbian Show were consequently drawn from the elite SoHo art scene in New York City, which the statement credited for "virtually no grass roots lesbians exhibiting."[76] The statement concluded:

> This condition is one that happens often in the lesbian community. It happens everyday [sic] in the world. Third world women are considered as an afterthought. Events are planned—well structured—and then third world women are asked to "fill in the spaces" with our presence. It is

racism—dishonesty covered with a well-meaning byline. It is offensive and degrading.

We are all victims of this situation and hopefully, in the future, we can work together for changes in our lesbian community.[77]

According to these authors, the way to address the concerns raised is not weak post-hoc attempts at representation that resemble tokenism. The absence of "grass roots lesbians" alongside the "we" of the lesbian community suggests that addressing the issues raised in the statement might look like engaging in the messy and often difficult processes of relating across difference to arrive at a shared space, and identity, that more accurately represents the heterogeneity of lesbians.

Reformulating Political Praxis beyond Rights

At a 1979 New York University Institute for the Humanities conference, Audre Lorde—one of the leading Black feminist voices and poets during this period—delivered a speech that touched on many of the themes introduced in *This Bridge Called My Back* and *Azalea* to put forward her specific vision for a more robust political agenda that was attentive to difference and targeted the institutions and ideologies that maintained oppression. She discussed the ways that lesbian feminist separatism relied on many of the false binaries and categories that mobilized patriarchal and colonial dominance. In this, one of her most famous speeches, Lorde used the metaphor of the "master's tools" to argue that sex and race categories were tools of patriarchal oppression and that the only effective political solution would be to harness differences as sources of strength: "Advocating for mere tolerance of difference between women is the grossest reformation. It is a total denial of the creative function of difference in our lives. For difference must not be merely tolerated, but seen as a fund of necessary polarities between which our creativity can spark like a dialectic."[78] Differences for Lorde were a source of creative potential from which to advance a political agenda, rather than features of identity that ought to be minimized and absorbed for the superficial unity put forth by a separatist politics and lesbian feminist identity organized around sex and foregrounding rightful citizenship claims. The feminist politics she imagined as an alternative instead focused on solidarity, in which the goal was to improve quality of life and opportunities for survival equitably, but especially for those most precariously situated in relation to power. Lorde

outlined the following political vision for honoring and mobilizing difference: "Those of us who stand outside the circle of this society's definition
of acceptable women; those of us who have been forged in the crucibles of
difference; those of us who are poor, who are lesbians, who are black, who
are older, know that *survival is not an academic skill.* It is learning how to
make common cause with those other identified as outside the structures,
in order to define and seek a world in which we can all flourish. It is learning
how to take our differences and make them strengths."[79] Lorde's refusal to
link these politics explicitly with coalitional mobilizations that might be
viewed as preserving an understanding of discrete identities, as well as her
focus on "society's definition" and "structures," directed politics toward
mobilizations against all sources of oppression. That is, whereas coalitions
can be put together and disassembled quickly due to the tendency to rely
upon the maintenance of boundaries between groups, the politics advocated
by Lorde prioritized ongoing solidarity and enduring opposition to patriarchal and racial domination as they were mediated by laws and institutions
or abetted by the single-axis logic at the core of rightful citizenship claims.
The metaphor of identities and experiences as "forged in the crucibles of difference" powerfully evokes the image of metalwork, or the act of melting together disparate elements through the use of extremely high temperature or
pressure to give shape to a final form that cannot physically be pulled apart.[80]
In these ways, the boundaries between groups are not adhered to, as they
are with coalitions, but are generative of political processes in which shared
understandings about subjectivity and political goals are negotiated, articulated, and better understood.

These theories of working across difference continued to evolve as the
1970s drew to a close, with some favoring Lorde's approach to solidarity and
others articulating a more coalitional praxis. The emphasis on embracing
difference and multifocal thinking was emphasized, regardless of the approach favored. At the West Coast Music Festival in 1982, civil rights activist
and founder of the all-women a cappella ensemble Sweet Honey in the Rock
Bernice Johnson Reagon addressed the prevailing climate of lesbian separatism in feminist spaces. Radical lesbian feminist discourse of the woman-
identified woman figured prominently in her speech. Using the metaphor of
a closed room to connote separatist politics, Reagon began her argument for
reconceptualizing lesbian and feminist identity by indicating the ways that
lesbian separatism foreclosed considerations of race and class: "There is no
chance that you can survive by staying *inside* the barred room. . . . In fact, in
that little barred room where you check everybody at the door, you act out

community. You pretend that room is your world. Of course the problem with the experiment is that there ain't nobody in there but folk like you, which by implication means you wouldn't know what to do if you were running it with all of the other people who are out there in the world."[81] For Reagon, the trouble with separatist politics was that while its practice helped to nurture identification within the group, or "community," that nurturing relied upon the exclusion of an other, most often articulated through difference, captured in the metaphor of the "barred room." As Reagon pointed out, "[A]in't nobody in there but folk like you." Although the lesbian separatist ethos (particularly as it was expressed by radical lesbian feminists) emphasized opposition to sexist society and patriarchal ideology as its principal political interest, as Reagon suggested in the conclusion of this quote, the elevation of "woman" neglected to attend to various dimensions of marginalization. As she speculated, "you wouldn't know what to do if you were running it with all the other people who are out there in the world." Separatism, in other words, contributes to ignorance of politics outside of one's own narrowly defined interests.

The political solution that Reagon suggested in 1980 highlighted the importance of engaging in coalitions with various groups to target a common enemy and expand the narrowly defined interests articulated by radical and lesbian feminists. In contrast to the "barred room," however, coalitions are inherently difficult and uncomfortable: "You have to give it all. It is not going to feed you; you have to feed it. And it's a monster. It never gets enough. It always wants more. So you better be sure you got your home some place for you to go to so that you will not become a martyr to the coalition. Coalition *can* kill people; however, it is not by nature fatal."[82] For Reagon, coalitional advocacy was something akin to mutually assured destruction—a "monster" that had the potential to kill. However, the political efficacy lay in these tensions: "That's why we have coalitions. Cause I ain't gonna let you live unless you let me live."[83] Rather than exclusion, coalitions are a step in the direction of fostering political agendas—however tenuous—because coalitions help to keep politics and activism accountable by promoting conversations across groups that comprise an alliance. Thus, although coalitions can be spaces of difficulty because they maintain the boundaries between groups, coalitions also provide the opportunity to learn about "all the other people who are out there in the world."

The two visions for political praxis offered by Lorde and Reagon are united by their emphasis on finding ways to tap difference as a resource or imagine ways to implement the metaphorical bridges conceived by the authors contributing to feminist texts like *This Bridge Called My Back*. Arguing that feminist praxis should attend to interlocking ideologies of oppression and focus on ensuring survival for as many people as possible directed attention away from rightful citizenship claims by denying the very logic of those political demands: the perception that oppression and marginalization stemmed from singular sources, such as sex. Black and Third World feminists engaged in world-building that could hold their identities and experiences outside of rightful citizenship logic, and in so doing put forward a political praxis focused on solidarity and oriented toward disrupting harmful ideologies, such as racism, sexism, classism, and White supremacy.

Conclusions: Lesbian Feminist Legacies

Two competing constructions of lesbian feminist identity and politics were evolving as the 1970s drew to a close. Black and Third World feminists continued to challenge the perceived dominance of the woman-identified woman central to radical lesbian feminist identity by advocating for political identities and agendas that took a more intersectional approach. These political solutions favored tapping differences as a source for political mobilization through grassroots activism, solidarity, and coalitions, and presaged what scholars and activists alike would come to call the "Third Wave" of feminism, in which a distinctly anticategorical approach to feminism and sexuality (i.e., queer) would be advanced against the foil of the "Second Wave." The following chapter shows how bisexual political actors and bisexuals themselves tapped into these evolving ideas about solidarity and opposition to rigid identities to confront their exclusion from straight, gay, and lesbian spaces. This thinking also foreshadowed the introduction of intersectionality to academic, activist, and, eventually, popular lexicons to connote a multifocal approach to understanding power and difference.

At the same time, and as I will show in the chapter on transgender political identity construction, radical lesbian feminists continued to put forth the normative construction of lesbian feminist identity as White and biologically female by defining "lesbian" as synonymous with universal White woman. These associations were strengthened by posing lesbian identity in opposition to transgender people, specifically transgender women, and evacuating "woman" of race, class, gender identity, and citizenship status.

This construction had the effect of severing membership ties with butch and femme lesbians as well as women of color. It also set the stage for future struggles over the inclusion of transgender women in feminist political mobilizations and agendas. Rightful citizenship claims played a key role in justifying these exclusions, with many avowed feminists arguing that the introduction of transgender women to political and social spaces presented an existential threat to feminism by displacing non-transgender women's rights claims.[84] Hitching "woman" to biology and rightful citizenship claims has cast a long shadow over feminist organizing. In 2017, a coalition of radical feminists, lesbians, Christians, and conservatives formed Hands Across the Aisle, an organization committed to "tabling our ideological differences to stand in solidarity against gender identity legislation, which we have come to recognize as the erasure of our own hard-won civil rights."[85] Hands Across the Aisle is just one example of this type of rhetoric, which explicitly pits "women's rights" against "gender ideology" (code for "transgender people") to cast transgender people as a threat to feminism.

More broadly, this chapter and the one before it demonstrate that construction of the gay and lesbian identity groups as mutually exclusive—with gay identity cohering around same-sex desire and lesbian identity unified by biological sameness—was a product of efforts by political actors to collapse identity along a single axis to ensure the success of rightful citizenship claims. In this chapter, the effects of rightful citizenship claims on narrow identity construction are illustrated in the countless ways that lesbian feminists positioned that identity and associated political agenda as one invested in claiming rights that were being wrongfully denied to them by men to prop up patriarchal domination. The dual erasure of lesbians from gay political and social spaces as well as from women's movements presaged the introduction of biological similarity to claim a discrete lesbian identity, one that would be separate from men and thus the vanguard of feminism. The woman-identified woman sealed lesbian identity off from difference, even while—as this chapter shows—Black and Third World lesbians, butch and femme lesbians, and transgender women worked within and alongside those spaces to put forward a more capacious understanding of political action and lesbian identification.

The following chapter picks up these threads by examining the development of yet another identity forged against the backdrop of exclusion and erasure: bisexuals.

4

"The B Isn't Silent"

Bisexuality, from a Cultural Movement to Political Practice

Between 1988 and 1992, three events occurred that reveal how bisexuality developed from a social identity associated with artists and free-love circles in the 1970s to a discrete political identity and associated political movement in the 1990s. In 1988, the Northampton, Massachusetts, annual Pride celebration steering committee voted to add "bisexual" to the title of that year's march. Northampton was (and still is) known locally as "Lesbianville" due to its significant lesbian population, many of whom banded together to protest the inclusion of bisexuals in the title and schedule of Pride events. Their efforts to resist the formal introduction of bisexuals fueled a protracted conflict that was ultimately settled by a 1992 citywide referendum that affirmed the addition of "bisexual" to the name of the city's annual Pride celebrations.[1]

The March on Washington for Lesbian, Gay, and Bi Equal Rights and Liberation took place the following year. As was the case in Northampton, the addition of "bisexual" was hotly contested. The march organizers ultimately agreed to include only "bi" in title and justified discursively stripping bisexuality of its relationship to sex by insisting it was important and strategically advantageous to avoid associations with sexual promiscuity (and sex positivity) in the context of the AIDS epidemic.

That same year, the mayor of St. Paul, Minnesota, Norm Coleman, made headlines for refusing to take part in the largely symbolic gesture of declaring June a month of "Gay, Lesbian, Bisexual, and Transgender Pride Celebration."[2] Coleman explained that he would not join Minneapolis mayor Sharon Sayles Belton in endorsing that year's Pride festivities due to the inclusion of "bisexual" and "transgender" in the title, which Coleman argued were "lifestyle choices," unlike gay men and lesbians, who, Coleman argued, were a protected class of citizens.[3]

In contrast to gay men and lesbians, who introduced those political identities in the context of laws and social practices that privileged

Terms of Exclusion. Zein Murib, Oxford University Press. © Oxford University Press 2023.
DOI: 10.1093/oso/9780197671498.003.0005

heterosexuality, bisexual activists constructed bisexuality in drawn-out struggles against twin forces: the stigmas and discrimination they faced from gay men and lesbians, on one hand, and the invisibility they confronted in heterosexual spaces when they engaged in opposite-sex relationships, on the other. These unique circumstances made the processes of bisexual political identity construction different from gay and lesbian identity development. Whereas the political actors spotlighted in the previous two chapters collapsed gay and lesbian identities along a single axis through the deployment of rightful citizenship claims, bisexual political actors avoided rightful citizenship claims in the interest of maintaining a relatively more open and contingently defined identity. They did so with the hopes of combating the exclusionary logic of rightful citizenship claims, which required minimizing the visibility (and interests) of those with intersecting racial, gender, and/or class identities that were seen as imperiling the claims to similarity.

Bisexuals applied this different approach to political identity construction. They confronted their erasure within gay and lesbian spaces and political action by asserting bisexuality as a unique and boastfully anticonformist identity with a corresponding alternative political agenda that should be considered adjacent to gay and lesbian political objectives. Key to this intervention was the assertion that bisexuals were historically involved in gay and lesbian political mobilizations but erased or unrecognized due to negative stereotypes. Bisexual political actors seized these stigmas as opportunities to redefine perceptions of bisexuality as a more authentic expression of human sexuality. They argued that unlike gay men and lesbians, whose emphasis on assimilation and rightful citizenship claims worked to distance those identities from sex, bisexuals celebrated sex positivity and embraced what they asserted was natural sexual and gender diversity. This orientation led to fruitful alliances and a welcoming climate for a variety of groups relegated to the margins of the ever-narrowing boundaries of gay and lesbian identities as efforts toward assimilation ramped up. As a result, transgender people, sex workers, and people practicing non-monogamy were all welcome in bisexual political mobilizations precisely because they were excluded from gay and lesbian organizing.[4] This relatively more open approach to the construction of boundaries around the bisexual group is reflected in the ways that rights were discussed. If mentioned at all, rights were often referred to in terms of the right to self-expression—both sexually and with respect to gender identity—as well as the right to engage in consensual sexual activity without social or legal prohibitions.

By their own account, these very same qualities would be the basis for the ongoing erasure of bisexuality. This was especially the case during the "gay '90s," the moment of unprecedented visibility for mainstream liberal gay and lesbian political mobilizations, which were fighting against conservative opponents pushing antigay legislation at both the local and national levels. National gay and lesbian organizations such as the National Gay and Lesbian Taskforce (NGLTF), Lambda Legal, and the Human Rights Campaign (HRC) met these challenges by emphasizing rightful citizenship claims to assert that gay men and lesbians were being discriminated against solely due to sexual identity. They argued that these prejudiced laws were unjust due to the innate and immutable nature of sexuality. Bisexuals were perceived as compromising these claims to similarity by disrupting the evolving narrative that sexuality (and gender) are static, and consequently they were elided in political mobilizations under the banner of gay and lesbian politics. Although bisexuals reported facing hostility when they made forays into predominantly straight spaces and relationships, it was their experiences in gay and lesbian political activity that shaped how they understood bisexuality as a sexual identity as well as the basis for political action.

Redefining the meanings associated with bisexuality and asserting the visibility of bisexuals in the face of their exclusion from gay and lesbian political mobilizations emerged as a focus in bisexual political discourse as political actors worked to shape what would come to be known of bisexual identity, political objectives, and political praxis. Addressing negative stereotypes that denied the validity, visibility, and legibility of bisexuality became the main objective. Many of the speeches given, articles written, and bisexual publications started during the 1980s and throughout the 1990s convey anger and frustration over being left out of gay and lesbian social and political circles for two main reasons: first, the perception that bisexuals were "fence-sitters," that is, hypersexual and thus incapable of sustaining relationships; second, that they were developmentally in flux and merely passing through straight or gay/lesbian relationships on their way to being gay, lesbian, or straight. Bisexuals named the oppression they experienced due to these negative stereotypes "biphobia," rooted in the ideology of "monosexism," which they coined to describe what they viewed to be a less evolved approach to sexuality based entirely on static perceptions of gender. To combat the oppressive force of monosexism, bisexual political actors celebrated bisexuality as a radical and dynamic alternative to what they argued was an excessive emphasis on stasis and the status quo demonstrated by mainstream gay and lesbian political organizations and their members, particularly as they crafted political agendas focused on rightful citizenship claims.

Bisexual political actors worked to enhance the visibility of bisexuality and bisexuals in a political and social milieu dominated by gay and lesbian representations. In large part, this took the form of refusing to concede sexuality to innate and immutable influences and, by association, the drive toward assimilation and rightful citizenship claims. Turning instead to theories of sexuality and gender as contingent and socially constructed drew attention to the uniqueness of bisexuality and the need to radically alter repressive ideologies that affect a wide variety of marginalized groups, including White supremacy, heteronormativity, ableism, and sexism. Constructing bisexuality as open to intersectional perspectives on identity paradoxically also created the conditions for its erasure, once again, from mainstream gay and lesbian political mobilizations due to increasing investment of those movements in seeking inclusion in the liberal political and social order via political agendas focused on rightful citizenship claims. As a result, although bisexual political actors would ultimately achieve the addition of "bisexual" to the names of gay and lesbian organizations and political actions, their inclusion proved to be nominal, at best, and absent any true incorporation of the unique perspective on politics developed by bisexuals invested in contesting pernicious binaries, exclusionary logics, and static approaches to identity.

This chapter examines how the political actors taking part in the bisexual political organizations and magazines that proliferated during the 1980s and 1990s constructed what was coming to be known of bisexuality and promoted bisexual political agendas as progressive and more inclusive variations of gay and lesbian politics. The prevailing context of multiculturalism in the 1990s as well as new theories of gender from the academy informed these efforts by bisexual political actors, who advocated for the representation of a wide array of bisexual people and gender identities in publications and political actions. My analysis of bisexual discourse from this period reveals that those cast out of the narrow boundaries of gay and lesbian identification often found their way into the pages of bisexual publications and leadership roles in bisexual political organizations owing to this relatively more open approach to identity and political action. Even when bisexual political organizations failed to live up to these ideals due to problems in leadership or internal debates over agendas, the inevitable conflicts over how and to what degree groups were represented in bisexual political action were often resolved in ways that preserved opposition to pernicious binaries and retained value for not reproducing exclusion. As the remainder of this chapter will show, a general aversion to rightful citizenship claims abetted these practices and helped bisexual political organizations resist the narrowing impulse found in many gay and lesbian political mobilizations.

Combating Myths

Two interrelated themes emerge in the discourse of bisexual political actors as they engaged in stigma transformation to meet the challenge of exclusion from gay and lesbian movements. The first is the articulation of bisexuality as a more authentic and honest expression of human sexuality, which political actors emphasized to combat the stereotype of bisexuals as pathologically oversexed and therefore incapable of being trusted. Bisexual discourse of desire worked to flip these scripts by articulating an understanding of sexuality based on attraction regardless of gender. Bisexual political actors embraced this sexual openness and sex positivity as a way to denounce the shame that gay and lesbian critics assigned to bisexuals while also disparaging gay men, lesbians, and straight people for limiting desire and human sexuality to gender.

In the second approach to stigma transformation, political actors put forward bisexuality as a celebration of an antinormative way of life that was emphatically against dichotomies. These articulations focused on the harms that stem from binary thinking, including racial, sexist, and heteronormative oppression, and posed bisexuality as a liberatory alternative to those ideologies. In so doing, bisexual political actors were careful to distinguish identity politics—defined as the politics of being—from a political vision focused on undoing harmful hierarchies. They achieved this contrast by posing bisexual politics in opposition to the liberal gay and lesbian movements, which they argued strayed too far from their radical roots in favor of deploying rightful citizenship claims, pursuing assimilation, and creating exclusive "gay ghettos" with strictly enforced boundaries that resulted in more exclusion than inclusion. Bisexual organizations and publications were instead constructed as open to all who wished to participate.

Newly formed bisexual political organizations channeled significant resources into directly combating the exclusion of bisexuals from gay and lesbian political and social spaces. One of the most prominent bisexual political organizations was BiNet USA, which was founded at the 1987 National

March on Washington for Gay and Lesbian Rights. It was during that event that the 75 members of the march's bisexual contingent articulated frustration at being excluded from the titles of gay and lesbian actions. One of the main tasks taken up by the newly minted bisexual organizations was educating the public about bisexuality. The next march—the 1993 March on Washington for Gay, Lesbian, and Bi Equal Rights and Liberation—was seized as an opportunity to engage in outreach to other bisexuals and alter some of the stigmas associated with bisexuality among the predominantly gay- and lesbian-identified audience. It was at that event, which drew people from all around the country to celebrate sexual identities, that the East Coast Bisexual Network (ECBN) circulated a flier written by Joe Woodhouse and Karina Roberts titled *Bisexuality: Some Questions Answered* to begin this process of education. Although it was initially distributed at the 1993 march, it endured as a key text that bisexual political actors drew upon in future mobilizations. It was also featured in educational packets distributed by BiNet USA for volunteer lobbyists to use (see Figure 4.1).[5]

Q: So what exactly is a Bisexual?

A: A Bisexual is someone who is sexually and emotionally attracted to people of both genders.

Q: So they're equally interested in men and women?

A: Not necessarily. Some are, some aren't. Some say they're attracted to men and women in different ways, others say gender just isn't relevant to who they're interested in.

Q: Doesn't being interested in both genders mean they're only half as interested in either?

A: Most Bisexuals will probably say that when they're interested in someone, they're interested in them 100%. Just like you and I.

Q: Aren't people really either heterosexual or homosexual?

A: No. It's well recognized in medical and psychological circles that bisexuality is a very real and genuine sexuality. But anyway, there are plenty of Bisexuals around who can tell you that.

Q: Isn't it just a phase?

A: No more than being heterosexual or homosexual is.

Q: But isn't it a transition to being lesbian or gay?

A: Maybe for some people. Some lesbians or gay men "come out" as Bisexual first, but most Bisexuals remain bisexual for the rest of their lives.

Q: But surely they're just confused, they haven't made up their minds yet?

A: Don't make the mistake of assuming there are only 2 options to choose from. Bisexuality is an option in it's own right. A lack of information about Bisexuality is probably the cause of most confusion a bisexual might feel.

Q: Didn't Freud think we're all Bisexual?

A: Not quite - Freud thought we were all born Bisexual, and may develop a preference later in life. No one is really quite sure about this, but most people have had at least some feeling for both genders at some stage in their lives.

Q: Suppose I have - does that mean I'm bisexual too?

A: Strictly speaking, maybe. But what you call yourself is up to you. Some may feel the attraction they feel for one gender isn't enough to call themselves Bisexual. Some people have other reasons for not identifying as Bisexual, as well.

Q: Like what?

A: Some people may want to feel "normal" and think of themselves as heterosexual. Others for political or social reasons may wish to identify with the Lesbian & Gay communities.

Q: Doesn't the term "Lesbian & Gay" include "Bisexual" as well?

A: That's a hot issue for some people. Some people think so, but there are plenty (bisexual and otherwise) who disagree. Lesbians fought for the right to be explicitly named, because they felt invisible. That battle is still going on for Bisexuals.

Q: So why aren't the Bisexuals more visible?

A: Well, no-one walks around with "Bisexual" stamped on their foreheads. It's very easy to miss them.

Figure 4.1 Page from BiNet, *Bisexuality: Some Questions Answered*, in Stephen Donaldson Papers, box 16, folder 8 (Bisexuality 1990s), New York Public Library.

The value of the flier stemmed from the comprehensive way it underscored the problems facing bisexuals and why those issues were relevant to gay men and lesbians. It began by addressing the most negative consequences of failing to maintain openness to sexual difference, stating on the first page that a recent study found that 30% of youth suicides stemmed from issues around sexuality and feeling abnormal in comparison to one's peers. The authors then connected these alarming rates to a lack of information about bisexuality. After quoting a question from a young person, "I'm attracted to women, but I can't be a lesbian because I'm still attracted to men . . . what am I?," the authors explained that the flier was assembled to provide unbiased information about bisexuality in the interest of challenging the harmful stereotypes that bisexuals face.

The remainder of the flier used a question-and-answer format, and the questions provide a snapshot of the stigmas that bisexual political actors were hoping to confront and change. These ranged from defining bisexuality as "someone who is sexually and emotionally attracted to people of both genders" to setting the record straight on how Freud viewed bisexuality.[6] Across each question-and-answer pair, the focus remained on succinctly capturing perspectives on bisexuality as an authentic expression of sexuality, a distinct identity, and unjustly excluded from gay and lesbian social spaces and political actions. Analogies were deployed to convey the latter; for example, the answer to whether or not bisexuals were already included in "lesbian and gay" politics was: "Some people think so, but there are plenty (bisexuals and otherwise) who disagree. Lesbians fought for the right to be explicitly named, because they felt invisible. That battle is still going on for Bisexuals."[7] The analogy here reflects a strategic choice to compare bisexuals to another group recognized for their struggle against erasure at the hands of powerful hegemonic forces. Even more important, describing bisexuals as engaged in an ongoing struggle for visibility and recognition posed the group as the new frontier in political action. This comparison suggests that in the same way that lesbians broke away from gay men to assert their unique political interests, so too must bisexuals, even while the use of analogy recast and solidified the boundaries between these two groups.

The struggle to distinguish bisexuals from gay men and lesbians also took the form of addressing misconceptions about bisexuals and bisexuality in the ECBN flier. For instance, one question asked if being bisexual meant that one had to split one's affections between two partners. The authors reply, "Most Bisexuals will probably say that when they're interested in someone, they're interested in them 100%. Just like you and I."[8] This conversational approach invited readers to see themselves alongside the authors and, importantly, as potentially similar. As a result, the analogy combats the stigma that bisexuals are indecisive and noncommittal by using a personal appeal to imply that bisexuality is as natural as the attraction the reader feels. It also succeeds in holding gay, lesbian, and bisexual identification as separate by comparing them as unique, but similar, sexualities.

Three questions about the temporality of bisexual identification succinctly captured the pejorative narratives that circulated in the 1990s (and in contemporary discourse). These included questions about bisexuality as a phase, a relay point before identifying as gay or lesbian, and a momentary confusion. Each of the answers maintained an emphasis on the naturalness of bisexuality as a facet of human diversity. For example, in a tersely worded reply, the authors rebutted the assumption that bisexuality is a phase, simply stating, "No more than being heterosexual or homosexual is."[9] Their approach to the question of bisexuality as a staging point between heterosexuality and gay or lesbian identification again drew on analogy to make a point about the salience of bisexual identification: "Maybe for some people. Some lesbians or gay men 'come out' as Bisexual first, but most Bisexuals remain bisexual for the rest of their lives."[10] This appeal to the reader uses analogy to align the experience of coming out as bisexual with the experience of coming out as gay or lesbian. Despite assumed stereotypes, the flier frames all three categories as discrete and bounded sexual identities, which can then be galvanized along political lines, for political means.

Distributing informative and action-oriented fliers at events targeting gay- or lesbian-identified people was a form of soft power campaigning to buttress efforts to have "Bi" included in the name of the 1993 March on Washington. Another flier, simply titled *Bisexual Pride*, opened by proclaiming, "WE'RE BI, NOT SHY, SO DON'T DENY IT: SAY HI, OUR ALLY!" The remainder of the flier took each of these points in turn, first by addressing the question of what it means to be bisexual, then moving on to the question of why bisexuals are not shy, why the reader should not deny the existence of bisexuality, and who might consider themselves potential allies. Like the ECBN pamphlet, this one-page flier worked to construct knowledge of bisexuality as the basis for a political movement and, most important, a manifestation of human variation and therefore wrongfully stigmatized identity. For example, in a section explaining why bisexuals are no longer shy, the unnamed authors wrote, "Bisexuals are now coming out of both closets in unprecedented numbers. The bi movement has been around since the early 1970s, but it is now nationally (and soon internationally) organized and is highly active in the New York City area."[11] Having drawn an implicit parallel to gay and lesbian experience by describing bisexuals as coming out of not one but two closets, the authors explained that this enduring movement existed because bisexuals were "not content to be misleadingly labeled as heterosexuals or homosexuals, though we move in both communities, for we find this a denial of our human wholeness and our basic sexuality."[12] In addition to confronting negative stigmas of bisexuality, this description compels readers to understand the salience, boundedness, and essential nature of bisexuality. It also highlighted their sexuality, which march organizers denied bisexuals by indexing them as "Bi."

Bisexual political actors cited enduring exclusion from political action as one of the main sources of oppression that bisexuals endure. According to the authors, the marginalization of bisexuals is produced by dichotomous thinking that recognizes only hetero- or homosexuality as a basis for social and political identity. This limited view on sexuality was credited to the emphasis on rightful citizenship claims, which—according to the authors—can only ever permit recognition for one axis of difference. History was once again marshaled to make this point: "For a hundred years after the categories of 'homosexual' and 'heterosexual' were first set up in 1869, dualistic thinking (which insisted on forcing people in all their complexity into one pidgeonhole [sic] or another) denied the reality of bisexuality." This use of history would be a powerful claim at the March on Washington, which was convened as a celebration of gay men and lesbians who endure seemingly endless oppression from laws and social practices designed to shore up heterosexual norms. The critique put forward in the flier, however, posited that the binary of gay/not-gay that is often mobilized in rightful citizenship claims to target these oppressions precludes the possibility for recognizing the diversity of human sexuality. The authors assert that if the reader has not heard of bisexuals, it is because they are complicit in entertaining only two possibilities for sexuality and identification, and thus endorsing monosexism.

The social and political consequences of adhering to dualistic thinking and eliding bisexuals were underscored by the authors: "This denial, on the part of heterosexuals and homosexuals alike, can be compared with the suppression of reality of other stigmatized and oppressed groups, including women and homosexuals themselves." Here, the authors use an analogy to link bisexuals with the gay men and lesbians who traveled to Washington from all over the United States to participate in the march. Doing so aimed to target gay and lesbian readers, who might be especially sensitive to the suggestion that they were unwittingly perpetuating conditions of marginalization by adhering to binary ways of organizing identities. The remainder of the flier focused on what readers could do to help combat these trends: "Gays and lesbians have frequently disparaged bisexuals and put down their heterosexual inclinations, barred them from leadership roles in the lesbian and gay rights movement, and assumed that everyone who is homosexually involved must proclaim an exclusivist gay or lesbian identity."[13] Bisexuals, in other words, are caught in a double bind that "denies the real and valued parts of our love and we cannot accept it."[14] The work for gay men and lesbians was thus clearly laid out. According to these bisexual political actors, they must work to foster recognition of bisexuals by promoting their visibility.

The solutions proposed by the authors were rooted in a need to combat stereotypes around bisexuality, particularly the assumption that bisexuals were traitors who were actually straight. They should instead be understood as linked to gay and lesbian struggles: "Most of the oppression faced by bisexuals comes from the heterosexual world, based on our sexual nonconformity and motivated by homophobia."[15] Deploying homophobia as a root of bisexual oppression links bisexuals, gay men, and lesbians against a common oppressive ideology. The authors assert, "[W]e have a strong commitment to fighting this homophobia and are natural partners in the lesbian and gay movement in securing freedom for all of us to love whom we choose." They concluded, "The bi movement is an ally of rather than a faction of that movement because we must maintain our own identity and in the process serve as a helpful bridge between the homosexual minority and the heterosexual majority."[16] Reframing bisexuals as allies in gay and lesbian struggles is a powerful assertion of bisexual political identity, one that is separate from gay and lesbian identity. In claiming allyship, the pamphlet asserts that bisexuals are not gay or lesbian. The metaphor of the bridge—potentially borrowed from Black and Third World lesbian feminist organizing—also suggests that bisexuals were interested in drawing the boundaries of bisexual identity as discrete and independent of gay and lesbian identities while also working alongside them in political struggle. Even more important, the authors promise that bisexuals could serve as a valuable resource for advancing gay and lesbian interests due to the opportunities bisexuals have to prevail upon straight sensibilities. Although the authors do not specify how, exactly, this might be achieved, the use of a bridge as a metaphor recalls the feminist ideal of seeing difference as a source of productive strength rather than a deleterious force.

Challenging Internal Stigmas

Using the 1993 March on Washington as an opportunity to educate about bisexuality and assert bisexual political interests reflects that the event was perceived by many to be akin to a bisexual Stonewall. *Anything That Moves*, a magazine that was published by the Bay Area Bisexual Network between 1991 and 2001 and circulated internationally, devoted a significant amount of space to reporting on the planning and events of the 1993 March. These articles provide insight into how bisexual political actors discussed the march behind the scenes to a primarily bisexual audience. Many of the themes that emerge in these articles echo the efforts at stigma transformation conveyed in the fliers that were distributed at the march. Instead of educating gay men and lesbians, these statements were designed to invite bisexual-identified people into political action and offer a glimpse into the processes of bisexual identity construction and agenda development during the early 1990s.

Demonstrating critical mass at the 1993 March was promoted in bisexual publications as a truly unique opportunity to positively impact the bisexual political movement. One article published in *Anything That Moves* before the march was reprinted from *Bi Women: The Newsletter of the Boston Bisexual Women's Network*, one of the oldest and largest bisexual political organizations active in the 1990s. The authors, Laura M. Perez and Victor Raymond, celebrated the historic potential of the march to bring together an unprecedented number of people devoted to contesting homophobia and emphasized the role that bisexuals should play in the event. They urged bisexuals to consider attending, writing, "The March on Washington will be a snap-shot of the state of queer liberation. Part of that snap-shot will include the bisexual community and our efforts to be recognized for our involvement in a larger struggle."[17] Having linked bisexuals to the purpose of the march, the authors highlighted the political importance of participation: "While some say that it would be easier to seize the day under the guise of gay and lesbian rights, we will be marching as bisexuals, speaking out for *our* specific rights and freedoms along with those of our lesbian, gay, and transgendered sisters, brothers, and siblings."[18] The rare reference to rights in this article is likely due to the political climate of the early 1990s, during which conservative opponents were ramping up efforts to withhold "special rights" from gay men and lesbians, such as same-sex marriage and nondiscrimination measures.[19] Perez and Raymond reasoned, "These state-wide struggles should make it clear to all of us that—whether we're bisexual, gay, lesbian, or transgendered—they will try to burn us all anyway."[20]

Although the authors underscored the rights that were at stake for bisexuals in these statewide struggles, they also resisted the narrowing impulse that I argue accompanies rightful citizenship claims. Later in the article, Perez and Raymond encouraged people to attend by saying, "The March on Washington gives us the chance to be out, loud, and proud as bisexuals, queer bisexuals who cannot, will not and do not want to change our queer identities."[21] Using "queer" to qualify "bisexual" indicates a stance on political action that resists categorization and the foreclosure of belonging that typically attends the construction of identity categories. This was reflected in Perez and Raymond's vision for the march:

> Picture this: thousands of bisexuals from all over the country, all over the world, from all sorts of different communities, old and young; working class and monetarily wealthy; African Latina/o, Asian indigenous and the unending rainbow of people of all colors; people with disabilities and able-bodied people; people living with HIV/AIDS; monogamous and non-monogamous; celibate and promiscuous, religious and atheist; womyn, men, and transgender people. It may be our struggle for sexual freedom and liberation and their inherent links to sexism, racism, classism, ableism, ageism and all other isms, that unites us. We as a queer community will come together to clearly and beautifully reflect the range of peoples of the Americas and the world.[22]

The litany of subject positions within an invitation to bisexual political action—at an event celebrated internally as the "bisexual Stonewall"—reflects a political vision that places emphasis on contesting "all other isms": the ideologies that foment pernicious hierarchies and contribute to widespread inequities and oppression. Bisexuals would resist the narrowing effects of rightful citizenship claims by instead working toward liberation for as many oppressed people as possible. These claims were possible only through the construction of bisexuals as a group separate from gay men and lesbians.

The National Conference Celebrating Bisexuality, which was scheduled to take place the day before the march and other official events, hosted
a number of workshops that reflected this approach to the introduction of
bisexuals on the political stage. Katie Mechem, a bisexual activist from San
Francisco, described her experience attending the conference in an article
for an *Anything That Moves* section devoted to debriefing the March on
Washington. As might be expected, several related conferences were held
in the days before and after the march to take advantage of lesbian, gay, bisexual, transgender, and queer people from all over the country convening in
one place. The bisexual conference, however, was also symbolically important as it honored what many bisexual political actors identified as the germinal moment of their movement at the 1987 March on Washington for Gay
and Lesbian Rights. It thus served as an opportunity for bisexual political actors to revisit their achievements and make plans for future political action.

Mechem captured the breadth of the workshops at the conference,
describing an array of topics that included discussions about identity, sex and
relationships, and HIV activism, sharing that she was "still savoring the articles in the registration packet, on bi history, inclusion in lesbian/gay organizations, 'Black and Bi,' transgender liberation, and white privilege."[23] With
respect to the last, Mechem stated that combating racism ought to inform bisexual politics: "A workshop on white racism I attended addressed issues cru-
cial in this society and for the bisexual movement as well. If the movement
is truly for freedom, we must strive and learn ways to avoid reproducing the
oppressions many of us were raised with."[24] Although Mechem was reflecting
on a workshop devoted to addressing what she refers to as "white racism,"
likely a panel devoted to discussing White privilege, it is noteworthy that her
comments assume a White audience. This was further reflected in her overall
proscription for the movement based on the lessons she learned at the conference: "[I]f we are to avoid becoming a single-issue movement that narrows
the struggle to the lowest common denominator, we must work to broaden
our understanding of our sisters and brothers and of ourselves."[25] According
to Mechem, holding open possibilities for the complexities of experiences
and identities through self-reflection is the key to avoiding a narrow movement, likely an implicit reference to gay and lesbian organizing. The use of
family metaphors—referring to "our sisters and brothers"—suggests that
although there might be differences, all are intimately connected by their
shared bisexual identity.

Despite Mechem and others sharing that they were largely pleased with the weekend's events, there were low points that reminded bisexual participants that although they were included in the march title, they still had a long way to go in combating negative stereotypes. Lani Ka'ahumanu, one of the most visible and active bisexual writers and activists at the time, and one of the original founders of a bisexual political organization called BiPOL in San Francisco in 1983, was scheduled to give a speech on the March on Washington mainstage. In "How I Spent My Two Week Vacation Being a Revolting Token Bisexual" she recounted for *Anything That Moves* readers her experiences of marginalization during march activities and the degree to which bisexuals were erased from the gay and lesbian political agenda. Her article began by inviting readers to see themselves alongside her on the stage: "I say 'we' were on the afternoon stage because we were. I did not feel alone up there for a minute."[26] Her repeated use of "we" to describe her audience helps to construct the boundaries of her bisexual audience, which took shape in her description of the afternoon's events through an emphasis on bisexual exclusion. She continued, "There was a definite sense of bistory in the making as I networked and challenged the biphobia, and reminded forgetful MCs and speakers that it was the lesbian, gay, and bisexual March, and appreciated those who said 'bisexual' throughout their speeches."[27] Bisexual discourse is replete with cunning wordplay that exploits how one can append "bi-" to most words to change the meaning. Ka'ahumanu referring to "bistory" falls within this tradition, along with newsletter titles such as *North Bi Northwest* and speaking of the appearance of Dianne Feinstein at the 1984 San Francisco Pride March as a visit from "Bianne Feinstein."[28] In this case, Ka'ahumanu uses the wordplay to name bisexuality as a discrete and bounded experience and identity, complete with its own history, or bistory.

Even with these small victories, Ka'ahumanu's article concluded on a sober note, describing how her speech—the only one to be given by an out bisexual—was almost cut due to an improvised cast of gay and lesbian speakers extending the program longer than city officials would allow. Her account of defying the request to shorten her speech to two minutes demonstrates how political actors use stigma transformation in response to erasure and exclusion to construct the boundaries of what comes to be known of a group. She relates approaching the stage to deliver her speech: "With each step I was filled with a powerful sense of love for bisexual people, for our courage and bravery, for the visible and viable bisexual community we have built, and for the strong bisexual pride movement we have organized. Oh no, I did not feel alone up there at all."[29] Narrating her refusal to be silenced so evocatively draws bisexual-identified readers once again onto the stage with her. As she recounts swelling with pride—bisexual pride—the reader is meant to understand that it is not just one speaker who might not have had a voice that day, but the entire bisexual movement. The message is thus clear: bisexuals need to continue to fight to assert the legitimacy of their identity, relationships, and political demands in the face of continued efforts to erase them. Doing so ensures that they are not alone, but are part of a broader community.

Mechem's and Ka'ahumanu's reflections on the March on Washington are examples of how bisexual political actors used stigma transformation to change meanings associated with bisexuality and to give shape to a bisexual political agenda that would stage a departure from the assimilationist tactics and rightful citizenship claims espoused by liberal gay and lesbian political movements. By projecting bisexuality as adamantly opposed to dichotomous thinking and constraining sexual and gender norms, bisexual political actors gave voice to a political agenda focused on ameliorating the oppressive traditions and norms that contributed to their erasure from both heterosexual and gay/lesbian spaces. They did not view their exclusion as unique, but as being alongside all marginalized groups, especially transgender people and people of color.

Emphasizing oppressions as interlocking and in opposition to binaries made space within the burgeoning bisexual political movement and identity for those excluded liberal gay and lesbian movements, which were increasingly focused on advancing rightful citizenship claims. Revisiting the opening anecdote about the 1989 Northampton Pride celebration through the lens of the political agenda crafted by bisexual political actors clarifies some of the connections they made in the spirit of crafting a political movement from the outcasts of liberal gay and lesbian political agendas. Just one year after the addition of bisexuals to the march title was approved by voters in the 1992 referendum, the title would be revised once again. This time, "Transgender," "S/M," and "Leather" were included, a development that predicted some of the conflicts over political agendas that were to take place as bisexuals continued to craft a political identity and agenda.

Death Bi Erasure

In addition to stigma transformation, the 10-year span of time that bisexual political actors worked to construct the boundaries of bisexual political identity and develop a corresponding bisexual political agenda was marked by various conflicts over who would be considered members of the group and which issues would be foregrounded as bisexual political organizations became more active. The most consistent and visible conflicts during the 1990s concerned the relationship of the burgeoning national bisexual movement to established gay and lesbian political organizations. Many bisexual activists and thinkers writing after the 1993 March on Washington celebrated the successful efforts at stigma transformation for altering meanings associated with bisexuality and giving voice to a discrete set of political objectives. Even so, they simultaneously expressed deep frustration with what amounted to only nominal inclusion in the official march activities. As bisexuality became more visible in the years after the 1993 March, so too did calls from bisexual political actors for recognition of their unique political interests and inclusion alongside gays and lesbians in the names of organizations, events, and political actions. They advanced these claims in the pages of bisexual publications as well as during protest actions held at events and conferences convened by gay and lesbian political organizations, such as the NGLTF's annual Creating Change conference. Bisexual activists used these moments of disruption to highlight the deadly effects of failing to take bisexuals into consideration, such as neglecting to extend AIDS education and resources to bisexuals, who were considered outside of the scope of gay and lesbian outreach. In other cases, failure to recognize bisexuality resulted in the epistemic erasure of bisexuals, such as when the annual Lambda Book Award, "The Lammies," miscategorized an important edited volume called *Bi Any Other Name: Bisexuals Speak Out* as a lesbian anthology, thereby erasing the essays in the volume that also addressed men in relationships with women and men.[30] These conflicts served the valuable purpose of solidifying the boundaries of bisexual political identity and putting forward an alternative political agenda focused on contesting dominant norms as well as the narrow boundaries of gay and lesbian identities.

Debates over the degree to which the bisexual political movement should be aligned with gay and lesbian political organizations like NGLTF and HRC defined the developing bisexual political identity and corresponding agendas. The centrality of rightful citizenship claims to lesbian and gay organizing and the narrow boundaries of those identities figured prominently in these discussions. An article in a 1994 issue of *Anything That Moves* by Liz A. Highleyman titled "Building a National Bisexual Movement" summarized the state of bisexual political activity: "In 1994 there are many issues on the bisexual agenda. There is a growing emphasis on multicultural organizing and activism, and many are working actively to increase the participation of people of color in bisexual communities. Transgendered and differently-gendered people have long been active within bisexual communities, but today their concerns are receiving increased attention, especially from bisexuals whose goal is to challenge rigidly polarized notions of sex/gender and sexual orientation."[31] As with efforts at stigma transformation, Highleyman posed bisexuality as distinct from gay and lesbian political mobilizations, which figure implicitly in the backdrop of her summary as those who are attached to inflexible views on gender and sexuality, presumably due to the reliance on rightful citizenship claims. Holding bisexuality apart and referring to a unique bisexual political agenda allowed Highleyman to define its scope as much broader than the one espoused by movements with narrow views on identity. Outreach to bisexual people of color and the enduring presence of transgender people in bisexual social and political spaces are marshaled as evidence of what the new bisexual movement was doing and, by implication, what gay and lesbian political actors neglected to do.

Highleyman's essay concluded by offering her take on the current status of bisexual political mobilizations:

> The bisexual movement in the past has almost as a matter of course considered itself closely allied with the gay and lesbian movement. Yet after continued resistance by gay men and lesbians to bisexual inclusion, some bisexuals have begun to question whether bi resources are best spent pleading for inclusion from the gay and lesbian movement. The idea that bisexuals would be better served by an independent bi movement that can focus on bisexual issues—whether or not they coincide with the issues of gay men and lesbians—is one theory. Another is that bisexuals should work toward the creation of a broad-based sexual and gender liberation movement—harking back to movements of the 1970s—that includes bisexuals and all other sexual minorities as equal partners.[32]

Highleyman poses the creation of a national bisexual political movement in the mold of gay and lesbian organizations as a rhetorical straw man to put forward a vision of the bisexual political movement as one that will focus on dismantling oppressive ideologies and serve as many different groups as possible. The history bisexuals should look to, according to Highleyman, is not the one where bisexuals mobilized alongside gay men and lesbians while also hiding their bisexuality, but rather the period of Gay Liberation, when all who chose to participate would be included in political action to upend oppressive ideologies. The vision for a national bisexual movement was oriented toward liberation, not assimilation and rightful citizenship claims. The evolving emphasis on liberation contra assimilation did not mean that efforts to have bisexuals included alongside gay men and lesbians in political action ceased. Even while some bisexual political actors, like Highleyman, proudly proclaimed an increasingly antinormative position, others agitated for broader recognition and expressed a desire for inclusion. Having "Bisexual" added to the titles of Pride marches was central to these efforts.

The site of one such controversy occurred in conjunction with a 1994 march called Stonewall 25, which invited people from all over the world to New York City to celebrate the 25th anniversary of the Stonewall riots. The march was also planned to coincide with a meeting of the United Nations, which organizers exploited as an opportunity to call for the inclusion of "homosexuals" in the protected groups listed in the UN Declaration on Human Rights. In a somewhat ironic move, given the stated goal of having "homosexual" included in a text of political significance, the Stonewall 25 organizers refused calls from organizers to add "bisexuals, transgendered, and drag queens" alongside "gay and lesbian" in the subtitle of the march, which sparked outcry from bisexual (and transgender) political organizations across the country.

A full-page letter from the San Diego chapter of BiPOL published on the first page of a 1994 issue of *Anything That Moves* lambasted the decision to exclude bisexuals from the title of the march and reminded the Stonewall 25 organizers of what the anniversary of the Stonewall riots truly marked, repeating an oft-cited origin story that identified transgender people and drag queens as the true instigators of the riots. The authors recounted, "The Stonewall rebellion resulted when a group of courageous people fought their police harassers. This group included drag queens, transgender people, bisexuals as well as lesbians and gay men. . . . Celebrating the anniversary of this event without celebrating or even mentioning drag queens, transgendered people, and bisexual people is rewriting history!"[33] While this narrative of Stonewall has always been subject to contestation, with different sides claiming credit for throwing the first punch—or high heel, as the case may be—the BiPOL letter constitutes one of the first additions of bisexuals to the debate over what happened that night at the Stonewall Inn. Claiming the integral role of bisexuals rested on linking these groups together in their shared marginalization by gay and lesbian political actors.

Having inserted bisexuals into the Stonewall origin story, the authors go on to critique the main justification for their exclusion. At issue was not the addition of these groups to the various programs published in conjunction with Stonewall 25, but rather the exclusion of them from the title of the march. The authors quote one of the Stonewall 25 organizers justifying the exclusion: "Having separate labels for groups of people with the 'gay' community is a western way of thinking, with which other cultures don't necessarily identify."[34] Another organizer was quoted as saying, "Adding drag performers, transgendered people and bisexuals to the title would be confusing to people from countries which don't have words or translations for the term."[35] After expressing several lines of sympathy for the monumental task the organizing committee faced in convening an international event, the authors of the BiPOL letter asked, "How will 'drag queens,' 'transgender,' and 'bisexual' be translated where they are used in the literature? Why would they not be translatable if included in the title?"[36] In light of these inconsistencies, which the letter authors argued exposed efforts by the organizers to decouple bisexuals, transgender people, and drag performers from Stonewall 25 and the public image of the march, they concluded with a final demand: "The title of Stonewall 25 should either include all groups within our community, or none."[37]

These conflicts were not limited to the United States. Just two years after the protracted public debates associated with Stonewall 25, a conflict took place in conjunction with the 1996 London Pride celebration. An article reprinted in *Anything That Moves* from the British publication *Bi Community News* urged readers to reconsider seeking partnerships with gays and lesbians and highlighted the stakes of doing so. Unlike the debate waged by BiPOL against the Stonewall 25 organizing committee, which featured interest groups on both sides of the conflict, the discussion about the London Pride celebration tilted in favor of the voices of bisexual activists who highlighted the perils of maintaining the status quo. One author, Jo Eadie, speculated in her essay that foundational differences in how gay, lesbian, and bisexual identities were understood accounted for enduring conflicts among those groups. Referring to the gay and lesbian community, she wrote, "It sometimes seems that it's a community which can only exist by marketing itself as a unique and distinct desire, a notion that suits heterosexuals very well because they can go on distancing themselves from their own queer longings."[38] In a radical departure from how gays and lesbians might see themselves as fundamentally different from straight people, Eadie discursively linked them together to assert that they are aligned in maintaining a distinct hetero/homosexual split. This is because rightful citizenship claims as a political strategy require narrowly conceiving of identities and shedding difference to get marginalized groups over the finish line in rights struggles. As a result, this rigid binary erases bisexuality and, with it, a dynamic understanding of desire and attraction. Eadie's critique continued by further locking gay men and lesbians in stasis: "As long as 'the homosexual' is a separate species, everyone is happy."[39] This observation critiqued the foundation of assimilationist logic required by advancing rightful citizenship claims, namely the construction of gay men and lesbians as essentially driven to same-sex attraction and relationships. Underscoring gay men and lesbians as locked in time urged bisexual readers to remember the importance of bisexuality's distinctiveness, namely positive associations with dynamism and respect for diversity. Eadie deployed the negative construction of gay men and lesbians as a species to make her point: "Now, when bisexuals are trying to remind everyone that erotic attraction can appear at the most unexpected places, we're leaping at the chance to have our own species, 'the bisexual,' which will go on placating the straight world by not trying to blow apart its categories."[40] For Eadie, working to link bisexuals with gays and lesbians further reifies the assumption that sexual identities are essential and immutable. These efforts merely rearticulate the pernicious binary that gay men, lesbians, and straight people have put in place that entails harm to bisexuals. Bisexuals, instead, should remember that they are proudly antinormative. Eadie drove this point home by concluding with a provocation and call to action: "Maybe instead of limiting bisexual pride to one day, one place, one time of the year, we ought to be looking at how to make more places proud of their unrecognized bisexuals."[41]

Who Is Bi, and Why? Internal Conflicts

Even while these conflicts with gay and lesbian political organizations provided a chance for bisexual political actors to put forward a more radical vision for political action focused less on identity and centered on liberation, bisexual publications and organizations were embroiled in internal conflicts over the dominance of White, nontrans bisexuals in leadership positions. The ongoing emphasis on bisexual politics as opposed to normativity and in the interest of sex positivity echoed throughout writings published by bisexual thinkers and political actors during the 1990s as they grappled with failures to incorporate antiracist and trans-affirming perspectives.

One of the most visible early conflicts over bisexual political agendas and the composition of the bisexual group took place in 1990 and concerned the question of self-identified transsexual women participating in the Seattle Bisexual Women's Network (SBWN).[42] Although the relationship between bisexual women and radical lesbian feminists was a fraught one due to the perception that bisexual women were traitors who engaged in relationships with nontrans men, the question of whether and how to include trans women in "women's spaces" revealed the extent to which some bisexual political actors remained attached to the radical feminist idea of gender as a strict biological binary.[43] The ensuing conflicts between those who held onto the idea that biology determines sex/gender and those who opposed them further crystallized understandings of bisexual identity and politics as emphatically anti-dichotomous. The conflicts over trans inclusion also occurred alongside debates in other organizations about the degree to which bisexual spaces were open and safe for people of color. As a result, the importance of the SBWN conflict was subsequently cited by political actors throughout the 1990s as they articulated commitment to trans inclusion and foregrounded the voices of transgender bisexuals in protests staged against the narrowness of the mainstream gay and lesbian political agenda.[44]

According to a 1991 issue of the SBWN newsletter, *North Bi Northwest*, the conflict began in 1990 when a self-identified "male-to-female transsexual" asked to participate in SBWN activities.[45] Although the organization's mission statement stipulated, "All women are welcome to attend SBWN activities," the participation of a transsexual woman was posed to the group's broader membership as a matter of debate.[46] This contradictory development is explained in part by the remainder of the mission statement, which expressed a commitment to broader oppression: "The discrimination we face as women and as sexual minorities is only one facet of oppression: all bigotry is our enemy. We stand behind the racial and ethnic liberation movements and the struggle for economic equality," before concluding, "However, in any work we do, feminism and the interests of women will be our central concern."[47] Naming an interest in contesting all oppressions gives way in the mission statement to a singular focus on women, who are implicitly understood to be White due to the suggestion that concern with race and ethnicity are separate or severable foci, which echoed radical lesbian thinking on woman-identified women. This commitment foreshadowed some of the adjacent conversations taking place in SBNW and other bisexual political organizations around race and the explicit Whiteness found at many bisexual political organizations.

The stated attachment to a very particular understanding of feminism and "women" was revealed throughout the year of debate that took place among SBWN members and outside voices, many of whom learned about the issue and wrote to various bisexual publications to express their views on the conflict. An article titled "Final Decision on Transsexuals in SBWN" by Beth Reba Weise appeared in the spring 1991 issue of *North Bi Northwest* and detailed the process undertaken by the group to reach a decision on the question of trans inclusion. These steps included a meeting with three transgender guests invited to field questions, two discussion meetings for members, and a final vote among the 22 participants. Weise reported that the proceedings were conducted in the interest of achieving consensus, but were marked by intense discussion and concluded with one member of SBNW opting to leave the organization based on the decision. The new policy announced by Weise stipulated conditional acceptance for trans women in SBNW, providing they lived "as a woman" for one year.[48] In spite of this development, trans women were still precluded from taking part in certain SBNW activities, including a newcomers group and social events that might be designated by organizers as for "women-born women only," which included dances and sleepovers.[49] Although Weise elaborated on the reason for excluding trans women from the newcomers group, stating that the group was established to provide a space for "women who said they felt threatened and overwhelmed by the overtly political nature of the Sunday night meetings," she failed to address how excluding trans women from the primary on-ramp to the organization contradicted the decision to allow trans women to join SBWN. Without her addressing the discrepancy of allowing trans women to join the group but also barring them from the newcomers meetings, readers were left to assume that the policy allowing trans women to join the group was at best a superficial gesture. This was likely due to the influence of radical feminist thinking about the biological determinants of sex/gender, a point that was made all the more clearly in the justification for the policy, which stated, "The reasoning behind the decisions of the group included keeping the Newcomers Group a safe and non-threatening space for women who are new to the sexual minority community."[50] Weise's repeated references to safety were couched in concern for nontrans women and drew on radical feminist discourse, like that promulgated by Robin Morgan in her 1973 speech, which promoted the idea that trans women exploit "women-only" spaces as hunting grounds to perpetrate sexual assaults. Weise recognized the problem of safety within the newcomers group before instituting the policy that allowed trans women to join SBWN. This suggests one of two things: either safety was not actually an issue, or safety was a central issue but one that was rooted in the dynamics of the group already in place, which had nothing to do with trans women themselves. The disingenuousness of this concern for safety was conveyed in the summary of the new guidelines, which concluded, "SBWN has made a strong commitment to consensus and diversity with this vote, and we hope that the transsexual community will support us in our process and respect the decisions we have made."[51] In this way, the definitive separation between bisexual women and trans women was set. Addressing the "transsexual community" in this final line portrayed them as outside of the group, effectively drawing a line between the "us" of SBWN, who are meant to be understood as biologically female (i.e., "women") and the transsexual community, who are implied to be outside of those boundaries.

The 1991 SBNW decision was hotly contested within the organization. It was also picked up on by other bisexual organizations, which seized on the very public SBNW controversy to clarify their own views on inclusion and articulate policies regarding the scope of the developing bisexual group and associated political agendas. Many of these debates took place in the same issue of *North Bi Northwest* where SBNW's final decision was published. These letters to the editor were prompted in large part by an opinion piece in a previous issue by Lenore Norrgard titled "Are We Still a Women's Group?," which explicitly articulated many of the radical feminist and biological essentialist arguments that appeared in the final decision. These lengthy letters to the editor weighed in on the question of trans inclusion, all of which went against the final SBNW decision to articulate different viewpoints for including trans women in bisexual spaces. The arguments put forward hit on several themes, including critiques of biology as a basis for identity and, by association, experiences of marginalization, as well as resistance to binary modes of thinking that abetted the exclusion of transgender people from bisexual spaces.

One letter writer, the Bay Area artist Claudia Smelser, used analogies to her identity as a bisexual to argue in favor of including trans women. In response to the assertion in Norrgard's article that trans women appropriate women's experiences as a political act, Smelser speculated, "I don't think

that people undergo such radical transformations based on theories of social repression, but rather because they must. I did not decide to call myself
a bisexual because it is a socially radical or politically correct thing to do."[52]
In this analogy, Smelser draws on the work of bisexual political actors who
emphasized the naturalness of bisexuality as an aspect of human diversity to
oppose stigmas of it as merely a phase or strategic way to avoid identifying
as gay/lesbian. She uses that history to articulate that trans women are also
fulfilling an innate drive toward personal authenticity. According to Smelser,
the true political stakes should be understood strictly in relation to patriarchal oppression: "To be born female in our society may be generally viewed
by the mainstream as a regrettable circumstance, but to actively and willfully
choose to abandon male status is the ultimate outrage, even more threatening than the existence of gay men to societies that value men and den-
igrate women."[53] Smelser then linked the position of trans women to that
of bisexuals: "Such a choice undermines the assumption of male superiority
in the same way that bisexuality undermines dualistic thinking."[54] To be a
trans woman is to rebut patriarchal dominance and the value placed on men
and masculinity in the same way that to be bisexual is to resist modes of binary thinking that limit sexuality to straight or gay/lesbian. The kinship that
Smelser and others like her envisioned as uniting bisexuals and trans people
was also understood against the backdrop of exclusion from gay/lesbian
spaces, and the need to come together in opposition to those forces. Smelser's
conclusion reflected these sentiments: "SBNW has no particular obligation
to include transsexuals if the group is too uncomfortable with the idea, just
as lesbian groups have no particular obligation to include us. (I find it particularly ironic that this same issue of *North Bi Northwest* [in which the original
antitrans letter was published] included a long article by Robyn Ochs and
Pam Ellis that argues for the inclusion of bisexuals and the world 'bisexuality'
in the Lesbian and Gay Studies Conference.)"[55] Once again making use of
analogy, Smelser portrays the rejection of trans people from bisexual spaces
as an act equally repressive as refusing bisexuals access to lesbian and gay
spaces. She drove this point forcefully home and highlighted the hypocrisy of
such actions by reminding readers that one of the main concerns on the bisexual political agenda was agitating for "bisexual" to be included alongside
"gay and lesbian" in the titles of events. That SBNW was unwilling to see the
contradiction in their actions was cited by Smelser as a source of deep personal embarrassment, and she concluded her letter with the announcement
that she was leaving the organization.

Other writers complimented Smelser's focus on the political consequences of excluding trans women from bisexual spaces by encouraging readers to think deeply about gender. These letters focused primarily on the question of what makes a man or woman, and who are bisexuals to put themselves in the position of adjudicating those questions. One writer began her letter on the conflict with a nod to her radical feminist roots by stating, "I am a strong supporter of womyn-only space," using the strategy of eliminating "man" from her syntax before asserting, "yet I feel that a ban on male-to-female transsexuals is wrong. If they are now living as womyn, and have gone through such drastic steps to do so, I feel that we should accept them."[56] The author extended her personal views to the broader organization's practices: "[W]hatever I may feel is right, not allowing transsexuals is not possible. Does SBNW plan to perform a genetic screening test on all of its members?"[57] Doing so would be practically impossible and have negative intangible effects on the group as well, as policing gender would "foster an environment of mistrust and intrusiveness."[58] What takes shape in this letter is the view that such exclusionary policies would work against the very safety that Weise's announcement of the policy sought to protect, not just for trans women but for all those in SBNW who, in theory, would be in the position of somehow demonstrating that they qualify as women. Other reports of the conflict also noted that there was one member of SBNW who was forced to reveal that she was trans as a result of the controversy, which further highlighted the slippery task of attempting to police membership on the grounds of gender.[59]

Although the SBNW conflict resulted in the enduring marginalization of trans women in that organization, the visibility of the debate focused greater attention on emerging theories of gender identity from the academy and by trans thinkers. Over the following decade, bisexual political actors grappled with questions about gender and, over time, forged a long-standing alliance with trans people and the movements representing them. These partnerships took two forms. The first was the active inclusion of trans voices in bisexual publications. These trans thinkers, many of whom also identified as bisexual, helped to give shape to emerging understandings of how the bisexual commitment to opposing binaries could be applied to social and political obstacles facing trans people in the 1990s. The second was the elevation of trans people in the effort to combat the exclusions wrought by the ever-narrowing gay and lesbian agenda as it became increasingly focused on rights and assimilation. Although avoiding rightful citizenship claims facilitated the relatively more open approach to the identity group boundaries constructed by bisexual political actors, conflicts were still waged over how and to what extent diverse voices would be represented by bisexual political organizations. These public debates marked the introduction of a national bisexual political movement.

One such conflict involved the name of BiNet USA, a national political membership organization founded in 1987, and the question of including the word "multicultural" in the name. The North American Bisexual Network was founded at the 1987 March on Washington for Gay and Lesbian Rights and envisioned by the 75 people who participated in the march's bisexual contingent as a national organization with a main chapter to coordinate activities and represent bisexual issues in Washington and local chapters to serve as regional resource hubs. At the first annual conference, in 1990, which convened the leaders of each of the regional offices in San Francisco, the name was changed to the North American Multicultural Bisexual Network to reflect a broader concern with oppression. The addition of "multicultural" was debated at the following annual conference, held in Seattle, and consequently the group's name became BiNet USA in 1991. The revision was once again debated, at the 1992 conference in Minneapolis, with no consensus reached. Participants took up the question once more, in Washington, D.C., in 1993; the historical records from that meeting provide little indication as to how the issue was resolved aside from the formal incorporation of "BiNet USA" that same year. The organization continued to provide resources and advocate for bisexuals until 2020, when activities were suspending due to internal conflict over the political agenda and the place of race within the organization.

That BiNet ultimately folded due to conflicts around race was foreshadowed by the conflicts over the organization's name. Tracing the word "multicultural" as it appears and drops out of BiNet USA discourse provides tremendous insight into how bisexual political actors approached pursuing their stated goals of inclusion and liberation as well as the obstacles they faced. Laura M. Perez, one of the authors of the ECBN flier *Bisexuality: Some Questions Answered*, attended the 1992 Minneapolis meeting that failed to resolve the question of including "multicultural" in any part of the organization's name. She reflected on the discussions that took place at that meeting in an essay for an edited volume on bisexual politics, describing it as "particularly disturbing" and speculating that "part of the reason there was so much opposition to 'multicultural' was the composition of the group itself."[60] Of the 50 participants, only she and two others self-identified as people of color, and according to Perez, she was the only one of those three who advocated retaining "multicultural" in the name. Opponents of the addition argued that including the word would imply that the organization prioritized racial issues, which contradicted the organization's stated focus on bisexuality for the purposes of advancing rightful citizenship claims.

Perez and others took issue with the conflation of multiculturalism and race while also drawing attention to the symbolic effect of striking "multiculturalism" from the title for Black, Asian, Latine, and Native BiNet USA members. An essay circulated to participants of the 1992 meeting in Minneapolis by elias farajaje-jones, "Multikulti Feminist Bis No More?," urged readers to consider what was at stake in the name change. farajaje-jones opened the essay by evocatively describing the feeling of joy upon discovering the North American Multicultural Bisexual network: "there were plenty of other bisexual groups, but this was the only one that made my heart thrill, made me feel that at last i was home. as a queer of colour, writer/ cultural critic and aids guerrilla, the mere existence of the name made me feel that this was a movement to which i would want to dedicate my energies."[61] farajaje-jones went on to explain that this enthusiasm stemmed from the belief that "bis were in the forefront of a movement that was affirming and recognizing relations of difference, of showing how there can be no real unity without a respect for, and recognition of diversity. this is something that has always been of radical importance to us bis."[62] For farajaje-jones, as for other bisexual thinkers who worked to enact stigma transformation, to be bi was to embrace diversity, not only as a core aspect of one's identity but also as an approach to social and political life. Using "us bis" to describe who holds these views reflects the success of efforts at stigma transformation, which flipped negative stereotypes about bisexuality to pose the group as one that welcomed diversity, had a positive attitude toward sex and desire, and opposed harmful binaries that perpetuate oppression.

To some extent, the construction of the bisexual group as one defined by diversity as a matter of necessity was used by opponents of adding "multicultural" in the BiNet's name. A memo circulated by ben e factory for the 1993 meeting summarized the many versions of the organization's names since 1991 and the efforts to thwart the inclusion of "multicultural": " 'Multicultural' as part of the NAMBN name referred to the diversity of Bi people and to the group stand against racism. However, this was seen by a significant number of people, including people of color, as a prioritizing of racism over other oppressions to which there was no reference."[63] factory provided the vote tallies for each of the options put forward at the Minneapolis meeting. "BiNet USA: The Multicultural Bisexual Network" received the greatest number (but not a majority) of votes, followed by "Alliance of Multicultural Bisexuals" and a three-way tie for the following options: "BiNet USA for the Liberation of Bisexuals and All Oppressed People," "BiNet USA: The Multicultural Feminist Bisexual Network," and "National Alliance of Multicultural Bisexuals."[64] As the vote tally suggests, a clear consensus failed to emerge, with much of the debate focused on the implications of adding "multicultural" and "feminism" to the name of the organization.[65] factory explained the conflict at length:

> Those supporting the return of "Multicultural" but not the addition of "Feminist" introduced the position that while the former was deleted in renaming it should be returned because it *can* refer to the cultures of all oppressed peoples (including women's culture, working class culture, differently abled culture, youth culture, etc.), and, therefore, is not a prioritizing of racism over other oppressions. Moreover, "Multicultural" must be understood to refer to all oppressed people, and, therefore, to include feminism, because if it is understood as referring only to racism, then listing "Feminist" and "Multicultural" *is* a prioritizing of sexism and racism over other oppressions which all agreed was unacceptable.[66]

Competing definitions of multiculturalism defined the debate over the organization's name: Does it connote racial diversity or an embrace of many different cultures with presumably equal weight? farajaje-jones advocated for an expansive interpretation, which potentially shaped the discussion at the Minneapolis meeting where farajaje-jones's essay was circulated. Even so, despite these efforts to expand the meaning of multiculturalism, the summary provided by factory suggests that a vocal contingent leaned toward the former definition of multiculturalism as synonymous with race. Drawing on well-worn anti-intersectional logic built into strategies oriented toward rightful citizenship claims, the participants then used this definition to argue that including it in the name of the organization implied an iterated focus on oppressions, especially when appearing alongside "feminism." The primary focus, these voices argued, should be on their shared bisexual identification, which echoed the logic of GAA leaders who prohibited members from bringing the complexity of their identity and experience to the organization in favor of prioritizing gay identification.

farajaje-jones's essay underscores the effects of conflating multiculturalism (and feminism) with race (and gender). In it, farajaje-jones argued
that "multiculturalism" connoted respect for a plurality of cultures, asserting
that "culture does not refer exclusively to race or ethnicity. who decided anyway that multiculturalism only referred to race?" farajaje-jones speculated,
"this is an extension of the heteropatriarchal understanding of multiculturalism as merely sprinkling some different colours onto an already-existing
gigantic white sheet." Like Perez, who critiqued the BiNet proceedings as
dominated by White people, farajaje-jones uses a not so subtle metaphor
of the "white sheet" to imply that the playing field upon which the debate
took place was one defined by White members of the organization.[67] farajaje-
jones then leveraged this observation about who, exactly, was responsible for dropping "multicultural" from the name to draw attention to the
parallels between them and the broader straight, gay, and lesbian forces that
most acknowledged as their main oppressors and the very reason they organized as bisexuals: "don't you see the parallels with the ways in which the
lesbigayristocracy rejects or trivializes bisexuality?"[68] This analogy linked
the bisexual political actors opposing multiculturalism with gay and lesbian
powerholders—compared here to landed nobility—all of whom shared what
farajaje-jones implied was a toxic value for pernicious binaries and rejection
of difference. farajaje-jones contrasted these abstract figures to bisexuals,
reminding readers, "many of us live, love, create, laugh, and struggle while
living at the intersection of many different forms of oppression." This statement directly contradicted the anti-intersectional logic used by opponents
of including "multicultural" in the name, who argued that to do so would
imply an iterated focus. farajaje-jones concluded on a personal note to draw
attention to the implications of organizing around identity understood along
a single axis: "i do not have the luxury of dealing with just one form of oppression at a time, nor do i spend my time prioritizing my oppressions."[69]
For these reasons, farajaje-jones intended to leave BiNet USA: "i fear that
the absence of intentionality about being multicultural can be interpreted as
a sign that 'we're really just all the same and THOSE people need to get over
themselves.'"[70]

These parting lines disrupted the presumed unity of the bisexual group in
a very visible debate over the name of *the* organization founded to represent
bisexuals in national politics and pointed to some of the more implicit ways
that rightful citizenship logic functions to narrow who is considered part of
an emerging group. Although rights discourse was seldom used by bisexual

political actors, farajaje-jones' departure from BiNet USA was performed as an act of resistance aimed at forces seeking to narrow the purview of the organization to those who are "just all the same" with the exception of bisexuality. According to farajaje-jones and others who were in agreement, to reject "multiculturalism" and "feminism" from the name of the organization was to participate in the very same anti-intersectional logic that inform rightful citizenship claims. That these disruptions occurred at the moment that BiNet USA emerged on the national stage as a federally incorporated nonprofit organization indicates that some of the perils of translating local, grassroots movements to the national stage entail narrowing the scope of who is considered part of the group based on the assumption that doing so will somehow make the boundaries and demands more obtainable. The following examination of how bisexuality was represented across political venues highlights how conflicts over the name and the place of racism, classism, sexism, and other issues on BiNet's agenda shaped what came to be known of bisexuality as well as gay and lesbian identities.

Thinking Representation

Ongoing conflicts regarding the scope of bisexual political action carried over into efforts by political actors to represent bisexuality in local and national politics. Two themes emerged in this discourse. The first captures the degree to which bisexual political actors prioritized making bisexuality visible as both an identity and a legitimate expression of sexuality, especially in the context of "monosexism," or what they viewed to be the privileging of sexuality defined in relation to gendered object choice. In positioning bisexuality against monosexism, political actors emphasized the dynamism of bisexuality as well as the view that all oppressions are interconnected. Whereas gay and lesbian political actors focused on rightful citizenship claims that collapsed those identities along a single axis of sexuality, bisexual political actors articulated rights claims outside of the juridical realm. These included calls for the right of self-expression and self-determination, a right to engage in consensual sex, and promoting the view that all oppressions are interconnected.

The second theme concerned the relationship of the increasingly visible bisexual group to gay and lesbian political mobilizations, especially in light of the construction of bisexuality as more open to difference than gay and lesbian identities. Bisexual political actors worked to highlight the ways that bisexuals, gay men, and lesbians were equally subject to discrimination from those who wish to maintain the primacy of the heterosexual nuclear family. These articulations focused on the effects of being named alongside gay men and lesbians in bans against serving openly in the military as well as in policy, such as Colorado's Amendment 2, which explicitly precluded gay men, lesbians, and bisexuals from nondiscrimination protections. Even while they made these claims, bisexual political actors were careful to note a desire to not reproduce the conditions of exclusion to which they were subjected by gay and lesbian political mobilizations.

Analyzing these two themes indicates that the resistance bisexual political actors faced from mainstream gay and lesbian political actors created the conditions for solidifying what came to be known of bisexual, gay, and lesbian identities. Mainstream gay and lesbian politics would increasingly connote an investment in rightful citizenship claims made in the name of immutable characteristics. Bisexuality, in contrast, was represented as a socially and politically meaningful way to describe an approach to sexuality that eludes categorization and eschews identity politics. While the controversy around BiNet's name suggests that some actors chose to construct bisexuals along a single axis, the following examples of people representing bisexuality across political venues shows that the underlying logic of bisexuality as necessarily oriented in opposition to pernicious binaries created the conditions for a relatively more flexible approach to identity.

Representing Bisexuality in a Biphobic World

In 1984, Maggi Rubenstein, one of the founders of the San Francisco BiCenter, was invited to address the city's Lesbian/Gay Freedom Day Parade. The text of her speech was printed in its entirety in an issue of *Bi-Monthly News* and noted as the first time that an openly bisexual person was invited to speak at the annual Pride celebration. Rubenstein opened her speech by recognizing the significance of her role in representing bisexuals to an audience convened under the banner of lesbian and gay liberation, especially in a city widely recognized as a hub for gay and lesbian life. Throughout her brief speech, she reiterated the assertion that bisexual people are the unnamed forced behind many of the successes achieved in the name of gay and lesbian social and political acceptance. She posed this as an overall benefit to gay men, lesbians, and bisexuals, explaining, "Now, because of hard political work by many bisexual people, our voices are being heard across the country."[71] Calling attention to the invisible part played by bisexuals served to unite them with gay men and lesbians in political mobilizations. Rubenstein emphasized the necessity of working together: "Today more than ever before, as we all face the AIDS crisis, we need each other for support and for unity. As allies we can build a coalition of all sexual minorities joining together without apology, demanding our rights in a homophobic and biphobic world."[72] Describing AIDS as a pandemic and a tragedy that affects gay men, lesbians, and bisexuals allowed Rubenstein to assert bisexuality as a discrete and legitimate identity that resists absorption into gay and lesbian identities. Listing homophobia and biphobia together linked these groups while also giving a specific name to the oppression that bisexuals endure.

Having established the interrelated history of activism by gay men, lesbians, and bisexuals, Rubenstein used analogies to familiar gay and lesbian struggles to emphasize the need to recognize and support bisexual political actions: "Like lesbians and gays, bisexual people are also everywhere. Despite the reactionary anti-sex forces in charge of this country, a network of bisexual organizations, in community with our lesbian and gay friends, exists and is growing, and THE SUPPORT MUST GO BOTH WAYS."[73] Rubenstein's hope for this exchange of support was to foster greater acceptance as well as building "a society that accepts the sexual diversity of all its people."[74] According to Rubenstein, that vision could be best achieved by putting aside internecine conflicts over the differences between gay, lesbian, and bisexual identities, and instead focusing on their shared objectives. The analogies she deployed functioned as they do elsewhere in political discourse, and to great effect. Whereas gay men and lesbians used analogies to the Black civil rights battles to pose gay men and lesbians as similar to Black people, which required the conceptual severing of sexuality and race, Rubenstein leveraged analogies to cast bisexuality as distinct from gay and lesbian identities. This rhetorical maneuver created the conditions for linking bisexuals in political action with gay men and lesbians. In doing so, Rubenstein also represented bisexual political interests as concerned with issues adjacent to sexuality, while also holding open possibilities for considering intersecting concerns related to race, gender, and colonialism. She clarified these points for her audience later in her brief speech, saying that the progressive bisexual political agenda included "support for the passage of federal, state, and local sexual minority rights bills, passage of the ERA [Equal Rights Amendment], increased funding for AIDS research and treatment, freedom of choice in reproductive rights, the civil rights—including sexual rights—and civil liberties of all people, a stop to US intervention in Central America, and an end to nuclear madness."[75] This brief list of political goals spanned a variety of concerns held by many groups, including gay men and lesbians, as well as liberal feminists. Furthermore, naming civil rights as intersecting with sexual rights connoted a commitment to struggles by Black, Asian, and Latine people, all of whom were active in San Francisco politics in some way or another. Specifying that mobilizations for civil rights includes consideration for sexual rights resisted the narrowing tendency of rightful citizenship claims by nesting the latter within the former. Having linked these groups in an articulation of the bisexual progressive agenda, Rubenstein then used this list to speculate that bisexual political interests were not so different from those held by the gay men and lesbians in the audience, and in closing, requested that bisexuals be considered for inclusion in the title of next year's march. She ended her speech on a liberatory note, announcing, "Together we will win our common struggle for peace, for freedom for all people, and for validation of the full spectrum of sexual orientations."[76]

The "B" Isn't Silent

The construction of bisexual political identity and political interests as more expansive alternatives to gay and lesbian identities and agendas resonated in subsequent representations of the group by bisexual political actors, especially as bisexual political mobilizations became more visible in national politics. The prevailing context of the "gay '90s," in which conservative opponents mobilized to stop any rights gains for gay men, lesbians, and feminists shaped how bisexual political actors developed and represented their political agendas.[77] Perhaps most visibly, in 1992, Colorado voters approved Amendment 2, which constitutionally prohibited any city, town, or county in that state from taking any action to recognize what the bill referred to as "homosexuals or bisexuals" as a protected class. The amendment was immediately met with a lawsuit and the case against it wound its way to the U.S. Supreme Court, where it was ultimately deemed unconstitutional in the Court's 1996 *Romer v. Evans* decision. During the intervening four years, bisexual political actors seized being named alongside gay men and lesbians to claim that the fates of those groups were linked together in the face of conservative forces that would just as soon strip them all of rights and protections. The opportunity to pose both groups as sharing in vulnerability was only magnified by the announcement of Don't Ask, Don't Tell in 1993, which prohibited any "homosexual or bisexual" from disclosing their sexuality while serving in the U.S. armed forces. Although both Amendment 2 and the passage of DADT curtailed the rights of bisexuals to participate in certain aspects of social and political life, the discourse from this period shows that bisexual political actors went to great lengths to retain a focus on the ways that heteronormativity, racism, sexism, and classism interact to create conditions of oppression. In focusing on these oppressive ideologies instead of rights, they articulated their agenda as an alternative to the rightful citizenship claims advocated for by gay and lesbian political actors in response to the very same developments.

The text of Lani Ka'ahumanu's 1993 speech at the March on Washington for Gay, Lesbian, and Bi Equal Rights and Liberation illustrates how bisexual leaders represented this alternative political orientation. The speech was published in its entirety in *Anything That Moves* alongside farajaje-jones's piece lambasting the decision by BiNet to drop "multicultural" from the name of the organization. Whereas farajaje-jones targeted bisexuals, Ka'ahumanu addressed a predominantly gay- and lesbian-identified audience. I analyze her articulation of a bisexual political agenda as one designed to shape meanings associated with bisexuality for outside audiences while also recognizing that the publication of the speech in its entirety in a bisexual publication served a valuable purpose in defining how bisexuals themselves might understand their political grievances and the steps they must take, as bisexuals, to address them.

Ka'ahumanu opened her speech by reiterating Rubenstein's argument that bisexuals have always been active, yet invisible, in gay and lesbian struggles, and added her own distinctive take: they were not invisible but actively erased by gay men and lesbians in positions of power. She struck a pronounced political note in her definition of bisexuality itself, stating, "Bisexual pride speaks to the truth of behavior and identity. No simple either/or divisions, fluid-ambiguous-subversive, bisexual pride challenges both the heterosexual and homosexual assumption."[78] Because of this, "[r]ecognition of bisexual orientation and transgender issues presents a challenge to assumptions not previously explored within the politics of gay liberation." Ka'ahumanu underscored the stakes of not considering issues pertinent to transgender and bisexual people by rhetorically asking her audience to consider who, exactly, stands to benefit from exclusionary politics. The answer, she asserted, was that such divisions play directly into the hands of "right wing fundamentalists who see all of us as queer."[79] She also named the anti-intersectional forces at play: "What is the difficulty in seeing how my struggle as a mixed race bisexual women of color is intimately related to the bigger struggle for lesbian and gay rights, the rights of people of color and the rights of all women? This is not a competition. I will not play by rules that pit me against any oppressed group."[80] To engage in this type of categorization is to erase bisexuals as well as all those people whose identities are shaped at the intersection of race, class, and gender. The same either/or divisions that obscure bisexuals, according to Ka'ahumanu, are the very same forces that set groups in opposition to each other when they could be united in struggle. Even so, Ka'ahumanu critiqued the "lesbigayristocracy" for being "invested so much in being the opposite of heterosexual that they cannot remove themselves; that they can't imagine being free of the whole oppressive heterosexist system" that was responsible for oppressing all minority groups.[81] Bisexuals, in contrast, were ideally positioned to challenge these oppressive dichotomies imposed externally in the form of heteronormativity and maintained internally by erasing transgender and bisexual people who, according to Ka'ahumanu, were "not passing for anything other than who and what we are [and] have our necks and our lives on the line. Our visibility is a sign of revolt."[82] Linking bisexuals and transgender people together as the most visible sexual and gender minorities named the consequences of the rightful citizenship claims advanced by the "lesbigayristocracy." In sum, posing gay men and lesbians as similar to straight people except for who they pursued for relationships and sex, made those leaders complicit in perpetuating oppression that impacted the more visible, and thus more vulnerable, sexual and gender minorities.[83]

The unique vulnerability of bisexuals and transgender people was only intensified by efforts toward assimilation as gay men, lesbians, *and* bisexuals continued to be targeted for legally enshrined discrimination, which Ka'ahumanu named as Amendment 2, Don't Ask, Don't Tell, and restrictions on bisexual people fostering or adopting children. She concluded her litany of oppressions by also locating bisexuals as targets for physical violence, drawing on the mainstream gay and lesbian movement's rhetoric of hate crimes to explain that bisexuals also "get beaten and killed for loving women and for loving men. Bisexuals are queer, just as queer as queer can be."[84] As in other places throughout this analysis of bisexual political identity, naming bisexuals as queer served the purpose of drawing sexual and gender minorities together in an anticategorical stance. Ka'ahumanu's use of "queer" also helped to rebut stigmas about bisexuals. They were not fence-sitters who occasionally benefited from heterosexual partnerships, as pejorative stereotypes of bisexuality held. Repeatedly naming bisexuals as queer positioned them as vanguards of sexual and gender minorities, with their antidichotomous approach to relationships and sex upending conventional narratives about desire, all of which made them even more vulnerable to assault. Ka'ahumanu concluded her speech by asking gays and lesbians in the audience to "decide how large our extended family is" and reminding them that every person in the audience convened in Washington in the interest of achieving civil rights and liberation, which could be achieved only by a critical mass mobilizing together: "Our visibility is an act of resistance. Remember assimilation is a lie."[85]

Ka'ahumanu was not alone in promoting bisexuality as an alternative to the exclusions built into mainstream gay and lesbian organizing. Similar statements would be reiterated by bisexual political actors throughout the 1990s as they mobilized to have bisexuality recognized in a playing field dominated by gay and lesbian political organizations. One such action took place at the NGLTF's 1997 Creating Change conference, which was (and still is) convened annually to bring activists, lobbyists, and gay men, lesbians, bisexuals, and transgender people together to craft political agendas, network, and attend workshops on activism. The conference proceedings were reported extensively in *Anything That Moves*, where bisexual and transgender authors and activists celebrated staging a successful protest action to draw attention to the prevailing climate of exclusion they found in gay and lesbian spaces. The disruptions to the conference proceedings conducted by bisexual, transgender, and intersex participants demonstrate how political actors use representations across various political venues to shape what comes to be known of a political identity and agenda. Lani Ka'ahumanu once again figured prominently in these efforts. She reported that Yosenio Lewis, a bisexual transgender activist associated with the National Latino/Latina Lesbian and Gay Organization, convened a meeting of transgender and bisexual Creating Change participants to prepare for a conversation with the gay and lesbian liaison to the White House, Richard Socarides. The newly formed bisexual and transgender caucus created an opportunity for people to share their negative experiences of discrimination. Lewis and Ka'ahumanu worked alongside representatives from the National Center for Lesbians and

FTM International, among many other organizations, to organize an action in which individuals from those groups would seize the stage during a plenary session to describe their experiences of biphobia, anti-transness, and racism during the conference.

The action began by asking all members of the audience who identified as bisexual, transgender, or intersex to stand up. After pausing for people to rise from their seats, one participant, identified only as Jen, described how a prevailing anti-intersectional climate silenced her voice during a breakout session: "During the youth sessions, I identified myself as a Korean-American bi-dyke queer, and was told that the people of color institute had happened the day before, and that we were to leave those issues at the door. When I attended the queer of youth color institute, the facilitators included only lesbian and gay when they were speaking. I felt as if I had been denied the right to be present."[86] Gerard, another participant, narrated a similar scene he witnessed: "In another workshop, a transsexual man of color was attempting to illustrate his experience of racism by tying it to his gender issues. He was cut off in mid-sentence and told that by bringing up gender, he was diverting the discussion away from racism."[87] After offering chances for other participants to report similar experiences in which anti-intersectional attitudes resulted in silencing and erasure, Gerard again took the stage to recognize NGLTF for convening the conference and concluded by calling on participants to consider the following call to action:

> We would like all of you who are still seated to consider this challenge: The people standing around you have had the courage to acknowledge our presence in our queer community. They have come to understand that we have been named by our common enemies. We ask all of you who are seated to remember to say the words "transgender and bisexual," to learn to understand our issues as your own, to speak out for us as we have all spoken out for you. Please show your solidarity with bisexual, transgender, and intersexed people who are fighting for the rights of all queer people, and stand with us now.[88]

By all accounts, the 1997 Creating Change conference was a watershed moment for bisexual and transgender politics and marked the culmination of almost two decades of organizing by bisexual political actors to achieve recognition. Several articles and speeches from this time celebrated the 1997 action as a powerful moment of representation that reverberated throughout the remainder of the meeting. The bisexual and transgender caucus protest also foreshadowed the future of bisexual, transgender, gay, and lesbian political organizing. Shortly after the 1997 conference, NGLTF amended its mission statement to include bisexual and transgender people, stating, "The National Gay and Lesbian Task Force (NGLTF) is a leading progressive civil rights organization that has supported grassroots organizing and advocacy since 1973. Since its inception, NGLTF has been at the forefront of every major initiative for lesbian, gay, bisexual and transgender rights."[89] HRC would follow in 2003.

Conclusions: The (Conditional) Terms of Inclusion

This chapter opened with three vignettes that present the fraught place of bisexuals and bisexuality in relation to gay men and lesbians as a puzzle: Why would gay men and lesbians work so hard to exclude bisexuals from political action only to eventually include them in the names of the most prominent gay and lesbian organizations?

I argue that part of the answer lies in tracing the development of bisexuality as a political identity with an eye to how the logic of rightful citizenship claims lurks in unseen places. Take, for example, the theorization of monosexism as the ideology that bisexuals contested to position themselves alongside—and yet distinct from—gay and lesbian identity. One way to think about this new understanding of human sexuality is as a framework for analyzing difference and power, with implications for political action. According to bisexual political actors and thinkers, gay men and lesbians adhere to and promote monosexism as a strategic maneuver to position those identities as proximate to heterosexuality through the claim that they are analogous to their straight counterparts but for the sex of the people they desire. The dynamic view of desire, relationships, and gender that bisexuals celebrated imperiled these claims by advocating for a more nuanced and intersectional approach to sexuality and recognition, which in turn created incentives for gay and lesbian political actors to erase bisexuals from political agendas and social circles. Bisexual political actors responded by critiquing monosexism and, along with it, the strategy of rightful citizenship claims that required shedding difference to make gains. They argued that doing so was hypocritical for movements so focused on visibility, recognition, and inclusion. In so doing, they aimed to put pressure on gay and lesbian political leaders by creating a dilemma for them to confront: how to address the issues raised by bisexuals while also continuing to put pressure on lawmakers for rights gains.

The most prominent national gay and lesbian political organizations responded by including "bisexual" in titles and mission statements as the 1990s came to a close. While this move addressed the grievances raised by bisexual political actors who argued for their place alongside gay men and lesbians, doing so came at the cost of losing the distinctiveness they worked so hard to establish, specifically the anticategorical stance that allowed sexuality to float freely without gender as an anchor. Bisexuals were folded in, but only conditionally.

These developments foreshadowed the future of gay, lesbian, and bisexual political identities and agendas as the 1990s came to a close, namely the increasing focus on rightful citizenship claims as national-level gay and lesbian political organizations gained visibility and funding. The following two chapters examine these shifts with respect to the development of two political identities: transgender and LGBT. Like bisexual political identity, the boundaries of transgender identity that I examine in the next chapter were shaped by an overarching context of exclusion born of rightful citizenship claims and the need to highlight gender-normative, White, affluent gay men (and some lesbians). Transgender political actors met these challenges by underscoring the hypocrisy of their exclusion while also working to align certain transgender people with the growing gay and lesbian movement. Accepting rightful citizenship claims as the most logical political strategy thus contributed to the shedding of difference and set the stage for the introduction of transgender identity to political conversations in very narrow terms.

5

Transgender Political Identity as Coalition

In 1994, Phyllis Frye, the founder of the International Conference on
Transgender Law and Employment Policy, circulated an open letter to protest the exclusion of transgender people from the title of a march to be held
in New York City that spring. Stonewall 25: The International March on the
United Nations to Affirm the Human Rights of Lesbian and Gay People was
organized by the International Lesbian and Gay Association (ILGA) and
used the Stonewall anniversary as an occasion to target the United Nations
with a call to include gay and lesbian people in the UN Universal Declaration
of Human Rights.[1] Though the ILGA mission statement, platform, and
organizing documents for the march emphasized the inclusion of bisexual,
drag, and transgender communities alongside lesbians and gay men in the
Stonewall 25 activities,[2] Frye passionately argued that the exclusion of transgender people from the title of the march underscored the lack of attention to
transgender concerns by lesbian and gay interest groups in Washington: "The
title is important. If we do not make the title, we do not make the language.
If we do not make the language, we are left out of legislation? [sic] Is transgender defined in 'sexual orientation' or is 'gender identification' anywhere
to be found in the proposed federal civil rights legislation being pushed in
Congress by 'lesbian and gay' activists? Without being disingenuous, I think
not. If I am wrong, I will celebrate being corrected."[3] In addition to making
a strong claim for the incorporation of transgender people in gay and lesbian political actions and interests, Frye's statement on the eve of Stonewall
25 succinctly captures the relatively inchoate status of transgender as a political identity in the early 1990s. Although "transgender" was occasionally
used to describe individuals since the 1970s, the terms "transsexual" (to describe a person who has pursued either surgery or hormones to alter their
sex) and "transvestite" (a man who dresses in women's clothes or a woman
who dresses in men's clothes) were more regularly used, and historians argue
that it was not until the early 1990s that "transgender" began to circulate as
a social and political identity.[4] Frye's question in 1994 about how to define
"transgender"—as either gender identity or sexual orientation—shows how

Terms of Exclusion. Zein Murib, Oxford University Press. © Oxford University Press 2023.
DOI: 10.1093/oso/9780197671498.003.0006

the boundaries of transgender identity were relatively unsettled in political discourse as recently as 30 years ago.

This chapter examines the ways that transgender activists and political leaders worked to construct meanings associated with transgender identity during the 1990s, particularly as they made concerted efforts to formulate the boundaries of transgender as both a cohesive identity and a burgeoning political movement, or what transgender-identified activist Leslie Feinberg described in 1991 as an umbrella term to unite "gender outlaws: transvestites, transsexuals, drag queens and drag kings, cross-dressers, bull-daggers, stone butches, androgynes, diesel dykes or berdache."[5] In this chapter, I foreground these disparate groups in my analysis of how political actors brokered them into a new political identity and, over time, crafted a political agenda. The first section examines conflicts over meanings of biological sex, gender identity, and sexual orientation in the discourse of the early thinkers of transgender identity. I show how conflicts over the definitions of each of these terms were resolved through the introduction of "transgender" to advance what was understood to be the socially constructed and contingent nature of gender identity, which rejected the idea that gender is ultimately rooted in biological markers such as chromosomes and physical traits.

The next section traces the ways that political actors attempted to translate the emerging understandings of transgender identity into political action. Although the leaders and thinkers working to usher transgender people into political action paid homage to the activist roots of transgender politics, particularly for the power of activism to seize narratives from medical professionals and radical feminists, they advocated shifting focus toward formal politics, namely lobbying in Washington. Key to this discourse was the argument that transforming stigmas could not happen "in the streets" and that more serious and respectable approaches to political action alone would achieve social and political legitimacy for transgender people.[6] Rightful citizenship claims were central to this strategy.

The final section details the representation of political interests by transgender organizations at the close of the decade. By comparing how transgender identity was represented across varying sites, this analysis illustrates how internal exclusions and marginalization—particularly for transgender men, transgender people of color, and people who were gender-nonconforming—within the transgender group were produced alongside the construction of transgender political identity. Once again, these omissions were produced through debates over how to best position the transgender group to advance rightful citizenship claims. The analysis begins with a focus on conflict and transgender identity construction.

Transgender: Conceptual Conflicts and Shifts

Although the first use of the word "transgender" is disputed by scholars, it is widely agreed that Virginia Prince, the founder of various organizations and publications for men who enjoyed wearing women's clothing, revived it in the 1970s to echo the introduction of gender identity in scientific circles.[7] Initially advanced by Robert Stoller, a psychiatrist working in the areas of sex and sexuality, the concept of gender identity was used to consolidate the varying terms that medical and psychiatric professionals used to describe the "tremendous areas of behavior, feelings, thoughts, and fantasies that are related to the sexes and yet do not have primarily biological connotations."[8] Stoller's introduction of gender identity attempted to sever biological sex from psychosocial or performed gender identity, allowing biological sex and gender identity to be considered discrete categories in both scientific and academic circles. For Prince, then, the term "transgender" described the sense of moving across (i.e., transiting) masculine and feminine identities (i.e., gender) without surgery or other medically mediated steps to align gender identity and gender presentation. Although Prince's transgender appellation faded away in favor of existing terms that dominated medical and psychiatric contexts, including "transsexual" and "transvestite," a few years after Prince's initial use, in the early 1990s some activists and movement leaders revived it as an umbrella term that captured many different versions of gender identity.

The reintroduction of "transgender" as a social and political identity built directly on the analytic separation of biological sex and gender identity established in the United States during the early 20th century. In her history of transsexuality in the United States, historian Joanne Meyerowitz explains that the term "sex" was expansively defined by doctors to include both anatomy and behavioral traits at the beginning of the 20th century, only to shift in midcentury, when doctors and social scientists began to explore different ways to parse physical traits from behaviors, and by the close of the century deployed three categories to explain what had been previously been understood simply as sex.[9] Embodied and inherited traits, such as chromosomes, genes, hormones, and physical markers, were indexed under biological sex. The individual's internal sense of masculinity and femininity, and the social roles associated with each, were conceptualized as gender identities. A third distinct category emerged at the end of the 20th century as "sexuality," defined by desire, attraction, and related behaviors. Historian Susan Stryker argues that the significance of the separation of sex, gender identity, and sexuality in contemporary transgender identity points to "the central issue of transgender politics—that the sex of the body does not bear any *necessary* or *deterministic* relationship to the social category in which that body lives."[10] Whereas biology was previously viewed as determinative of gender, the evolving understanding of transgender identity maintained that gender identification does not inhere in the body but is instead situated in the realm of self-expression and social roles.

Holly Boswell's 1991 "The Transgender Alternative" was featured in the second issue of *Chrysalis Quarterly*, a journal catering to self-identified transsexual subscribers to "promote the nonjudgmental and nondiscriminatory treatment of persons with gender dysphoria, and advocate respect for their dignity, their right to treatment, and their right to choose their gender."[11] *Chrysalis Quarterly* was published in conjunction with the *AEGIS Newsletter*, both of which were overseen by Dallas Denny, a prominent transgender activist and thinker. Denny founded the American Educational Gender Information Service (AEGIS) in 1990 to disseminate information to trans-identified people. The organization and publication functioned similarly to the contemporary internet in that they were important information hubs where people could learn about gender identity, gather knowledge about doctors, and connect socially.[12] The collection of essays by transgender activists and thinkers and their wide circulation can thus be read as influential sources for people learning about the evolving construction of transgender identity during the early 1990s as the meanings associated with "transgender" were taking shape.

Boswell's essay in *Chrysalis Quarterly* was especially influential due to her role as the founder in the early 1990s of one of the first support groups for transgender people. Her introduction of "transgender" as an alternative to transsexual identity and medicalized discourse built on an influential essay by trans thinker Sandy Stone, who in 1987 wrote "The Empire Strikes Back: A Post-Transsexual Manifesto," which is often credited with efforts to root narratives of trans experience in the voices of trans-identified people and thus laying the epistemic groundwork for the development of Transgender Studies. Boswell's essay begins by reiterating the debates over gender identity and biological sex initiated by Stone that would shape transgender political identity moving forward: "The middle ground I am referring to is transgenderism. I realize this term (heretofore vague) also encompasses the entire spectrum: crossdresser to transsexual person. But for the purposes of this article—and for what I hope will be a continuing dialogue—I shall attempt to define transgender as a viable option between crossdresser and transsexual person, which also happens to have a firm foundation in the ancient tradition of androgyny."[13] In contrast to Stone who focused on "transsexual," Boswell used spatial metaphors to articulate transgender as a singular middle ground, but also an all-encompassing spectrum, which highlighted the tensions between "transgender" as an umbrella term or an identity category defined along a single dimension that would characterize the "continuing dialogue" regarding transgender identity moving forward. At this point in Boswell's essay, transgender identity does not contain within its boundaries *all* possible gender identifications. Rather, her conceptualization of transgender is located on a spectrum anchored by the poles of biological sex ("the transsexual person") and gender identity ("the crossdresser") as its own, discrete category that would be similar to the "androgyne," or an individual who purposefully blends masculine and feminine characteristics. The stakes of this conceptualization of transgender identity become clear when Boswell writes, "Many people confuse sex with gender. Sex is biological, whereas gender is psychosocial. So if biology does not truly dictate gender or personality, then dichotomies of masculinity and femininity only serve to coerce or restrict the potential variety of ways of being human."[14] In forcing a rupture with biology and "sex," Boswell echoes the Combahee River Collective Statement, which used "demand" to describe the coercive effects of grounding feminism in biology. But this is where the parallels end. Unlike the CRCS's objection to biology, Boswell rests her argument on the observation that linking biology to gender identity limits full expressions of human diversity.

For Boswell, then, confronting these constraints requires a comprehensive solution that contradicts dichotomies of masculine/feminine and male/female that limit the full expression of humanity. She surmised toward the end of her essay, "I believe the truth of a solution to our dilemma is all-encompassing—not polarized. We know, deep in our hearts, that we are more than our culture dictates. We can reject those limitations, in all their manifestations, if we have a vision that transcends—if we believe we must go beyond."[15] Reiterating her vision of transgender identity as "all-encompassing" contradicts her earlier formulation of it as an identity located between the poles of transvestite-identified people and transsexual-identified people, and again underscores the inchoate and continually evolving constructions of transgender identity. As Boswell wants to indicate here, refuting the ubiquitous binaries that have structured the lives of transgender- and transsexual-identified people is not only about transcending them. It is also about claiming a legitimate, comprehensive position that defies these binaries in order to achieve unity. It is clear from her conclusion that she envisions transgender identity as flush with social and political possibilities that will be enabled by linking transgender political goals with human rights efforts. Such a call provides some insight into why it is that she concludes on the note of transgender as an "all-encompassing" identification. However, what is not entirely clear is where she stands on the question of whether or not transgender should be a category to capture multiple identities or should construct its own boundaries to contain a narrowly conceived membership.

Despite ambiguities over how this identity should be conceived, Boswell's essay foreshadowed two aspects of transgender as a political identity that would continue to evolve in the following years. The first is the efforts of political actors to pursue unity across different groups under "transgender" as an umbrella term and the competing tendency to present transgender as a narrowly defined political identity to mobilize successful rightful citizenship claims. The second aspect foreshadowed by Boswell was the ongoing tensions between casting transgender identity as broad and inclusive or narrow and exclusive of racial, sexual, and class difference. These tensions over the boundaries of the transgender political identity and its proper membership demonstrate the ways that political actors play a significant role in shaping what comes to be known of groups, particularly as they make choices to include some groups and seek distance from others.

Leslie Feinberg, a transgender and butch-identified activist and author of Stone Butch Blues, built on the political possibilities outlined by Boswell in "Transgender Liberation: A Movement Whose Time Has Come," a widely circulated pamphlet that was first published in 1992 and later appeared in a book on transgender politics. Whereas Boswell alternated between transgender as an all-encompassing identity category that would defy boundaries as well as a category located at the center of two poles anchored by crossdressers and transsexuals, Feinberg framed the question this way: "We are talking here about people who defy the 'man'-made boundaries of gender. Gender: self-expression, not anatomy."[16] By situating gender identity in opposition to categories of male and female imposed from the outside (and by "man," no less), Feinberg refines the positions previously outlined by Boswell and lays the intellectual foundations for two important features of transgender political identity that were evolving during the early 1990s. First, the boundaries designating biological sex are, in fact, social constructions (i.e., "self-expression") and not natural, preexisting truths. In addition to settling some of Boswell's ambivalence around both gender identity and biological sex, this repudiation of biological sex helped to set the stage for the second defining feature of transgender politics in Feinberg's eyes: if biological sexes are social constructs, then gender identities are determined by the presentation and perception of one's gender, which can change on a daily basis, if one wishes, as a facet of self-expression that can be erotic, social, or—importantly—political. In other words, gender identity can offer the opportunity for people to take control of the constructed categories that previously acted upon their lives as constraints and definitions imposed from the outside.[17]

Feinberg's theoretical moves to establish both biological sex and gender identity as social constructs suggested the political possibilities of transgender identity and people identifying with it: "In recent years a community has begun to emerge that is sometimes referred to as the gender or transgender community. Within our community is a diverse group of people who define ourselves in many different ways. Transgendered people are demanding the right to choose our own self-definitions."[18] For Feinberg, transgender is not a singular and discrete identity to figure in between self-identified transsexuals and cross-dressers, or alongside lesbian and gay identities, as Boswell asserted. It is a community of identities that coheres around shared experiences of oppression that stem from the maintenance of gender norms, and as such includes anybody who has ever been subject to standards of hegemonic masculinity and femininity. According to Feinberg, then, a necessary first step for transgender liberation is about "trying to find words, however inadequate, that can connect us, that can capture what is similar about the oppression we endure."[19] Focusing on narratives and discourse, Feinberg's construction of transgender identity attempts to settle the conflict between transgender as a singular identity and an umbrella category by contesting the model of politics that locates political claims in presumably static identities. An avowed revolutionary Communist, Feinberg endeavored to locate political demands in relation to the institutions that structure and maintain gender normativity, consequently resulting in the oppression of all people who are perceived as challenging dominant gender norms. The significance of this construction of transgender identity and political agenda cannot be overstated, as this radical approach toward the institutions that create and maintain binary gender would come to define transgender politics in subsequent years, when some transgender political actors embraced a radical antistructural approach to political action and others maintained an attachment to radical citizenship logic to cast transgender along a single axis of identity: gender.[20]

Another important contribution of Feinberg's focus on structural inequality was the opportunity to challenge the exclusion of trans people from political action based on the assumption that sexuality and gender are mutually exclusive. Feinberg explains, "Transgendered people are mistakenly viewed as the cusp of the lesbian and gay community. In reality the two huge communities are like circles that only partially overlap. While the oppressions within these two powerful communities are not the same, we face a common enemy. Gender-phobia—like racism, sexism and bigotry against lesbians and gay men—is meant to keep us divided. Unity can only increase our strength."[21] Antiviolence campaigns mobilized by concern with homophobia were at the top of gay and lesbian political agendas during the early 1990s. Recasting homophobia as "gender-phobia" and speculating about the strength of a unified gay, lesbian, and transgender political movement spoke directly to gay and lesbian political groups that had long histories of excluding trans people from their ranks. Feinberg's focus on gender normativity and heteronormativity as interlocking forces posed a significant challenge to gay and lesbian political organizations that foreclosed membership to transgender people based on the assumption that sexuality and gender are two different axes of identity. By association, then, statements such as these constructed meanings associated with transgender identity as well gay and lesbian identities. They are not mutually exclusive or tangential to each other, but instead overlapping and mutually imbricated in social and political struggles. Much like Gay Liberation discourse, articulating this challenge to the gay and lesbian political identities and agendas while also reconceptualizing the source of the dominant, and shared, threat for all groups was an effort to forge a type of prefigurative politics premised on challenging stigmas and the tendency to pathologize both sexual and gender identities. In this case, Feinberg expanded the discourse of transgender as an umbrella identity—explicitly inclusive of many variations of gender

identity—to consider gay and lesbian political concerns alongside transgender identity and political interests. Envisioning transgender, lesbian, and
gay politics as overlapping identities critiqued the history of gay and lesbian
political organizations excluding transgender people and prefigured an alternative form of political action focused on unity and inclusion.

In sum, reviving transgender as the preferred way to refer to all iterations
of gender variance in the 1990s marked a significant shift away from the
terms derived by doctors and psychiatrists, such as "transvestite" and "transsexual," and imagined a future for transgender as an explicitly social and political identity. Transgender identity, in other words, would not be imposed
from the outside but rather constructed by transgender people's narratives,
experiences, and political demands. This rupture with medicalized discourse of gender normativity, as well as the erasures enacted by radical
lesbian feminists and gay assimilation, offers an example of political actors constructing political identities through conflicts to assert particular
meanings with a group. According to these thinkers, transgender identity was
not rooted in pathology but rather a *political* identity that was constructed by
political actors to bring people together in political and social action. Key to
constructing the boundaries of this identity was the use of narrative and discourse by and from transgender-identified people.

The next section focuses on publications and internal memos from two
newly minted transgender political organizations to examine the influence
of this early discourse on political action conducted in the name of transgender people. My reading of the *AEGIS Newsletter* and lobbying notes from
a new interest group, the Gender Political Action Committee, or GenderPAC,
shows that efforts to translate the construction of transgender identity as an
umbrella to contain many different types of gender and sexual variance did
not come without complications. Two competing understandings of transgender political identity evolved in the discourse of political actors. One
version vehemently advocated for maintaining an open and inclusive understanding of transgender identity and political action that would contest
the institutions that rely on binary gender norms to maintain coercive power
over gender and sexual expression. These political actors advocated radical
social change to accomplish their goal of an oppression-free world. Perhaps
unsurprising by now, another version of transgender identity put forward by
political actors channeled rightful citizenship logic to foreground a universal
transgender subject evacuated of intersecting identities, especially race, but
including class, HIV status, religion, and ability.

Stigma Transformation: Making Transgender Political

AEGIS was incorporated as a 501(c)(3) organization in 1990, around the same time Boswell's and Feinberg's articulations of transgender identity and political interests were circulating. Dallas Denny, founder of both AEGIS and *Chrysalis Quarterly*, explained in the first issue that the *AEGIS Newsletter* would serve as an information clearinghouse on transgender history, political action, and AEGIS itself. Although the newsletter ran for only 13 issues and ceased in 1998 with the advent of the internet as a centralized source for information on identity, doctors, and politics, the newsletter was distributed broadly and featured essays from transgender-identified people who played a pivotal role in shaping the emergent meaning of transgender into an active political identity and associated agenda of interests.

The second issue of the *AEGIS Newsletter*, in 1994, featured a brief article by Denny that succinctly articulated the need to develop a visible political movement. After observing that all movements start with pioneers willing to take risks, Denny articulated a vision of transgender politics that would logically progress from activism toward formal political advocacy to accomplish a variety of goals, including advancing rights claims, combating defamation, and disseminating information to alter stigmas associated with transgender people. Political organizations in the mold of interest groups would be key to this evolution, and Denny positioned AEGIS as central to the work, explaining to readers, "We at AEGIS have been constructing a framework which can allow that to happen. But before it does, we must have a community which can work together for our common good."[22] In much the same way that Gay Liberationists encouraged people to come out as gay or lesbian, Denny promoted embracing transgender identity to show a critical mass of trans people backing the social and political changes sought, without explicitly addressing who, exactly, was best positioned to come out and comprise that community.

The question of who would make up the membership of a transgender political movement was answered in the third issue of the newsletter, which began with a front-page announcement from the AEGIS board concerning a new membership program. The invitation explained the board's motivation: "The world will not take transgendered persons seriously until we take ourselves seriously. The world is not impressed by recaptioned cartoons, stylized drawings of women who are supposed to be transgendered, and magazines containing contact ads and advertisements for phone sex lines.

Any gain in ad revenues or readership by including such things is more than offset by a corresponding loss of respect."[23] The ideal member of the new transgender political movement is serious and respectable, requirements that are made all the more salient by the contrast to more libidinal and supposedly frivolous aspects of transgender life depicted in publications that might be considered apolitical, exploitative, or low-brow. AEGIS would instead focus on objectives to "create a world in which transgendered persons are treated with respect and in which it is illegal to discriminate against transgendered persons," goals that would be achieved by using "serious tools for outreach."[24]

Matthew Hindman's research on the history of lesbian and gay interest groups addresses membership programs similar to the one introduced by AEGIS in 1994. In particular, Hindman shows how those organizations recruited their members by targeting those best positioned to meet the financial demands of membership and see themselves in the mold of the respectable citizen who avoids political activism in the streets and favors funding litigation and lobbying. Because this results in relatively more privileged people being invited into organizational membership, such privileged members are then cited by organizational leaders as the reason for political action that tends to benefit them at the expense of others who cannot afford to participate.[25] In the AEGIS membership announcement, pairing traits such as seriousness and respectability with rightful citizenship claims, captured in the objective to legally prohibit discrimination against trans people, reveals how interest group membership invitations also function anti-intersectionally by explicitly targeting those who see themselves as denied rights solely in relation to their transgender identification (see Figure 5.1). Read in this light, words like "seriousness" and "respectability" serve as proxies for qualities such as gender-normative, employed, and not sexually promiscuous or engaged in sex work. That these individuals are most likely White professionals with relative class privilege was confirmed by the tiers listed on the following page, which started at $36 a year for general membership and went as high as $500 a year for a benefactor, who it is noted will be able to deduct $440 of the donation on their taxes.[26] In addition to providing members with subscriptions to *Chrysalis Quarterly* and the *AEGIS Newsletter* as well as a membership card, the invitation to membership promised, "Because we have a membership base, our voices are raised in unison with yours," which would be channeled to "protest against discrimination, when we fight against unjust laws, and when we claim our

Why Membership?

What are the advantages of your membership for AEGIS?

● We get a stronger voice.

Because we have a membership base, our voices are raised in unison with yours and will be more easily heard when we protest against discrimination, when we fight against unjust laws, and when we claim our rights.

● We get feedback from you.

Via voting and membership meetings, we learn more about your concerns and interests, both in regard to the operation of AEGIS and in regard to your personal needs.

● We can work together toward effective solutions.

Many heads are better than one. You may have the perfect solution to a problem which has been plaguing us, and if you do, we want to hear it.

● We get your help.

Which membership comes pride. With pride, comes willingness to work within the framework of an organization to help others, and to financially support the organization.

● We get "consumers" and "caregivers" talking to one another.

Excuse the medical model terms, but we needed them to make our point that AEGIS is the perfect forum for helping professionals and transgendered persons to meet on equal footing and discuss complicated issues regarding access to medical treatments.

What do you get from Membership?

● You get our publications.

You get two copies of our outstanding journal, *Chrysalis*, and 4 copies of our newsletter, *AEGIS News*. You also get medical advisories and special bulletins throughout the year.

● You get an ID card.

AEGIS issues identification cards to all members. The card may come in handy some time when you need the authority of a membership organization behind you.

● You get discounts on our products.

We sell lots of interesting things. You'll find out about our new products before anyone else, and you'll get them for less than others will pay. You'll also get a discount on membership in the Transgender Historical Society.

● You get a vote.

You have a say-so in the way AEGIS is run.

● You get the satisfaction of helping others.

We mail dozens of information packets each week. Those packets change lives, and money from your subscription will be paying the duplication costs and mailing fees.

● You get to change the world.

Ideas about transgendered and transsexual people are changing. AEGIS has played a considerable part in making that change happen. And things are going to change even more. We're going to make the world a better place. Together.

A note to helping professionals:

AEGIS has a professional division which is concerned with issues of treatment and with education of caregivers. Our professional division will take a leading role in redefining the relationship between transgendered persons and the professional community (and consider, these are not mutually exclusive categories; there are hundreds of transsexual and transgendered physicians, psychologists, researchers, ministers, electrologists, counselors, therapists, and social workers). Please join so we can work together in an atmosphere of mutual respect to solve our considerable problems.

Page 2

AEGIS Membership 1996

Categories & Benefits

General ($36/year)
includes
Subscription to *Chrysalis* (2 issues)
Subscription to *AEGIS News* (4 issues)
Membership/Identify Card
Free access to Library & Archive
10% discount on all merchandise

Professional ($60/year)
includes benefits above plus
Transgender Treatment Bulletin and
*Shhh! The Bulletin of the National
Transgender Library & Archive*
15% discount on all merchandise

Supporting ($100/year)
includes benefits above plus
20% discount on all merchandise
$40 tax deduction

Sponsoring ($250/year)
includes benefits above plus
Listing in *AEGIS News*
1st class mailing of materials
25% discount on all merchandise
$190 tax deduction

Benefactor ($500/year)
include benefits above plus
Note of appreciation in *Chrysalis*
$440 tax deduction
30% discount on all merchandise

Student ($24/year)
includes General Membership benefits
(Subject to verification)

Minor ($24/year)
includes General Membership benefits
Must be under 18
(Subject to verification)

Incarcerated & Transgendered?
You can *receive AEGIS News* free

Memberships are for the calendar year

**Please add $10 if you are
outside the U.S. & Canada**

AEGIS News 1/96

Figure 5.1 *AEGIS Quarterly* 1, no. 6 (1996): 2.

rights."[27] The vision for a transgender political agenda thus took shape in a particular form in the AEGIS announcement: it would be propelled forward in political venues such as legislatures and courtrooms (and not the streets), by members who consider themselves serious and respectable, those with financial means, and people concerned with making right claims.

AEGIS was not the only organization working to bring transgender people together in political action during the 1990s, and the evolution of the normative transgender subject at the core of transgender political organizing was echoed in essays featured in the *AEGIS Newsletter* by political actors at other organizations. Chief among the topics taken up in these lengthy essays was the portrayal of a natural progression from local and grassroots activism to formal political activity at the national level, in which the authors crafted elaborate arguments for why transgender people and interests ought to embrace political action and, along with it, rightful citizenship claims. One prominently featured essay by Jessica Xavier, the director of It's Time, America!, a transgender rights organization lobbying in Washington, described transgender activism as evolving from "a rag-tag collection of brave individuals" to "groups with members, agendas, actions, and goals."[28] Xavier's teleology posed activism as disorganized in contrast to formal political advocacy to justify the two goals she put forward in an analysis of transgender politics she titled "So You Wanna Be in Politics? A Realistic Assessment of Transgender Political Involvement." First, Xavier argued that the emerging transgender political movement should be one that works alongside other established interest groups, namely the HRC and NGLTF, to advance rights claims on behalf of transgender people. The second goal pertained to developing a critical mass of transgender people to not only comprise the political movement and urge responsiveness from those in power but also to fund political activities in Washington. Weaving these two goals together in a six-page essay that prescribed the transgender political agenda illustrates how rightful citizenship claims contribute to narrow and exclusive identity construction.

Xavier's essay contributed to the construction of a normative transgender subject—one who is White, employed, and gender-normative—by posing direct action in contrast to political activities such as lobbying and litigation, which were described as respectable and effective forms of political activity. She built her case for using formal political activity to advance rightful citizenship claims by describing protest as risky and, in some ways, inherently selfish: "Direct action focuses the public's attention directly on an outrage committed against members of our transgender community," which included "violence against transgendered persons and transphobia in the media."[29] Although activist groups such as Transexual Menace and Transgender Nation successfully drew attention to these issues, Xavier suggested that the audience for such actions might be limited: "Despite careful planning, something can go wrong. The point of our protests may be lost on nontransgendered persons who don't understand us or the outrage we are protesting, and many in our own community are alienated by it."[30] In Xavier's view, disruptive political action to draw attention to urgent issues such as violence against trans people and pejorative media representations that enable such violence runs the risk of highlighting those members of "our own community" who are most marginal: those who engage in trading drugs or sex for survival as well as those who are most visibly transgender due to the inability to afford (or lack of desire to obtain) medical interventions to "pass." Xavier concluded her discussion of activism before turning to political advocacy by observing, "Whatever form they take, direct actions allow their participants to feel good about being out, being 'in your face' (or more appropriately, in *their* face) and most importantly, about being themselves. It's a powerful way to shuck your shame while sticking a sharp stick in the public's eye."[31] The potential for stigma transformation achieved through protest actions takes on a double-edged quality in Xavier's essay. On one hand, protest actions can affirm one's existence and articulate political grievances in ways that feel good; however, this form of political activity fails to achieve tangible political gains. Her turn to "lobbying and the traditional approach to political action in this country" in the next paragraph reveals that the more selfless and effective form of political action is seeking legal remedies to social and political grievances.[32]

Xavier's subsequent discussion of the importance of lobbying drew on rightful citizenship claims to justify abandoning activism: "As citizens living in a constitutional democracy, transgendered Americans possess certain rights, including the right to vote, by which we elect our representatives. As taxpayers, we pay their salaries, and therefore they work for us."[33] In much the same way that AEGIS's appeals to serious and respectable political action functioned anti-intersectionally, so too does Xavier's reliance on citizenship logic. According to Xavier, transgender people are legitimate claimants of rights by virtue of their status as citizens and taxpayers, a statement that leaves aside the possibility that people who might identify as transgender could also potentially be undocumented or experience second-class citizenship due to race, ethnicity, religion, and/or ability. Even further, Xavier's approach to representation as a market transaction in which citizens pay taxes and are thus entitled to certain benefits fails to consider the disproportionate number of transgender people who cannot obtain formal employment due to obstacles that range from incorrect identification documents to discrimination against transgender people in hiring practices. It also naturalizes market capitalism and forecloses consideration for alternative possibilities on the transgender political agenda. These rhetorical moves consequently drew some transgender people into political action while simultaneously—and explicitly, through the contrast with activism around violence—organizing others out.

These narrow boundaries of the transgender group were furthered in Xavier's discussion of how to fuel successful lobbying efforts in the mold of other powerful interest groups, such as the HRC. She speculated, "[P]erhaps most of all, successful lobbying requires a community united in its support of these efforts. We are a very small community and we need everyone to make it work."[34] The terms of this unity and engagement and, by extension, who comprises the community were clarified in financial terms: "Money is the single most important requirement for lobbying efforts. Lots of it. Money is perhaps the best barometer of a community's commitment to achieving a collective goal."[35] Once again, activism served as a useful foil for Xavier to emphasize formal political action. After noting her expertise as somebody who grew up in Washington, D.C., and studied government at the University of Maryland, located just outside of D.C., Xavier stated, "By itself, education does not make it lobbying. But add money to the left side of the equations, and instantly, all things are possible."[36] Although members of activist-led organizations such as Transgender Nation and Transexual Menace were already actively conducting what they called "gender education" through activism to build awareness among the broader public and politicians, Xavier uses her status as a Washington insider to flatten political engagement to an algebraic formula, in which one substitutes money for x to achieve a desired end.[37] The difference between political action and political efficacy, according to Xavier, is money, with a strong preference for the latter as the main activity for those who are interested in learning more about how to be in politics. The transgender movement described in Xavier's extensive elaboration coheres around financial engagement and the willingness of those within the evolving transgender community to provide it.

Xavier's fundraising pleas and the emphasis on rightful citizenship logic came together in the end of the essay to pose the transgender person at the center of this political action along a single axis: gender identity. Analogies to well-funded gay and lesbian organizations, such as the HRC and the NGLTF, functioned as reference points to describe what would be needed to develop a strong national transgender movement: "Gay men and lesbians know their rights are at stake because they know they are a minority, and they share a minority consciousness. Most of us within the transgender community are still hiding our shame under a blanket of heterosexuality, refusing to admit our minority status, and thus our vulnerability. And that is the greatest threat to the transgender political movement. Unless we can disabuse ourselves of this denial, the transgender political movement will ultimately fail."[38] This aspiration for transgender political mobilization links political awareness with rights. That this focus on rightful citizenship claims requires constructing identities along a single axis is underscored by the parallels drawn between transgender identity and "gay men and lesbians" who "know they are a minority," which poses transgender as analogous and thus separate from gay and lesbian identification. To some degree, this comparison served an instrumental purpose by explaining to readers that their interests would not be advocated by gay and lesbian interest groups. While the long history of active exclusion and passive neglect from gay and lesbian interest group agendas largely confirmed Xavier's point, the comparison of the two groups rhetorically cast them as mutually exclusive and consequently set the stage for future battles over membership for people who are transgender or gender-nonconforming and also lesbian- or gay-identified, even while it successfully posed transgender as a unique political group that is subject to discrimination.

Although other essays on how to mobilize a strong national transgender political presence reflected the narrow boundaries of transgender identity Xavier advanced, there were also moments of rupture when political actors articulated anxieties about who might be left behind by the increasingly dominant rhetoric of transgender political action. Denny's Vision 2001 series, which surveyed the seven major transgender organizations operating in the 1990s, identified many of these weaknesses of representation, particularly with respect to disability, class, race, and ethnicity. The impetus for the audit, according to Denny, was a protest action by the Transexual Menace, which targeted a meeting of the International Foundation for Gender Education to draw attention to the organization's lack of attention to issues of class, race, homophobia, and transphobia.[39] The question of how to best represent the needs of all members—particularly those perceived to be on the margins of transgender identity—came to the fore in the penultimate installment of the Vision 2001 series as a result.

After stating that good working relationships across the seven organizations was one of the strengths of transgender organizing, Denny concluded her descriptive overview of transgender organizations with the following observation:

> One thing that is *not* working is the very thing that gets protested frequently: the transgender community pays little attention to its most vulnerable and most needy factions: trans youth, those forced by poverty born of discrimination into sex work, persons of color, and those who are HIV-positive. The ongoing protests about these issues provide a clear message that more needs to be done. Obviously, the national organizations could do more for the disenfranchised—and AEGIS *is* committed to doing more. But someone, somewhere, is going to have to start an organization which address[es] issues of homelessness, prostitution, drug abuse, street violence, and HIV as its *major focus*. It won't be those whose dance cards are already filled.[40]

Using descriptors like "vulnerable" and "most needy" gestures to the urgency of these marginalized transgender people. Maintaining the goal of mobilizing for legal changes while positing that *separate* organizations ought to be developed to represent each of these groups reflects the influence of rightful citizenship claims by suggesting that organizations can only ever cater to populations understood along a single axis of identity. In this case, the national movement is intended to advocate on behalf of those whose lives and experiences are not shaped by intersecting factors that shape identities and experiences, including age, race, and HIV status. The implied focus on the presumably universal transgender subject who is White, middle-aged, and not living with HIV/AIDS is justified by the creation of ever more organizations to cater to those who are excluded.

When coupled with Xavier's emphasis on a transgender interest group presence in Washington, Denny's recommendation that separate organizations should be formed to represent different segments of the transgender community and join in alliance with each other reflects one of the key issues facing transgender politics going into the end of the decade. On the one hand, political actors in the early 1990s used the rupture with sex and biology to craft an understanding of transgender identity that functioned like an umbrella category to name, contain, and empower many expressions of gender variance. However, by the mid-1990s, the effort to translate this broad, inclusive identity category into a unified political movement with formal advocacy organizations to represent it tended toward organizing transgender political interests along a single axis of identity: transgender.[41] The result of this work was a narrow focus on an emerging universal transgender subject who was understood to be a White, educated, middle-class woman who could most successfully make rightful citizenship claims.

Transgender Representation: Two Takes

As the 1990s came to a close, many of the foundational aspects of transgender political identity outlined by Boswell and Feinstein had evolved into salient characteristics that gave transgender identification meaning and defined its boundaries. Key among these was the severing of presumed links between biological sex and gender identity, which broadened the scope of transgender identity to include anybody whose gender expression challenged dominant norms of masculinity or femininity. These conceptual moves reflected significant work by scholars to theorize the proper objects of sex and gender and situated transgender identity decidedly in the realm of self-expression.[42] Another key feature of transgender political identity at the end of the 1990s was an emphasis on broad inclusion, which stemmed from the historic stigmatization and exclusion of transsexual- and transgender-identified individuals from progressive politics. The rhetorical importance of inclusion to transgender politics is illustrated in the articulation of it as synonymous with transgender identity with the introduction of "trans-inclusion," as well as the symbolic emphasis on inclusion foregrounded by many of the social groups and political organizations that formed to represent transgender people during the late 1990s.

Although many of the organizations representing transgender people during this period held these two characteristics central to their mission statements and agendas of interests, the Vision 2001 audit revealed that they also struggled with how to ensure that the various interests of such a diverse group could be effectively represented. These challenges were amplified by the relative lack of knowledge about transgender people and political issues when compared to the ascendency of gay and lesbian politics during the "gay '90s." The late 1990s and early 2000s were consequently a critical juncture during which political actors confronted these obstacles and made choices that would shape future understandings of both transgender as a social and political identity as well as the agenda of interests to be advanced in the name of "transgender politics."

Integral to the evolution of transgender political identity during this period was the activism and intellectual work of Riki Wilchins.[43] In 1994, Wilchins cofounded the Transexual Menace, a direct-action group that formed after news about the murder of a young transgender man, Brandon Teena, received national attention.[44] Two years later, in 1996, Wilchins played a critical role in brokering the coalition of organizations that would eventually be represented in national politics by a new organization called Gender Political Action Committee. Wilchins was subsequently appointed executive director of GenderPAC and in 1997 published a book of essays called *Read My Lips* that put forward a vision for transgender politics at the close of the decade and into the next century. Wilchins's essays provide insight into the evolution of transgender politics through the eyes of an activist turned executive director at the forefront of translating the founding characteristics of transgender identity—gender identity as self-expression and broad inclusion—into an interest group in Washington.

The following analysis of how transgender identity and interests were represented during the late 1990s and early 2000s in Washington proceeds in two parts. In the first, I examine *Read My Lips* with attention to how Wilchins articulates GenderPAC's founding principles and vision for transgender political identity and interests. Wilchins identified three main objectives for GenderPAC to pursue. The first goal for the organization would be posing the transgender political identity and agenda of interests as broad and inclusive. The second would be fighting on behalf of "diversity" rather than issues pertaining specifically to transgender identity. The third task would be targeting oppression stemming from gender discrimination, which, in line with thinkers like Feinberg and those at the forefront of transgender studies, such as Susan Stryker, Wilchins argues is the root of *all* marginalization. The vision of representation for transgender people that Wilchins put forth was intended to push back against the homogenizing tendency of identity-based interest groups and rightful citizenship claims.

In the second part, I analyze the archived lobbying notes from GenderPAC's political mobilizations in the 1990s to examine the extent to which GenderPAC lobbyists succeeded at implementing this broad and inclusive political agenda while representing transgender people across political venues, specifically Congress. Comparing Wilchins's book, which was tailored for those interested in learning more about transgender identity and issues, to lobbying notes documenting how political actors represented transgender people and political issues for audiences of primarily nontrans individuals further shows how identities are constructed at the site of representation and the effect of rightful citizenship claims. In particular, the GenderPAC lobbying records show how the fluid and inclusive boundaries of transgender identity that continued to evolve in Wilchins's discourse allowed lobbyists to shift the ways that transgender identity was projected in order to maximize potential gains. These strategic maneuvers often entailed collapsing transgender identity into sexual identity, such as gay and lesbian, to argue that transgender people must be included in protections offered by the Employment Non-Discrimination Act (ENDA) and hate crimes legislation. In other instances, GenderPAC lobbyists confronted ignorance about transgender people and the issues affecting them as an opportunity to educate about the political identity group and associated political interests. Although the intellectual framework of broad inclusion was well established by the end of the 1990s, the lobbying notes show how political actors represented transgender as a unique identity through analogies to sexual identities and an explicit focus on the experiences of White transgender people. This latter representation of transgender identity discursively constructed transgender solely in relation to gender identity and to the exclusion of intersecting identifications. Transgender, in sum, evolved in lobbying discourse as implicitly associated with the concerns of White transgender people alongside the growing emphasis on rightful citizenship claims as the group gained more attention in Congress.

These tactical discursive shifts support two key arguments in this book regarding identity construction. The first is that identities do not inhere in certain bodies or in essential traits but rather are continuously produced by the decisions political actors make to represent, and consequently construct, identities in strategic ways. The second pertains to the effect of rightful citizenship claims on how identities are constructed and understood. While Wilchins represented transgender identity as multifaceted and shaped against the backdrop of gender norms that hurt all people, lobbyists working for GenderPAC cast transgender identity along a single axis for the purposes of advancing the rightful citizenship claims that were central to efforts to pass trans-inclusive ENDA and hate crimes laws.

The Gender in Transgender

Wilchins's commitment to representing transgender identity and political interests as oriented against *all* oppressions is made clear at several points in *Read My Lips*. This vision for politics, according to Wilchins, would serve as a radical departure from the politics undertaken in the name of lesbians and gay men as rightful citizenship claims. In the chapter titled "The Birth of the Homosexual," for example, Wilchins offers an overview of the trajectory of gay and lesbian political organizing that highlights the ways in which it has failed to address the needs of transgender-identified people: "Gay liberation has increasingly focused on mainstream acceptance which will gain for acceptable queers full civil rights, while largely bypassing the issues of those queerer queers who might upset that civil rights apple cart by distressing the straight power structure."[45] In these opening lines, Wilchins divides "queers" into two camps—"acceptable queers" and "queerer queers"—to make a point about the need to modify existing political agendas so they address gender identity. For Wilchins, acceptable queers are interested in advancing a gay civil rights agenda that seeks recognition and inclusion by heterosexuals within heterosexual institutions, such as marriage and the military. This is different from challenging the foundations of these institutions, as do queerer queers—presumably people who are transgender and gender-nonconforming—in order to unsettle the rigidity of the male/female binary as it is mediated through institutions. Michael Warner's 1993 *Fear of a Queer Planet* argues that "queer" resists definition through an orientation that challenges dominant norms. In so doing, queer defies its own categorization or evolution into a norm. Cathy J. Cohen's "Punks, Bulldaggers, and Welfare Queens," however, argues that "queer" has been interpreted by some mainstream political actors as the binary opposite of straight, in contrast to rejecting binaries and norms, as Warner outlines.[46] What Wilchins signals with "acceptable queers" is the ways in which the use of "queer" functions in political rhetoric. For many interest group leaders and lobbyists, the strategic use of "queer" pays homage to activists and academics working in the emerging field of queer theory and political praxis, while also putting forward rightful citizenship claims that are legible within a liberal democratic system and benefit only a narrow swath of the groups under consideration. This Janus-like deployment of "queer," according to Wilchins, sidelines gender variance as a way to avoid upsetting dominant gender norms while also paying lip service to diversity that justifies interest group activity. Wilchins defined the stakes of this divide: "You see this in the approaches of the national gay groups, which appear less interested in the diversity of our community, or in the intersection of oppressions which meet in our complex lives and bodies, than in forwarding a narrow-band gay rights agenda."[47] By implication, although the HRC and the NGLTF publicly claimed to advocate for the interests of gay- and lesbian-identified people, in reality they only buttressed the straight power structure. For Wilchins, then, these organizations served as a foil against which transgender political interests gained meaning. The transgender political agenda would not seek assimilation into dominant heterosexual norms, which included preserving the rigidity of binary gender. Rather, transgender political interests unsettled the gender binary, addressed intersections of oppression, and were more attentive to what Wilchins referred to in the language of 1990s multiculturalism as "diversity."

The importance of diversity for the political agenda put forth by Wilchins is underscored by outlining the stakes of failing to take it into account. In the essay "Why Identity Politics . . . Sucks," Wilchins outlines the repercussions for neglecting to embrace diversity as a central political concern: "I have no interest in being part of a transgender or transexual movement whose sole purpose is to belly up to the Big Table and help ourselves to yet another serving of Identity Pie, leaving in our wake some other, more marginalized group to carry on its own struggle alone."[48] Wilchins refuses a serving of "Identity Pie," a proper noun served by those who convene at the proverbial table of inclusion, to assert that the end of politics is not to have identities recognized. In fact, for Wilchins, "the Big Table" is not the solution but the problem in that the decisions made there are always to the disadvantage of those not invited to participate. Wilchins argues that due to these deficiencies, politics ought to orient political action toward challenging structures and policies that mitigate the full range of possible expressions, characteristics, and desires.

This expansive view on political mobilization under the heading of "diversity" as a political interest applies the conceptualization of transgender identity as an umbrella category to the realm of politics. That is, just as transgender as an umbrella category emphasizes the contingency of social categories by maintaining openness for all expression of gender, Wilchins conveys that transgender political interests should be similarly derived. Differentiating transgender politics from the paradigm of identity politics requires modifications to the ways that political actors tend to utilize it to mobilize political action: "Our movement shifts its foundations from identity to one of functions of oppression. Coalitions form around particular issues, and then dissolve. Identity becomes the result of contesting those oppressions, rather than a precondition for involvement. In other words, identity becomes an effect of political activism instead of a cause. It is temporary and fluid, rather than fixed."[49] For Wilchins, then, transgender identity is not a static identification. It is shaped by oppression of diversity and solely concerned with challenging the conditions that naturalize narrow constructions of identity, specifically the gender binary. This effectively reconfigures the relationship between identities and politics. Instead of political interests emanating from identifications and being represented in politics accordingly, Wilchins conceives of transgender politics as radical activism that is attentive to a variety of interests and targets institutions that structure and maintain oppression and marginalization, such as sex-segregated bathrooms, locker rooms, sports, and dormitories and documentation of sex on birth certificates, passports, and driver's licenses.[50] In these ways, Wilchins outlined a political agenda for transgender people that emphasized orienting political actions toward challenging the institutions that normalize and naturalize the gender binary.

This vision largely upheld the early thinking on transgender identity and politics put forward by Boswell and Feinberg. In November 1996, the national gay and lesbian news magazine, *The Advocate*, featured an article announcing the founding of GenderPAC. In the story, Wilchins described the impetus behind the formation of the new interest group: " 'A lot of people are stuck in the mind-set that there's a gay community, a lesbian community, and a transgender community,' she says. 'I'm hoping we have an idea for a movement against all the 'isms.' " [51] In line with Wilchins's vision in *Read My Lips* for transgender politics, the mission statement for GenderPAC defined it as a nonprofit organization "dedicated to 'gender, affectional, and racial equality' "[52] that would channel resources to lobby representatives Washington.

An important backdrop to the formation of GenderPAC was the U.S. Supreme Court's landmark decision in *Romer v. Evans*. In May 1996, the Court ruled six to three that a Colorado constitutional amendment (Amendment 2) which precluded protected status for lesbians, gay men, and bisexuals did not serve a legitimate state interest and thus violated the Equal Protection Clause of the Fourteenth Amendment. Antonin Scalia's dissent asserted that Colorado's Amendment 2 did not deny protections but rather ensured that special privileges would not be conferred upon lesbians and gay men in the future. Writing for the majority, however, Justice Anthony Kennedy explained that the amendment's intent to disqualify lesbians and gay men from protected status increased the potential for gay men and lesbian women to be discriminated against and, further, denied them basic protections given to all members of the polity under the law. Although the *Romer v. Evans* decision was an important victory that marked a significant departure from previous Court rulings with respect to the status of gay men, bisexuals, and lesbians, the differing ways in which Kennedy and Scalia conceptualized sexuality for the purposes of the ruling raised alarms among transgender, lesbian, and gay political advocacy organizations that were searching for the most strategic ways to advance their agendas. Kennedy referred to "homosexual *status*," granting it consideration as an immutable trait and a legitimate social identification that would prompt heightened scrutiny from the Court (with implications for the ways lawmakers would view sexuality when making policy). Scalia consistently referred to "homosexual *conduct*" and, in direct contradiction to status, or identity, suggested that lesbians, bisexuals, and gay men could simply choose to behave differently, which would prevent them from being subjected to discriminatory actions, statutes, and laws. In other words, according to Scalia's logic, same-sex desire ought to be considered akin to behaviors that amount to a crime, and not an identity category in the eyes of the law—like race, for example—as the Court's 1986 ruling in *Bowers v. Hardwick* required.

Though Scalia was writing for the slim minority in the case, the political actors at the helm of gay, lesbian, and transgender interest groups recognized how dissents function as "politics for another day," which can be used by lawmakers to anticipate upcoming social and political developments and legislate either for or against them accordingly. The possibility that sexuality might be viewed as a behavior rather than an immutable characteristic in jurisprudence and by lawmakers sent shock waves through transgender, lesbian, and gay interest groups as a result. They expressed concerns that continuing work on the Hate Crimes Statistics Act (HCSA), as well as ENDA, which would protect lesbian and gay employees from discrimination in the workplace and in hiring, would be negatively affected and even made impossible to achieve. These fears were founded in the knowledge that Scalia's dissent and consistent reference to "homosexual conduct" denied the grounding assumptions of these proposed bills: that to be gay or lesbian is immutable and thus in need of protections from discrimination under the law. Thus, by the close of the 1990s an important shift had occurred. Whereas the beginning of the decade was marked by the influence of poststructural gender and feminist theory and the associated rejection of categories—especially those determined by biology—at the end of the decade, transgender, lesbian, and gay interest groups were in the position of reviving the biological determinants of gender identities and sexual orientation as a matter of political strategy. The social construction of these identities, which were once considered to be progressive and radical, were pulled out of the spotlight due to new conservative discourse that conflated social construction with behavior and thus choices that could be abandoned at will. These discursive shifts toward biology and immutability also set the stage for prioritizing rightful citizenship claims at the expense of political objectives that sought to educate or enact radical structural changes to mitigate social, political, and economic marginalization.

Transgender Lobbying with Gay Men and Lesbians

Records of GenderPAC's lobbying efforts indicate that it was also impacted by the diverging views on homosexuality articulated by Kennedy and Scalia. GenderPAC's director of lobbying, Dana Preisling, reported on the *Romer v. Evans* decision in a memo circulated to coalition members: "Part of a successful approach to eliminating the oppression transgendered persons suffer may involve understanding (and the science to do so isn't there yet), and then explaining to the wider audience (GLB and straight), to what extent being transgendered is not a matter of choice, but stems from biological differences."[53]

Here it is important to recall that early conflicts over transgender political identity emphasized the separation of biological sex from gender identity and attached "trans" to the gender side of this divide. Susan Stryker and activists such as Pat Califia identify the salience of this separation as one of the principal mobilizing forces behind transgender politics: gender as self-expression, *not* biology.[54] According to Preisling, the consequences of the distinctions drawn by Kennedy and Scalia, however, suggest that yet another radical reorientation of transgender political identity might be necessary to effect political change. Rather than maintaining the definition of transgender identity as a social category—one that is contingent and fluid—Preisling implies that the representation of transgender identity could possibly be shifted to emphasize biological roots of identity as a way to gain a more sympathetic audience. Although discussions about shifting the meanings associated with transgender identity back to biological influences were not pursued, the Court's decision in *Romer v. Evans* indicated to lobbyists like Preisling the necessity of framing transgender identity strategically for different audiences.

Preisling kept meticulous notes on all lobbying activities, and her documentation of efforts to have transgender people included in two pieces of legislation in 1996—HCSA and ENDA—demonstrate how the rightful citizenship claims mobilized to pass these two pieces of legislation entailed strategically representing transgender identity as either embedded within gay and lesbian identities or mutually exclusive from them. In discourse to lawmakers and coalition partners, Preisling and other GPAC lobbyists strategically collapsed transgender along an alternating single axis of identity—sexuality *or* gender—to represent the group as amenable to inclusion in civil rights advances. There would be no messy discussions about intersectionality or the structural roots of sexism, as was the case in early political discourse advanced by Wilchins and others, but rather a simplification of transgender identity with the hopes of getting it past the finish line of civil rights legislation.

A flashpoint for the ongoing conflict over meanings to be associated with transgender political identity at the site of representation was the 1996 introduction of ENDA in Congress. The historic precursor to ENDA, the Gay Rights Bill, was first introduced by Representatives Ed Koch and Bella Abzug in 1974 and proposed the addition of sex, sexual orientation, and marital status to Title VII of 1964 Civil Rights Act. By the 1990s, the legislation evolved into ENDA and outlined protections for gay men and lesbian women from employment discrimination. The 1996 debate and vote in the Senate was the first time legislation of its kind (with specified protections pertaining to real or perceived sexual orientation) made it out of committee in 20 years.[55] Preisling's notes indicate that by mid-May, lobbyists working for GenderPAC accepted that including gender identity alongside sexual orientation was a distant possibility and began exploring forming coalitions with the national lesbian and gay interest groups to inject consideration for transgender people in the upcoming congressional debate. The reports of these meetings demonstrate the attempts by GenderPAC to educate potential coalition partners about transgender identity as well as the willingness to strategically frame transgender identity along a single axis to maximize political efficacy.

Preisling reported on one such meeting with Rich Tafel, the executive director of the conservative lesbian and gay interest group Log Cabin Republicans, in which the boundaries of transgender identity were elaborated for the purposes of educating a broader gay- and lesbian-identified audience.

Preisling relates an anecdote from the conclusion of their meeting: "On the depressing side, one of Rich's colleagues asked whether transfolk think they are part of the larger queer community, and if so, why? This provided an opportunity for a brief lecture on (1) who we are, (2) how many of us identify as TG and gay, lesbian or bisexual, and (3) how the bigots who harass and kill us certainly consider us queers."[56] This elaboration of the relationship between transgender, gay, and lesbian groups recalls Feinberg's articulation of the overlap of interests across those groups, specifically with respect to violence. Feinberg explained that transgender men and women, lesbian women, and gay men were targeted for violence by bigots not for their private behavior but because their appearance suggested a challenge to the gender binary (and consequently heterosexuality). Four years later, Preisling reiterated this logic to educate a potential coalition partner about the necessity of including transgender people in legislation like ENDA, a point made forcefully by locating "queers" as the recipient of bigotry. Preisling uses this logic to avoid addressing the question of whether or not transgender people see themselves as part of the broader queer community and instead reframes the meaning of "queer" to connote a position outside of dominant gender norms that includes gay men, lesbians, and transgender people.

The source of resistance to adding gender identity *alongside* sexual orientation is made clear in a similar meeting with NGLTF's director of lobbying, Melinda Paras. Preisling reports that Paras "admitted that many gays and lesbians still see transfolk as obstacles to gaining legislative protection for gays and lesbians, rather than as members of the same community and allies in the struggle for such protection. Hoping to change that perception . . . . I explained that on May 5–6, 1997 we'll have more than 100 constituent-lobbyists on Capitol Hill, and we're willing to carry water for the rest of the queer community while we're there. (I've made the same offer to HRC's Elizabeth Birch.)"[57] David Valentine's genealogy of transgender as a category shows how gay and lesbian political actors embraced transgender for its capability of containing visible gender variance as separate from sexuality, which in turn facilitated the rightful citizenship claim that gay men and lesbians are just like heterosexual people but for their sexuality.[58] In this excerpt, Preisling aligns GenderPAC with lesbian and gay interest groups by reframing focus on a broad "queer" community in a way that mirrors Wilchins's explanation of how political actors use "queer" instrumentally to indicate concern for diversity. In this case, the word "queer" functions as something akin to a reminder of the links that bind gay men, lesbians, and transgender people together despite efforts by gay and lesbian political actors to distance themselves. Having asserted the relationship of transgender-identified people and interests to lesbian and gay political advocacy under the banner of queer politics, Preisling communicates to GPAC members that they should be prepared to demonstrate the fact that they belong by their willingness to "carry water." Articulating a readiness to work on behalf of, and indeed serve, lesbian and gay political interests challenges the seemingly dominant view that transgender people are an obstacle to passing legislation. Preisling argues that they should be viewed instead as useful allies and potential coalition partners. In the context of a growing reliance on biological roots of identity, the offer to "carry water" alongside the deployment of "queer" takes on a different valence, one that emphasizes belonging on behavioral terms rather than biological determinants, and might explain the strategic deployment of "queer" to connote the relationship among the groups.

Attempts to support a reauthorization of HCSA in 1996 provided another opportunity for GenderPAC and transgender advocates to educate potential coalition partners about transgender people and the need to include them in protections. These strategies alternated between posing transgender people as separate from gay men and lesbians, and thus in need of unique protections, and portraying transgender identity as a facet of sexual identity. These varying definitions were largely determined by who comprised the targeted audience. For example, Preisling circulated a lengthy update to all GenderPAC member organizations to discuss strategies for having transgender people included in an upcoming 1997 White House conference on hate crimes. In addition to citing statistics on hate-motivated violence collected by coalition partners, Preisling requested that member organizations weigh in on having transgender people who have been targeted for violence attend the conference. Preisling explained her plan, saying, "I'd like to locate folk who have been victimized by hate crimes, preferably crimes that were unequivocally based *not* on perceived sexual orientation (i.e., the attackers did *not* yell 'Fag!' or 'Dyke!'), but rather, on gender identity, characteristics, or expression."[59] Preisling went on to elaborate that the need to invite individuals who were targeted exclusively due to gender presentation was a result of the unique nature of hate crimes protections, which require that claimants demonstrate "evidence that the perpetrator has an animus against a group, and **selected the victim as representative of that group.**"[60] The focus on finding individuals who might confidently claim that they were targeted for violence on the basis of their gender identity and not sexuality can be read as indicative of the power of rightful citizenship claims on hate crimes protections, wherein those targeted for violence must demonstrate that they would not be singled out were it not for their gender identity. Preisling's efforts to distinguish transgender identity from sexual identity resulted in a very limited strategy, one that permitted consideration only for those members of the transgender group whose experiences were defined along a single axis. Preisling explained this need: "The argument is often made in policy circles here that gender different folk do not need specific protections as such, because they will be covered by sexual orientation-based laws."[61] Although this understanding of gender identity as a facet of sexuality was fostered by Preisling's efforts to persuade HRC and NGLTF to support the inclusion of transgender people in ENDA, Preisling went on to explain that hate crimes were different from nondiscrimination protections and required a new strategy that highlighted the unique stigmas transgender people face. Preisling speculated, "In order to counter that argument in this context, we must demonstrate that gender-different folk are being specifically targeted as such. Brandon Teena's murder makes a fairly good example. It is difficult to argue that anti-lesbian bias was involved in his murder, for he lived and presented as a man. Arguably he was killed because he violated the gender-based stereotype that a male sense of self and masculine expression exist only in individuals assigned to the male sex at birth (a stereotype we all know to be nonsense)."[62] Preisling posits that Teena's murder illustrates the unique stigmas leveled against transgender people due to the perception that he took what was not his to take: masculinity. The violence consequently stems from unique animus against transgender people, who are the only ones in the eyes of the law who can perpetrate such an act and thus provoke violent responses designed to preserve binary gender rooted in biology. Preisling's parenthetic observation at the end of her statement alludes to the shared knowledge that Teena's murder was much more complex due to his intimate relationship with his murderer's ex-girlfriend and might have been shaped by a desire to assert heteronormativity as well as binary gender. Although Preisling nods to these nuances of transgender identity for the benefit of her internal audience, her intention to pose Teena as an ideal victim of hate violence for the White House audience reifies the construction of transgender along a single axis and closed off from intersecting identities, namely race. In the context of a conference on hate crimes and the logic of rightful citizenship claims, Teena's murder is the prototypical example of hate violence directed at transgender people due to the absence of intersecting identities. In other words, Teena is easily understood as a victim of hate violence directed at transgender people due to his Whiteness. While this discussion of transgender identity allowed possibilities for gender and sexuality to intersect, it did so while also posing these identities along a single axis of race.[63]

Maintaining single-axis understandings of transgender identity was also used strategically to appeal to other interest groups with which GenderPAC might make fruitful alliances on the topic of hate crimes. For instance, in a bid to sign on to a letter directed to Senator Ted Kennedy's office regarding HCSA by the Anti-Defamation League (ADL), Preisling once again strategically modified the meanings associated with transgender identity in an attempt to have it considered by a potential coalition partner, explaining in her lobbying notes, "I had earlier made the case (to ADL) for inclusion by conceptually expanding the definition of sexual orientation without using red-flag terms like 'cross-dresser' or 'transsexual.' Apparently ADL has chosen not to act on that request."[64] Here, Preisling vacates transgender identity of its associations with those who are perceived to most visibly live outside of binary gender norms. She does this to nest the version of transgender she is lobbying on behalf of within sexual orientation, which is more legible to the ADL audience. This strategic modification conveyed a powerful message to the ADL as well as the member organizations comprising GenderPAC. Whereas transgender identity carried connotations of inclusion *within* the transgender community, this example of representation to external audiences shows how the transgender umbrella can be used to obscure the boundaries to exclude more precariously situated members. The strategic choice to elide the membership of cross-dressers and transsexuals attempts to situate transgender as an identity alongside sexuality rather than as a facet of self-expression or gender identity.[65] Those omitted from consideration with this new definition would be the most vulnerable members of the transgender group, such as transgender people of color, who are disproportionately targeted for violence, and gender-nonconforming people, who do not "pass" as male or female and thus attract increased scrutiny and violence. Although the ADL ultimately ignored Preisling's plea, the large national lesbian and gay groups—HRC and NGLTF—used their influence to arrange a series of meetings with lawmakers to assert the urgency for transgender inclusion in HCSA based on similar logic.

Lobbyists from HRC arranged one such meeting for GenderPAC with House Judiciary Committee members to discuss transgender inclusion. The reports from the meeting indicate that Preisling's efforts to locate transgender identity within sexual orientation were not entirely fruitless. While the representatives present at the meeting made plain their view that the addition of transgender people to HCSA was not a political reality, especially given the Republican majority, they speculated to GenderPAC representatives that transgender-identified people might benefit from the "actual or perceived sexual orientation" language in the HCSA.[66] Preisling reported this development to coalition members as positive and indicative of the tremendous amount of work that remained to be done on the Hill to educate representatives about transgender identity.

In the meantime, GenderPAC lobbyists seized the opportunity presented by this strategy as they turned their energy to the upcoming ENDA vote. Appealing to the willingness of representatives to collapse and link sexual orientation with transgender identity required a challenging balance of priorities and illustrates one of the ways that the boundaries of political identities are shaped at the site of representation. On one hand, GenderPAC representatives were keenly aware that they stood to benefit from the intimate association with sexual orientation, especially given the power and influence of groups like HRC. On the other hand, GenderPAC and transgender advocates were also motivated by knowledge of transgender political identity as an umbrella category in its own right, which cohered in relation to gender, not sexual orientation.

In written testimony regarding transgender inclusion in ENDA, representatives writing on behalf of GenderPAC used the opportunity to educate members of Congress on these boundaries of transgender identity by providing a thorough breakdown of relevant terminology: "The term 'transgendered' includes not only transsexuals and cross-dressers, but also hermaphrodites and intersexed persons. Because ENDA addresses only the issue of sexual orientation, none of these persons would be protected against discrimination directed against them as transgendered persons."[67] Here again, the expansive and inclusive boundaries of transgender are put forth. Having explicated the boundaries of transgender identity for lawmakers, the testimony goes on to offer a compromise that exploits the opportunity to combine sexual orientation and transgender identification for the purposes of advancing rightful citizenship claims. It concludes with GenderPAC's recommendation: "The omission of transgendered persons from ENDA could be remedied by broadening Section 17(9), ENDA's definition of sexual orientation, to include gender characteristics, behavior, expression or identity, regardless of chromosomal sex."[68] That is, rather than naming transgender identity or gender characteristics alongside sexual orientation, GenderPAC advises modifying the conventional understanding of sexual orientation to include transgender-identified people. The shift from defining transgender identity capaciously and then collapsing it for inclusion in legislation illustrates the effects of rightful citizenship claims on how identities come to be understood. In this case, transgender is simultaneously an expansive umbrella category and a facet of sexuality, which ultimately paves the way for inclusion for those transgender people who are most closely aligned to normative gender while also deploying logic that sets the stage for excluding all those whose intersecting identities complicate the claims for inclusion.

This definition of transgender also retained a focus on biology, illustrated by Preisling's observation, "Protecting transgendered persons against job discrimination would not be unprecedented. The discrimination at issue arises from the application of stereotypical notions of what having a particular chromosomal or birth sex entails."[69] To some extent, this caveat helped to educate policymakers about what they perceived to be the actual source of discrimination against gay men, lesbian women, and transgender-identified people. Discrimination, as communicated by GenderPAC lobbyists, did not stem from responses to private behavior but from the multiple ways that expressions of gender are policed on a daily basis. Casting gender in biological terms and absorbing transgender into sexual orientation, however, had the negative effect of silencing the unique political concerns of transgender people as they were put forth by activists and political actors, particularly with respect to those with multiple and intersecting identities. The turn away from structural critiques, and with them the focus on how institutions structure and maintain the primacy of binary gender, heterosexuality, and gender norms, meant also abandoning efforts to abolish the documentation of sex on identity documents and challenging sex segregation more broadly. Instead, casting transgender identity as a facet of sexuality focused on achieving assimilation and recognition for those members who were positioned proximate to dominant norms of White supremacy, patriarchy, and heteronormativity. Even with this strategic formulation, ensuring legal changes to White, gender-normative, and monogamous transgender people proved an uphill battle, and the 1990s closed without any meaningful movement on including transgender people in ENDA or the HCSA.

Conclusions: Collapsing the Umbrella

This chapter has revealed the contrast between an internal representation of transgender identity, such as that of Wilchins, and an external representation, such as that by GenderPAC lobbyists. The latter shows how the construction of transgender political identity as an inclusive umbrella category without a static referent became an opportunity to shift and modify transgender identity in order to present it strategically to wider political audiences. However, this discursive move was not necessarily successful. Such open-ended possibilities for the meanings associated with transgender, like those put forward by GenderPAC lobbyists, produced challenges, as political actors had to both maintain an emphasis on unconditional inclusion while also encountering pressures to marginalize and silence certain segments of the transgender population (framed as unwieldy and nonnormative) in order to gain a voice in Washington.

With this in mind, this chapter showed how representing transgender political identity to lawmakers often entailed the collapse of multifaceted transgender identity initially imaged by transgender political actors into a single axis, or anti-intersectionally. In some cases—such as the vision for political action of Dallas Denny's organization—this resulted in the elevation of gender identity as the defining feature of transgender identity, and the simultaneous marginalization of other identifications, particularly those pertaining to ability, age, and race. The strategic omission of these groups and identifications thus posed transgender identity as discrete and mutually exclusive of other identifications.

The example of GenderPAC lobbying shows another approach to the narrow construction of transgender identity: that of conflating gender identity with sexuality. Such a move was perceived to be more legible and, by association, strategically advantageous given the growing success of lesbian and gay interest groups in Washington. These strategies, however, shifted attention away from the principal political changes sought by transgender activists and political actors. In particular, nesting gender identity within sexual orientation for the purposes of advancing inclusion and recognition in legislation (such as the HCSA and ENDA) elided the political priorities of transgender people at the time. This included efforts to ensure unmitigated access to healthcare and administrative changes to eliminate the documentation of sex on state documents.

This trade-off in the name of strategy consequently constructed transgender identity narrowly for lawmakers and the broader public. Whereas transgender identity was initially conceived as a broad identity category, inclusive of all iterations of gender identification, by the end of the 1990s transgender identity was becoming increasingly associated with transgender men and women who could be rendered legible to lawmakers and the broader public. This turn to legibility was not excusive to transgender identity. The next chapter explores efforts by political actors to unite lesbian, gay, bisexual, and transgender groups into a coalition and cohesive identity-based group, LGBT, and the issues of inclusion and exclusion that vexed this new alliance and political identity group.

6

Framing Unity

LGBT and Queer

In March 1998, the NGLTF issued a press release detailing the third meeting of the National Policy Roundtable, "a semi-annual meeting of executive directors and leaders of national GLBT groups sponsored by the Policy Institute, a think tank inside NGLTF dedicated to research, policy analysis, and strategy development."[1] Bringing together anywhere from 20 to 40 executive directors at a time to represent their respective interest groups and organizations, the National Policy Roundtable was envisioned by Urvashi Vaid, the director the Policy Institute and the founder of the National Policy Roundtable, as "a forum for the creative and strategic thinking which is the basis of united action." The agenda taken up at the March 1998 meeting reflected these goals with action items such as developing strategies for the upcoming midterm elections, studying how public policy is shaped by the debates over the origins of sexual orientation, race and leadership in national LGBT movement organizations, and how to respond to an "increasingly shrill and hostile right."[2]

These four agenda items provide a general overview of the goals prioritized by the leaders of national lesbian, gay, bisexual, and transgender interest groups convened at the Roundtable meetings during the late 1990s and early 2000s. Specifically, questions about how to frame the origin of sexual and gender identities, how to showcase the diversity of the LGBT group, and how to respond to the growing mobilization of the Conservative Right and Evangelical Christians against LGBT people are significant because they indicate the importance that members of the National Policy Roundtable placed on generating a shared set of issues for the organizations to advance in coordination with each other. Taken together, these agenda items highlight the broader purpose of the National Policy Roundtable: to join lesbian, gay, bisexual, and transgender organizations into a cohesive political group united by a common agenda.

Terms of Exclusion. Zein Murib, Oxford University Press. © Oxford University Press 2023.
DOI: 10.1093/oso/9780197671498.003.0007

The transcripts of the biannual meetings that took place between March 1998 and March 2001 are archived in their entirety at the Cornell University Human Sexuality Collection and contain over 500 pages of meeting notes and related emails. The relative comprehensiveness of these documents is impressive, which is to say that in an archive filled primarily with random and sporadically collected news clippings, organization fliers, meeting agendas with handwritten notes, and internal communications that appear first as mimeographed memos and evolve into printed emails, the transcripts stand out for the extent to which they portray a cohesive narrative of what took place.[3] I am often struck by this aspect of the meeting notes, which likely entailed significant financial cost to generate, and I view the comprehensiveness as suggesting that the political actors convened were perhaps aware that they were making history as they engaged in ongoing debates and negotiations over how to accomplish the task of developing a shared political agenda to bring lesbian, gay, bisexual, and transgender issues into the political mainstream. And yet the emergence of two alternatives—LGBT and queer—as the dominant ways to describe political and social agendas concerned with sexuality and gender identity indicates that to some degree they failed in their endeavor to forge this united front. The introduction and popular adoption of LGBT was used descriptively to capture the presumably four discrete identity-based groups coming together in political action, while proponents of a separate queer identity drew on academic queer theory to connote an anticategorical and, in some interpretations, a distinctly antinormative approach to sexuality and gender. These two very different terms would circulate in popular and political discourse separately for almost two decades before being ultimately merged into yet another initialism, LGBTQ, shortly after the 2015 Supreme Court decision in *Obergefell v. Hodges*, which settled the question of same-sex marriages and created opportunities to expand the LGBT agenda and initialism.

In this chapter, I examine the discussions that took place among the political actors who took it upon themselves to lay the institutional and rhetorical foundations for a unified and cohesive movement, which ultimately gave rise to two alternative political identities: LGBT and queer. I argue that the evolution of these two discrete political agendas was shaped by ongoing conflicts over the focus placed on rightful citizenship claims and efforts toward assimilation, particularly as political actors articulated and confronted the exclusions those strategies would entail. These exclusions resulted first in arguments and then in ruptures, as the initial involvement of leaders from lesbian, gay, bisexual, and transgender organizations led to the eventual peeling off of national bisexual and transgender organizations, as well as those representing Black, Latine, and Asian lesbians, gay men, bisexuals, and transgender people. In naming their experiences of marginalization within political action advanced in the name of "LGBT politics," the statements from these political actors as they departed the Roundtable meetings also support the argument that I make throughout this book regarding the effects of rightful citizenship claims on political agendas: narrowing whose interests are represented to those who are White, gender-normative, monogamous, and male-identified.

Most important, these transcripts show that the executive directors at these meetings were aware of the exclusionary effects of focusing on rightful citizenship claims. I draw this conclusion based on several instances when representatives from bisexual, transgender, and Black political organizations described the consequences of a turn to rightful citizenship claims in great detail, namely their exclusion from the agenda taking shape in the name of LGBT politics. The repeated efforts to alter the emphasis on rights claims were met with silence and inaction, and, over time, these silences accumulated into a shared understanding that "LGBT politics" would be the name of efforts to mobilize rightful citizenship claims to primarily benefit White, gay men (and some lesbians), while "queer" would index all other political issues. Advocates of the LGBT framing explicitly acknowledged these exclusions and recognized that the inclusion captured in "LGBT" was nominal at best. Even so, they urged its adoption as a way to signal critical mass in a political context increasingly dominated by a deepening coalition of conservative Republicans and the Christian Right. The contested election of George W. Bush, an avowed Evangelical Christian, in 2000 was perceived as confirming the need for a united front and redoubled efforts to consolidate a unified political agenda oriented toward protecting rights won and advancing others, such as same-sex marriage and gay men and lesbians serving openly in the military. The intensifying mobilization by the political arm of Evangelical Christians to resist these efforts lent greater urgency to political battles and helped to shape political activity advanced in the name of the LGBT group for the following two decades.

Conflicts over a Unified Movement

George W. Bush was recognized as one of the most religious presidents elected to the office and a champion of the Christian Right even before the attacks on the World Trade Center and Pentagon in 2001 that inaugurated "the War on Terror" and two subsequent decades of state-sponsored Islamophobia. The positions he staked out in opposition to the trope of extremist Islam *as a Christian*, including the elevation of the heterosexual nuclear family, opposition to abortion and reproductive freedom, and prohibitions against same-sex sexuality, were celebrated by his proponents as the arrival of over 70 years of mobilization by the Christian Right on the political stage.[4]

The National Policy Roundtables were convened in the context of this unified and growing political influence by the Christian Right and the opposition to political gains for lesbians, gay men, bisexuals, and transgender people in the 1990s. The perceived unity of Evangelical Christians—particularly in their efforts to stigmatize homosexuality and wage attacks against the various groups participating in the Roundtable—figured prominently in the motivations to convene with the hopes of engaging in unified action that might mount an equally broad defense. Another factor driving the meetings was the second term of the Clinton administration, which was initially perceived as a champion of lesbian and gay people. Clinton's early signing of Don't Ask, Don't Tell, the policy that prohibited gay men, lesbians, and bisexuals from serving openly in the military, was perceived by lesbian, gay, and bisexual political leaders as a betrayal of their electoral support, especially as they had supported him in the wake of multiple sex scandals. In addition to these national issues, conservatives at the state and local levels were introducing—and in many cases, passing—a steady stream of legislation and referenda seeking to roll back or prohibit any rights gains for gay men and lesbians.

Urvashi Vaid, who served as executive director of the NGLTF from 1989 to 1992, returned to the organization as director of the new Policy Institute, which aimed to forge connections across activists, political organizations, and academic research on sexuality to combat these antigay political trends. She initiated two sets of meetings as part of this work: the National Policy Roundtable to bring executive directors together and the Religious Roundtable to foster conversations among faith leaders. She opened the first National Policy Roundtable meeting by elaborating her vision: "It is my hope that ideas and collaboration will emerge from this roundtable. The first goal is to create a space, to meet, share information that can continue in an on-going manner. . . . The second goal is building trust among our organizations and us as leaders. The final goal is to establish a mechanism for the national leaders to think strategically and creatively."[5] The minutes from the first National Policy Roundtable, held in September 1997, show how some participants advocated for a strategy to combat conservative opposition by forming an equally large and powerful coalition of lesbian, gay, bisexual, and transgender political organizations. The coalition proposed by the executive directors in attendance was imagined as one that would pursue goals both inside and outside of formal politics, as well as contribute to the ongoing construction of lesbian, gay, bisexual, and transgender political identities and political agendas.

Kate Kendell, the newly appointed executive director of the National Center for Lesbian Rights, was charged with moderating the first meeting, which she opened by describing how the threat from the Right shaped her organization and her hopes for what the Roundtable would accomplish in light of these challenges. According the Kendell, her organization was in a perpetual defensive crouch against the Radical Right, which was organized and able to "speak with one voice on queer issues." Kendell's comments—like others in the transcripts—appear in annotated form; with her explaining at one point, "Our community is not adequately poised to respond. Gay agenda is not capable of definition. Lack of coalescence—issues defined for us. How can we speak with one voice while honoring our differences? Would like to have an agenda for the community."[6] Posing the need to unify as "the community" alongside the assertion that the Right is organized and "speaks with one voice" sketched the political landscape for participants at the meeting as comprised of two sides in opposition to each other. The response to the unity of the Religious Right underscored the need for participants of the Roundtable to come together in political action—to "coalesce"—and develop a shared political agenda that would shift from defense to offense.

Kendell's short introductory comments were immediately followed by open discussion focused on the feasibility of a shared agenda. The points raised by the executive directors during this discussion indicate that many believed any potential cooperation would first need to contend with the divisions between groups up to that point. "Identity politics," which was used pejoratively in the 1990s to describe a myopic and self-interested approach to social and political problems, figured prominently in the background of these discussions, with each respective identity-based group accusing the others around the table of failing to care about issues beyond the scope of their own interests. For example, Jessica Xavier, from It's Time, America!, a national interest group advocating for transgender-identified people discussed at length in the previous chapter on transgender politics, echoed Kendell's wish for a shared agenda but exhorted the participants of the Roundtable,

"[W]e really need to stop trashing each other. We cannot possibly ask our straight society to respect us if we don't."[7] In much the same way that coming out was advocated due to the power of performing the self-acceptance one wishes to see in the world, Xavier proposed embracing respect for each other, explaining, "Internalized self hatred can victimize us."[8] In addition to making each of the groups at the literal and figurative table equivalent in perpetrating harm against each other, Xavier's solution encouraged the political actors at the meeting to use their relationships to engage in stigma transformation and prefigure the acceptance and inclusion those groups sought in broader social and political arenas.

Xavier's call to bring together presumably similarly positioned groups was met by skepticism from other executive directors whose organizations were not directly oriented toward formal political action but rather fostered social spaces for lesbian, gay, bisexual, and/or transgender people to access resources and make connections. Rea, from the National Youth Advocacy Coalition, immediately followed Xavier's comments with the observation "Something going on of ghettoizing in our organizations" to describe the fractured political landscape.[9] Richard, from the National Coalition of Community Centers—an incubator for local community centers that served as safe spaces for lesbian, gay, bisexual, and transgender people—followed Rea's observation by speculating that unified action might not only be impossible but also undesirable. He declared, "It is a messy movement and I like it that way. Facing a monolithic right, only two principles: free market and no government. Our agendas are not economically based." He added that those assembled around the table were characterized by "[c]are about people."[10] The best way to enact this agenda of caring for people, according to Richard and others who agreed with him, would be to retain the autonomy of the organizations represented at the meeting. Embedded in this wish was also a desire to maintain an attachment to a type of messiness, or what might be understood better as the more libidinal and antinormative aspects of lesbian, gay, bisexual, and transgender life that might satirize the monogamous, heterosexual nuclear family long before embracing it as their defining characteristics.

For many participants at the Roundtable, the conflicts over the proper scope of political action between identity groups that were articulated by Xavier, Rea, and Richard—coupled with external opposition in the form of the Conservative Right—created the need for unified action in any form, and there was a contingent of attendees at this first meeting who urged forging a formal coalition in response. These advocates represented smaller organizations with relatively limited resources, and they argued that the main benefit of a coalition would be enhanced power and influence in politics. Gary, from American Boyz—an organization founded as a social and political space to foster dialogue among a community of gender-variant men, transgender men, and gender-queer-identified people—proposed that a united front could be accomplished by making the effort to "acknowledge differences, take on issues that aren't necessarily our own. If we share resources, create more than we have."[11] Gary's suggestion recasts the conflicts stemming from differences across the groups in productive terms: by actively reprioritizing objectives, the groups present, according to Gary and other like-minded participants, stand to educate each other about their respective agendas and consequently amplify their influence in politics with the ability to speak more directly to issues where the disparate agendas overlap. In so doing, Gary explains, the participants stand to overcome the problematic boundaries dividing groups and consequently generate "more than we have."

This concluding observation, taken alongside the problems of unified action identified by the other executive directors, suggests that an added benefit of a shared strategy to draw together independently operating lesbian, gay, bisexual, and transgender organizations might be the development of a *new* collective identity and corresponding political agenda to represent the groups and project an illusion of critical mass when faced with opponents. The divisions that give rise to conflicts among groups would be absorbed by this new collective identity and a reconfigured political agenda to go along with it. And yet, Tonye, who represented Transgender Officers Protect and Serve, summarized the main issue facing all of the organizations at the table this way: "We in this room do not enjoy any rights. One simple issue, civil rights. Need to think central core at this time and work as a collective."[12] Tonye's remark on the heels of Gary's proposal to pool resources underlines the tensions participants faced as they negotiated coordinated political action at the first meeting of the Roundtable, namely the inherited legacy of rightful citizenship claims. As the previous chapters illustrate, the focus on rights and inclusion elevated members who were most proximate to normative citizenship, specifically those who were White, middle class, gender-normative, and monogamous. Those who could meet these requirements were privileged by the rubric of rightful citizenship claims regardless of whether they identified as gay, lesbian, bisexual, and/or transgender. And, as I have argued throughout this book, those cast to the margins through

the exclusions produced by rightful citizenship claims did not fade into ob-
scurity or allow their interests to be absorbed. Rather, they maintained (or
created) alternative political organizations to advance their interests. The ac-
rimony between groups, expressed by the executive directors convened at
the first meeting of the Roundtable, reflected the proliferation of identity-
based groups and differing agendas.

Retaining the autonomy of the organizations and, by extension, the presumably discrete identities they represented, foreshadowed the introduction of "LGBT" as an initialism. The formalized association of those four
groups linked them together in political action without requiring the ex-
pansion of any organization's political scope or agenda. Continued mobilization of rightful citizenship claims, now under the aegis of the "LGBT
community," set the stage for the ongoing construction of that new group
along a single axis of sexuality. As the increasingly common circulation of
that initialism—sometimes as GLBT—gained traction in these meetings and
in popular discourse, so too did the awareness that the groups were not all
equally arrayed and that what appeared on the surface as a horizontal orientation to each other might in fact be more like an ordered list, with "gay"
and "lesbian" featured interchangeably at the beginning, but "bisexual" and
"transgender" always at the end. The tensions of collective action to bring
a critical mass of lesbians, gay men, bisexuals, and transgender people into
the political realm and articulate their interests grew alongside the visibility
of this newly reconfigured construction of sexuality in social and political
discourse. Of particular concern was the resurgence of Christian Right discourse about "homosexuality" and the family. Central to the September 1998
National Policy Roundtable was the question of how to respond to the recent
surge of "gay conversion therapies" and the promulgation of narratives by
self-identified "ex-gays" in the media. These two issues threatened decades of
work by political activists invested in presenting sexual and gender identities
as salient, legitimate, and enduring over time.

Stigma Transformation against the Backdrop of "Conversion Therapy"

In the late 1990s, an organization called Love Won Out promoted "conversion" programs and "therapies" as part of a media blitz to challenge the
increasing social and political visibility of lesbians and gays.[13] Many iterations

of these "conversion therapies" proliferated between the 1970s and 1990s, all of which drew on pseudo-scientific discourse to validate the Christian Right's beliefs about the presumably natural and necessary complementary gender roles masculine and feminine.[14] A common feature across these programs was an emphasis on facilitating an "ex-gay's" proper gender role (i.e., husband or wife, son or daughter) and, by association, membership in his or her family, which was considered the central unit for the dissemination of values espoused by the Christian Right.

In 1998, a coalition of conversion therapy providers known as the National Association for Research and Therapy of Homosexuality, or NARTH, launched a national media campaign, called "Truth in Love," to circulate narratives by successful "ex-gays." Taking out full-page ads in national publications and purchasing television airtime for commercials, the stories told by "former" gay men and lesbians served two functions. First, they helped to reify a Christian Right collective identity by casting the presumed transformations from lesbian or gay to heterosexual as a way to mitigate the misery of living outside of a strong and supportive Christian community.[15] Second, whereas Gay Liberation rhetoric of coming out encouraged people to identify as lesbian or gay based on their behaviors and desires, the "ex-gay" narratives advocated for people to view their celibacy—the enduring denial of desire—as the act that defined their identification as "ex-gay."

The promulgation of these narratives and the strong institutional backing of the organizations comprising NARTH disrupted the tight relationship between same-sex desire and gay and lesbian identities that was so hard-won by gay and lesbian political actors, and in doing so, furthered the repression of same-sex desire and relationships. In particular, the introduction of Love Won Out in 1998 and the accompanying assertion that there were no biological roots for same-sex attraction were perceived by political actors at lesbian, gay, bisexual, and transgender political organizations as an effort to define same-sex sexuality as a set of stigmatized and deviant behaviors rather than the roots of salient political and social identities. Political actors also perceived reconfiguring understandings of sexuality in these ways as imperiling efforts to achieve marginalized group status that would draw on Strict Scrutiny and Equal Protection clauses to justify recognition by the courts and by policymakers. By the time of the third Roundtable meeting, the very existence of lesbian, gay, bisexual, and transgender identities as social identity categories and potentially legible minority groups was viewed to be under attack.

Reflecting these anxieties, the September 1998 Roundtable agenda channeled the attention of participants to the most strategic way to (re) frame lesbian, gay, bisexual, and transgender identities in response to the stigmatizing rhetoric of conversion therapy. These conversations focused on two topics: confronting ex-gay narratives and debates regarding the immutability of sexual and gender identities. Although these issues might seem unrelated on the surface, I argue that they were linked by ongoing conflicts regarding the scope of LGBT political agendas with implications for who would comprise "LGBT politics." Two new frames emerged from these conversations: LGBT rights as human rights and LGBT people as upstanding and moral citizens.[16] The deployment of rightful citizenship claims in these new forms created the conditions for collapsing the emerging alliance of lesbian, gay, bisexual, and transgender organizations along the single axis of sexuality. LGBT increasingly took shape as an anti-intersectional political identity and agenda as a result.

The afternoon session of the September 1998 Roundtable meeting focused on combating ex-gay narratives and consisted of the "Report on the Right Wing," which featured commentary from two experts, Surina Khan and Chip Berlet from Political Research Associates, an organization specializing in research on White supremacist and Christian Right groups. Khan and Berlet opened the meeting with a broad overview of the strategy driving the promotion of conversion therapy. They summarized it as a new opportunity for opponents of lesbians and gay men to gloss their bias and discrimination as compassionate action that cared for the well-being of people and the broader social order, understood to be organized in relation to sexist norms that elevated men over women. In response, Berlet advised participants to prioritize reaching people who might be sympathetic to ex-gay discourse and making deliberate efforts to educate them on the legitimacy of sexual and gender identities, which would then inoculate them against the idea that sexuality is a choice and that conversion therapies were performed out of care for gay men and lesbians. Berlet and Khan drew on their status as experts and coached the attendees of the Roundtable to accomplish this goal by targeting religious people (presumed throughout these conversations to be Evangelical Christians and Catholics) and those in "Middle America" as the recipients of messaging that would confront ex-gay narratives by turning attention to human rights.

As might be expected, the deployment of the human rights framework served as a proxy for advancing rightful citizenship claims, which created the

conditions for foregrounding members of the group who were most proximate to the characteristics of universal man. This discursive turn worked hand
in hand with the populations targeted—religious people in the Midwest—to
elevate White, gender-normative, and monogamously partnered lesbians
and gay men with children as representative of the evolving LGBT political
agenda focused increasingly on claims that they were entitled to the same
rights as heterosexual couples and their families.

The costs of knitting rights claims together with bids for assimilation were
illustrated by a lengthy comment from Felicia Park-Rogers, the executive director of Children of Lesbians and Gays Everywhere, who expressed an interest in targeting religious people in the Midwest. She posed questions about
the discursive tactics they should use to address tensions that arose when
promoting gay and lesbian identities as distinct and legitimate while also
advancing arguments focused on emphasizing the similarity of gay men and
lesbians to straight people and families. Park-Rogers asked the group, "How
do we minister to those folks? Concerned about matching their rhetoric
with rhetoric of our own," and then segued to a specific example: "In family
work—we have family values, we are in a time when people are concerned
about values. Aside from protecting individual rights and privacy, how do
we shift the discussion into values without being reactionary and proscrip-
tive to talk about collective society values."[17] These comments succinctly
capture how the discursive shift to a human rights paradigm promoted by
Khan and Berlet required collapsing family values and rights into "collective
society values" for the purposes of positioning gay men and lesbians alongside their straight peers. In referring to this political work as tantamount to
the act of ministering, Park-Rogers underlined who would be recruited into
this work: those who were familiar with Christian practices of introducing
nonbelievers to scripture and bridging it with lessons about social and political life to incorporate those teachings into their worldview. Although
Park-Rogers professed an interest in engaging in those conversations, her
questions about how, exactly, to deploy the claim to similarity also betrayed
an underlying concern with who might be excluded by such messaging. At
the very least, those left out would include people who were religious but
not Christian, nonbelievers, and those for whom the trappings of normative
family life might be unattainable or unattractive.

Berlet addressed these concerns about the exclusions that accompany
efforts at assimilation later in the meeting, encouraging participants to
view the message more broadly: "The message should be to extend freedom

and democracy and equality and that everyone gets to take part in that discussion. GLBT movement is about freedom from fear. WWII medals said freedom of religion, freedom of expression, and freedom from want and fear. We want not freedom from sexuality we want what you want, freedom from fear."[18] Rightful citizenship logic in this response takes yet another form. Here, Berlet draws on the trope of soldiers fighting to preserve and extend democracy to reassure participants at the meeting that their messages would resonate precisely because they strike universal themes of freedom, democracy, and equality, but most important the freedom to exist without fear. And yet the history of legal racial segregation, immigration quotas, and subjugation of women in the postwar U.S. context belies the universal appeal of the strategy Berlet urged Roundtable participants to adopt. This history and its enduring legacies, which were likely familiar to some of the participants at the third Roundtable, reveal the narrowly defined audience targeted by the appeal to human rights. It is not marginalized groups harmed by ideologies of White supremacy, patriarchy, ethnonationalism, and heteronormativity but those who know themselves to be both protectors and recipients of the rights of citizenship afforded by the state by virtue of their Whiteness, their class status, and their normative (i.e., binary) gender presentation.

The assumption that lesbian, gay, bisexual, and transgender groups were comprised primarily of people who might reasonably expect access to the rights of citizenship (or human rights) were it not for their sexuality or gender identity informed a session held on the second day of the Roundtable titled "Immutability and Its Discontents." During this session, participants debated how to address arguments from the Christian Right that same-sex desire could be replaced with opposite-sex desire through techniques of "conversion therapy." Participants viewed the presumed fungibility of sexuality in conversion therapy rhetoric as equal parts preposterous and deeply threatening, while also accepting responsibility for creating the conditions in which opponents could swoop in to contest the legibility of sexual identity.

John D'Emilio, a renowned historian of sexual politics and professor of history, led this session by tracing the evolution of gay identity as a horizon of possibility during the Gay Liberation period, when gay men and lesbians encouraged all people to see themselves as potentially gay, then later being gay as a preference, and finally being gay as an orientation in the contemporary moment. In giving this history, D'Emilio recounted how the same reasons for rejecting the phrase "sexual preference," with the connotation of sexuality as fungible, gave rise to the clinical language of "sexual orientation" by political actors in the 1980s and 1990s to assert the fixed and innate nature of sexuality and the injustice of marginalization as a result. Although the introduction of orientation preceded the claim of being "born this way" by 20 years, the political actors convened at the third Roundtable recognized that embracing orientation as a descriptor may have inadvertently invited the increasingly public scientific debates about the biological roots of same-sex desire. These studies included examinations of people's digits (supposedly lesbians' ring fingers are longer than their index fingers) earlobes (attached or not attached) and found possibilities in a "gay gene" that might be discovered during the newly inaugurated international efforts to map the human genome in the 1990s.

The political problems posed by a "gay gene" and the promulgation of same-sex desire as fungible in "ex-gay" narratives were succinctly captured at the Roundtable meeting as a debate over nature versus nurture and how to frame sexuality. While holding aside any definitive declaration on the issue, participants posited that the question could be rendered moot by focusing on the inherent morality of gay men and lesbians demonstrating self-knowledge and personal authenticity and engaging in loving relationships that were monogamous and the basis for strong family ties. Much like the turn to a human rights framework, embracing morality and model citizenship entailed assumptions about who comprises the population of gay men, lesbians, bisexuals, and transgender people that the groups arrayed around the table were charged with representing. The perception that these groups were made up of predominantly White, educated, middle-class people in loving families drove the morality framing and also functioned recursively to focus attention on those who most closely approximated those characteristics.

For example, Dixon Osborn, from the Service Members Legal Defense Network, summarized the debate over the origins of sexuality and gender identity as he and other participants saw it: "Often posed question to the community is, is this biology or choice. Seems to me to be separate sets of questions that pose false either-ors." The main challenge was that "opponents suggest that identity of self is a matter of choice or if we act on it then it's a choice."[19] Osborn proposed reframing sexuality and identification as an act of morality or personal authenticity that stands to benefit society more broadly: "[The] discussion we should have is one about morality, that it's morally good to be who we are."[20] Proponents of Osborn's morality framing extended these arguments to the necessity of personal authenticity for the maintenance of healthy families in which each person is valued for their uniqueness. One unnamed participant suggested that they "have to make the argument that we are redefining the family, but not tearing down the family, talking about families coming in different shapes."[21] In other words, lesbian, gay, bisexual, and transgender-identified people and their families are valuable members of a heterogeneous and multicultural democratic society who deserve consideration under the law, with the emphasis on families grounding the proposed frame. This construction of sexuality and gender identity as manifestations of good morality and model citizenship effectively sidestepped the question of mutability and challenged Christian Right discourse by underscoring that gay men and lesbians also have families, just different families. Locating families central to this political strategy aimed to confront the opposition by using their talking points, namely the importance placed on the family as the primary social and political unit, which consequently foregrounded those with strong family ties or people with children. People who could not claim family ties because their families rejected them upon coming out or those for whom the costs of starting a family were onerous or perhaps not even desired were not considered by those advocating for a morality framing. They were instead organized out of the political mobilization advanced in their name.

Morality framing was also mined for its potential to sidestep questions about the roots of sexuality that might be necessary to address in legal battles. The relatively recent 1986 Supreme Court loss in *Bowers v. Hardwick* served as the backdrop for these discussions. In brief, Michael Hardwick was charged with violating Georgia's antisodomy statute after a police officer entered his bedroom without a warrant. The ACLU immediately identified this incident as an opportunity to advance a test case that would challenge antisodomy statutes across the states, with lawyers representing Hardwick arguing that the constitutional right to privacy was violated by such statutes that prohibit acts between consenting adults in their homes. In the end, the Supreme Court's 5–4 decision upheld Georgia's antisodomy statute, shocking gay and lesbian interest groups, many of which were convened at the Roundtable meetings.[22] In addition to denying a right to privacy, the Court's decision was interpreted by political actors as calling into question the very existence of gay and lesbian (i.e., "homosexual," in the Court's parlance) identities.

Focusing on morality bypassed the question of the status of gay identity and homosexuality and was advanced as a new legal strategy to confront these developments. Chai Feldblum, the director of the Georgetown University Law Center, argued that the most strategic approach would be posing those groups as offering a net benefit to the overall social order that the Christian Right and Conservatives claimed to value. This approach would sidestep questions of individual versus collective rights by deploying morality to fold gay men and lesbians into the fabric of family values. This logic and its resonances with rights discourse proposed positioning morality and rightful citizenship claims on equal footing in LGBT discourse. Feldblum drove this point home: "To me, what we then need to do is [say] that taking this action is good for the individual, good for the family, and good for society. It's morally good. Good for the individual because the act of loving an individual and being loved. That act of loving and creating a family is good for the family. And having loving families is good for society. Intervention would be suppressing good things."[23] Vaid followed Feldblum's comments by affirming the potential for this framing and observing "[t]hat nature/nurture is less the question than presenting the meaning of homosexuality." For Feldblum and others who accepted the arguments set forth during her presentation, the meaning of gay and lesbian identification was akin to the promise of coming out: allowing self-love, acceptance, and pride to model a utopian social and political order where all who resemble White nuclear families are valued.

Although the morality framing gained momentum among a majority of the participants, there were others who returned to the debate over immutability to highlight the question of who, exactly, is best positioned to be considered morally good and a net benefit to the existing social order. Much like Richard's appreciation for the messiness of the movement, these participants drew attention to the heterogeneity of those represented by the organizations at the Roundtable to question who, exactly, would be represented as morally good. Jonathan Krall, from National Coalition for Sexual Freedom, interjected his view among the many comments celebrating the potential power of the morality framing in the service of rightful citizenship claims: "If you're really going to actually support bi and trans have to drop the immutability thing, don't see a way around it." Krall went on to explain, "So much about being intersex or transgender it's not just a matter of feeling like I'm born with it, some of it's trying things out. Interesting thing from the fetish perspective, why you are into kinky stuff. The best theory you didn't mention, sexual imprinting concept, something happens to you in a good way."[24] Leaving aside the question of what it means to "sexually imprint" or the misrepresentation of what it means to be born with an intersex condition, the questions Krall asked drew attention to those who might resist static identification or the requirement to claim similarity under the rubric of morality and, with it, rightful citizenship claims. Those excluded would be bisexuals for whom sexuality is organized around the refusal of monosexism and an adamant wish to be represented as *different* from gay men, lesbians, or straight people. Krall's comments expanded the scope of those who would be negatively impacted by an emphasis on morality and rightful citizenship claims by naming a large segment of people who might engage in behaviors understood to be indicative of same-sex sexuality or gender variance, but who do not acquire those labels as marks of their personal identities. These include those who consensually participate in fetish or kink scenes or are "just trying things out."[25]

In addition to documenting the narrowing effects of rightful citizenship claims, my analysis of the Roundtable meeting up to this point captures the discursive slippages that centered gay men and lesbians and included consideration for bisexuals and transgender people only as an afterthought. The occasional mentions of bisexuals or transgender people in the transcripts underscore the extent to which they were erased in these discussions; they always appear as prompts for participants to consider how the ideas and strategies taking shape through the deployment of rightful citizenship claims not only exclude bisexuals and transgender people but might also work against their political interests. Comments in this vein identified these concerns while also offering potential solutions to the problem of exclusion that was increasingly understood to accompany rightful citizenship claims. As I have shown throughout this book, these alternative approaches often took the form of proposals to consider the shared sources of oppression, which were not individuals or groups, such as Anita Bryant, who inaugurated using tropes of gay people as pedophiles to secure the repeal of a Miami-Dade County law that prohibited discrimination on the basis of sexual orientation in 1977, or Evangelical Christians, but more amorphous ideologies of White supremacy, capitalism, and heterosexism blended with patriarchy. In putting forward these more liberatory goals, advocates argued for the formation of coalitions organized around political issues shared by a wide array of groups and resisted the tendency to collapse identities along a single axis.

Toward the end of the meeting, Xavier outlined these issues in her comments about the morality framing taking place in conjunction with a conversation about immutability: "Many of us who are transsexual feel that gender identity is immutable. Gender, gender identity, and sex have been interchanged and I don't like that. Mutability of sex itself has more implication for us."[26] Xavier was referring to the confluence of medical doctors, insurance companies, and state bureaucrats acting as gatekeepers that would only allow transgender people to access hormones, surgeries, and updated state documents based on evidence that one's gender presentation must be brought into line with one's innate understanding of gender identity.[27] Immutability, in this view, entailed the claim that one was "born in the wrong body," even if that declaration was made solely to satisfy gatekeepers.[28] As a result, to occlude immutability in the proposed political strategies that foreground morality would be to deny consideration for one of the most important issues facing transgender people as they sought gender-confirming healthcare.

Xavier continued by underscoring the broader political issues at play: "Marriage is based on sex. If sex is immutable then that's fine. If sex is changed, then I don't think we've got a solid basis for a social contract."[29] The social contract, according to Xavier, was defined by heteropatriarchal norms that privileged the presumed complementarity of men and women making up marriages and, by necessity, males and females comprising reproductive nuclear families. In spanning both gender and sex and casting both as strictly binary, the social contract consequently entailed epistemic erasure for transgender people who could only ever be understood as transing that rigid binary.[30] To expand the scope of political action, Xavier proposed refocusing on issues that could bring the issues raised by gay men and lesbians at the Roundtable in line with the issues transgender people confronted. She explained, "What [we are] really talking about here is gender variance, not just transgendered or transsexual or intersexual people do that. When we talk about gender variance when men take jobs as nurses when men have long hair."[31] Echoing other trans thinkers, such as Leslie Feinberg and Riki Wilchins, Xavier posed the static maintenance of the gender binary as a universal problem that affected all those expressing some form of gender variance, broadly construed, and forwarded an alternative framework that directed attention away from the social contract, morality, and rights claims and was oriented toward the sources of shared oppression. She declared, "This is the paradigm that we're talking about, heterosexism as the common oppressor. If we frame this as a larger societal pressure that reaches to straight people yet [sic]. If we all realize that we're fighting the same enemy in different ways. That language has more implications for society. It's gender."[32]

I want to pause here to note that it is difficult to read what happened in the room aside from the specific comments reported in the verbatim meeting notes. The person creating the transcript does not mention if there was silence after Xavier finished talking. Did people make eye contact and communicate nonverbally about what to say, or not say, next? Or did the next speaker begin talking immediately? In strictly objective terms, the transcripts show that Xavier's suggestion to reconsider the ideological roots of the oppression that limit opportunities for a larger population of people that extend beyond the purview of the organizations convened at the Roundtable meeting was met with no response. Nor were the concerns she raised about how these decisions might affect transgender people, nonbinary people, and gay men or lesbians who might not be considered normatively gendered. Instead, the conversation returned to the topic of morality and how to develop tactics to bring that focus to the work conducted by the organizations present.

The failure to take up Xavier's suggestions implies that the participants at the meeting were implicitly in agreement that morality—deployed through the discursive vehicle of rightful citizenship claims couched in human rights, self-awareness, and families that contribute to and maintain the broader social order—would be the backbone of the agenda for LGBT politics moving forward. The silence also suggests that they were tacitly in agreement about neglecting the concerns raised by bisexual and transgender participants. Xavier, Krall, and Richard were not alone in pointing to the heterogeneity of the lesbian, gay, bisexual, and transgender groups. The tendency to presume racial homogeneity or that the interests of the White executive directors would necessarily apply to Black, Asian, and Latine gay men, lesbians, bisexuals, and transgender people was named by Black and Latine executive directors to highlight the problems associated with the growing investment in assimilation. The ultimate departure of these dissenting voices from the LGBT coalition taking shape at the Roundtable meetings was not without final efforts to address the exclusions that accompany rightful citizenship logic. Many of these conversations took place at the following meeting, which was devoted to addressing race in LGBT politics.

Deafening Silences: Debates over Race and the Burgeoning LGBT Movement

The agenda for the September 1999 Roundtable meeting charts two days of discussions focused on the broad question of how to address the ways that "race and racism show up in our movement."[33] Of particular concern was the racial composition of the leadership, which skewed White.[34] This is visible through a special effort to invite representatives from Black and Latine interest groups to lead the attendees in a conversation about two issues: the structural factors that channeled White members into leadership positions and developing a plan for the next three to five years to address these causes.

Barbara Garcia, from the National Latino/a Lesbian and Gay Organization, and Phil Wilson, the executive director of the AIDS Social Policy Archive and founder of the National Black Gay and Lesbian Leadership Forum, were invited to chair the first panel of this Roundtable meeting. Deborah Johnson, the founder of what is described in the meeting minutes as a "motivational institute," was hired as an expert on diversity to facilitate the meeting. Their opening comments framed what they hoped would be the focus of the subsequent days of discussion: the problems with a single-axis perspective on identity and the perils of striving for assimilation and rightful citizenship claims. This intervention was intended to shift discussion away from the question of representation (how to include *more* people of color) to a focus on survival (how to craft political agendas that would invite people to participate by advocating for issues that impact their lives).

Johnson began the session by sketching her perspective on the differences between how White people and people of color approach race and sexuality, explaining that White people "considered P.O.C. [people of color] as some sub-set of the movement or community. So when race issues came up it was: 'where are the P.O.C. among us, where are they?'" In contrast, "P.O.C. looked at the issue; for them it was more like a[n unclear] diagram, an intersection, not a subset of anything."[35] Johnson's description was accompanied by drawings for participants to reference (see Figure 6.1). One illustrated "White people's perspective" as a set of concentric circles, with "people of color" set within the circle labeled "GLBT movement," which is set within a circle labeled "Everybody." This perspective assumes that there are people of color who identify as gay, lesbian, bisexual, and/or transgender, but that they are separated from the broader GLBT movement by a border that nests them within. As a result, the political project becomes finding ways to reach across that border to pull people into "the movement," which consequently removes them from the space representing people of color.

In contrast, Johnson challenged Roundtable participants to alter their perspectives to see how people of color view identity and political problems. The diagram illustrating "people of color's perspective" also showed three circles, but arrayed them differently to locate the GLBT movement in the

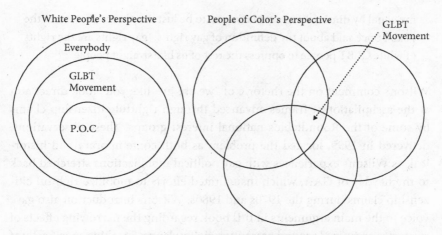

White People's Perspective   People of Color's Perspective   GLBT Movement

Everybody

GLBT Movement

P.O.C

Figure 6.1 Diagram from "National Policy Roundtable Minutes, September 24th and 25th, 1999," Human Sexuality Collection #7301, box 299, folder 15, Cornell University, Ithaca, NY, n.p.

space where the three circles overlap, in what might now be understood as an intersectional approach to identity and politics. Johnson walked participants through an explanation of the diagrams to underscore that the objective of doing better outreach to people of color, as stipulated by the meeting agenda, relied upon the assumption that those individuals could choose to prioritize sexuality over race and cross the border into the LGBT movement. The more intersectional-like perspective represented in the overlapping circles would not force this choice, but instead require attention to issues shaped by White supremacy in combination with heterosexism.

Johnson was not alone in advocating for participants to reconceive their approach to agenda development. Wilson followed Johnson's framing comments by describing his experiences of being forced to choose between his racial and sexual identities while doing work with the LGBT organizations at the Roundtable. His opening assessment succinctly introduced the relationship between agendas, strategies, and who is represented as part of the group:

What is our message? The core of the message is that "We are just like you." Well, if you can imagine this statement being said in the current Congress— with its old white men. What does it mean to be just like them? These are old racists. What does it mean to be just like them? The goal is not to make me equal by diminishing my blackness, to be just like them. That is not the goal. I once said about the definition of gay rights: "gay rights are the rights of white GLBT people to oppress the rest of us like straight people."[36]

Wilson's comment on the rhetoric of "we are just like you" took direct aim at the assimilationist frames advanced through rightful citizenship claims by some of the Roundtable's national interest groups. These observations, delivered in 1999, located the problem as both contemporary and historical, as Wilson's experiences with gay political mobilizations stretched back to the heyday of GAA, which inaugurated efforts to mobilize rightful citizenship claims during the 1970s and 1980s. Wilson's introduction also gave voice to the main arguments in this book regarding the narrowing effects of strategies organized around presenting rights claims. Speaking specifically of Congress, Wilson described how bids for equality within the framework of rightful citizenship claims required him to privilege his sexuality at the expense of his racial identity. Wilson urged participants to see that the content of their political agendas need to be revised, lest they continue to perpetuate oppression against the very groups the September 1999 Roundtable claimed to be interested in representing.

Garcia supported Wilson's call to view the meeting as a chance to revise the content of what constitutes the LGBT political agenda by asking participants to consider the issue of immigration in practical terms. She opened by repeating a common refrain in the 1990s regarding the rapidly diversifying population of the United States, particularly with respect to projections that Asian and Latine communities would exponentially increase in the next 20 years. Garcia pointed out that these developments presented opportunities for the groups at the Roundtable to take up issues outside of their current purview, including immigration: "I worked with farm workers, and there were lesbians and gay people in that community [and yet] . . . I don't see our movement caring about immigration: what about the number of people who die at the border, a number of whom are GLBT."[37] Turning attention to immigration would address the pressing political issue of life and death at the U.S.-Mexico border and built on Wilson's call for change by highlighting the urgent political, social, and mortal need to expand the LGBT political agenda. By altering politics at the border, these organizations might stand to shift who, exactly, was understood as comprising the polity as well as the LGBT group.

I would like to pause once again to draw a thread between the anecdote about Jennicet Gutiérrez in the book's introduction and Garcia's comments on immigration, as I believe these connections will elaborate the stakes of the arguments made throughout this book. Garcia and Wilson challenged participants at this Roundtable meeting to consider the role of Whiteness in the development of what was coming to be known as the LGBT political agenda. They also alluded to the stakes of this formulation by underscoring who would be excluded in the long term through the mobilization of an agenda centered on rightful citizenship claims. Sure enough, in 2015, just 16 years after Garcia encouraged the political actors at the Roundtable to consider immigration as an issue on the LGBT political agenda, Gutiérrez was booed and ultimately removed from a White House celebration convening leaders of the LGBT movement, many of whom were likely present at the 1999 Roundtable devoted to discussing how to incorporate race in the LGBT movement. They were convened to celebrate the coincidence of Pride month opening and the Supreme Court's imminent announcement that same-sex marriage would be made legal. This focus on same-sex marriage showcases the extent to which the advice given by Johnson, Wilson, Garcia, and others at the Roundtable meeting—to shift away from rightful citizenship claims—was ultimately ignored as the LGBT political agenda continued to develop.

This is not to say that intersectional approaches to political organizing in the name of the "LGBT community" were completely discarded or slowly faded away. The days of discussion that followed Johnson, Wilson, and Garcia's recommendation to abandon inclusion models and consider more intersectional views indicates that there were several junctures at which the executive directors made a series of choices to prioritize a shared political agenda organized around rightful citizenship claims and leave the existing model of political engagement intact. These decisions ranged from how to address the influence of funders on agenda development to calls to form a separate movement to address progressive issues in light of HRC's perceived dominance. The latter tactic was advocated by Vaid, who reiterated throughout the discussions that perhaps the best way to address the issues raised by those who were excluded from the mainstream agenda would be to view the discussion as pertaining to the characteristics of the movements, plural. At the beginning of group discussion, Vaid suggested the following approach to agenda development in light of the concerns raised:

We must identify the central issue that is coming up for activists and leaders in our movement: If we're not going to be a self-defined social justice movement then people are going to work in another arena (I'm worried that this means people will leave and have left.) What we can do then is create a progressive wing of the GLBT movement and resign ourselves to work with THE movement on the "sexual orientation" issue in COALITION and that there will be other ways in which THE movement cannot be together. And we can work with other groups on the race and economic justice issues.[38]

Vaid's proposal for addressing the single-axis approach to identity shaped by rightful citizenship claims is the formation of yet another movement that embraces progressive issues, presumably one that would elevate issues related to race, bisexuality, and gender identity. Although perhaps the most politically expedient option, Vaid's suggestion did little to address the emerging consensus at the meeting that there were, in fact, people within the organizations doing the work, and that those individuals felt abandoned by the lack of fusion to bring "THE movement" in line with the issues that concerned them most immediately.

These concerns also carried with them some worry about what it would mean to allow HRC's civil rights agenda and rightful citizenship advocacy to define the meanings associated with LGBT politics. Many attendees identified the HRC as the main organization responsible for mobilizing an assimilationist political agenda, with several expressing anger at the fact that HRC failed to send a representative to a Roundtable meeting dedicated to the topic of race and representation.[39] One unidentified participant targeted HRC as the main promulgator of assimilationist strategies and underscored the ways in which rightful citizenship claims further marginalized people of color out of political agendas:

HRC has built a racist structure. We have to talk about this, about how that place had an event in this city, this city [Washington, D.C.,] in which there were no black faces there. The social justice is that black gay men, when they are left out, not represented, they are left alone and they are left to die. This is where social justice does not happen. I have to look at where, I am as a person, choose to invest in. A lot of what we have is built on the infrastructure of the black civil rights movement. Yet, what is ironic is that neither do the civil rights movements have any investment into black gay men and poor gay men.[40]

For this speaker, the rightful citizenship claims and assimilationist political agenda advanced by HRC were closely related to the failure to foreground race at its events, in its leadership, and among its membership—all of which created its "racist structure." This speaker explained that the consequences extended beyond there being no Black people present at an HRC event. For them, the lack of descriptive representation for Black gay men had implications for the substantive representation offered, and the speaker articulated these costs for Black gay men in bleak terms: social isolation and eventual death. The silencing of political concerns to address the struggles of Black and poor gay men was the main cost of rightful citizenship claims and assimilationist political agendas such as the one advanced by HRC. This, consequently, prompted a question that echoed Wilson's opening remarks: Assimilation for whom? As this speaker indicated, the assimilation pursued by HRC was premised upon inclusion and recognition in a political system that had historically marginalized the needs and standing of people of color, poor people, women, people with disabilities, and those who were not considered citizens or members of the polity because they were undocumented or formerly incarcerated. These exclusions were reflected in the text of the transcripts themselves; whereas the bulk of quotes were properly attributed in the majority of National Policy Roundtable transcripts, the September 1999 meeting referred to many speakers simply as "participant." I read indexing comments in this anonymous way as indicative of the failure of the National Policy Roundtable organizers to take seriously their task of inviting organizations representing Black, Asian, and Latine groups to "the table" in any enduring fashion. They are instead unmarked voices, recorded for posterity, to show that at one point in time, organizers of LGBT politics attempted to take issues pertaining to inclusion seriously.

All the Representation Money Can Buy

On the surface, the majority of the executive directors attending this particular Roundtable generally agreed that interest groups should strive to fulfill the promise of the progressive wing proposed by Vaid. However, conflicts among attendees took place over how, exactly, to mobilize an agenda to oppose institutionalized and systemic racism and sexism. The task of implementing this political agenda was perceived by some participants as an especially daunting goal in the context of a political field dominated by large national organizations, specifically HRC, which many perceived as working against broad inclusion and attracting a disproportionate share of funding dollars to support that work. The role played by funding quickly became the main target for change. One attendee introduced the discussion of money in organizations, urging participants to "look at the movement, which institutions have the funding, those that don't, those that are white run, have white issues . . . etc. We see the hierarchy of oppression in terms of funding."[41] An executive director offered a more specific example of the role that funding played in deciding the agenda for organizations: "My organization got big gift from gay male couple with promise for more. Six months later we took position against death penalty and funding was pulled. Spoke to individual about this, wrote letter. He said this was not a gay issue. I said we are lesbian, but also feminist and that agenda is more broad. He said that was unfortunate."[42] Funders not only influenced the initial development of agendas but could also withhold money to punish organizations and limit the issues they addressed. As this executive director explained, funders had specific ideas about the content of "gay issues" and used their money and influence to advance those issues, often elevating rightful citizenship claims and assimilation. Another executive director built on this point to describe how funders are attracted by the simplicity of single-issue politics: "Loss of funders when we incorporate more complex missions. The very notion of identity politics has helped to create this kind of isolationist structure."[43] For this speaker, the political backdrop of identity politics—with its focus on narrowly constructed groups, whether gay men, lesbian women, or transgender-identified men or women—gave rise to funders concerned solely with advancing the interests of their respective identity group. The advantage of this strategy was that it projected well-bounded gay, lesbian, or transgender groups and furnished opportunities for like-minded people to find each other and mobilize together politically. However, these statements also illustrate the influence of funders in narrowing the agenda of political interests to accommodate very specific identity categories, with consequences for the particular type of lesbian, gay, bisexual, and transgender people represented in politics.

These organizations used access to funding and resources to construct and reward what Matthew Hindman refers to as "interested citizens," those who would conform to norms of respectability and formal political action, such as voting, litigation, and lobbying.[44] Funding consequently shapes not only the political agenda but also the construction and representation of gay, lesbian, bisexual, and transgender people in politics by prioritizing rightful citizenship claims and political goals with measurable ends to satisfy funders. Shifting attention away from efforts to oppose the death penalty, funding decisions such as the ones reported by the executive directors at this meeting obscured the long history of lesbian women, gay men, bisexuals, and transgender-identified people as subject to disproportionate scrutiny and punishment by law enforcement and the courts.[45] This effectively silenced and further marginalized the most vulnerable lesbian, gay, bisexual, and transgender-identified people.

Eliding so many groups that fell outside the purview of rightful citizenship claims had two related effects on the meanings associated with the evolving "LGBT community" in popular discourse. The first is the projection of a normative lesbian, gay, bisexual, and transgender interest group member that is considered mutually exclusive with people who are incarcerated or subject to police and legal scrutiny. Second, the result of this projection is the erasure of these groups from the agendas of national LGBT political organizations, with implications for who is represented as lesbian, gay, bisexual, and transgender. In this case, elevating people who are not incarcerated in political goals—when joined to the history of political actors constructing these identities as implicitly White, middle class, and gender-normative— represents gay men and some lesbians as White, middle class, law abiding, and gender-normative. This construction excludes a broad swath of people who identify as lesbian, gay, bisexual, and/or transgender, including people who are gender-nonconforming, people of color, people who are poor, and people who are undocumented.

The extent to which funding decisions bolstered the representation and construction of lesbian, gay, bisexual, and transgender identities in these narrow ways was demonstrated through further examples presented by Roundtable participants. One executive director voiced concerns over the role of funders to hiring decisions that resulted in the predominantly White leadership: "When a person of color applies for an ED [executive director] job, a board of that organization may be struck with great fear. They won't be able to fundraise."[46] The phrase "great fear" to describe a job candidate from a racially marginalized group provides a particularly stark example of ways that the influence of funders was felt beyond the content of agendas; they also shaped the racial (and gender) demographics of the leaders and employees on staff at various organizations. This participant went on to offer a solution to this problem: "Allies need to be developed to promote the candidacy of these individuals" and then see their work through, explaining that "these allies may need to come together again to assist with fundraisers."[47] Although this executive director was quick to identify the root cause of the predominantly White leadership—the influence of funders—their solution did not challenge the role of money in organizations. Rather, this participant suggested reforming the practices of lesbian, gay, bisexual, and transgender organizations to accept the influence of funding and to seek out ways to make those relationships, organized around money, more diverse. In other words, the solutions posed emphasize individual solutions to address the systemic features that keep White people in power. The subsequent plenary discussion, in which small groups reported their suggestions for augmenting diversity in LGBT politics, conveyed this focus on reform and individual-level responses, with the executive directors offering a variety of solutions designed to make fundraising easier for people from underrepresented groups.

Vaid challenged the attendees of this Roundtable to look outside of the concerns with budgets to the more urgent issue of attracting a diverse membership for each organization and explained the need for this diversity: "Racism in leadership reflects racism in life. Who the constituents that you serve will affect how you can transform [sic]. How can we add or change focus of organizational priorities to serve a broader constituency."[48] For Vaid, the solution was to encourage executive directors to see possibilities for democratizing their organizations by making them attractive to many more potential members. This would offset the disproportionate influence of having only a handful of funders. Funding, in Vaid's vision, could shift from a focus on big money donors to smaller donations accumulated through grassroots campaigns. Changes in the membership to a broader constituency would necessarily entail shifting agendas of political interests that—in turn—stood to mitigate what was perceived as the implicit and explicit racism of the assimilationist-oriented movement.

Many participants took this opportunity to articulate their reflections on race in the movement alongside the task of developing a "vision." Once again, the imperative of adding *more* people to the organization was identified as the incorrect approach. One participant argued that race needed to be central to the issues identified by the group because people of color already comprised the memberships of the organizations at the table: "I was struck when hearing we were going to deal with racism, and I was struck in the agenda 'unmasking how race affects our movement.' I had no idea that I was not part of the movement. The idea that race is something we can play with, that we can make part of the agenda, when for [many] of us it is something we cannot ever walk away from. There is inherent racism in these assumptions. This is a great learning experience for Anglo focused organizations, but it does not involve organizations working in these areas."[49] For this participant, convening meetings dedicated specifically to discussing "how race affects the movement" belied the goal of helping executive directors and leaders to develop a more inclusive movement because it was premised on the idea that people of color needed to be brought in, when, according to this speaker, people of color already populated these organizations and shaped the agendas. Building on some of the points regarding the incompatibility of assimilation agendas, rightful citizenship claims, and race raised by Wilson in his opening to the Roundtable, this participant drew attention to how staging discussions in this way located race as something outside "the movement" to be considered by leaders *post hoc*, and consequently only served to reify the very divisions they sought to address.

The serious charge that there was an "inherent racism" in these assumptions grabbed the attention of the other executive directors. One immediately followed this statement to echo their own frustration with locating race outside of lesbian, gay, bisexual, and transgender politics:

> I want to support what you are saying and add to it. It is right and productive to be creating a vision. That vision has been articulated for about 30 years by progressive queer people of color. Audre Lorde, Barbara Smith. You could fill a library with what we have said. There is a level of frustration about when that translated into, "Okay, enough talking, let's do it." The notion that economic injustice is a queer issue is not a new fight. Ten years ago we had this fight at the task force. Now it is 1999 and we are not talking about economic injustice. . . . The more that we do this type of thing, the more relevance this movement will have to Latino people.[50]

Comments like this urged participants to see how issues pertaining to economic injustice had been displaced over the previous 10 years. The shifts away from issues such as these and ENDA, according to this speaker, rendered the goals advanced by the organizations at this Roundtable irrelevant to Latine people, and by association, other minority groups.

Another executive director expressed similar frustration with the task of generating a more inclusive vision for LGBT politics, saying, "[T]here is something about the topic . . . people of color telling white people how to

do the work is an old model which hasn't worked." Vaid responded, "I disagree with the notion that this is what the meeting was about. I think what
your [sic] bringing up is about what we mean by 'THE' movement . . . and in
that sense it would have been better to talk about 'movements' rather than
THE movement."[51] When taken in the broader context of this discussion at
the Roundtable, Vaid's comments do more than the work of a good meeting
facilitator who attempts to refocus the group on the task at hand. By urging
the executive directors present to see that there was no one monolithic movement ("'THE' movement"), Vaid once again introduced the possibility of
multiple versions of politics organized in relation to sexuality and gender
identity that could be represented by the various groups at the Roundtable.

The reminder that there could be many different versions of "the movement," contra the predominant influence of the HRC in politics ("'THE'
movement"), was adopted by participants as a useful way to describe
what they saw as the main obstacles to the work of incorporating racial
concerns in their agendas and attracting more marginalized groups to their
memberships. The political actors at this meeting on race in the movement
used HRC as a foil for developing their own queer political identity and
agenda to better reflect the existing diversity of the lesbian, gay, bisexual, and
transgender communities.

For example, immediately after the discussion of there being many possible
LGBT movements, one participant urged executive directors to see that a

> [p]aradigm shift needs to happen. There is a limit to what "civil rights" as
> the pinnacle to the movement. This is the pinnacle for the HRC. There is a
> place for one organization to have that focus. But it is not what these people
> need to be doing. "Liberation"—old word new era. Social change. Our
> focus cannot be either civil rights or equality . . . of course this is not just
> about "equality" this is about my mother, jobs, food, prison. Today, okay, we
> will just get ENDA passed. But there needs to be an articulation about what
> it means to be part of a broader social rights movement. . . . That may not be
> what we are GLBT movement. We may need to do that in other venues. We
> need to develop a training institute to develop leadership. But we must do
> it with understanding that our goals are different from that of some others.
> We need a different paradigm.[52]

Here, the speaker targets the emphasis on rightful citizenship claims, or "civil
rights and equality," as the terrain covered by HRC and proposes, once again,

that executive directors consider an alternative approach that foregrounds efforts at liberation or a political agenda oriented toward enhancing the lives and opportunities afforded to as many people as possible. Significantly, this speaker does not advance liberation and associated political interests as achievable only through a radical restructuring of the institutions that organize and maintain marginalization, as their Gay Liberation predecessors did, but instead acknowledges that some within-system political goals ought to be prioritized, specifically antidiscrimination legislation such as ENDA. These goals, however, should be advanced only in conjunction with a discursive shift to a more intersectional politics.

Other participants built on this by articulating the discursive shift called for as a turn to a specifically queer politics, which they argued would provide a necessary counterpoint to the hegemonic paradigm of rightful citizenship claims. Queer politics would instead orient political demands based on a critical understanding of proximity to power.[53] For example, one executive director spoke about recent mobilization of death penalty opposition as an instance of different organizations, which were in many cases unlikely partners, uniting as a coalition: "I was very struck in the press by the death penalty stand and the impact of several organizations getting together. There has always been a mainstream and a more progressive wing within the queer movement. The difference is now we are not made of volunteers but are organizations and the hills are bigger. The weight can start to shift about what is a 'queer issue' if a group of organizations can get together and make a public statement in which two issues are declared as 'queer issues.'"[54] By locating the coalitions mobilizing protests against the death penalty under the heading of "queer issues," this speaker underscored the long-standing separation between mainstream and progressive politics. This also echoed Vaid's earlier musings about an alternative coalition of interest groups and political organizations as a progressive flank to work in conjunction with "THE movement." However, what is most notable about this speaker's articulation of the possibilities for many different movements was their referring to the progressive political agenda as one comprised of "queer issues." Although throughout the meeting people used "queer" and its connotations of opposition to hegemonic conceptions of "normal" to articulate their individual self-identification as queer, or a simple way to index an understanding of identity that does not adhere to rigid categorization, this was one of the first instances in the Roundtables when an executive director used it to modify a proposed agenda of issues. This use of "queer" is thus notable for being implicitly posed in opposition to assimilationist political agendas, rightful citizenship claims, and "LGBT politics."[55]

Using the word "queer" in a meeting dominated by the discourse of "LGBT politics" and devoted to discussing the lack of attention to intersecting identities, namely race, indicates an important development taking place at this meeting on the eve of the turn of the century. The reintroduction of "queer" in this context indicates a subtle discursive shift underway, in which meanings associated with "LGBT" were increasingly attached to the single-axis understanding of identities that I have shown characterize the evolution of lesbian, gay, bisexual, and transgender identities. "LGBT," in other words, was increasingly associated with the political interests of White, middle-class, gender-normative members of that group.

The adoption of "queer" from academic discourse was then taken up as a way to signal resistance to that dominant model and register an over-arching interest in all those people cast to the margins of the LGBT group. Discussions at this Roundtable meeting indicate that the political actors convened understood the shifts they were fostering. One executive director put an optimistic spin on the end of the two-day meeting: "One of the things that still fills me with hope is that conservative perspectives in GLBT move-ment is that they are still explicitly defined as the conservative perspectives [sic]. We shouldn't concede this. Around the issue of race, there is not a choice around if it is addressed or not addressed, it is there. *To be inactive is to have made a decision on it.* Raising the bar on race also will screen people out as well, but I would rather lose those people."[56] Reading this comment in the context of a conflict over how to develop and represent an agenda of interests pertaining to marginalization and inequality further establishes the queer and LGBT divide articulated by other executive directors, particularly as they attempted to address the history of marginalization within lesbian, gay, bisexual, and transgender political organizations. HRC's silence on is-sues pertaining to race, captured by the failure to send a representative to a meeting convened on the subject, was interpreted as a decision to advance political interests from what was evolving as a conservative and assimila-tionist perspective grounded in rightful citizenship claims. The conservative and assimilationist approach epitomized by HRC, in turn, was used by po-litical actors as the guide for what an alternative agenda of political interests would emphatically *not* be. Significantly, it recasts that divide as one that separates those interested in maintaining the status quo—rightful citizen-ship claims and assimilation—and those political actors who are compelled to take up issues concerning race, power, and oppression under the aegis of "queer" politics. These repeated divides between organizations, political agendas, and members effectively centered race as the reference point for locating interest groups and their corresponding agendas as assimilationist and LGBT or queer.

Representing LGBT, Representing Queer

The evolution of "queer" in explicit contrast to "LGBT" that evolved out of the 1999 Roundtable reverberated in subsequent meetings, which convened leaders to discuss political strategies in the context of the upcoming 2000 elections.[57] The minutes from National Policy Roundtable meetings held between March 2000 and March 2001 illustrate two important developments that further shaped the construction and development of identities and agendas associated with sexuality and gender identity during this time.

The first is that queer political identity was increasingly associated with broad political agendas that aimed to address the priorities of those with multiple and intersecting identities. As such, these political goals were less concerned with introducing narrowly defined sexual and gender identities to make claims for rights and inclusion, and more focused on effecting political changes that would alter the social, political, and economic institutions that structure and maintain inequality for a broad range of people. These goals included the end of mass incarceration and ceasing the documentation of sex and gender on state documents. During this moment of rapid change, queer identity and the associated agenda of political interests developed as a radical critique of anti-intersectional identity politics. The continued evolution of the queer political agenda channeled efforts of queer political actors *away* from intervening in assimilationist LGBT political identity and agendas. This led to the second major development for sexual and gender identities during this time: the continued construction of LGBT political identity and political agendas as *solely* concerned with sexuality. "LGBT politics" increasingly came to connote a singular focus on issues pertaining to sexuality through the advancement of an agenda oriented toward rightful citizenship claims. These political objectives included civil unions and, later, legal marriage for same-sex couples, antidiscrimination legislation to protect lesbians, gay men, and transgender people in employment, and removing barriers to openly gay and lesbian people serving in the military. By the end of the 1990s, "queer" was understood as a commitment to intersectional organizing, while "LGBT" was increasingly understood along a single axis of sexuality.

The National Policy Roundtable meetings held immediately before and after the 2000 elections show how these two developments influenced the diverging constructions and associated representations of LGBT and queer political identities and political agendas. While queer political agendas reflected a continued interest in finding ways to be relevant to people across race, gender identity, class, and ability, the following analysis of this meeting transcript shows how the departure of queer advocates from participation in the Roundtable freed the remaining interest groups to move forward with their construction of LGBT political identity and interests through the narrow frame of same-sex sexuality.

The political actors convened at the March 2000 meeting were especially concerned with developing effective strategies to influence the upcoming November elections in ways that were perceived to benefit the LGBT group. This specific political context, as well as a failure in leadership to carry the focus on racial justice from the September 1999 meeting into the March 2000 meeting, resulted in an emphasis on defining the LGBT group as an influential segment of the electorate. Virginia Apuzzo, from NGLTF, opened the meeting with the observation, "We are 11% of the Democratic primary and 2% of the Republican primary in California. 11% of voters identify as African, Latino, or Jewish. Here we are as a voting bloc right up there with every other voting bloc."[58] Apuzzo's strategy placed established voting blocs (Black, Latine, and Jewish voters) alongside LGBT voters as equals while simultaneously framing LGBT voters as separate from those who vote along racial and ethnic lines. Getting LGBT voters to the polls was subsequently identified as the paramount goal to pursue. The executive director of HRC, Elizabeth Birch, elaborated on her organization's vision for the LGBT group's influence. Her comments outlined the stakes of the upcoming election in specific terms: "What is at play is 57 seats. How can GLBT community invest on the edge to swing those seats? HRC's PAC is 8% of our budget. Goals are to: Energize the GLBT community to participate in the elections . . . [to] support openly GLBT candidates."[59] Birch built on her plan by introducing the possibility that this voting bloc, alone, could determine the outcomes of elections.

The connection between the LGBT group as part of the electorate and the construction of LGBT identity is demonstrated in Birch's subsequent outline for the plan to "energize" LGBT voters. She detailed one such campaign,

saying, "National Coming Out program in election year includes voting promotion among youth. Also working with NGLTF on campuses. Important
investment."[60] Here, Birch was referring to National Coming Out Day, which
is held annually on October 11 and was established in 1988—at the height
of HIV/AIDS activism—as an opportunity to assert the social and political visibility of gay men and lesbians by coming out en masse on that day.
This dramatic alteration to the meanings attached to "coming out" cannot
be overstated. The grassroots vision for coming out was imagined as a rite
performed to overcome personal discomfort as well as a political statement
to alter stigmas directed at lesbian, gay, bisexual, and transgender people by
modeling self-acceptance and rejection of the shame associated with sexuality and gender identity. In contrast, the version of coming out promoted
by HRC and NGLTF encouraged people to come out solely as voters who
happen to be gay, lesbian, bisexual, or transgender. In this instance, the introduction of LGBT to index sexuality reads not so much as an effort at rhetorical expediency or even a gesture toward greater unity, but instead as yet
another move to sever connotations with the sexual aspects of sexuality.
According to Birth and HRC, LGBT people are citizens entitled to certain
rights, which include the right to influence the outcomes of elections by
voting as a bloc.

There were other ways that these political actors envisioned the power of
a mobilized LGBT group in electoral politics, specifically with respect to potentially opposing the various ballot initiatives introduced across the states
that sought to define marriage as between one man and one woman. To help
executive directors craft a coordinated response, the March 2000 Roundtable
featured a special session on how to most effectively challenge these ballot
initiatives. Many of the discussions focused on how to use public opinion to
the advantage of the LGBT group. As the transcripts show, participants relied
on public opinion data gathered by Roundtable leaders regarding issues such
as same-sex marriage and social security benefits to support the pursuit of
rightful citizenship claims. This strategy reveals the assimilationist goal for
LGBT group to be recognized and given standing within the existing political system.

For instance, Vicki Shabo, a pollster commissioned to conduct a study of
attitudes toward LGBT people, reported her findings: "While participants in
every group said that gay and lesbian and same sex couples are just like other
people and resisted characterizations that distinguish gays and lesbians from
heterosexuals, it is clear that [there] are still strong positive and negative

stereotypes associated with gays and lesbians. People feel threatened by overt sexuality and public displays of affection."[61] The results of this focus group appear contradictory on the surface: on the one hand, respondents report no differences between gay men and lesbians and heterosexual; on the other hand, the same respondents still embrace negative stereotypes of gay men and lesbians. What is important here is the ending observation, that respondents expressed discomfort and defensiveness in response to "overt sexuality and public displays of affection." This concluding note illustrates that the central opposition to gay men and lesbians is the perception of deviant sexuality, which locates gay men and lesbians outside of the realm of proper citizens.

To combat the general public's associations of the LGBT group with deviance, Shabo recommended reframing the LGBT group as one concerned primarily with rightful citizenship claims in the language of equal rights. She explained how variations in wording could potentially change the outcomes at the polls: "If civil rights laws are equal or special rights, see a lot of improvement. In May of 1995 we had a 3% lead and now in Nov 1999 a 22% lead on equal rights response. People support hospital visitation rights, social security benefits, inheritance rights. The numbers are better among those that know GLBT people."[62]

Shabo's study shows how the growing acceptance of certain family rights—namely, hospital visitation for ailing partners or visits by gay or lesbian parents to sick children—was used to develop the most advantageous and potentially successful LGBT agenda, one that would, perhaps unsurprisingly by now, focus on asserting the similarities across heterosexual families and LGBT families. For instance, Shabo also observed, "When we asked people to define marriage, they spoke in very gender neutral terms. Definition of marriage should work more in our favor. People described marriage in terms of commitment and values not gender. Looking to future suggested an ethic of commonality across relationships. This is a window for us in the future."[63] Shabo's speculation that respondents in the general public are looking to see similarities between straight and LGBT people suggests that drawing out these potential overlaps might be an effective strategy for leaders at the Roundtable to adopt, especially her conclusion that analogies such as these might help to create opportunities—"a window"—in the future. Shabo's emphasis on drawing out the parallels between straight people and a very particular understanding of LGBT people directed the participants at the Roundtable to adopt a strategy focused on goals that fell squarely within the bounds of rightful citizenship claims.

There were, however, some participants who expressed concerns over asserting similarities between straight people and LGBT people. These moments of pushback indicate that the tendency toward rightful citizenship claims or the assimilation frame, in the case of the LGBT group, was not an inevitable path for the political actors convened at this meeting. Rather, these instances of disagreement, rupture, and contradiction show how the construction of a political identity along a single axis of identity is produced through strategic choices made by political actors—choices that elevate some members and issues at the expense of others. This is illustrated most compellingly in the growing split between LGBT identity and politics, focused on advancing rightful citizenship claims, and queer identity and politics, which channeled energies toward developing alternative political agendas that targeted oppressive ideologies and structures.

One respondent, for instance, explained that a better strategy for combating ballot initiatives might be found in accessing established activist networks: "One thing I haven't been hearing is that timeline probably started sooner. Had Prop 209. What level of organized queer involvement was there in those campaigns, laying groundwork for anti-gay initiatives? I am of the mindset that we will never win anything alone. Coalition problem."[64] The unidentified speaker in this excerpt refers to the mobilization that worked for the passage of California's Proposition 209, an anti–affirmative action measure that amended the state constitution to prohibit state government institutions from considering race, sex, or ethnicity in public employment, contracting, or education. The speaker theorizes that it was actually the networks of activists—people of color and other political operatives—put in place to oppose Proposition 209 that laid the groundwork for mounting a resistance to Proposition 22, also known as the Knight Initiative, which defined marriage as strictly between one man and one woman. Significantly, the use of "queer" by this speaker articulating alternatives to a rights-based strategy illustrates the deepening divide between queer and LGBT political identity. The LGBT strategy advocated by the majority of political actors present at this Roundtable tended toward rightful citizenship claims, and with them, a narrowly bounded understanding of LGBT identity as commensurate with heterosexuality. In contrast, this speaker interjects the possibility that the gains made in conjunction with the Knight Initiative were the result of coalitions comprised of people of color and lesbian, gay, bisexual, and transgender people who united in opposition to rolling back affirmative action with Proposition 209. The final observation, "we will never win anything alone," suggests that the efforts to assert the LGBT group as a group with a unique set of political goals might not be as effective as reformulating political agendas to make issues of concern relevant to as many people as possible.

The growing focus on rightful citizenship claims resulted in the withdrawal of some members from the Roundtable. I read these departures as further evidence of the growing alignment of "LGBT politics" with the interests of a narrowly defined segment of gay men and lesbians enacted through the elevation of rightful citizenship claims as the dominant political strategy. For instance, Deb Kolodny from BiNet identified her concerns with the increasingly exclusive character of the "LGBT group" that resulted from the repeated comparison to straight people in mobilizations to achieve rights, and used the open time at the end of the meeting to announce her intention to leave the Roundtable: "I have enjoyed all these meetings tremendously. I feel that these meetings have helped in developing professional relationships, but only 3 presenters included bi and trans language. The NPR [National Policy Roundtable] participants I feel personally have really gotten better at this. I still leave with sadness of the funding panel and a lot of opportunity in tactical decisions. Do people understand what I mean when I say that bisexuals have potential to reconstruct our whole notion of sexual liberation and strategies? There is a level of understanding that doesn't exist."[65] In this vision of bisexuality, the adherence to monosexism and with it the reliance on the rigid gender binary should be replaced by political mobilizations designed to alter the conditions of stigmatization and oppression for all people exploring nonhegemonic sexualities and gender identities. Kolodny's departure cemented the understanding that not all of the identities captured in the LGBT initialism were equally arrayed, and suggested that there was a growing awareness that bisexuals and transgender people were only nominally included in the name of the group but not substantively represented in the strategies developed or the discussions held, particularly through the focus on rightful citizenship claims and assimilation.

Kolodny was not the only Roundtable participant to announce that the March 2000 meeting would be their last based on dissatisfaction with what was becoming an increasingly assimilationist political agenda. Roger Leishman, co-chair of the Federation of State Lesbian, Gay, Bisexual, and Transgender Political Organizations, also used the conclusion of the meeting to announce his departure from the group and his reasons for doing so: "This is also my last meeting. I was troubled that we didn't integrate race into this discussion since it was the center piece of the last meeting. The work that . . . I do, working with people at state level, this has been in the discussion and has come up very naturally and appropriately and a lot more attention is being paid to the states than when we joined the Roundtable."[66] For Leishman, the scant attention the Roundtable paid to issues pertaining to race was incongruous with the simultaneous increase in attention to state politics because conversations about race were necessary features of LGBT politics at the local level and should be at the national level as well. This departure on the basis of relative lack of attention to race—along with Kolodny's comments with respect to bisexuality and transgender issues— shows the effects of the increasingly narrow LGBT political identity and political agenda constructed and represented by the national organizations convened at the National Policy Roundtable in action. By asserting the similarity of LGBT people to straight people under the rubric of rightful citizenship claims (now understood as emphasizing the status of lesbians, gay men, bisexuals, and transgender people as voters and potentially making a bid for legal marriage) the political actors invested in constructing the LGBT political identity group and agenda succeeded in collapsing that identity along the single axis of same-sex sexuality. As Kolodny's and Leishman's departures signal, the increasingly tight association of the LGBT group with sexuality, defined exclusively as taking form in same-sex relationships, came at the exclusion of issues pertaining to race, bisexuality, and gender identity, among many other issues raised at the meetings up to this point, including immigration, disability, financial struggles, and an overarching resistance to conformity demanded by bids for assimilation in the name of rightful citizenship claims. This increasingly singular focus was further secured one year later, at the March 2001 Roundtable meeting, where the executive directors met to process the outcome of the November 2000 election and the implications for political agendas moving forward.

Rightful Citizenship Claims and LGBT Representation

The March 2001 National Policy Roundtable meeting was the first held after the election of George W. Bush. The executive directors used the two days to craft a political agenda that would be successful in what they perceived to be an inhospitable political climate for LGBT people. These discussions revolved around how to appeal to Republican lawmakers, which was ultimately settled with the decision to cement sexual identity as the defining characteristic of the LGBT group. In addition to being amenable to rightful citizenship claims, advocates of this strategic framing argued that maintaining the centrality of sexuality would potentially attract more members to the group and thus allow for the projection of critical mass in political mobilizations. "LGBT" was consequently prized as a chance to signal unity even while these efforts entailed the exclusion of various groups that were seen as contradicting the singular focus of the group. These exclusions implicitly impacted people of color through the normalization of White gay men and lesbians as the proper members of the LGBT group; however, most telling was the willingness of those invested in this unitary construction to explicitly jettison representation and membership for bisexual and transgender people.

The meeting began with the executive director of the Log Cabin Republicans, Rich Tajfel, who first briefed participants on his knowledge of the Bush administration and then provided some insight into the potential victories that could be won in the next four years. His introduction included a panel discussion about the current state of the Republican Party and featured a returning speaker, Vicki Shabo, who offered the polling data used in the March 2000 meeting, as well as a new guest speaker, David Boaz, from the Cato Institute, a Libertarian think tank.

Boaz opened the panel with the following summary of how the representation of the LGBT political identity group and political agenda would benefit from strategic shifts in language to appeal to the new Republican administration:

> When I was asked to do give [sic] this presentation, I was surprised that I was asked to advise you on tactics and goals. We do agree on goals. We at least agree that increasing tolerance on GL issues is one of our goals. There are groups on the right and the left who don't share this as a goal. I think this is consistent with the best of American values. I think one principle is that goals should be for the common good. We should agree that we are seeking common good, not just handouts for special interests. The latter is what Republicans think that gays want.[67]

As posed by Boaz, the solution to disputes over the promotion of "tolerance" for gay men and lesbians—on both the Right and the Left—is to develop a shared investment in what he terms the "common good," which is defined in opposition to "special interests." He explained, "You'll make more headway if you look at overall law and not at just specific issues. Talk about things as a moral thing and individual rights and equality—this would make it easier for libertarian and conservative Republicans to support your issues."[68] Here, Boaz returns to terrain familiar to the political actors at the Roundtable and urges them to see how they stand to benefit from directing energy toward legal gains premised on morality, individual rights, and equality—rightful citizenship claims—and *not* efforts to enhance visibility for the LGBT group in politics and society by pushing an agenda of political and social issues specific to sexuality or gender identity.

Boaz's elaboration of how to make this revised political agenda appeal to the new Republican administration, as well as the trade-offs these revisions would entail, reveals the meaning of "special interests" for Libertarians and Republicans. "Republicans can tolerate the word gay, but when bisexual and transgender come in they just start thinking about hyphenated Americans. It triggers their identity politics issue especially where transgender is concerned."[69] "Special interests," in other words, are identities that are salient to some members, but are perceived to disrupt the status quo conveyed by an unqualified "American" identity. "Gay" is therefore tolerable for some Republicans because it functions as a similar, but different, expression of sexuality, while "bisexual and transgender" are perceived as introducing uncertainty and challenges to the dominant model for relationships.

To some extent, Boaz's suggestions at this meeting were in line with the strategic focus on rightful citizenship claims that was steadily gaining in popularity at the Roundtable. His recommendation to exclude bisexual and transgender members, organizations, and issues from the political organizing taking place at the Roundtable, however, was met with opposition from some members, who reminded the attendees that the group was defined to some degree by sexual and gender diversity. Boaz responded by shifting the meaning of diversity. After conceding that keeping people who are transgender on the LGBT agenda would be a reasonable goal for a different type of movement, he suggested, "You also need to recognize diversity in the gay movement. Libertarians and Republicans feel there is a lot of pressure for ideological conformity within the gay community. This drives them away from wanting to work with you."[70] According to Boaz, the way to succeed in the current political climate would be to expand the meaning of diversity to facilitate the inclusion of Libertarians and Republicans in the LGBT group, presumably due to the assumption their goals and complaints might be more legible to the Republican administration. Though on the surface Boaz's comments are a simple plea for the LGBT group to embrace Republicans and Libertarians, his efforts to redefine diversity also effectively elevated sexuality as the common identification uniting the group, which is evidenced in his conspicuous use of "gay" rather than "LGBT." As a result, for Boaz and other Conservative members of the Roundtable, gay and lesbian Republicans and Libertarians should be considered when crafting the political agenda because they have similar sexual identities as the meeting attendees. Gay and lesbian identification must be held constant in order to allow party affiliation to vary, which effectively locks a very narrow understanding of sexuality as the defining feature of the group.

There were some members of the Roundtable who protested the elevation of sexuality as the defining feature of the LGBT group and political agenda, particularly because it resulted in the exclusion of those who are multiply marginalized. One participant followed Boaz's presentation by predicting that a focus on rightful citizenship claims and the elevation of sexuality as the common factor would exclude non-White racial groups saying that "the common good is defined as what the majority is which is perceived as white males. How to frame the common good in ways that don't leave out Americans?"[71] The explicit point about how White men do not provide adequate examples for political goals advanced by a group made up of many different sexual, gender, and racial identities was lost, however, in Tajfel's response to the question. He explained, "The way to get to common good is to not go in as the self interested group," and went on to assert that while "African American women with breast cancer can join a health coalition," they must ultimately yield to the demands of the group by separating their unique interests as Black women from the larger issue of breast cancer.[72] Extending the implications of this response to the LGBT group suggests that sexuality, yet again, ought to be the shared characteristic motivating political action, much like breast cancer is a shared characteristic in his example. That this elevation requires the erasure of race in Tajfel's formulation is not accidental. In other words, it is not lesbian, gay, bisexual, and/or transgender identification that brings the LGBT group together in this formulation, but rather expressions and experiences with same-sex sexuality that should motivate politics. Representing sexuality as unitary was viewed as a strategy that would ultimately be more successful in the context of a Republican administration. The question of how it is exactly that people might choose between their intersecting identities was not raised, nor answered, suggesting that there was implicit agreement that they might simply be left out of those mobilizations.

With these suggestions in mind, the executive directors used the remainder of the meeting for two tasks. The first was to discuss ways to elevate sexuality as the defining feature in representations of the LGBT group, and the second was to make plans for how this formulation of LGBT identity and political agenda might provide the basis for enhanced coalition work. The elevation of sexuality alongside the renewed interest in forming coalitions reinforced the construction of the LGBT group as unified in narrow ways, which was achieved through efforts to position the LGBT group alongside—and not overlapping with—intersecting identity-based groups. LGBT, in other words, would be a unique, anti-intersectional political identity and agenda to advance issues pertaining solely to sexuality, specifically those held by gay men and lesbians who were interested in advancing rightful citizenship claims across political venues.

Eric Rofes, the former executive director of NGLTF, articulated the following vision for the LGBT group in line with the suggestions made for prioritizing sexuality: "I adhere to big tent picture of the GLBT community. I don't believe that gay male leaders should look de-sexed or pretend that they are in a monogamous relationship if they aren't. If we are in a participatory democracy, that means that people who organize their sexual lives in ways outside of heterosexual norms should allow full access to our communities."[73] For Rofes, the LGBT community is united underneath the tent of sexuality, which is defined as "outside of heterosexual norms." Diversity would and should be encouraged and permitted according to this metaphor, but only in relation to sexuality, which excluded gender identity, gender, and race as a result.

Other visions for coalition proposed by the political actors present at this meeting were premised on creating alliances across groups that *also* experienced oppression based on sexual stigmas, but not sexuality. These distinctions helped to keep the LGBT group separate from potential coalition partners. A participant identified as Amber, for example, argued for coalitions as follows:

> [W]e need to be talking in a vibrant way about where we have natural allies and build a movement that expands from this core to bring any more

constituencies that are attacked around sexuality. We're really not the only ones. The reason we remain isolated is because we haven't built voices to broaden the scope. As long as gayness is used as sex and straight people are there to represent everything else, we are in trouble. Our ability to envelop other voices on sex before we are attacked is important. Our ability to defend ourselves would shift because we would not be in isolation around the frame of "dangerous" sexuality.[74]

Amber identifies the motivation to form potential coalitions solely in relation to sex and sexuality, but she does not specify who comprises these other groups or who could help form these potential coalitions. In this way, she highlights the persistent failure to reach out to others who are similarly attacked in relation to sex while still effectively silencing the specific groups targeted for "dangerous sexuality." The losses entailed by this omission are evident in the missing alliances between LGBT people and women of color during this period, many of whom were stigmatized as promiscuous single mothers growing rich off the U.S. welfare state.[75]

Structural Shifts and New Directions

I have thus far argued that because of their focus on rightful citizenship claims, the LGBT group inevitably transformed their push for coalition-based organizing into an anti-intersectional conflation of "LGBT" with sexuality. The repeated assertion of the utility to be gained by forming coalitions with groups understood as "other" established and maintained the illusion that these groups were separate and not overlapping. In particular, the resistance to understanding sexuality as intersecting with race, gender, and class exerted a regulatory influence on what came to be known of the LGBT identity and agenda.

The elevation of sexuality and the renewed interest in forming coalitions were reflected in the conclusion of the meeting, as the participants debated revising the structure of the meetings to maximize their political efficacy. In some ways, these debates read as normal activities that any organization engages in to audit their work after a set period of time. However, because the archive does not contain meeting transcripts past this March 2001 date, I read the final discussion regarding the structure of the National Policy Roundtable moving forward as auguring the future of LGBT politics, particularly as the organizations at the meeting sat the precipice of the 21st century and the massive social, political, and economic paradigm shifts that would follow the events of September 11, 2001. The issues that executive directors discussed at the final session of the final meeting addressed two questions that determined the shape of the Roundtable and LGBT politics at this critical juncture.

First, a number of participants withdrew from the Roundtable in favor of focusing on organizations and movements more directly affiliated with queer, or liberatory, approaches to political action. In some cases, the departure of these individuals was received with hostility by those in attendance. For example, at the conclusion of this meeting, during which a discussion about these absences took place, one unidentified participant offered to say why certain members refused to attend meetings, and implied that the participants would not be receptive to the information. This participant vaguely threatened to "tell you why they aren't coming, if you want to have the conversation," to which another retorted, "No, we don't."[76] These tense exchanges over the previously engaged members of the Roundtable suggest that the proposed coalitions might not seek queer movements and organizations as allies, only furthering the divide between the LGBT agenda and queer identity and politics.

The second question concerned how to structure the National Policy Roundtables to promote more of the coalitional-type work discussed at the March 2001 meeting. Here, again, the question of attendance and who would be invited took center stage. After a quick debate, the participants voted on inviting two representatives, preferably including an executive director, to attend each meeting. Phrasing these revised rules as contributing to the National Policy Roundtables as a "shared power structure" established the formal coalition between groups in attendance. Furthermore, these revisions created the conditions for very particular types of organizations to participate in the National Policy Roundtables. Specifically, those rules included a formalized institutional structure and designated executive directors and other officers as invitees to future meetings. Much like the story of eben clark in chapter 2, who evocatively described how parliamentary procedure silenced his voice at GAA meetings, this structural shift foreclosed participation by political movements without formalized structures from the National Policy Roundtables, as well as from the political agendas taking shape there. These decisions resulted in the exclusion of many of the queer political organizations engaged in activism at the time.

These two shifts in the structure of the National Policy Roundtables show how the divides between LGBT political identity and queer identity were not natural evolutions of fundamentally different identifications—and political interests—away from each other. Instead, this division resulted from hotly contested political developments and was institutionalized by political actors making lasting changes to who would be invited into the LGBT group and which interests would be advanced on their behalf. Significantly, the diverging LGBT and queer agendas were established through mutual opposition. Attaching "LGBT" to HRC's mission statement in 2003 cemented the association of the LGBT with assimilation, rightful citizenship claims, and the elevation of sexuality as the defining feature of the group. "Queer," on the other hand, would be adopted by grassroots social movements to connote an anticategorical stance and commitment to political goals that would target the institutions, laws, and practices that oppress all marginalized groups: people of color, women, people who are poor or homeless, people who are undocumented, and people with disabilities.

In practice, these diverging views on structure and political praxis meant that organizations advocating for assimilation and inclusion would be helmed by and speak to the issues of White gay men and lesbians. The constellation of organizations and movements aligned with a queer orientation to political action and power would be predominantly led by Black, Asian, Latine, and Native transgender-, bisexual-, and queer-identified people. The successes of the rightful citizenship claims advanced by those interested in assimilation, in this light, did not occur because that strategy is more advantageous or feasible but rather due to decisions by leaders in those movements to collapse LGBT identities along a single axis. Doing so permitted the entrance of White gay men and some lesbians into institutions of citizenship, such as marriage and the military. Queer political mobilizations did not vanish into thin air or dissolve into the mainstream LGBT movement; instead, they shifted focus to more local concerns or forged new pathways in prison abolition, the decriminalization of sex work, economic redistribution, and activism on behalf of migrants. These distinctions would come to define the politics of sexuality and gender identity for the foreseeable future.

Conclusions: LGBT and Queer Futures

The analysis in this chapter shows how political actors working to advance political agendas concerned with sexuality and gender identity adopted either a queer politics frame or an assimilationist frame mobilized through rightful citizenship claims to represent sexuality and gender identity in politics. Critically, these decisions were largely made by considering who, exactly, ought to be included in political activity, and the conflicts emerging from these decisions contributed to a proliferation of sexual and gender identities. I argue that during this time "queer" became increasingly associated with people with multiple identifications, especially people of color, people who are undocumented, people who are poor, and people who are disabled. The boundaries of queer identity were constructed as intersectional and, as a result, contributed to a political agenda founded in opposition to the institutions that structure and maintain subordinate status for those who are multiply marginalized. Queer politics was not about particular identities; it was conceived of as a shared orientation against ideologies that structure and maintain hierarchies of belonging, such as White supremacy, heteronormativity, binary gender, classism, ableism, and citizenship. Queer politics thus turned attention to challenging the death penalty, mass incarceration, police violence, and the documentation of sex, all of which were viewed as using violence and coercion to maintain a gendered and racialized status quo.

In contrast to "queer," the evolving LGBT identity achieved meaning through the elevation of sexuality as a core facet of identity that was understood to be mutually exclusive from other identifications. This further contributed to the construction of a prototypical LGBT group member, who was projected as White, gender-normative, able-bodied, educated, and of relative class privilege. The tight relationship between the construction of LGBT identity along a single axis was further reflected in the political agendas developed to represent the interests of the group. Throughout this chapter, I underscore how the LGBT group evolved in conjunction with a growing focus on rightful citizenship claims and pursued political goals such as open inclusion in the military and relationship recognition. The LGBT group was also projected as a significant and influential segment of the electorate, one that could determine outcomes of elections. The LGBT political identity and agenda, in other words, was constructed so as to operate most effectively within the constraints of liberal democracy. In this way, LGBT political action reified and extended the oppressive system that put into motion many of the inequalities that the movement sought to contest.

In light of these splits, the executive directors at the March 2001 meeting of the Roundtable advanced two diverging approaches to political action. One approach would highlight rightful citizenship claims by pursuing electoral gains, visibility, and civil rights objectives, such as inclusion in the military and advancing the work on marriage equality. These issues would be taken up by organizations such as HRC, which would eventually revise its mission statement in the mold of rightful citizenship claims to announce its role as the "largest national lesbian, gay, bisexual, and transgender civil rights organization."[77] The alternative approach, indexed as queer, would be centrally concerned with broad social inequality and consequently target issues related to sexuality and gender identity as these identity categories intersected with race and class. These organizations would commit to working together in coalitions to advance these broad, social justice–based goals.

Thus, by the close of the 1990s, the dynamics of within-group marginalization that primarily shaped the experiences of lesbian, gay, bisexual, and transgender people of color, people with disabilities, gender-nonconforming people, and undocumented people were reconfigured. While HRC would continue to represent and elevate the construction of lesbian, gay, bisexual, and transgender people in narrowly racialized, gendered, and classed ways, other movements and political organizations were developed to work in coalition to push back against these constructions to advance much broader political goals concerned with social justice and equity for women, people of color, people with disabilities, undocumented people, and most important, those who were multiply marginalized.

7

Rightful Citizenship Claims, Then and Now

In June 2022, President Joe Biden invited Jennicet Gutiérrez—the undocumented transgender woman whom the Secret Service escorted out of the White House at the behest of President Obama and to the cheers of onlookers in 2015—to his annual Pride celebration. She declined the invitation. In a widely circulated open letter to explain her decision, Gutiérrez reminded Biden that transgender people in Immigration and Customs Enforcement detention are still housed in deadly conditions. She ended with the following observation: "You could easily stop their suffering by instructing the Department of Homeland Security to implement a policy of liberating trans people, people living with HIV and other medical conditions, as well as other vulnerable people. Ending trans detention and using your executive powers to protect LGBTQ people would have a greater impact on our community and would save many lives rather than hosting an event to deliver a well-crafted speech with broken promises."[1] The event went on without Gutiérrez, and there was no mention of transgender people incarcerated by ICE. Instead, Biden used the event as an opportunity to sign the Bill of Rights for LGBTQI+ Older Adults, an executive order that made an array of promises aimed at improving the lives of lesbian, gay, bisexual, transgender, queer, intersex, and all other sexual and gender minorities not named in the initialism of the title. These included prohibitions against the use of federal funds to support conversion therapy programs, adding an "X" marker for transgender and gender-nonconforming people to use on state documents in plane of M or F, and providing training and technical support for jurisdictions to "better serve LGBTQI+ youth involved in the juvenile justice system."[2] When Gutiérrez called for liberation, Biden responded with rights. And just as in 2015, when Obama gathered a room full of self-identified gay, lesbian, bisexual, and transgender advocates and activists to mark the Supreme Court's

Terms of Exclusion. Zein Murib, Oxford University Press. © Oxford University Press 2023.
DOI: 10.1093/oso/9780197671498.003.0008

impending decision that would make same-sex marriage legal, those very same political actors applauded what they celebrated as key rights wins.

I want to use these Pride celebrations as an opportunity to return to the puzzle that I posed at the beginning of this book: Why would a room full of lesbian, gay, bisexual, and transgender political actors familiar with the rich history of disruptive protests condone silencing an undocumented transgender woman and ignore her call for the end of ICE incarceration? Concluding with these events at the White House underscores that little has changed with respect to the tensions that opened this book concerning who comprises lesbian, gay, bisexual, transgender, and LGBT identity-based groups and which interests ought to be advocated on their behalf. First, I argue that the deployment of rightful citizenship claims as a political strategy results in the elevation of interests held by White gay men (and some lesbians) who most closely mirror the hegemonic norms of citizenship: monogamous relationships, gender normativity, (re)productive nuclear families, legal citizenship status, and property ownership. These members then become representative of the identity-based groups to the broader public and, in so doing, reaffirm the normative contours of citizenship when they are seamlessly folded into institutions and laws. As a result, rightful citizenship claims create the conditions for casting those excluded or designated as partial citizens to the margins of the polity.

I also argue that the state secures the marginalization of those who are constructed outside of the group and the polity when lawmakers respond to rightful citizenship claims. Biden's executive order, for example, addresses important issues, such as state-level discrimination against LGBTQI+ youth. This includes committing federal resources to combat legislation such as Florida's "Don't Say Gay" bill, which establishes the right of parents to sue school districts that allow teachers to discuss sexuality and gender identity. However, the Bill of Rights signed by Biden also uses the language of rightful citizenship claims to expand the scope of the state's regulation and surveillance of LGBTQI+ lives by allocating funds to "better" juvenile incarceration. This provision disproportionately impacts Black, Latine, and Native LGBTQI+ youth, who make up a relatively higher percentage of incarcerated LGBTQ people in juvenile detention.[3] Aspiring to improve incarceration under the rubric of rightful citizenship claims extends the reach of the carceral state and leaves myths of criminality intact. This stands in stark contrast to contemporary calls for the end of mass incarceration made by activists such as Gutiérrez and many others, who use the language of abolition and liberation—and not rights—to mobilize against the long-term erasure and disappearance of LGBTQI+ people that is shaped by cycles of incarceration (and poverty).

The preceding chapters emphasize that these erasures occur not *despite* significant rights wins in the past decade—such as opportunities to serve openly in the military and marriage equality—but *because* of those rights wins. In drawing this distinction, my third argument is that naturalizing rightful citizenship claims as the most logical or strategic objectives functions anti-intersectionally to obscure alternative political interests that might benefit those who are multiply marginalized. These include political solutions that avoid the language of rights and address the most vulnerable members of identity-based groups, such as decoupling healthcare from private insurance, eliminating sex markers on state documentation, and ending the militarized policing of borders.

Throughout six chapters, I have drawn on primary sources to reveal how this work has been done intentionally, strategically, and at great cost to those who are pushed to the margins of developing identity categories. Although proponents of rightful citizenship claims pose them as necessary and logical, and thus without debate, my focus on political discourse in the development of lesbian, gay, bisexual, transgender, and LGBT political identities shows that choices to prioritize rightful citizenship claims were subject to significant contestation. I highlight these moments of rupture within groups to intervene in the prevailing tendency to cast these differences as diverging approaches to political praxis that are indexed as assimilationist versus radical. I show that time and time again, decisions to prioritize rightful citizenship claims were made by political actors who were well aware of the costs. After all, the people who would eventually be excluded were in the room. They engaged in prolonged debates about agendas, and the transcripts of these debates exist in the archives. This book uses those exchanges to illustrate that what is often glossed as differences in political sensibilities—a preference for formal political action versus grassroots activism—is actually rooted in decisions regarding who, exactly, merits inclusion in the group. Through careful discourse analysis, I showed who is achieving power and how they use that power to omit those who are intersectionally marginalized, all in the service of rightful citizenship claims.

This book ends in 2001 with the introduction of "LGBT" as the predominant way to refer to sexuality and gender identity in U.S. politics. In many cases, the archive after 2001 is locked and cannot yet be accessed. While this limits my ability to examine how activists and advocates internally discussed political strategy in the intervening 20 years, there are several recent developments that provide some clues as to how the theories and analysis in this book generalize to present-day LGBT politics. The following three case studies span political, social, and popular culture to illustrate the far-reaching effects of rightful citizenship claims on who is considered members of the LGBT group: the evolution of Pride flags, Taylor Swift's 2019 music video *You Need to Calm Down*, and the recent U.S. Supreme Court decision in *Dobbs v. Jackson Women's Health Organization*. Each of these case studies underscores how rightful citizenship claims fuel ongoing tensions regarding who is considered a member of the LGBT group and which interests ought to be advanced on their behalf.

Pride Flags

The proliferation of Pride flags designed to represent LGBT, bisexual, intersex, transgender, and asexual people (among an almost innumerable array of groups) reflect the hold that rights, citizenship, and belonging has on contemporary LGBT politics. Beginning with the introduction of the rainbow Pride flag in 1978, offshoots include a transgender flag with pink, blue, and white horizontal stripes; a bisexual flag with hot pink, purple, and blue horizontal stripes; and a flag that blends the transgender flag into the original rainbow flag in an offset triangle and adds two additional stripes—black and brown—to signal the inclusion of Black and Brown members. Flags are traditionally used to identify nations and function as banners displayed by soldiers and citizens to evoke feelings of patriotism, fealty, and belonging—especially during times of war. Similarly, these multiple versions of Pride flags serve the purpose of signaling identity and uniting groups through shared symbols that can be politically mobilized. In other words, just as flags that demarcate spatial borders have been used to establish nations and citizenship, Pride flags have been used to establish the boundaries of categorization under the LGBT umbrella. With this premise in mind, how do we make sense of the addition of black, brown, pink, white, and blue (but not the hot pink, purple, and blue stripes from the bisexual flag) to the general rainbow flag, and what are the social and political stakes of these additions? Do these additions resist the exclusionary practices of rightful citizenship claims, or do they further enforce them?

As I have shown throughout this book, an intersectional analysis reveals how questions of inclusion and exclusion cannot be engaged through the lens of sexuality alone, but must instead be expanded to account for race, class, and citizenship. For example, in 2017, Philadelphia's Office of LGBT Affairs added a black and a brown stripe to the rainbow Pride flag and introduced it in a press release, stating, "In 1978, artist Gilbert Baker designed the original rainbow flag. So much has happened since then. A lot of good, but there's more we can do. Especially when it comes to recognizing people of color in the LGBTQ+ community. To fuel this important conversation, we've expanded the colors of the flag to include black and brown."[4] Evident in this statement is an effort to address and reframe the long-standing erasure of Black and Brown people from political agendas and popular understandings of the group that I argue results from rightful citizenship claims mobilized by organizations like the Philadelphia Office of LGBT Affairs. The introduction of the two stripes, however, was hotly contested by political actors across the political spectrum. These conflicts go some way in revealing the enduring effects of rightful citizenship claims in producing the exclusions that give LGBT political identity meaning. Although Baker died before the new flag was introduced, his close friend Charley Beal spoke on his behalf to take issue with the flag and the symbolism of adding black and brown stripes. In an interview, he stated, "The stripes were not chosen for skin color—they were chosen to reflect the spectrum of color in nature."[5] He concluded with a passionate plea that Baker's name not be attached to the new flag as the design worked against his original intentions, as if to sever the link between Barker's suggested affinity for diversity—understood through Beal's interpretation to be solely sexual—and the new representation of that diversity captured in the Philadelphia flag.[6] Irene Monroe, the founder of the National Black Justice Coalition, also weighed in with comments that drew attention to the question of what it means to "add" and "include" Black and Brown people when they were active in the very first moments of gay and lesbian politics. "The Stonewall riot started on the backs of working-class African and Latino queers who patronized that bar," Monroe explained in an interview. "I think it's unfortunate that we have to be even more intentional. . . . [B]y putting those extra colors they're saying 'you're not doing it,' and that's just unfortunate . . . because of years of being tone deaf that the rainbow includes everybody."[7]

It is striking how Monroe's words converge with Beal's on the subject of the rainbow as a universally recognized representation of diversity, but with different connotations. For Beal, stating that the colors of the rainbow—red, orange, yellow, green, blue, indigo, and violet—were not meant to correspond to skin colors is more than a seemingly nonsensical observation. After all, people do not have rainbow-colored skin. However, digging deeper into his comments uncovers a subtext in which a political commitment to diversity is understood to be sexual, not racial. This sentiment echoes statements made by GAA political leaders cited in chapter 2 who asserted that unity would be achieved by focusing exclusively on sexuality at the expense of gender, race, and class. For Monroe, though, the rainbow functions much more metaphorically, with the colors meaning that Black, Latine, Asian, and Native people were always part of what would come to be known as "LGBTQ politics" in contemporary discourse. Her words echo those of farajaje-jones in chapter 4, who expressed dismay and anger at the decision to drop "multicultural" from the title of BiNet USA due to concerns that retaining it would suggest that Black and Brown people would be privileged over all other members. For farajaje-jones, the word "multicultural" spans difference to contain all the particularity of human experience, much like the rainbow functions as a symbol of natural heterogeneity for Monroe.

The example of Pride flags reveals how, on the level of identity, inclusion along the axis of sexuality results in anti-intersectional exclusion along the lines of race, class, and citizenship. Throughout this book, I have shown how such exclusions, mobilized through rightful citizenship claims, were used by stakeholders to make LGBT groups and individuals legible within the assumed and already settled landscape of American politics. The structures were not being transformed (as more marginalized stakeholders advocated); instead, the lens of inclusion was simply widened to account for those whose racial, class, and citizenship identities placed them proximate to Whiteness. I want to suggest that the proliferation of Pride flags has followed similar logics in regard to capital and neoliberalism. For example, many businesses choose to fly a simple rainbow Pride flag during June to demonstrate a commitment to sexual diversity. Others go further. In June 2022, with transgender people under attack by a spate of laws designed to legalize discrimination against them, several online retailers changed their website banners to a rainbow Pride flag with an inset transgender Pride flag to declare their awareness of transgender issues. While the proliferation of Pride flags may foster a sense of inclusion and visibility for many people (and this is not without value), on a structural level this visibility is far more about interpellating LGBTQ consumers than transforming the material realities of marginalized communities.

"You Need to Calm Down"

In June 2019—at the height of the summer Pride season and on the eve of the 2020 presidential election—country singer turned pop icon Taylor Swift released the music video for her new single, "You Need to Calm Down." In it, a who's who of LGBTQ stars populate a candy-colored-trailer-park-turned-gayborhood and engage in the trappings of queer life: Laverne Cox in a glittery pink evening gown waters her flowers, RuPaul judges a drag contest, Ellen DeGeneres gets a tattoo, and Jesse Tyler Ferguson (of ABC's *Modern Family*) weds his real-life husband, Justin Mikita, in matching powder-blue tuxedos. Toward the end, the straight White actor Ryan Reynolds peeks out from behind a canvas on which he is painting an abstract rendition of the Stonewall Inn.

The delights of this rainbow-colored LGBTQ utopia are periodically disrupted by their drab, colorless neighbors, a group coded as poor and working class through tropes of rural poverty: unkempt, missing teeth, and dingy, tattered American flag clothing. They appear as a mob and carry signs with the old antigay favorite, "Adam and Eve, Not Adam and Steve," alongside signs that read "Homosekuality is sin" and "Get a Brain Morans." As if the spelling errors did not make it obvious enough that these protesters should be understood as uneducated, the latter sign is brandished upside-down, presumably by a person unable to read. At one point, two of the youngest antigay protesters roll their eyes at the mob and cross the border into the LGBTQ gayborhood to participate in a glittery, fun-filled food fight.

As the music fades out, an all-pink screen displays the following call to action: "Let's show our pride by demanding that, on a national level, our laws truly treat all of our citizens equally. Sign the petition on change.org to urge the Senate to pass the Equality Act." The petition to support the Equality Act—legislation that would amend the Civil Rights Act of 1964 to prohibit discrimination on the basis of sex, sexual orientation, and gender identity in employment, housing, public accommodations, education, federally funded programs, credit, and jury service—was signed by close to one million people between 2019 and 2022. The video itself was also wildly popular; it has been viewed over 284 million times and won the 2019 MTV Video Music

Awards Video of the Year and Video for Good. In her acceptance speech, Swift described the goal of the Equality Act as "basically saying we all deserve equal rights under the law" in a tone suggesting that entitlement to those rights is a foregone conclusion and that everybody in the awards hall with her is equally positioned in relation to being denied those rights.[8]

Swift's video is a near-perfect distillation of the past 60 years of gay, lesbian, bisexual, and transgender political mobilizations under the rubric of rightful citizenship claims. I have argued throughout this book that the deployment of rightful citizenship claims results in the elevation of those members who can reasonably claim that they would be folded into the fabric of full citizenship were it not for their different sexuality. This results in the marginalization of those considered less proximate to normative citizenship (Black, Asian, Latine, Native, and Arab/Middle Eastern LGBTQ people) and the elevation of Whiteness as the marker of belonging in both the LGBT group and the American polity. Twenty years after the last National Policy Roundtable was convened and just four years after Obama's Pride celebration that opened this book, Swift's video recasts these hierarchies of belonging and provides insight into the state of LGBT politics in 2022. The video poses the multiracial LGBTQ all-star cast (and their straight White allies, such as Reynolds and, though subject to significant debate, Swift herself) as the proper residents of the queer utopia, who square off against the presumably backward and uneducated White straight masses that would deny them their rights in Trump's America. Striking a hopeful tone, the video promises that those rights can be achieved with the passage of the Equality Act, which will codify into law that the residents of Swift's LGBTQ gayborhood have won despite opposition.

Similar to the proliferation of Pride flags, Swift's video first appears to be about inclusion, as this brightly colored and diverse group of queer luminaries (arguably a Pride flag made animate) are placed in opposition to the voting bloc perceived as denying them their rights: conservative homophobic and transphobic Trump voters. However, there are two deceptive moves being made through this formulation. First, part of the appeal of this narrative of rightful citizenship claims as the route to LGBTQ utopia is the way it papers over those who are not present in the video, specifically undocumented, incarcerated, and Native LGBTQ people. Second, their erasure paves the way for Swift and the viewers themselves to pit residents of the LGBTQ gayborhood living their best lives against protesters coded as backward and uneducated. Swift seems to argue that it is these voters, and not the White supremacist and Nationalist structure of the U.S. government (grounded in rightful citizenships claims), that keeps LGBTQ people from full citizenship status. By focusing on the specter of the White, rural, and poor (likely Trump) voter, Swift's video reproduces the distraction that allowed for the Trump administration to stack the courts with conservative judges, hollow out the federal government, and erode democratic norms. Her video makes her viewers feel something (similar to the inclusion felt by Pride flags) by, first, celebrating LGBT people as symbols of modernity and progress and, second, suggesting that the state's provision of rights through the Equality Act will lead to critical change. However, as this book has shown, these achievements are impossible without the erasure of those LGBTQ people who are most vulnerable, all in the name of rightful citizenship claims.

Dobbs v. Jackson Women's Health Organization

The distraction I draw attention to above—the specter of the White, rural, and poor (likely Trump) voter—may be played for laughs in Swift's video, but the threat behind this strategy has become all too real. In June 2022, the U.S. Supreme Court overruled *Roe v. Wade* and *Planned Parenthood v. Casey* with *Dobbs v. Jackson Women's Health Organization*. The 6–3 majority justified their decision by reasoning that the U.S. Constitution does not confer a right to obtain abortions. Reactions to the ruling were swift and fell into predictable camps. Conservatives and Evangelicals celebrated the decision as the pinnacle of the 49-year mobilization to end abortion. Women's and reproductive health organizations took to social media to denounce the Court's decision and emphasized that the ruling would result in countless forced pregnancies and—in many cases—deaths that could have been avoided.

On the one hand, the *Dobbs* decision reveals how the rights advocated for and achieved through rightful citizenship claims are not settled and can, in the current political landscape, be overturned. On the other hand, the decision also opened up space for internal backlash—not from the White, rural, poor Trump voters framed as the enemy in public imagination (on display in Swift's video) but from self-identified antigender feminists, who carried the torch for the radical lesbian feminists (from chapter 3) by asserting that the biological aspects of sex are inseparable from what is commonly referred to as gender. They seized the moment of *Roe*'s reversal to make epistemic and political arguments that targeted transgender women. The epistemic line of reasoning followed a well-worn path: women are defined by the biological capacity to become pregnant, and this embodied difference entitles them to certain rights under the law. Transgender women do not require these rights, as they lack the biological features necessary for bearing children and are therefore not actually women. This epistemic position fueled the political argument, which tapped into the logic of rightful citizenship claims to pose rights gains and political attention as zero sum. Antigender feminists asserted that the uptick in attention to transgender women and transgender rights more generally corresponds to a proportionate loss of awareness for nontrans women's rights. They argued that this set the stage for abortion to be rolled back due to public attention devoted to transgender rights. Since transgender women are not, in their reasoning, women, those who extend rights to them are living in a state of false consciousness that must be corrected through vigorous education campaigns aimed at reclaiming public space from transgender women.[9]

Outrage from radical lesbian feminists and newly rebranded antigender feminists has simmered since Robin Morgan first took the stage at the 1973 West Coast Women's Music Festival to assert that transgender women are tantamount to rape in women's spaces. It has recently boiled over as political actors on the Far Right mobilize divisive rhetoric to pit nondominant groups against each other while they move the ball forward on global fascism.[10] Actor Bette Midler captured these dynamics unfolding in real time in a Twitter post shortly after the *Dobbs* decision was announced: "WOMEN OF THE WORLD! We are being stripped of our rights over our bodies, our lives and even our name! They don't call us 'women' anymore; they call us 'birthing people' or 'menstruators', and even 'people with vaginas'! Don't let them erase you! Every human on earth owes you!" According to Midler—and others like her—the evolution of gender-affirming language is to blame for losses in rights because these linguistic shifts erase the specificity of women, biologically defined. The logic of rightful citizenship claims fueled statements such as these through the explicit assertion that women are denied rights that they would be afforded were it not for their biological sex. It also points to the broader theme of exclusion that undergirds the examination of rightful citizenship claims at the center of this book. Across six chapters and in these three case studies, political actors have sought legibility, inclusion, and recognition in a liberal legal and political system that can address political grievances only along a single axis. With respect to Pride flags and Swift's utopia, that difference is sexuality. For antigender abortion advocates, it is woman understood as biological difference captured in the capacity for pregnancy. The persistent and enduring patterns of exclusion that follow these unitary and mutually exclusive articulations of identity—and, with them, political agendas—show that while rights wins may go some way in ameliorating the conditions of harm experienced by groups, they do so only superficially and conditionally. This is due to rightful citizenship claims foreclosing possibilities for challenging norms. Antigender feminists illustrate this when they assert that biology is not destiny (women should have rights over their bodies, as men do) but that biology is destiny (trans women are not women and therefore have no rights) to secure the right of bodily autonomy. Left unquestioned in this formulation is the logic of gender as a strict binary, let alone a rubric for allocating or exercising rights. Claiming rights as women, in other words, paints a target on their backs to lose rights as women. This is because rightful citizenship claims leave in place the political systems, ideologies, laws, and structures that create vulnerability. Rights wins in this view are at best Pyrrhic victories.

Thinking Outside of Rightful Citizenship Claims

The in-depth analysis of rightful citizenship claims in this book sheds light on a relatively underexplored aspect of social movement and interest group politics, namely the political strategies that shape the well-documented exclusions of certain members from identity-based groups.[11] Whereas scholars and pundits take for granted the centrality of rights claims by marginalized groups and theorize that political movements evolve from naming shared political grievances and mobilizing to make claims on the rights and responsibilities promised by citizenship, the analysis in this book paints a different picture, one marked by debates and ruptures as political actors and members themselves engage in conflicts over the boundaries of identity and the issues to be prioritized.[12] Highlighting these voices disrupts the teleological account of gay, lesbian, bisexual, transgender, and LGBT politics that celebrates certain victories—such as marriage equality and opportunities to serve in the military—as evidence of a steady march of progress for the LGBT group. This approach also underscores the costs of rights claims as a political strategy by devoting attention to moments when political actors identify the material and epistemic effects of the erasures associated with rightful citizenship claims. These include the enduring silence around bisexuality by mainstream gay and lesbian political organizations and inadequate attention devoted to addressing the most common obstacles that transgender and gender-nonconforming people confront daily. Failure to address the issues affecting these populations is not simply the byproduct of an incremental approach to political change; rather, as I argue throughout this book, these exclusions are a constitutive feature of political mobilizations organized around rightful citizenship claims.

The enduring dynamics of contestation and contingency embedded in movements organized around identity contain two implications for political praxis, particularly with respect to the use of rights discourse to frame political problems and solutions. First, I have shown numerous instances when advocates favoring rightful citizenship claims implicitly and explicitly recognize the limitations of such appeals, particularly with respect to addressing the interests of women, people of color, bisexuals, and transgender people, and yet these limitations persist due to the assumption that rights are the most politically expedient strategy available. What is more, they persist even when those who will be excluded object and articulate how they will be left behind. Second, contemporary developments—such as the Supreme Court's elimination of abortion rights and the subsequent fretting over same-sex marriage rights—call into question the resilience of rights wins. Structural solutions, and not rights, have the potential to address political problems in far more durable ways given these changes to rights. These include framing abortion as a public health issue, decoupling tax and insurance benefits from marriage, seeking the provision of universal healthcare, and abolishing the prison industrial complex. Extending these observations to the realm of political praxis indicates that political actors ought to consider revising the ways they deploy, develop, and make political claims in three ways.

First, this study suggests that rightful citizenship claims should be deprioritized as a movement strategy in favor of grassroots and agonistic approaches to agenda development. This means paying attention during moments of conflict, when segments of membership forcefully articulate that they are being left behind. These statements often provide thorough roadmaps for alternative strategies that political organizations can pursue. Additionally, these conflicts frequently take the form of members creating separate organizations to advocate a different political agenda. Interest group and social movement scholarship highlights many advantages of coalitions, not least of which is the opportunity to pool material and intangible resources.[13] Organizations that have been subject to critique might benefit by becoming earnest partners in coalitional mobilizations to address issues outside of rightful citizenship claims and, in so doing, share work in shaping what Courtenay Daum refers to as "vibrant counterpublics" where new discourses and dialogues of liberation can develop.[14] Partnerships such as these would disrupt the binary understanding of power that poses marginalized people against oppressors, and replace it with attention to the ways that ideologies such as White supremacy, heteropatriarchy, and nativism shape hierarchies of belonging.[15] Doing so might also help political leaders develop what Cricket Keating refers to as a "coalitional consciousness," whereby the education they receive from coalition partners changes how they understand and approach political problems.[16]

The second suggestion relates directly to the first and concerns prioritizing equity in outcomes versus equality in opportunities. One of the primary justifications for rights claims and incremental strategies hinges on the assertion that there is a strategic sequencing of objectives that must take place to achieve results. The intersectional approach used in this study shows, however, that these piecemeal approaches often succeed in bringing a very select few over the finish line of political wins. For example, while marriage equality applies to all same-sex couples, enduring structural obstacles—such as growing wealth disparities and ongoing anti-Black racism—mean that it is primarily White gay and lesbian couples that have been positioned to take advantage of this new right.[17] Developing political objectives with equity in mind attunes political leaders to different priorities. In the case of marriage equality, alternatives focused on equity would seek reforms to the tax code, which disproportionately benefit married couples, as well as pushes for universal healthcare to decouple employment status from accessing medical treatments.[18] Prioritizing these goals would benefit a broader range of the polity. They would also be relatively more resistant to aggressive backlash from opponents because, as Alison Gash suggests, they would take place "below the radar" and sidestep scrutiny.[19]

Finally, this study points to the perils of conceiving identity and political agendas narrowly and along a single axis. Although liberalism rewards the naming of rights claims in relation to subject positions that are understood as unitary and mutually exclusive, the lived experience of people affected by political, social, and economic marginalization reveals multiple and interlocking hierarchies of belonging as the culprits that foreclose opportunities to participate, let alone thrive, in democratic institutions. These include White supremacy, capitalism, patriarchy, the gender binary, heteronormativity, Christian normativity, ableism, nativism, and citizenship—among many others. Neglecting to consider how these ideologies shape what comes to be thought of as identity and political problems means that political practitioners and scholars will be increasingly out of touch with the political lives of those they claim to be interested in aiding and understanding. Employing intersectionality as an analytic perspective directs scholarly attention to these dynamics and offers ways to produce more nuanced understandings of political struggles. It also stands to benefit practitioners in identifying the roots of political problems. Taken together, these interventions potentially hold the key to building stronger and broader movements to effect political change. If recent and impending rollbacks of rights are any indication, we will need all the tools of queer, feminist, and trans world-building we can get.

Critical Discourse Analysis Codes Used

This appendix provides the codes using in the first and second stages of coding. They are organized by overarching themes or linguistic devices with nested codes specifying content.

First- and Second-Stage Codes

- Analogy
  o Analogy-BisexualGay
  o Analogy-Ethnic
  o Analogy-Minorities
  o Analogy-Race
  o Analogy-Religion
  o Analogy-Straight
  o Analogy-Women

- Conflict
  o Conflict-Agenda
  o Conflict-AntiWoman
  o Conflict-Exclusive
  o Conflict-Inclusive
  o Conflict-Meaning
  o Conflict-Members

- Linkages
  o Link-AntiClassism
  o Link-AntiSexism
  o Link-AntiTrans&Gay = Sexism
  o Link-BiQueer
  o Link-BisexualFeminism
  o Link-BisexualGenderFluidity
  o Link-BiTrans
  o Link-BQ
  o Link-Community
  o Link-Gay&AIDS = ExcWomen
  o Link-Gender
  o Link-GL
  o Link-GLB
  o Link-GLBT
  o Link-GLBTQ
  o Link-GQ
  o Link-Lesbian&Feminism
  o Link-Marginalization

- o Link-Race
- o Link-Racism
- o Link-Transgender
- o Link-TransgenderGay
- o Link-TransWomen
- o Link-Women

- Representation
  - o Rep-Congress
  - o Rep-External
  - o Rep-Internal
  - o Rep-Media
  - o Rep-Members

- RightfulCitizenshipClaims
  - o RCC-AmericanValues
  - o RCC-Belonging
  - o RCC-Citizens
  - o RCC-Rights
  - o RCC-RoleofGov
  - o RCC-SecondClassCitizens
  - o RCC-Voting

- StigmaTransformation
  - o ST-Bisexuals
  - o ST-Citizens
  - o ST-Coalition
  - o ST-Compassion
  - o ST-Human
  - o ST-LikeStraightPeople
  - o ST-Monogamous
  - o ST-Moral
  - o ST-NonPathological
  - o ST-Positive
  - o ST-Unity

Notes

Introduction

1. Liam Stack, "Activist Removed after Heckling Obama at L.G.B.T. Event," *New York Times,* June 24, 2015.
2. Laura P. Minero, Sergio Domínguez Jr., Stephanie L. Budge, and Bamby Salcedo, "Latinx Trans Immigrants' Survival of Torture in U.S. Detention: A Qualitative Investigation of the p," n.d., 25.
3. Stack, "Activist."
4. Justin Wm. Moyer, "Transgender Obama Heckler Jennicet Gutierrez Hailed by Some LGBT Activists," *Washington Post,* June 26, 2015.
5. White House, "Opening the People's House," September 24, 2014, https://obamawhitehouse.archives.gov/blog/2014/09/15/opening-peoples-house.
6. Although ICE reported a significant decrease in "removals and returns" in 2015, this decrease was more than offset by the uptick of 2015 Department of Homeland Security removals and returns in the aggregate, which includes Border Patrol statistics. See "DHS Releases End of Fiscal Year 2015 Statistics," U.S. Immigration and Customs Enforcement, December 22, 2015, https://www.ice.gov/news/releases/dhs-releases-end-fiscal-year-2015-statistics; Maria Hinojosa, "Obama Leaves Office as 'Deporter in Chief,'" NPR, January 20, 2017, https://www.npr.org/2017/01/20/510799842/obama-leaves-office-as-deporter-in-chief.
7. Matthew Rodriguez, "I Stand with Obama Heckler Jennicet Gutierrez," *Advocate,* June 26, 2015.
8. Dawn Ennis, "Booking Jennicet Was Wrong, but Was What She Did Worse?," *Advocate,* July 1, 2015.
9. "Jim Obergefell Responds to Supreme Court Decision on Same-Sex Marriage" *PBS Newshour,* June 26, 2015, https://www.youtube.com/watch?v=qMxWLJGuPJk&t=226s.
10. Samantha Allen, "LGBT Leaders: Gay Marriage Is Not Enough," *Daily Beast,* June 26, 2015, http://www.thedailybeast.com/articles/2015/06/26/same-sex-marriage-is-legal-now-what.html, emphasis mine.
11. "Statement by the Vice President on the Supreme Court Decision in Obergefell v Hodges," White House, June 26, 2015, https://www.whitehouse.gov/the-press-office/2015/06/26/statement-vice-president-supreme-court-decision-obergefell-v-hodges, emphasis mine.
12. Amy L. Brandzel, *Against Citizenship: The Violence of the Normative* (Urbana: University of Illinois Press, 2016), 34.

13. In this book, I capitalize racial categories such as "Black" and "White" to signal that they are constructed racializations with significant consequents for who has access to resources. See Eve L. Ewing, "I'm a Black Scholar Who Studies Race. Here's Why I Capitalize White," Medium, July 2, 2020, https://zora.medium.com/im-a-black-scholar-who-studies-race-here-s-why-i-capitalize-white-f94883aa2dd3.

14. Dean Spade, "Fighting to Win," in *That's Revolting! Queer Strategies for Resisting Assimilation*, ed. Matilda Bernstein Sycamore (Berkeley, CA: Soft Skull, 2004), 53.

15. Jonathan Capehart, "Mourning Stormé DeLarverie, a Mother of the Stonewall Riots," *Washington Post*, June 3, 2014; Julia Jacobs, "Two Transgender Activists Are Getting a Monument in New York," *New York Times*, May 29, 2019; Solvej Schou, "Rolland Emmerich's 'Stonewall' Finds Controversy," *New York Times*, September 18, 2015.

16. Alison L. Gash, *Below the Radar: How Silence Can Save Civil Rights* (New York: Oxford University Press, 2015); Brian F. Harrison and Melissa R. Michelson, *Listen, We Need to Talk: How to Change Attitudes about LGBT Rights* (New York: Oxford University Press, 2017).

17. The words used to strive towards gender inclusion are constantly in flux. Throughout this work, I use "Latine" as a gender-inclusive alternative to Latino/a/x. Latine has been developed by Spanish-speakers as a substitute for Latinx, which is impossible to pronounce in Spanish. I have no doubt that more terms will proliferate to address this issue, but as of this writing in 2023, Latine is the best possible term. See: "Latine vs Latine: How and Why They're Used," Dictionary.com, September 26, 2023, https://www.dictionary.com/e/latine-vs-Latine/.

18. Robert Tracinski, "Federalism Has Its Limits, and Abortion Will Soon Test Them," *Discourse*, June 24, 2022, https://www.discoursemagazine.com/ideas/2022/06/24/federalism-has-its-limits-and-abortion-will-soon-test-them/.

19. A brief note on terminology: I take great care throughout this book to reflect the terms and initialism used by political actors in each respective time period. As the following chapters will underscore in detail, the ordering of the various identities in the initialism has been hotly contested, with many asserting that "gay" belongs first as it captures same-sex sexuality, while others insert "lesbian" at the beginning to contest the historic dominance of gay men over the political group. "Q," for "queer," was appended to the initialism used by many of the interest groups and social movements discussed in this book in 2016. When I refer to LGBTQ in this book, it gestures to the use of that initialism by individuals and organizations themselves. In international contexts, other initialisms proliferate, with SOGI (Sexual Orientation and Gender Identity) used to identify what in the United States circulates as "LGBT" and its variants. It is due to these contingencies, contestations, and unsettled terms that I take great care to use terms that reflect specific political and social contexts over time.

20. Gabriele Magni and Andrew Reynolds, "Voter Preferences and the Political Underrepresentation of Minority Groups: Lesbian, Gay, and Transgender Candidates in Advanced Democracies," *The Journal of Politics* 83, no. 4 (October 2021): 17.

21. "Legislation Affecting LGBTQ Rights across the Country," American Civil Liberties Association, July 1, 2022, https://www.aclu.org/legislation-affecting-lgbtq-rights-across-country.

22. In formulating this argument, I draw on Leela Fernandes's disruption of the "wave narrative" in feminism, which poses feminist thinking as a teleology of inclusion and consequently elides the many thinkers who worked across and within what are typically glossed as second-, third-, and fourth-wave feminism. See Leela Fernandes, "Unsettling 'Third Wave Feminism,'" in *No Permanent Waves*, ed. Nancy A. Hewitt (New Brunswick, NJ: Rutgers University Press, 2010), 98–118.

23. Emily K. Hobson, *Lavender and Red: Liberation and Solidarity in the Gay and Lesbian Left*, vol. 44 (Berkeley: University of California Press, 2016).

24. Sina Kramer, *Excluded Within: The (Un)Intelligibility of Radical Political Actors* (New York: Oxford University Press, 2017), 6.

25. See also Joshua Gamson, "Must Identity Movements Self-Destruct? A Queer Dilemma," *Social Problems* 42, no. 3 (1995): 390–407.

26. Cristina Beltrán, *The Trouble with Unity: Latino Politics and the Creation of Identity* (Oxford: Oxford University Press, 2010); Cathy J. Cohen, *The Boundaries of Blackness: AIDS and the Breakdown of Black Politics* (Chicago: University of Chicago Press, 1999).

27. Kimberle Crenshaw, "Demarginalizing the Intersection of Race and Sex: A Black Feminist Critique of Antidiscrimination Doctrine, Feminist Theory and Antiracist Politics," *University of Chicago Legal Forum* 1989 (1989): 139–67.

28. Courtenay W. Daum, *The Politics of Right Sex: Transgressive Bodies, Governmentality, and the Limits of Trans Rights* (Albany: State University of New York Press, 2020).

29. Erin Mayo-Adam, *Queer Alliances: How Power Shapes Political Movement Formation* (Palo Alto, CA: Stanford University Press, 2020).

30. Wendy Brown, "Suffering the Paradoxes of Rights," in *Left Legalism/Left Critique*, eds. Wendy Brown and Janet Halley (Durham, NC: Duke University Press, 2002), 420–34; Judith Butler, *Excitable Speech: A Politics of the Performative* (New York: Routledge, 2013); David Eng, *The Feeling of Kinship: Queer Liberalism and the Racialization of Intimacy* (Durham, NC: Duke University Press, 2010); Lisa Duggan, *The Twilight of Equality? Neoliberalism, Cultural Politics, and the Attack on Democracy* (Boston: Beacon Press, 2004); Chandan Reddy, *Freedom with Violence: Race, Sexuality, and the U.S. State* (Durham, NC: Duke University Press, 2011).

31. Sumi Cho, Kimberlé Williams Crenshaw, and Leslie McCall, "Toward a Field of Intersectionality Studies: Theory, Applications, and Praxis," *Signs* 38, no. 4 (2013): 785–810, https://doi.org/10.1086/669608; K. Crenshaw, "Mapping the Margins: Intersectionality, Identity Politics, and Violence against Women of Color," *Stanford Law Review* 43, no. 6 (1991): 1241–99.

32. Dara Z. Strolovitch, *Affirmative Advocacy: Race, Class, and Gender in Interest Group Politics* (Chicago: University of Chicago Press, 2007); Spade, "Fighting to Win."

33. Cathy J. Cohen, "Punks, Bulldaggers, and Welfare Queens: The Radical Potential of Queer Politics?," *GLQ: A Journal of Lesbian and Gay Studies* 3, no. 4 (May 1, 1997): 437–65, https://doi.org/10.1215/10642684-3-4-437; Cathy Cohen, "The Radical Potential of Queer? Twenty Years Later," *GLQ: A Journal of Lesbian and Gay Studies* 25, no. 1 (2019): 140–44.

34. Angela Y. Davis, *Abolition Democracy: Beyond Empire, Prisons, and Torture* (New York: Seven Stories Press, 2011); Angela Y. Davis, *Freedom Is a Constant Struggle: Ferguson, Palestine, and the Foundations of a Movement* (Chicago: Haymarket Books, 2016).

35. Patricia Hill Collins, *Black Feminist Thought: Knowledge, Consciousness, and the Politics of Empowerment* (New York: Routledge, 2002); Patricia Hill Collins, *Fighting Words: Black Women and the Search for Justice*, vol. 7 (Minneapolis: University of Minnesota Press, 1998); Mari J. Matsuda, *Where Is Your Body? And Other Essays on Race, Gender, and the Law* (Boston: Beacon Press, 1997).

36. Samuel R. Delany, *Times Square Red, Times Square Blue*, 20th anniversary edition (New York: NYU Press, 2019); Steven M. Engel and Timothy S. Lyle, *Disrupting Dignity: Rethinking Power and Progress in LGBTQ Lives* (New York: New York University Press, 2021).

37. Janet Mock, *Redefining Realness: My Path to Womanhood, Identity, Love & So Much More*, Reprint edition (Atria Books, 2014), 256, emphasis mine.

Chapter 1

1. Eric E. Schattschneider, *The Semisovereign People: A Realist's View of Democracy in America*, revised edition (Hinsdale, IL: Wadsworth, 1975). See also David Bicknell Truman, *The Governmental Process: Political Interests and Public Opinion* (New York: Knopf, 1951).

2. Cohen, *Boundaries of Blackness*; Crenshaw, "Demarginalizing the Intersection of Race and Sex"; Strolovitch, *Affirmative Advocacy*.

3. Stephen M. Engel, *Fragmented Citizens: The Changing Landscape of Gay and Lesbian Lives* (New York: NYU Press, 2019); Anne Norton, *Reflections on Political Identity* (Baltimore, MD: Johns Hopkins University Press, 1988); Rogers M. Smith, *Stories of Peoplehood: The Politics and Morals of Political Membership* (Cambridge: Cambridge University Press, 2003).

4. Karen Zivi, *Making Rights Claims: A Practice of Democratic Citizenship* (New York: Oxford University Press, 2011); Brown, "Suffering the Paradoxes of Rights."

5. Brandzel, *Against Citizenship*.

6. Henri Tajfel and J. C. Turner, "The Social Identity Theory of Inter-Group Behavior," in *Psychology of Intergroup Relations*, ed. Stephen Worchel and William G. Austin (Chicago: Nelson Hall, 1986), 7–24.

7. Francesca Polletta and James M. Jasper, "Collective Identity and Social Movements," *Annual Review of Sociology* 27 (2001): 282–305. See also Jo Reger, "Identity Work, Sameness, and Difference in Social Movements," in *Identity Work in Social Movements*, ed. Jo Reger, Daniel J. Myers, and Rachel L. Einwohner (Minneapolis: University of Minnesota Press, 2008), 1–17.

8. Political process theory and resource mobilization theory use the concepts of political opportunity structure, framing, and mobilizing structures to argue that social movement mobilization is predicted and shaped by shifts in political and social

context. See Doug McAdam, *Political Process and the Development of Black Insurgency* (Chicago: University of Chicago Press, 1982); Doug McAdam, John D. McCarthy, and Mayer N. Zald, eds., *Comparative Perspectives on Social Movements: Political Opportunities, Mobilizing Structures, and Cultural Framings* (Cambridge: Cambridge University Press, 1996); David S. Meyer and Suzanne Staggenborg, "Movements, Countermovements, and the Structure of Political Opportunity," *American Journal of Sociology* 101, no. 6 (1996): 1628–60; Sidney Tarrow, *Power in Movement: Social Movements and Contentious Politics*, 2nd edition (Cambridge: Cambridge University Press, 1998); Charles Tilly, *From Mobilization to Revolution* (New York: McGraw Hill, 1978).

9. Reger, "Identity Work, Sameness, and Difference in Social Movements."
10. Jo Reger, Daniel J. Myers, and Rachel L. Einwohner, eds., *Identity Work in Social Movements* (Minneapolis: University of Minnesota Press, 2008). For new social movements, see Steven M. Buechler, "New Social Movement Theories," *Sociological Quarterly* 36, no. 3 (June 1, 1995): 441–64, https://doi.org/10.1111/j.1533-8525.1995.tb00447.x; Bert Klandermans, "New Social Movements and Resource Mobilization: The European and American Approach Revisited," *Politics & the Individual* 1, no. 2 (1986): 13–37; Alberto Melucci, *Nomads of the Present* (Philadelphia, PA: Temple University Press, 1989).
11. Polletta and Jasper, "Collective Identity and Social Movements."
12. Erving Goffman, *Frame Analysis: An Essay on the Organization of Experience* (Cambridge, MA: Harvard University Press, 1974), 21.
13. Robert D. Benford and David A. Snow, "Framing Processes and Social Movements: An Overview and Assessment," *Annual Review of Sociology* 26 (2000): 614.
14. Polletta and Jasper, "Collective Identity and Social Movements"; Deborah B. Gould, *Moving Politics: Emotion and ACT UP's Fight against AIDS* (Chicago: University of Chicago Press, 2009).
15. Verta Taylor and Nancy Whittier, "Collective Identity in Social Movement Communities: Lesbian Feminist Mobilization," in *Frontiers in Social Movement Theory*, ed. Carol McClurg Mueller and Aldon D. Morris (New Haven, CT: Yale University Press, 1992), 104–29.
16. Robert D. Benford, "Frame Disputes within the Nuclear Disarmament Movement," *Social Forces* 71, no. 3 (1993): 677–701, https://doi.org/10.1093/sf/71.3.677; Mary Bernstein, "Celebration and Suppression: The Strategic Uses of Identity by the Lesbian and Gay Movement," *American Journal of Sociology* 103, no. 3 (November 1, 1997): 531–65; Mary Bernstein and Kristine A. Olsen, "Identity Deployment and Social Change: Understanding Identity as a Social Movement and Organizational Strategy," *Sociology Compass* 3, no. 6 (2009): 871–83; Jo Reger, "Organizational Dynamics and Construction of Multiple Feminist Identities in the National Organization for Women," *Gender and Society* 16, no. 5 (October 2002): 710–27; Sheldon Stryker, Timothy Joseph Owens, and Robert W. White, eds., *Self, Identity, and Social Movements* (Minneapolis: University of Minnesota Press, 2000).
17. Gamson, "Must Identity Movements Self-Destruct?"
18. Bernstein and Olsen, "Identity Deployment and Social Change," 872.

19. Norton, *Reflections on Political Identity*.

20. William E. Connolly, *Identity\Difference: Democratic Negotiations of Political Paradox*, expanded revised edition (Minneapolis: University of Minnesota Press, 2002), 64.

21. Rogers Brubaker and Frederick Cooper, "Beyond 'Identity,'" *Theory & Society* 29 (2000): 5.

22. Using the language of positivist social science, the differences underscored here can be thought of as approaching identities as dependent variables—factors to be explained—rather than independent variables: factors that explain outcomes.

23. Norton, *Reflections on Political Identity*.

24. Iris Marion Young, *Justice and the Politics of Difference* (Princeton, NJ: Princeton University Press, 1990).

25. Nancy Fraser, "Recognition or Redistribution? A Critical Reading of Iris Young's Justice and the Politics of Difference," *Journal of Political Philosophy* 3 (1995): 166–80.

26. Cohen, *Boundaries of Blackness*, 10.

27. Ibid., ch. 3. For more on stereotypes of Black sexuality as a way to naturalize racial difference, see Patricia Hill Collins, *Black Sexual Politics: African Americans, Gender, and the New Racism* (New York: Routledge, 2004); Melissa V. Harris Perry, *Sister Citizen: Shame, Stereotypes, and Black Women in America* (New Haven, CT: Yale University Press, 2011).

28. For a more contemporary exploration of these dynamics of within-group marginalization in Black politics and its effects, see Keeanga-Yamahtta Taylor, *From #BlackLivesMatter to Black Liberation* (Chicago: Haymarket Books, 2016).

29. Beltrán, *The Trouble with Unity*.

30. Strolovitch, *Affirmative Advocacy*, 10.

31. Proponents of pluralism celebrate the proliferation of interest groups as opportunities to provide representation for groups and issues that are not addressed in a two-party system. See Robert Dahl, *A Preface to Democratic Theory* (Chicago: University of Chicago Press, 1956).

32. T. H. Marshall, *Class, Citizenship, and Social Development: Essays by T. H. Marshall* (New York: Doubleday, 1965).

33. Elizabeth F. Cohen and Cyril Ghosh, *Citizenship* (Medford, MA: Polity Press, 2019); Elizabeth F. Cohen, *Semi-Citizenship in Democratic Politics* (Cambridge: Cambridge University Press, 2009); Julie Novkov, "Sacrifice and Civic Membership: The War on Terror (2010)," paper presented at APSA 2010 Annual Meeting, https://ssrn.com/abstract=1643175, 4.

34. Patricia Hill Collins, "Like One of the Family: Race, Ethnicity, and the Paradox of US National Identity," *Ethnic and Racial Studies* 24, no. 1 (2001): 7, https://doi.org/10.1080/014198701750052479.

35. Judith N. Shklar, *American Citizenship: The Quest for Inclusion* (Cambridge, MA: Harvard University Press, 1991).

36. Collins, "Like One of the Family," 24.

37. Lauren Berlant, *The Queen of America Goes to Washington City* (Durham, NC: Duke University Press, 2002), https://www.dukeupress.edu/the-queen-of-america-goes-to-washington-city; Cristina Beltrán, *Cruelty as Citizenship: How Migrant Suffering Sustains White Democracy* (Minneapolis: University of Minnesota Press, 2020).

38. Collins, "Like One of the Family," 19.

39. Scott Lauria Morgensen, *Spaces between Us: Queer Settler Colonialism and Indigenous Decolonization* (Minneapolis: University of Minnesota Press, 2011); Adam Dahl, *Empire of the People: Settler Colonialism and the Foundations of Modern Democratic Thought* (Lawrence: University Press of Kansas, 2018).

40. Lisa Lowe, *Immigrant Acts: On Asian American Cultural Politics* (Durham, NC: Duke University Press, 1996), 11.

41. Ibid.

42. M. Jacki Alexander, "Not Just (Any) Body Can Be a Citizen: The Politics of Law, Sexuality and Postcoloniality in Trinidad and Tobago and the Bahamas," *Feminist Review*, no. 48 (1994): 5–23; Collins, "Like One of the Family."

43. Eithne Luibheid, "Introduction: Queering Migration and Citizenship," in *Queer Migrations: Sexuality, U.S. Citizenship, and Border Crossings*, ed. Eithne Luibheid and Lionel Cantú (Minneapolis: University of Minnesota Press, 2005), xiv.

44. Siobhan Somerville, "Sexual Aliens and the Racialized State: A Queer Reading of the 1952 U.S. Immigration and Nationality Act," in *Queer Migrations: Sexuality, U.S. Citizenship, and Border Crossings*, ed. Eithne Luibheid and Lionel Cantú (Minneapolis: University of Minnesota Press, 2005), 75–91.

45. While some scholars celebrate the provision of GI benefits to marginalized groups, especially Mexican American veterans, the denial of those benefits to Black veterans has been well documented as a political project to accommodate formal segregation in the Jim Crow South as well as de facto segregation in the North, the legacies of which account for the persisting racial wealth gap. See Trymaine Lee, "A Vast Wealth Gap, Driven by Segregation, Redlining, Evictions and Exclusion, Separates Black and While America," *New York Times*, August 14, 2019, https://www.nytimes.com/interactive/2019/08/14/magazine/racial-wealth-gap.html; Margot Canaday, *The Straight State: Sexuality and Citizenship in Twentieth-Century America* (Princeton, NJ: Princeton University Press, 2009); Steven Rosales, "Fighting the Peace at Home: Mexican American Veterans and the 1944 GI Bill of Rights," *Pacific Historical Review* 80, no. 4 (November 1, 2011): 597–627, https://doi.org/10.1525/phr.2011.80.4.597.

46. Both the Electoral College and the U.S. Senate are designed to insulate the federal government from popular influence by subverting direct democracy. Historically, these institutions gave outsized influence to voters in southern states to preserve slavery. These patterns endure in contemporary politics to marginalized Black voters. See Wilfred Condrington III, "The Electoral College's Racist Origins," *The Atlantic*, November 17, 2019.

47. Martin Luther King Jr established the Poor People's Campaign after these legislative victories to address the ongoing problem of poverty, which scholars interpret as evidence of the failure of rights wins to fully address pervasive inequities wrought by racial capitalism. See Gordon K. Mantler, *Power to the Poor: Black-Brown Coalition and the Fight for Economic Justice, 1960–1974* (Chapel Hill: University of North Carolina Press, 2013).

48. Reddy, *Freedom with Violence*; Lowe, *Immigrant Acts*; Cedric J. Robinson, *Black Marxism: The Making of the Black Radical Tradition,* revised and updated 3rd edition (Chapel Hill: University of North Carolina Press, 2020); Taylor, *From #BlackLivesMatter to Black Liberation.*

49. Zivi, *Making Rights Claims.*

50. Mayo-Adam, *Queer Alliances.*

51. Joseph Mello, *The Courts, the Ballot Box, and Gay Rights: How Our Governing Institutions Shape the Same-Sex Marriage Debate* (Lawrence: University Press of Kansas, 2016).

52. Brown, "Suffering the Paradoxes of Rights."

53. Gayatri Chakravorty Spivak, *Outside in the Teaching Machine* (New York: Routledge, 2012).

54. The notable exception here are Mayo-Adam's "intersectional translators" in *Queer Alliances*, who are typically not citizens; however, it should be noted that the alliances they form are often at the sites of rights claims made by dominant groups.

55. Brown, "Suffering the Paradoxes of Rights"; Butler, *Excitable Speech* (2013).

56. Hannah Arendt, *The Origins of Totalitarianism* (New York: Schocken Books, 1948).

57. Zivi, *Making Rights Claims*; Drucilla Cornell, "Bodily Integrity and the Right to Abortion," in *Identities, Politics, and Rights*, ed. Austin Sarat and Thomas R. Kearns, Amherst Series in Law, Jurisprudence, and Social Thought (Ann Arbor: University of Michigan Press, 1995), 21–84.

58. Cynthia Weber, *Queer International Relations: Sovereignty, Sexuality and the Will to Knowledge* (New York: Oxford University Press, 2016).

59. Strolovitch, *Affirmative Advocacy*; Sheldon Stryker, "Identity Competition: Key to Differential Social Movement Participation," in *Self, Identity, and Social Movement*, ed. Sheldon Stryker, Timothy J. Owens, and Robert W. White (Minneapolis: University of Minnesota Press, 2000), 21–40; Katherine Cramer Walsh, *Talking about Politics: Informal Groups and Social Identity in American Life* (Chicago: University of Chicago Press, 2004); Melissa S. Williams, *Voice, Trust, and Memory: Marginalized Groups and the Failings of Liberal Representation* (Princeton, NJ: Princeton University Press, 1998); Nadia Urbinati, "Representation as Advocacy: A Study of Democratic Deliberation," *Political Theory* 28, no. 6 (December 2000): 758–86.

60. Matthew Dean Hindman, *Political Advocacy and Its Interested Citizens: Neoliberalism, Postpluralism, and LGBT Organizations* (Philadelphia: University of Pennsylvania Press, 2018).

61. Bisexuals are excluded because they were seldom included in mainstream efforts to transform stigmas associated with marginalized sexuality.

62. Ange-Marie Hancock, "Intersectionality as a Normative and Empirical Paradigm," *Politics & Gender* 3, no. 2 (2007): 351; see also Evelyn M. Simien, "Doing Intersectionality Research: From Conceptual Issues to Practical Examples," *Politics & Gender* 3, no. 2 (June 2007): 264–71.

63. Rita Kaur Dhamoon, "Considerations on Mainstreaming Intersectionality," *Political Research Quarterly* 64, no. 1 (March 1, 2011): 240.

64. Cho, Crenshaw, and McCall, "Toward a Field of Intersectionality Studies"; Ange-Marie Hancock, "Empirical Intersectionality: A Tale of Two Approaches," *University of California Irvine Law Review* 312 (October 2013): 259–94.

65. Crenshaw, "Mapping the Margins," 1298.

66. Michel Foucault, "The Subject and Power," *Critical Inquiry* 8, no. 4 (1982): 780.

67. Mitch Berbrier, "Making Minorities: Cultural Space, Stigma Transformation Frames, and the Categorical Status Claims of Deaf, Gay, and White Supremacist Activists in Late Twentieth Century America," *Sociological Forum* 17, no. 4 (December 1, 2002): 553–91, https://doi.org/10.1023/A:1021025307028.

68. Brittney C. Cooper, *Beyond Respectability: The Intellectual Thought of Race Women* (Urbana: University of Illinois Press, 2017); Evelyn Brooks Higginbotham, *Righteous Discontent: The Women's Movement in the Black Baptist Church, 1880–1920* (Cambridge, MA: Harvard University Press, 1993); Dara Z. Strolovitch and Chaya Y. Crowder, "Respectability, Anti-Respectability, and Intersectionally Responsible Representation," *PS: Political Science & Politics* 51, no. 2 (April 2018): 340–44, https://doi.org/10.1017/S1049096517002487.

69. Williams, *Voice, Trust, and Memory*; see also Strolovitch, *Affirmative Advocacy*, 58–60.

70. Lisa Disch, "The Impurity of Representation and the Vitality of Democracy," *Cultural Studies* 26, nos. 2–3 (2012): 207–22.

71. Cho, Crenshaw, and McCall, "Toward a Field of Intersectionality Studies"; Dhamoon, "Considerations on Mainstreaming Intersectionality"; Hancock, "Intersectionality as a Normative and Empirical Paradigm"; Simien, "Doing Intersectionality Research"; Leslie McCall, "The Complexity of Intersectionality," *Signs: Journal of Women in Culture and Society* 30, no. 3 (2005): 1771–800; Strolovitch, *Affirmative Advocacy*.

72. Francisco Panizza and Romina Miorelli, "Taking Discourse Seriously: Discursive Institutionalism and Post-Structuralist Discourse Theory," *Political Studies* 61, no. 2 (2013): 301–18, https://doi.org/10.1111/j.1467-9248.2012.00967.x; Ruth Wodak, *Methods of Critical Discourse Analysis* (London: Sage, 2009).

73. Peregrine Schwartz-Shea and Dvora Yanow, *Interpretive Research Design: Concepts and Processes* (New York: Routledge, 2013); Dvora Yanow and Peregrine Schwartz-Shea, *Interpretation and Method: Empirical Research Methods and the Interpretive Turn* (New York: Routledge, 2015).

74. I outline these two modes in this section and specify the mechanics of how one conducts CDA in the appendix.

75. The political Right favors analogies to the Revolutionary War, captured in maxims such the Gadsden Flag's warning, "Don't Tread on Me," to highlight the emphasis on negative rights, or freedom from state interference.

76. Judith Butler, *Excitable Speech: A Politics of the Performative* (New York: Routledge, 1997).

77. Wodak, *Methods of Critical Discourse Analysis*.

78. A comprehensive list of my coding scheme can be found in the appendix.

Chapter 2

1. Elizabeth A. Armstrong and Suzanna M. Crage, "Movements and Memory: The Making of the Stonewall Myth," *American Sociological Review* 71, no. 5 (October 1, 2006): 724–51, https://doi.org/10.1177/000312240607100502; David Carter, *Stonewall: The Riots That Sparked the Gay Revolution* (New York: St. Martin's Press, 2010); Martin Bauml Duberman, *Stonewall* (New York: Plume, 1994).

2. Neil Miller, *Out of the Past: Gay and Lesbian History from 1869 to the Present* (New York: Alyson Books, 2006), 338–39.

3. Social clubs for gay men and lesbians proliferated during the post–World War II era through the end of the 1960s and were organized to maintain the privacy of members while also facilitating connections. See John D'Emilio, *Sexual Politics, Sexual Communities: The Making of a Homosexual Minority in the United States, 1940–1970* (Chicago: University of Chicago Press, 1983).

4. The Stonewall riots are used here to epitomize the shift toward public protests that precipitated the beginning of the Gay Liberation period; however, there were other, equally radical riots that precipitated the Stonewall riots. See Susan Stryker, "Transgender History, Homonormativity, and Disciplinarity," *Radical History Review* 2008, no. 100 (December 21, 2008): 145–57.

5. Ensuring privacy for members was a priority for these organizations because members risked losing their jobs, homes, families, and friends if their interest in same-sex relationships was revealed. Privacy was maintained through elaborate organizational structures modeled in similar ways to terrorist cells (D'Emilio, *Sexual Politics, Sexual Communities*, 63–64).

6. See Elizabeth A. Armstrong, *Forging Gay Identities: Organizing Sexuality in San Francisco, 1950–1994* (Chicago: University of Chicago Press, 2002).

7. Donn Teal, *The Gay Militants* (New York: Stein and Day, 1971), 50–51.

8. Ibid., 55.

9. Armstrong and Crage, "Movements and Memory."

10. Wini Breines, *Community and Organization in the New Left, 1962–1968: The Great Refusal* (New Brunswick, NJ: Rutgers University Press, 1989).

11. Eric Marcus, *Making Gay History: The Half Century Fight for Lesbian and Gay Equal Rights*, reprint edition (New York: Harper Perennial, 2002), 137.

12. Ibid., 134.

13. See Betty Luther Hillman, "'The Most Revolutionary Act a Homosexual Can Engage In': Drag and the Politics of Gender Presentation in the San Francisco Gay Liberation Movement, 1964–1972," *Journal of the History of Sexuality* 20, no. 1 (2011): 153–81; Terrance Kissack, "Freaking Fag Revolutionaries: New York's Gay Liberation Front, 1969–1971," *Radical History Review*, no. 62 (1995): 104–34; Justin Suran, "Coming Out against the War: Antimilitarism and the Politicization of Homosexuality in the Era of Vietnam," *American Quarterly* 53, no. 3 (2001): 452–88.

14. GLF is just one example for a Gay Liberation political organization. For others, see Hobson, *Lavender and Red*.

15. Kissack, "Freaking Fag Revolutionaries," 123.

16. Huey P. Newton, "A Letter to Revolutionary Brothers and Sisters about the Women's Liberation and Gay Liberation Movements," in *Traps: African American Men on Gender and Sexuality*, ed. Rudolph P. Byrd and Beverly Guy-Sheftall (Indianapolis: University of Indiana Press, 2001), 281–83.

17. Hobson, *Lavender and Red*, 18.

18. "Letter by Bob Martin, Chairman of the Youth Committee of NACHO Addressed to the Marchers on Washington, November 15, 1969," *Come Out!* 1, no. 2 (January 10, 1970): 4 in *The* Come Out! *Reader*, ed. Stephen Donaldson, Perry Brass, and John Knobel (New York: Christopher Street Press, 2012), 49.

19. Ibid.

20. "Come Out!," *Come Out!* 1, no. 1 (November 1969): 1 in Donaldson, Brass, and Knobel, *The* Come Out! *Reader*, 29.

21. "Homosexuals. . . ," *Come Out!* 1, no. 3 (April–May 1970): 8 in Donaldson, Brass, and Knobel, *The* Come Out! *Reader*, 70.

22. Ibid., 9.

23. *Come Out!* 1, no. 7 (December 1970): 4 in Donaldson, Brass, and Knobel, *The* Come Out! *Reader*, 133.

24. Ad Hoc Gay Men's Committee, "On Liberalism," *Come Out!* 2, no. 8 (Winter 1972): 3

25. *Faggots and Faggotry*, abbreviated here as simply *Faggot*, was a zine produced by Ralph Hall, a GLF member. It circulated in New York City during the 1970s.

26. Gay Switchboard, *Come Out!* 2, no. 8 (Winter 1972): 4 in Donaldson, Brass, and Knobel, *The* Come Out! *Reader*, 187.

27. Steven Gavin, "Thoughts on the Movement: the Year of the Queer," *Come Out!* 2, no. 8 (Winter 1972): 20 in Donaldson, Brass, and Knobel, *The* Come Out! *Reader*, 203.

28. Hobson, *Lavender and Red*.

29. Armstrong, *Forging Gay Identities*, 86–87; Kissack, "Freaking Fag Revolutionaries," 166–67.

30. Martha Shelly, one of the founders of GLF, detailed these debates to fund the Panther 21 (Marcus, *Making Gay History*, 137–38).

31. Gay Activists Alliance, "The GAA Alternative," in *Speaking for Our Lives: Historic Speeches and Rhetoric for Gay and Lesbian Rights (1892–2000)*, ed. Robert B. Ridinger (New York: Harrington Park Press, 2004), 150.

32. Gay Activists Alliance, "The GAA Preamble," in Ridinger, *Speaking for Our Lives*, 148.

33. Quoted in Kay Tobin and Randy Wicker, *Gay Crusaders*, reprint edition (New York: Arno Press, 1975), 36.

34. Gay Activists Alliance, "The GAA Alternative," 155.

35. Ibid.

36. Ibid.

37. Ibid., 155–56.

38. Quoted in Tobin and Wicker, Gay Crusaders, 180.

39. Ibid., 181.

40. Scholars have written extensively on how this effectively created two movements: one for White gay people and one for gay people of color. See Cohen, *Boundaries of Blackness*, 91–99; Stryker, "Transgender History, Homonormativity,

and Disciplinarity"; David Valentine, *Imagining Transgender: An Ethnography of a Category* (Durham, NC: Duke University Press Books, 2007).

41. Marquis Bey, *The Problem of the Negro as a Problem for Gender* (Minneapolis: University of Minnesota Press, 2020); Heath Fogg Davis, *Beyond Trans: Does Gender Matter?* (New York: NYU Press, 2017); C. Riley Snorton, *Black on Both Sides: A Racial History of Trans Identity* (Minneapolis: University of Minnesota Press, 2017).

42. Gay Activists Alliance, "The GAA Alternative," 155.

43. Ibid.

44. Ibid., 191.

45. Ibid., 168.

46. Quoted in Tobin and Wicker, *Gay Crusaders*, 36.

47. Arthur Bell, "An Open Letter to Gay Activists Alliance," in Ridinger, *Speaking for Our Lives*, 145.

48. The antihierarchical organization of radical groups such as GLF often resulted in charismatic members dominating conversations and consequently further silencing the most marginalized members of these movements. See Alice Echols, *Daring to Be Bad* (Minneapolis: University of Minnesota Press, 1989), 17, https://www.upress. umn.edu/book-division/books/daring-to-be-bad.

49. eben clark, "An Article," *Come Out!* 2, no. 7b (Spring–Summer 1971): 7 in Donaldson, Brass, and Knobel, *The* Come Out! *Reader,* 164.

50. Ibid.

51. Shane Phelan, "(Be)Coming Out: Lesbian Identity and Politics," *Signs: Journal of Women in Culture and Society* 18, no. 4 (1993): 774.

52. Stephen P. Dansky, "*Come Out!* And the Pursuit of Identity," in Donaldson, Brass, and Knobel, *The* Come Out! *Reader,* 17.

53. Quoted in Pat Maxwell, "Homosexuals . . . in the Movement," *Come Out!* 1, no. 3 (April–May 1970): 9 in Donaldson, Brass, and Knobel, *The* Come Out! *Reader,* 71.

54. Leo Louis Martello, "A Positive Image," *Come Out!* 1, no. 1 (November 1969): 16 in Donaldson, Brass, and Knobel, *The* Come Out! *Reader,* 44.

55. The Gay Commandos, "The October Rebellion," *Come Out!* 1.1 in Donaldson, Brass, and Knobel, *The* Come Out! *Reader,* 33.

56. Gay Activists Alliance, "The GAA Alternative," 157.

57. Isaac Julien and Kobena Mercer, "True Confessions: A Discourse on Images of Black Male Sexuality," in *Brother to Brother: New Writings by Black Gay Men*, ed. Essex Hemphill (Boston: Alyson Publications, 1991), 168.

58. Cohen, *Boundaries of Blackness*, 92.

Chapter 3

1. Quoted in Marcus, *Making Gay History*, 154.

2. I am not satisfied with referring to the many different mobilizations that comprised what was understood to be "the women's movement" under the same umbrella term. As such, I will qualify each movement by referring to its main proponents.

For example, when I discuss the segment of the movement led by White feminists and institutionalized in organizations such as the National Organization for Women (NOW), I will use "mainstream women's movement" and "Third World feminist movement" when referring to mobilizations in the 1970s on behalf of what was then referred to as Third World people (Black, Latine, Asian, and Native).

3. People who might self-identify in contemporary terms as transgender used transsexual during this period. I discuss the history and significance of these shifts in chapter 4.

4. Hancock introduces this term in her history of intersectionality that locates its origins in Black feminist thinking that paid attention to multiple axes of identity and interlocking oppressions long before the eventual introduction of "intersectionality" by Kimberlé Williams Crenshaw in 1989.

5. Lorna N. Bracewell, *Why We Lost the Sex Wars: Sexual Freedom in the #MeToo Era* (Minneapolis: University of Minnesota Press, 2021).

6. Steve Dansky, "Hey Man," *Come Out!* 1, no. 4 (June–July 1970), in Donaldson, Brass, and Knobel, *The* Come Out! *Reader,* 85.

7. Dennis Altman, "One Man's Gay Liberation," *Come Out!* 1, no. 7 (December–January 1970–71), in Donaldson, Brass, and Knobel, *The* Come Out! *Reader,* 150.

8. *The Ladder, Come Out!,* and *Motive* are the publications with national circulations, and it is likely there were many smaller, local publications that featured the essay as its popularity drove its diffusion across audiences.

9. Del Martin, "If That's All There Is," *The Ladder* 15, nos. 3–4 (December–January 1970–71): 5.

10. Ibid., 4.

11. Lillian Faderman, *Odd Girls and Twilight Lovers* (New York: Columbia University Press, 1991), 21.

12. Martin, "If That's All There Is," 6.

13. Martha Shelley, "Stepin Fetchit Woman," *Come Out!* 1, no. 1 (November 1969): 7.

14. Ibid.

15. Freidan also publicly speculated that lesbians were CIA infiltrators dispatched to disrupt the NOW. See Laurie Johnston, "Mrs. Friedan's Essay Irks Feminists," *New York Times,* March 8, 1973.

16. For a comprehensive firsthand account of the lesbian purges at NOW in the late 1960s and early 1970s, see Del Martin and Phyllis Lyon, *Lesbian/Woman,* 4th edition (New York: Bantam Books, 1977).

17. Kissack, "Freaking Fag Revolutionaries," 122.

18. I use "sex" here instead of "gender" as it was the predominant term used at the time. It was often the case that Women's Movement discourse used "sex" to describe both the condition of being designated female at birth and the social effects of consequently identifying/being identified as a woman.

19. Radicalesbians, "The Woman-Identified Woman," Digital Scriptorium, Special Collections Library, Duke University (1970), https://repository.duke.edu/dc/wlmpc/wlmms01011.

20. Ibid., 1.

21. Taylor and Whittier, "Collective Identity in Social Movement Communities," 181–82.

22. Faderman, *Odd Girls and Twilight Lovers*, 218.

23. I use "sex assigned at birth" because it highlights the contingency of doctors using sexed genitalia to identify the sex, and consequently the gender, of infants.

24. I use "nontrans" here in place of "cisgender" out of concern for the ways that "cis-" and "trans-" recast gender identities in sexed and raced ways. See Bey, *The Problem of the Negro as a Problem for Gender*.

25. Radicalesbians, "The Woman-Identified Woman," 4.

26. For first-person accounts of the Radicalesbian action at the Second Congress to Unite Women, see Sidney Abbott and Barbara Love, *Sappho Was a Right-on Woman* (New York: Stein & Day, 1972); Deborah Goleman Wolf, *Lesbian Community* (Berkeley: University of California Press, 1979).

27. Echols, *Daring to Be Bad*, 4. See also Lorna Norman Bracewell, "Beyond Barnard: Liberalism, Antipornography Feminism, and the Sex Wars," *Signs: Journal of Women in Culture and Society* 42, no. 1 (2016): 23–48.

28. Wolf, *Lesbian Community*, 66.

29. Ibid., 67.

30. Echols, *Daring to Be Bad,* 10.

31. Leslie Springvine, "Out from under the Rocks with Guns!," *The Ladder* vol. 14, nos. 3 & 4 (December 1969–January 1970): 10.

32. Wilda Chase, "Lesbianism and Feminism," *The Ladder* 14, nos. 3–4 (1969–70): 13.

33. Scholars speculate that Morgan's comments were motivated by rumors that her belonging at a lesbian feminist conference would be questioned due to her marriage to a man. Her speech, written the night before, is interpreted as an effort to shift the focus away from her feminist *bona fides* and turn attention against transgender women at the conference. See Finn Engke, "Collective Memory and the Transfeminist 1970s." *TSQ: Transgender Studies Quarterly* 5, no. 1 (February 1, 2018): 9–29.

34. Robin Morgan, *Going Too Far: The Personal Chronicle of a Feminist* (New York: Random House, 1977), 180–81.

35. "Transsexual" is used here because it was the predominant term used during this time; I address the shifts in language from "transsexual" in the 1970s to "transgender" in the 1980s and 1990s in chapter 4.

36. Morgan, *Going Too Far*, 180.

37. For an examination of the historical uses of blackface to mark the boundaries of various groups and American national identity, see Michael Rogin, *Blackface, White Noise: Jewish Immigrants in the Hollywood Melting Pot* (Berkeley: University of California Press, 1996).

38. Morgan, *Going Too Far*, 180.

39. There is a broad range of scholarship on butch and femme lesbians and relationships during this period. See Abbott and Love, *Sappho Was a Right-on Woman*; Nan Alamilla Boyd, *Wide-Open Town: A History of Queer San Francisco to 1965* (Berkeley: University of California Press, 2003); Madeline Davis and Elizabeth Lapovsky Kennedy, *Boots of Leather, Slippers of Gold: The History of a Lesbian Community* (New York: Routledge, 1993); Amber Hollibaugh and Cherrie Moraga,

"What We're Rollin' Around in Bed With: Sexual Silences in Feminism," *Heresies* 12 (1981): 58–62; Faderman, *Odd Girls and Twilight Lovers*; Joan Nestle, "Butch-Femme Relationships: Sexual Courage in the 1950's," *Heresies* 12 (1981): 21–25; Gayle Rubin, "Of Catamites and Kings: Reflections on Butch, Gender, and Boundaries," in *The Persistent Desire: A Femme-Butch Reader*, ed. Joan Nestle (Boston: Alyson, 1992), 466–82.

40. Rubin, "Of Catamites and Kings"; Valentine, *Imagining Transgender*; Jack Halberstam, *Trans: A Quick and Quirky Account of Gender Variability*, vol. 3 (Berkeley: University of California Press, 2017).

41. For other examples of the seminal figures in radical feminism, see Mary Daly, *Gyn/Ecology: The Metaphysics of Radical Feminism* (Boston: Beacon Press, 1978); Germaine Greer, *The Female Eunuch* (London: MacGibbon and Kee, 1970); Janice G. Raymond, *The Transsexual Empire: The Making of the She-Male* (New York: Teachers College Press, 1979); Monique Wittig, *The Straight Mind and Other Essays* (Boston: Beacon Press, 1992).

42. Harriet Desmoines, "Notes for a Magazine," *Sinister Wisdom* 1, no. 1 (July 1976): 3–4.

43. Ibid., 4.

44. "Mia Albright," *Sinister Wisdom* 1, no. 3 (Spring 1977): 12.

45. Ibid.

46. Ibid.

47. "Martha Shelley," *Sinister Wisdom* 1, no. 3 (Spring 1977): 14.

48. "Judy Antonelli," *Sinister Wisdom* 1, no. 4 (Fall 1977): 57.

49. Ibid., 59.

50. Ibid.

51. "Peggy Kornegger," *Sinister Wisdom* 1, no. 4 (Fall 1977): 57.

52. Elena Gambino, "Politics as 'Sinister Wisdom': Reparation and Responsibility in Lesbian Feminism," *Contemporary Political Theory* 20, no. 3 (September 2021): 524–46, https://doi.org/10.1057/s41296-020-00457-7.

53. Keeanga-Yamahtta Taylor, *How We Get Free: Black Feminism and the Combahee River Collective* (Chicago: Haymarket Books, 2017), 5–6.

54. Combahee River Collective, "The Combahee River Collective Statement of 1977," in *Home Girls: A Black Feminist Anthology*, ed. Barbara Smith (New York: Kitchen Table/Women of Color Press, 1983), 265.

55. Ibid.

56. Ibid., 277.

57. Most scholars credit Kimberle Crenshaw with the late 1980s/early 1990s introduction of "intersectionality" in academia; however, there has been recent interest in identifying what political scientist Ange-Marie Hancock terms "intersectional-like thinking" in women of color activism that predates the introduction of intersectionality as a theoretical and analytic concept in the academy. Ange-Marie Hancock, *Intersectionality: An Intellectual History* (New York: Oxford University Press, 2016).

58. "Combahee River Collective," "The Combahee River Collective Statement of 1977," 275.

59. There is a long history of alliances between White women and men to maintain White supremacy in the United States, beginning with the suffrage movement in the mid-19th century, when White women drew on White supremacist logic to argue that they should be extended suffrage before formerly enslaved Black men. In contemporary politics, these alliances look like the majority of White women voting for Trump in both 2016 and 2020, not despite his clearly anti-Black and anti-immigrant platforms but because of them. See Dara Z. Strolovitch, Janelle S. Wong, and Andrew Proctor, "A Possessive Investment in White Heteropatriarchy? The 2016 Election and the Politics of Race, Gender, and Sexuality," *Politics, Groups, and Identities* 5, no. 2 (2017): 353–63; Jane Junn, "The Trump Majority: White Womanhood and the Making of Female Voters in the US," *Politics, Groups, and Identities* 5, no. 2 (2017): 343–52.

60. Combahee River Collective. "The Combahee River Collective Statement of 1977," 277.

61. Ibid.

62. Ibid., 278.

63. Ibid., 281.

64. Barbara Smith, "Toward a Black Feminist Criticism," *Radical Teacher*, no. 7 (March 1978): 20–27.

65. Combahee River Collective. "The Combahee River Collective Statement of 1977," 281.

66. Ibid.

67. Editorial statement, *Azalea* 1, no. 2 (Spring 1978): n.p.

68. Cherríe L. Moraga, "Catching Fire: Preface to the Fourth Edition," in *This Bridge Called My Back*, ed. Cherríe L. Moraga and Gloria E. Anzaldúa, 4th edition (Albany: State University of New York Press, 2015), xix.

69. Mitsuye Yamada, "Asian Pacific Women and Feminism," in *This Bridge Called My Back*, ed. Cherríe L. Moraga and Gloria E. Anzaldúa (Berkeley, CA: Third Woman Press, 2002), 70.

70. Ibid., 77.

71. Separatists critiqued presenting in feminine ways as an attempt to appeal to men and patriarchal expectations of beauty. On the other hand, presenting as masculine was also condemned for the ways that it suggested that power and access could be obtained by imitating masculinity.

72. Chrystos does not use gender pronouns; I use "they" or "their" as a result.

73. Chrystos, "I Don't Understand Those Who Have Turned Away from Me," in *This Bridge Called My Back*, ed. Cherríe L. Moraga and Gloria E. Anzaldúa (Berkeley, CA: Third Woman Press, 2002), 66.

74. Cherríe L. Moraga, "La Jornada," in *This Bridge Called My Back*, ed. Cherríe L. Moraga and Gloria E. Anzaldúa, 4th edition (Albany: State University of New York Press, 2015), xxxvi (emphasis in original).

75. Salsa Soul Sisters, "A Lesbian Show," *Azalea* 1, no. 2 (Spring 1978): 12.

76. Ibid.

77. Ibid.

78. Audrey Lorde, "The Master's Tools Will Never Dismantle the Master's House," in *This Bridge Called My Back*, ed. Cherríe L. Moraga and Gloria E. Anzaldúa (Berkeley, CA: Third Woman Press, 2002), 107.

79. Ibid., 108.

80. This metaphor presaged Crenshaw's use of the "intersection" metaphor, which she used to explain how Black women are not doubly harmed by the effects of racism and sexism, much like a person standing in an intersection and hit by cars coming from both directions does not stop to consider which car hurt them more. In both instances, the final product is simply harm.

81. Bernice Johnson Reagon, "Coalition Politics: Turning the Century," in *Home Girls: A Black Feminist Anthology,* ed. Barbara Smith (New York: Kitchen Table/Women of Color, 1981), 361.

82. Ibid.

83. Ibid., 365.

84. In 2017, a coalition of radical feminists, lesbians, Christians, and conservatives formed Hands Across the Aisle and is just one example of this type of rhetoric, which explicitly pits "women's rights" against "gender ideology" (code for transgender people) to cast transgender people as a threat to feminism. See "Home" Hands Across the Aisle Women, accessed July 30, 2022, https://handsacrosstheaislewomen.come/home/.

85. Ibid.

Chapter 4

1. Jessica Sathanson, "Pride and Politics: Revisiting the Northampton Pride March, 1989–1993," *Journal of Bisexuality* 2, nos. 2–3 (October 17, 2001): 148, https://doi.org/10.1300/J159v02n02_10.

2. Anthony Lonetree, "Coleman Won't Sign Gay Month Proclamation," *Star Tribune,* May 4, 1994, 1B, in Steven Donaldson Papers 1965–1988, box 16, folder 8 (Bisexuality 1990s), New York Public Library.

3. Ibid.

4. Smith, Charles Anthony, Shawn Schulenberg, and Eric A. Baldwin. "The 'B' Isn't Silent," in *LGBTQ Politics: A Critical Reader,* ed. Marla Brettschneider, Susan Burgess, and Christine Keating, (New York: NYU Press, 2017), 89–109.

5. BiNet, *Bisexuality: Some Questions Answered,* n.d., in Stephen Donaldson Papers, box 16, folder 8.

6. Ibid.

7. Ibid.

8. Ibid.

9. Ibid.

10. Ibid.

11. *Bisexual Pride,* n.d., in Stephen Donaldson Papers, box 16, folder 9.

12. Ibid.

13. Ibid.

14. Ibid.

15. Ibid.

258   NOTES

16. Ibid.
17. Laura M. Perez and Victor Raymond, "Bisexuals Included in the March on Washington," *Anything That Moves*, no. 5 (1993), Archives of GLBT Historical Society, San Francisco, CA.
18. Ibid.
19. These conservative mobilizations were set in motion by Hawaii's 1991 state supreme court decision that extended marriage to same-sex couples as well as Amendment 2, the 1992 Colorado constitutional amendment that was passed by voters in a statewide ballot initiative, stipulating that no future antidiscrimination protections for gay men, lesbians, and bisexuals force.
20. Perez and Raymond, "Bisexuals Included in the March on Washington."
21. Ibid.
22. Ibid.
23. Katie Mechem, "March on Washington," *Anything That Moves* 6 (1993): 13, in Archives of GLBT Historical Society.
24. Ibid.
25. Ibid.
26. Lani Ka'ahumanu, "How I Spent My Two Week Vacation Being a Revolting Token Bisexual," *Anything That Moves* 6 (1993): 11, in Archives of GLBT Historical Society.
27. Ibid.
28. Lani Ka'ahumanu, "Tippecanoe and Ka'ahumanu Too," *Anything That Moves* 8 (1994): 18, in Archives of GLBT Historical Society, 18.
29. Ka'ahumanu, "How I Spent," 53.
30. Loraine Hutchins et al., "From Out/Look Magazine to Cable News Network, Everyone Wants to Know: What Do Bisexuals Want?," *Anything That Moves* 4 (1992): 5, in Archives of GLBT Historical Society.
31. Liz A. Highleyman, "The Evolution of the Bisexual Movement," *Anything That Moves* 8 (1994): 25, in Archives of GLBT Historical Society.
32. Ibid.
33. BiPol, "Dear *Anything That Moves*," *Anything That Moves* 8 (1994): 3, in Archives of GLBT Historical Society.
34. Ibid.
35. Ibid.
36. Ibid.
37. Ibid.
38. Jo Eadie, "All One Big Happy Family?," *Anything That Moves* 11 (1996), in Archives of GLBT Historical Society.
39. Ibid.
40. Ibid.
41. Ibid.
42. "Transsexual" was the dominant term until 1993, when political actors introduced "transgender." In this section I refer to the women requesting participation in SBNW as "trans" due to that lack of clarity in the historical record as to how they self-identified. The next chapter provides a more detailed analysis of these discursive shifts and their importance for how identity was understood.

43. Adrienne Rich's "compulsory heterosexuality" theorized that the only way to sub-vert patriarchy was to withdraw oneself from relationships from men. These gestures signaled that women refused to be recruited into buttressing masculinity and pa-triarchy, and evolved into one of the defining features of radical lesbian feminism. Bisexuals were scorned for compromising these efforts by engaging in relationships with men and presumably perpetuating the availability of all women to men. See Laura M. Perez, "Go Ahead: Make My Movement," in *Bisexual Politics: Theories, Queries, and Visions*, ed. Naomi S. Tucker, Liz Highleyman, and Rebecca Kaplan (New York: Haworth Press, Inc, 1995), 109–14.

44. Questions pertaining to the inclusion of transgender women in SBWN were framed as existential threats to it as an explicitly women's organization. The debates documented in this chapter implicate the tendency to collapse biology with gender that often had tragic consequences for transgender women and, in the present mo-ment, abet a rash of legislation across the US that criminalizes trans women's ex-istence. See Susan Stryker, "My Words to Victor Frankenstein Above the Village of Chamounix," *GLQ* 1, no. 3 (1994): 237–54.

45. These are the terms used by authors, which reflect the appropriate ways to name these groups at the time. In other places, I use "trans" as an umbrella term to capture trans-gender, nonbinary, and gender-nonconforming identities that might not have been named as such during the early 1990s but were likely part of these discussions.

46. "SBNW Statement of Purpose," *North Bi Northwest* 4, no. 2 (April–May 1991): 2, in Stephen Donaldson Papers, box 16, folder 9 (Bisexuality 1999s).

47. Ibid.

48. Beth Reba Weise, "Final Decision on Transsexuals in SBWN," *North Bi Northwest* 4, no. 2 (1991): 6, in Steven Donaldson Papers, box 16, folder 9 (Bisexuality 1999s).

49. Ibid.

50. Ibid.

51. Ibid.

52. Ibid., 6–7.

53. Claudia Smelser, "Dear SBWN," *North Bi Northwest* 4, no. 2 (1991): 7, in Steven Donaldson Papers, fox 16, folder 9 (Bisexuality 1999s).

54. Ibid.

55. Ibid.

56. Rebecca Kaplan, "Dear North Bi Northwest Womyn," *North Bi Northwest* 4, no. 2 (1991): 7, in Steven Donaldson Papers, box 16, folder 9 (Bisexuality 1999s).

57. Ibid.

58. Ibid.

59. Gary North, "Seattle Settles Transsexual Issue," *Anything That Moves* 3 (1991): 19, in Archives of GLBT Historical Society.

60. Perez, "Go Ahead," 112.

61. elias farajaje-jones, "Multikulti Feminist Bis No More?," *Anything That Moves* 5 (1993): 18, in Archives of GLBT Historical Society.

62. Ibid.

63. ben e factory, "Multiculturalism, Feminism, and the Naming of 'BiNet USA,'" memo, 1993, in Steven Donaldson Papers, box 16, folder 10 (Bisexual Network of the USA).
64. Ibid.
65. It will not be lost on students of politics that adding more options is a tactic to spread votes and prevent a definitive outcome. There is no explicit reference to this strategy being employed by participants at the Minneapolis meeting; however, the unexplained proliferation of names with very similar meanings suggests a scheme to achieve a failed election and force a reversion to the status quo.
66. factory, "Multiculturalism, Feminism, and the Naming of 'BiNet USA.'"
67. farajaje-jones, "Multikulti Feminist Bis No More?," 18.
68. Ibid.
69. Ibid., 19.
70. Ibid.
71. Maggi Rubenstein, "A Bisexual Speaks at L/G FDP," *Bi-Monthly News* 8, no. 5 (1984): 6, in Archives of GLBT Historical Society.
72. Ibid.
73. Ibid.
74. Ibid.
75. Ibid.
76. Ibid.
77. Amy L. Stone, *Gay Rights at the Ballot Box* (Minneapolis: University of Minnesota Press, 2012).
78. Lani Ka'ahumanu, "A 1992 March on Washington for Lesbian, Gay, and Bisexual Equal Rights and Liberation Speech," *Anything That Moves* 5 (1993): 16, in Archives of GLBT Historical Society.
79. Ibid.
80. Ibid.
81. Ibid.
82. Ibid.
83. David Valentine's ethnography of transgender as a category that emerged during this same period argues that the increasingly liberal gay and lesbian movement designated visible gender difference to transgender people as a way to shore up assimilatory claims that gay men and lesbians are "just like" straight people. We see the effects of these maneuvers today in the hundreds of bills that have been introduced to bar transgender people from accessing healthcare. See Valentine, *Imagining Transgender*.
84. Ka'ahumanu, "A 1992 March on Washington for Lesbian, Gay, and Bisexual Equal Rights and Liberation Speech," 16.
85. Ibid.
86. Quoted in Lani Ka'ahuani, "The Art of Creating Change," *Anything That Moves* 13 (1997):15, in Archives of GLBT Historical Society.
87. Ibid.
88. Ibid.
89. National Gay and Lesbian Task Force, "General Information," February 4, 1999, http://web.archive.org/web/19990202042554/http://www.ngltf.org/gi.html.

Chapter 5

1. ILGA was renamed International Lesbian, Gay, Bisexual, Trans and Intersex Association in 2008.

2. Listing bisexual, transgender, and drag communities alongside lesbian and gay was an effort to recognize that many people who choose to dress in men's or women's clothing do not necessarily identify as transgender. The organizers of the protests to include transgender people in the title of the Stonewall 25 march consequently included drag communities as a gesture of solidarity. See Leslie Feinberg, speech at Cornell University, April 20, 1994, Human Sexuality Collection #7572, Cornell University, Ithaca, New York. Franklin Fry, one of the lead ILGA organizers, defended the inclusion of bisexual, transgender, and drag communities in an open letter to march supporters; see "Letter to community members," May 1994, Human Sexuality Collection, National Gay and Lesbian Task Force Collection #7301, box 20, folder 2, Cornell University, Ithaca, New York.

3. Phyllis Frye, "Letter to followers of the unfolding Stonewall 25 events," May 12, 1994, Human Sexuality Collection, National Gay and Lesbian Task Force Collection #7301, box 20, folder 24, Cornell University.

4. [138] For a comprehensive history of the emergence of transgender as a complement or alternative to transsexual and transvestite, see Stryker, *Transgender History*, ch. 1.

5. Leslie Feinberg, "Transgender Liberation: A Movement Whose Time Has Come," in *The Transgender Studies Reader*, ed. Susan Stryker and Stephen Whittle (New York: Routledge, 2006), 206.

6. Andrew R. Flores, Donald P. Haider-Markel, Daniel C. Lewis, Patrick R. Miller, Barry L. Tadlock, and Jami K. Taylor, "Transgender Prejudice Reduction and Opinions on Transgender Rights: Results from a Mediation Analysis on Experimental Data," *Research & Politics* 5, no. 1 (January 2018), https://doi.org/10.1177/205316801 8764945.

7. Cristin Williams, a trans-identified historian, has written extensively on this subject on her personal website. See "Tracking Transgender: The Historical Truth" at cristinwilliams.com.

8. Robert J. Stoller, *Sex and Gender: The Development of Masculinity and Femininity* (London: Karmac Books, 1994).

9. Meyerowitz, Joanne J. *How Sex Changed: A History of Transsexuality in the United States* (Cambridge, MA: Harvard University Press, 2002).

10. Stryker, "Transgender History," 11.

11. Dallas Denny, "About Chrysalis," *Chrysalis Quarterly*, 2014, http://dallasdenny.com/Chrysalis/about-chrysalis/.

12. The internet and social media often serve as the first and in some cases only source of information about gender, transgender identity, medical possibilities, and fashion for transgender people. Denny's work, in particular, was instrumental in connecting trans-identified people. See Malatino, Hil, *Side Affects: On Being Trans and Feeling Bad* (Minneapolis: University of Minnesota Press, 2022).

13. Holly Boswell, "The Transgender Alternative," *Chrysalis Quarterly* 1, no. 2 (1991): 29.

14. Ibid.

15. Boswell, "Transgender Alternative," 30.

16. Feinberg, "Transgender Liberation," 205.

17. Feinberg foreshadowed Judith Butler's observation in *Gender Trouble*, "If the immutable character of sex as biological fact is contested, perhaps this construct called 'sex' is as culturally constructed as gender; indeed, perhaps it was always already gender, with the consequence that the distinction between sex and gender turns out to be no distinction at all." Judith Butler, *Gender Trouble: Feminism and the Subversion of Identity* (New York: Routledge, 1990), 11.

18. Feinberg, "Transgender Liberation," 206.

19. Ibid.

20. These shifts also presaged the introduction of transgender studies in the academy, which foregrounds critiques of institutions, laws, spaces, and social practices that give meaning to binary gender. See Susan Stryker, "Introduction," *TSQ: Transgender Studies Quarterly* 7, no. 3 (August 1, 2020): 299–305, https://doi.org/10.1215/23289 252-8552908.

21. Feinberg, "Transgender Liberation," 206.

22. Dallas Denny, "A Word from the Editor," *AEGIS Quarterly* 1, no. 2 (September 1994): 8.

23. Dallas Denny, "AEGIS Now Offers Membership," *AEGIS Quarterly* 1, no. 3 (March 1995): 1.

24. Ibid.

25. Hindman, *Political Advocacy and Its Interested Citizens*. See also Jane Ward, *Respectably Queer: Diversity Culture in LGBT Activist Organizations* (Nashville, TN: Vanderbilt University Press, 2008); Strolovitch, *Affirmative Advocacy*.

26. "Why Membership?," *AEGIS Quarterly* 1, no. 3 (March 1995): 2. For perspective, $36 in 1995 is the equivalent of approximately $71 in 2023; $500 is roughly $990 in 2023.

27. Ibid.

28. Jessica Xavier, "So You Wanna Be in Politics?," *AEGIS Quarterly* 1, no. 7 (April 1996): 1.

29. Ibid., 2.

30. Ibid.

31. Ibid.

32. Ibid.

33. Ibid.

34. Ibid., 3.

35. Ibid.

36. Ibid.

37. See Susan Stryker, *Transgender History* (Berkeley, CA: Seal Press, 2008) for more regarding the use of "transexual" and "transsexual" over time.

38. Xavier, "So You Wanna Be in Politics?," 6.

39. Dallas Denny, "Vision 2001, Part One," *AEGIS Newsletter* 1, no. 6 (January 1996): 1, personal archive of Dallas Denny.

40. Dallas Denny, "Vision 2001, Part Three," *AEGIS Newsletter* 1, no. 8 (September 1996): 7, personal archive of Dallas Denny.

41. For more on the ways scientific discourse was used to prop up these arguments, see Joanna Wuest, "The Scientific Gaze in American Transgender Politics: Contesting the Meanings of Sex, Gender, and Gender Identity in the Bathroom," *Politics & Gender* 15, no. 2 (2019): 336–60.

42. See Judith Butler, "Against Proper Objects," *Differences* 6, no. 2 (1994): 1–26; Annamarie Jagose and Don Kulick, "Thinking Sex/Thinking Gender: Introduction," *GLQ: A Journal of Lesbian and Gay Studies* 10, no. 2 (2004): 211–12.

43. It is important to note that all of Wilchins's political activism is united by an effort to destabilize the importance and necessity of social categories like transgender and transsexual. It should come as no surprise, then, that Wilchins refuses to identify as a transgender or transsexual activist and instead orients herself as an activist against gender oppression. Riki Anne Wilchins, "Interview with a Menace," in Wilchins, *Read My Lips: Sexual Subversion and the End of Gender* (Ithaca, NY: Firebrand Books, 1997).

44. See Stryker, *Transgender History*, ch. 5.

45. Wilchins, *Read My Lips*, 69.

46. Cohen, "Punks, Bulldaggers, and Welfare Queens."

47. Wilchins, *Read My Lips*, 87.

48. Ibid.

49. Ibid., 86.

50. Heath Fogg Davis, *Beyond Trans: Does Gender Matter?* (New York: NYU Press, 2017). For a discussion of the effects of sex segregation and for the effects of the administrative state, see Dean Spade, *Normal Life: Administrative Violence, Critical Trans Politics and the Limits of Law* (Boston: South End Press, 2011).

51. John Gallagher, "The Transgender Revolution," *The Advocate*, December 10, 1996, 51.

52. GPAC. "GPAC Homepage." Accessed July 3, 2014. web.archive.org/web/ . . . /www.gpac.org/.

53. Dana Preisling, "Report 96:09: Romer v Evans Decision," May 22, 1996, Internet Archive, www.web.archive.org/web/*/gpac.org.

54. Patrick Califia, *Sex Changes: Transgender Politics* (Jersey City, NJ: Cleis Press, 2013); Stryker, *Transgender History*.

55. Protections similar to the ones outlined by ENDA had been enacted by the Minneapolis City Council in 1975. These were adopted as Minnesota state law in 1993. In both instances, the city/state was the first in the country to ban discrimination based on sexual orientation or gender identity.

56. Dana Preisling, "Report 96:11: ENDA & More," May 30, 1996, Internet Archive, www.web.archive.org/web/*/gpac.org.

57. Ibid.

58. Valentine, *Imagining Transgender*.

59. Dana Preisling, "Hate Crimes Developments," July 1997, Internet Archive, www.web.archive.org/web/*/gpac.org.

60. Ibid.

61. Ibid.
62. Ibid.
63. For more on hate crimes laws as anti-intersectional, see Christina Hanhardt, *Safe Space: Gay Neighborhood History and the Politics of Violence* (Durham, NC: Duke University Press, 2013) and Amy Brandzel, *Against Citizenship*.
64. Dana Preisling, "Report 96:02," May 6, 1996, Internet Archive, www.web.archive.org/web/*/gpac.org.
65. Some have argued that listing "transgender" at the end of lists comprised of "lesbian, gay, and bisexual" implicitly defines transgender identity as a desire and not a gender identity, see Stryker, "Transgender History, Homonormativity, and Disciplinarity."
66. Dana Preisling, "Report 96:08: Hate Crimes," July 18, 1996, Internet Archive, www.web.archive.org/web/*/gpac.org.
67. Ibid.
68. Ibid.
69. Ibid., 3.

Chapter 6

1. "NGLTF Convenes Third National Policy Roundtable," *Oasis Magazine*, 1998. Accessed using The Internet Archive: www.waybackmachine.org.
2. The initialisms used in this chapter alternate between GLBT and LGBT. I use LGBT to be consistent.
3. Although the degree to which these transcripts captured the debates is impressive, there are also many errors: spelling, grammatical, and/or exclusions. Where appropriate, I have removed the typical *sic* designation and made logical corrections to enhance readability.
4. For more on the rise of the Evangelical Right, see Cynthia Burack, *Tough Love: Sexuality, Compassion, and the Christian Right* (Albany: State University of New York Press, 2014); Tina Fetner, *How the Religious Right Shaped Lesbian and Gay Activism* (Minneapolis: University of Minnesota Press, 2008); Christian Smith and Michael Emerson, *American Evangelicalism: Embattled and Thriving* (Chicago: University of Chicago Press, 1998).
5. "National Policy Roundtable," Human Sexuality Collection #7301, box 299, folder 12, Cornell University, 1.
6. Ibid., 8.
7. Ibid., 9.
8. Ibid.
9. Ibid.
10. Ibid.
11. Ibid.
12. Ibid.
13. The parent organization for Love Won Out was the Colorado Springs–based Focus on the Family.

14. Burack, *Tough Love*, 31.

15. Ibid., 44.

16. Scientific logic grounded in biology as static held these claims together. See Joanna Wuest, "'From Pathology to Born Perfect': Science, Law, and Citizenship in American LGBTQ + Advocacy," *Perspective on Politics* 19, no. 3 (2021): 838–53.

17. "National Policy Roundtable," n.p.

18. Ibid.

19. "National Policy Roundtable Minutes: September 17th and 18th, 1998," Human Sexuality Collection #7301, box 299, folder 13, Cornell University, 26.

20. Ibid.

21. Ibid., 24.

22. Joyce Murdoch and Deb Price, *Courting Justice: Gay Men and Lesbians v. the Supreme Court* (New York: Basic Books, 2002).

23. "National Policy Roundtable," September 1998, Human Sexuality Collection #7301, box 267, folder 12, Cornell University, n.p.

24. Ibid., 22.

25. Jane Ward, *Not Gay: Sex between Straight White Men*, vol. 19 (New York: NYU Press, 2015).

26. "National Policy Roundtable," September 1998, 23.

27. See Spade, *Normal Life*; Dean Spade, "Mutilating Gender," in *Transgender Studies Reader*, ed. Susan Stryker and Stephen Whittle (New York: Routledge, 2006), 315–32.

28. Much has been written about how people seeking gender confirmation would study diagnostic criteria to report them verbatim to gatekeepers and ensure access to hormones and surgery. This history suggests that some may have fabricated claims to inherent transgender identity and indicates a far more nuanced experience of transness. See Stryker, *Transgender History*; Julian Gill-Peterson, *Histories of the Transgender Child* (Minneapolis: University of Minnesota Press, 2018).

29. "National Polity Roundtable," September 1998, 23.

30. For more on the spatial dynamics attending trans identity when posed in opposition to "cis-," see A. Finn Enke, "The Education of Little Cis," in *Transfeminist Perspectives In and Beyond Transgender or Gender Studies*, ed. Anne Enke (Philadelphia: Temple University Press, 2012): 60–77.

31. "National Policy Roundtable," September 1998, 23.

32. Ibid.

33. "National Policy Roundtable Minutes, September 24th and 25th, 1999," Human Sexuality Collection #7301, box 299, folder 15, Cornell University, n.p.

34. Ibid.

35. Ibid.

36. Ibid.

37. Ibid.

38. Ibid.

39. The anger at HRC in this section of the minutes is palpable. For more on affect and social movements, particularly in lesbian and gay organizing, see Gould, *Moving Politics*, ch. 2.

40. "National Policy Roundtable Minutes," 1999, n.p.
41. Ibid.
42. Ibid.
43. Ibid.
44. Hindman, *Political Advocacy and Its Interested Citizens*.
45. Specific instances where the mismatch between crime and punishment are mediated by the perceived sexual orientation or gender identity of the accused are too numerous to list here. The case of CeCe McDonald (a Black transgender-identified woman), who received a 41-month prison sentence for stabbing a man in self-defense when he threatened and pursued her through a parking lot in the Seward neighborhood of South Minneapolis, is just one example. For more on the criminalization of sexuality and gender identity, see Canaday, *The Straight State*; Duggan, *The Twilight of Equality?*; Regina Kunzel, *Criminal Intimacy: Prison and the Uneven History of Modern American Sexuality* (Chicago: University of Chicago Press, 2008); Spade, *Normal Life*.
46. "National Policy Roundtable Minutes," 1999, n.p.
47. Ibid.
48. Ibid.
49. Ibid.
50. Ibid.
51. Ibid.
52. Ibid.
53. Warner, *Fear of a Queer Planet*; Cohen, "Punks, Bulldaggers, and Welfare Queens"; Cohen, "The Radical Potential of Queer?"
54. "National Policy Roundtable Minutes," 1999, n.p. Earlier that year, the Log Cabin Republicans and NGLTF—conservative and progressive organizations, respectively—held a public debate about the death penalty. They agreed beforehand on how to stage the conflict in order to emphasize what each organization saw as important issues in relation to the death penalty and lesbian, gay, bisexual, and transgender people. See Chris Bull, "A Matter of Life and Death," *The Advocate,* March 16, 1999.
55. This use of "queer" differs from how it was used by activists to signal a shared orientation to power against White supremacy and heteronormativity that would unite all those stigmatized for deviant sexuality. See Cohen, "Punks, Bulldaggers, and Welfare Queens."
56. "National Policy Roundtable Minutes," September, n.p.
57. The LGBT and GLBT initialisms were both used during this period. Both are indicated here to maintain consistency with the excerpts from political actors, some of whom used GLBT.
58. "National Policy Roundtable Minutes, March 16, 2000," Human Sexuality Collection #7301, box 299, folder 16, Cornell University, 4.
59. Ibid.
60. Ibid., 9.
61. Ibid., 16.
62. Ibid.

63. Ibid.

64. Ibid., 19.

65. Ibid., 27.

66. Ibid.

67. "National Policy Roundtable Minutes," March 1, 2001, Human Sexuality Collection #7301, box 299, folder 20, Cornell University, 3.

68. Ibid., 3–4.

69. Ibid., 4.

70. Ibid.

71. Ibid., 7.

72. Ibid.

73. Ibid., 31.

74. Ibid., 44.

75. Cohen, "Punks, Bulldaggers, and Welfare Queens"; Ange-Marie Hancock, *The Politics of Disgust: The Public Identity of the Welfare Queen* (New York: New York University Press, 2004); Joe Soss, *Unwanted Claims: The Politics of Participation in the U.S. Welfare System* (Ann Arbor: University of Michigan Press, 2002).

76. "National Policy Roundtable Minutes," March 2001, 46.

77. Human Rights Campaign, "HRC Story." Accessed May 31, 2021. www.hrc.org/hrc-story.

Chapter 7

1. Jennicet Gutiérrez, "No Pride in Detention of Transgender, Queer Communities," *Washington Blade,* June 15, 2022, https://www.washingtonblade.com/2022/06/15/to-biden-no-pride-in-detention-of-transgender-queer-communities/.

2. White House, "Fact Sheet: President Biden to Sign Historic Executive Order Advancing LGBTQI+ Equality During Pride Month," June 15, 2022, https://www.whitehouse.gov/briefing-room/statements-releases/2022/06/15/fact-sheet-president-biden-to-sign-historic-executive-order-advancing-lgbtqi-equality-during-pride-month/.

3. Alexi Jones, "Visualizing the Unequal Treatment of LGBTQ People in the Criminal Justice System," *Prison Policy Initiative*, March 2, 2021, https://www.prisonpolicy.org/blog/2021/03/02/lgbtq/.

4. Alex Abad-Santos, "Philadelphia's New, Inclusive Gay Pride Flag Is Making Gay White Men Angry," June 20, 2017, *Vox*, https://www.vox.com/culture/2017/6/20/15821858/gay-pride-flag-philadelphia-fight-explained.

5. Ibid.

6. Ibid.

7. Julie Compton, "Controversy Flies over Philadelphia's New Pride Flag," NBC News, June 15, 2017, https://www.nbcnews.com/feature/nbc-out/controversy-flies-over-philadelphia-s-new-pride-flag-n772821.

8. "Taylor Swift Calls Out Trump in VMAs Speech," *ET Canada,* August 27, 2019, https://www.youtube.com/watch?v=YtYTKSHQVBQ.

9. Katelyn Burns, "The Rise of Anti-Trans 'Radical' Feminists, Explained," *Vox News,* September 5, 2019, https://www.vox.com/identities/2019/9/5/20840101/terfs-radi cal-feminists-gender-critical.

10. *New York Times* columnist Pamela Paul rehearsed these antitrans arguments in her July 3, 2022 piece, "The Far Right and the Far Left Can Agree on One Thing: Women Don't Count." She asserted that while the Far Right is the natural enemy of women, so too are "woke" feminists and transgender people who advocate for gender-affirming language.

11. Beltrán, *The Trouble with Unity*; Cohen, *The Boundaries of Blackness*; Hindman, *Political Advocacy and Its Interested Citizens*; Schattschneider, *The Semisovereign People*; Strolovitch, Wong, and Proctor, "A Possessive Investment in White Heteropatriarchy?"

12. P. G. Klandermans, "Identity Politics and Politicized Identities: Identity Processes and the Dynamics of Protest," *Political Psychology* 35, no. 1 (2014): 1–22; Gamson, *The Strategy of Social Protest*; McAdam, *Political Process and the Development of Black Insurgency.*

13. Erin M. Adam, "Intersectional Coalitions: The Paradoxes of Rights-Based Movement Building in LGBTQ and Immigrant Communities: Intersectional Coalitions," *Law & Society Review* 51, no. 1 (March 2017): 132–67, https://doi.org/10.1111/lasr.12248; Marie Hojnacki, "Organized Interests' Advocacy Behavior in Alliances," *Political Research Quarterly* 51, no. 2 (1998): 437–59; Michael T. Heaney and Geoffrey M. Lorenz, "Coalition Portfolios and Interest Group Influence over the Policy Process," *Interest Groups & Advocacy* 2, no. 3 (2013): 251–77, https://doi.org/10.1057/ iga.2013.7; Strolovitch, *Affirmative Advocacy.*

14. Daum, *The Politics of Right Sex*, 159.

15. Spade, *Normal Life.*

16. Cricket Keating, "Building Coalitional Consciousness," *NWSA Journal* 17, no. 2 (2005): 86–103.

17. Associated Press, "Nearly 1 Million U.S. Households Composed of Same-Sex Couples," NBC News, September 17, 2020, https://www.nbcnews.com/feature/nbc-out/nearly-1-million-u-s-households-composed-same-sex-couples-n1240340.

18. Paisley Currah, *Sex Is as Sex Does: Governing Transgender Identity* (New York: New York University Press, 2022).

19. Gash, *Below the Radar.* For the advantages of statutory approaches to ensuring rights, see Jason Pierceson, *Before Bostock: The Accidental Precedent of Price Waterhouse v. Hopkins* (Lawrence: University Press of Kansas, 2022).

Works Cited

Abad-Santos, Alex. "Philadelphia's New, Inclusive Gay Pride Flag Is Making Gay White Men Angry," *Vox*, June 20, 2017, https://www.vox.com/culture/2017/6/20/15821858/gay-pride-flag-philadelphia-fight-explained.

Abbott, Sidney, and Barbara Love. *Sappho Was a Right-on Woman*. New York: Stein & Day, 1972.

Adam, Erin M. "Intersectional Coalitions: The Paradoxes of Rights-Based Movement Building in LGBTQ and Immigrant Communities: Intersectional Coalitions." *Law & Society Review* 51, no. 1 (March 2017): 132–67. https://doi.org/10.1111/lasr.12248.

AEGIS Quarterly 1, no. 2 (September 1994).

AEGIS Quarterly 1, no. 3 (March 1995).

Albright, Mia. "Mia Albright," *Sinister Wisdom* 1, no. 3 (Spring 1977).

Alexander, M. Jacki. "Not Just (Any) Body Can Be a Citizen: The Politics of Law, Sexuality and Postcoloniality in Trinidad and Tobago and the Bahamas." *Feminist Review*, no. 48 (1994): 5–23.

Allen, Samantha. "LGBT Leaders: Gay Marriage Is Not Enough," *Daily Beast*, June 26, 2015, http://www.thedailybeast.com/articles/2015/06/26/same-sex-marriage-is-legal-now-what.html.

Antonelli, Judy. "Judy Antonelli." *Sinister Wisdom* 1, no. 4 (Fall 1977).

Arendt, Hannah. *The Origins of Totalitarianism*. New York: Schocken Books, 1948.

Armstrong, Elizabeth A., and Suzanna M. Crage. "Movements and Memory: The Making of the Stonewall Myth." *American Sociological Review* 71, no. 5 (October 1, 2006): 724–51. https://doi.org/10.1177/000312240607100502.

Associated Press, "Nearly 1 Million U.S. Households Composed of Same-Sex Couples," NBC News, September 17, 2020, https://www.nbcnews.com/feature/nbc-out/nearly-1-million-u-s-households-composed-same-sex-couples-n1240340.

Beltrán, Cristina. *Cruelty as Citizenship: How Migrant Suffering Sustains White Democracy*. Minneapolis: University of Minnesota Press, 2020.

Beltrán, Cristina. *The Trouble with Unity: Latino Politics and the Creation of Identity*. Oxford: Oxford University Press, 2010.

Benford, Robert D. "Frame Disputes within the Nuclear Disarmament Movement." *Social Forces* 71, no. 3 (1993): 677–701. https://doi.org/10.1093/sf/71.3.677.

Benford, Robert D., and David A. Snow. "Framing Processes and Social Movements: An Overview and Assessment." *Annual Review of Sociology* 26 (2000): 611–39.

Berbrier, Mitch. "Making Minorities: Cultural Space, Stigma Transformation Frames, and the Categorical Status Claims of Deaf, Gay, and White Supremacist Activists in Late Twentieth Century America." *Sociological Forum* 17, no. 4 (December 1, 2002): 553–91. https://doi.org/10.1023/A:1021025307028.

Berlant, Lauren. *The Queen of America Goes to Washington City*. Durham, NC: Duke University Press, 2002. https://www.dukeupress.edu/the-queen-of-america-goes-to-washington-city.

Bernstein, Mary. "Celebration and Suppression: The Strategic Uses of Identity by the Lesbian and Gay Movement." *American Journal of Sociology* 103, no. 3 (November 1, 1997): 531–65.

Bernstein, Mary, and Kristine A. Olsen. "Identity Deployment and Social Change: Understanding Identity as a Social Movement and Organizational Strategy." *Sociology Compass* 3, no. 6 (2009): 871–83.

Bey, Marquis. *The Problem of the Negro as a Problem for Gender*. Minneapolis: University of Minnesota Press, 2020.

Boswell, Holly. "The Transgender Alternative." *Chrysalis Quarterly* 1, no. 2 (1991): 29–31.

Boyd, Nan Alamilla. *Wide-Open Town: A History of Queer San Francisco to 1965*. Berkeley: University of California Press, 2003.

Bracewell, Lorna Norman. "Beyond Barnard: Liberalism, Antipornography Feminism, and the Sex Wars." *Signs: Journal of Women in Culture and Society* 42, no. 1 (2016): 23–48.

Bracewell, Lorna N. *Why We Lost the Sex Wars: Sexual Freedom in the #MeToo Era*. Minneapolis: University of Minnesota Press, 2021.

Brandzel, Amy L. *Against Citizenship: The Violence of the Normative*. Urbana: University of Illinois Press, 2016.

Breines, Wini. *Community and Organization in the New Left, 1962–1968: The Great Refusal*. New Brunswick, NJ: Rutgers University Press, 1989.

Brown, Wendy. "Suffering the Paradoxes of Rights." In *Left Legalism/Left Critique*, edited by Wendy Brown and Janet Halley, 420–34. Durham, NC: Duke University Press, 2002.

Brubaker, Rogers, and Frederick Cooper. "Beyond 'Identity.'" *Theory & Society* 29 (2000): 1–47.

Buechler, Steven M. "New Social Movement Theories." *Sociological Quarterly* 36, no. 3 (June 1, 1995): 441–64. https://doi.org/10.1111/j.1533-8525.1995.tb00447.x.

Bull, Chris. "A Matter of Life and Death." *The Advocate*, March 16, 1999.

Bunch, Charlotte. "Women's Rights as Human Rights: Toward a Re-vision of Human Rights." *Human Rights Quarterly* 12 (1990): 486.

Burack, Cynthia. *Tough Love: Sexuality, Compassion, and the Christian Right*. Albany: State University of New York Press, 2014.

Burns, Katelyn. "The Rise of Anti-Trans 'Radical' Feminists, Explained." *Vox News*, September 5, 2019, https://www.vox.com/identities/2019/9/5/20840101/terfs-radical-feminists-gender-critical.

Butler, Judith. "Against Proper Objects." *Differences* 6, no. 2 (1994): 1–26.

Butler, Judith. *Excitable Speech: A Politics of the Performative*. New York: Routledge, 1997.

Butler, Judith. *Gender Trouble: Feminism and the Subversion of Identity*. New York: Routledge, 1990.

Califia, Patrick. *Sex Changes: Transgender Politics*. Jersey City, NJ: Cleis Press, 2013.

Canaday, Margot. *The Straight State: Sexuality and Citizenship in Twentieth-Century America*. Princeton, NJ: Princeton University Press, 2009.

Carter, David. *Stonewall: The Riots That Sparked the Gay Revolution*. New York: St. Martin's Press, 2010.

Chase, Wilda. "Lesbianism and Feminism." *The Ladder* 14, nos. 3–4 (1969–70).

Cho, Sumi, Kimberlé Williams Crenshaw, and Leslie McCall. "Toward a Field of Intersectionality Studies: Theory, Applications, and Praxis." *Signs* 38, no. 4 (2013): 785–810. https://doi.org/10.1086/669608.

Chrystos. "I Don't Understand Those Who Have Turned Away from Me." In *This Bridge Called My Back*, edited by Cherríe L. Moraga and Gloria E. Anzaldúa, 65–67. Berkeley, CA: Third Woman Press, 2002.

Condrington III, Wilfred . "The Electoral College's Racist Origins," *The Atlantic*, November 17, 2019.

Cohen, Cathy J. *The Boundaries of Blackness: AIDS and the Breakdown of Black Politics.* Chicago: University of Chicago Press, 1999.

Cohen, Cathy J. "Punks, Bulldaggers, and Welfare Queens: The Radical Potential of Queer Politics?" *GLQ: A Journal of Lesbian and Gay Studies* 3, no. 4 (May 1, 1997): 437–65. https://doi.org/10.1215/10642684-3-4-437.

Cohen, Cathy. "The Radical Potential of Queer? Twenty Years Later." *GLQ: A Journal of Lesbian and Gay Studies* 25, no. 1 (2019): 140–44.

Cohen, Elizabeth F. *Semi-Citizenship in Democratic Politics.* Cambridge: Cambridge University Press, 2009.

Cohen, Elizabeth F., and Cyril Ghosh. *Citizenship.* Medford, MA: Polity Press, 2019.

Combahee River Collective. "The Combahee River Collective Statement of 1977." In *Home Girls: A Black Feminist Anthology*, edited by Barbara Smith, 265–74. Kitchen Table/Women of Color Press, 1983.

Compton, Julie. "Controversy Flies over Philadelphia's New Pride Flag." *NBC News*, June 15, 2017, https://www.nbcnews.com/feature/nbc-out/controversy-flies-over-philadelphia-s-new-pride-flag-n772821.

Collins, Patricia Hill. *Black Feminist Thought: Knowledge, Consciousness, and the Politics of Empowerment.* New York: Routledge, 2002.

Collins, Patricia Hill. *Black Sexual Politics: African Americans, Gender, and the New Racism.* New York: Routledge, 2004.

Collins, Patricia Hill. *Fighting Words: Black Women and the Search for Justice.* Vol. 7. Minneapolis: University of Minnesota Press, 1998.

Collins, Patricia Hill. "Like One of the Family: Race, Ethnicity, and the Paradox of US National Identity." *Ethnic and Racial Studies* 24, no. 1 (2001): 3–28. https://doi.org/10.1080/014198701750052479.

Condrington III, Wilfred. "The Electoral College's Racist Origins," *The Atlantic*, November 17, 2019.

Connolly, William E. *Identity\Difference: Democratic Negotiations of Political Paradox.* Expanded revised edition. Minneapolis: University of Minnesota Press, 2002.

Cooper, Brittney C. *Beyond Respectability: The Intellectual Thought of Race Women.* Urbana: University of Illinois Press, 2017.

Cornell, Drucilla. "Bodily Integrity and the Right to Abortion." In *Identities, Politics, and Rights*, edited by Austin Sarat and Thomas R. Kearns, 21–84. Amherst Series in Law, Jurisprudence, and Social Thought. Ann Arbor: University of Michigan Press, 1995.

Crenshaw, Kimberle. "Demarginalizing the Intersection of Race and Sex: A Black Feminist Critique of Antidiscrimination Doctrine, Feminist Theory and Antiracist Politics." *University of Chicago Legal Forum* 1989, (1989): 139–67.

Crenshaw, K. "Mapping the Margins: Intersectionality, Identity Politics, and Violence against Women of Color." *Stanford Law Review* 43, no. 6 (1991): 1241–99.

Currah, Paisley. *Sex Is as Sex Does: Governing Transgender Identity.* New York: NYU Press, 2022.

Dahl, Adam. *Empire of the People: Settler Colonialism and the Foundations of Modern Democratic Thought.* Lawrence: University Press of Kansas, 2018.

Dahl, Robert. *A Preface to Democratic Theory*. Chicago: University of Chicago Press, 1956.

Daly, Mary. *Gyn/Ecology: The Metaphysics of Radical Feminism*. Boston: Beacon Press, 1978.

Daum, Courtenay W. *The Politics of Right Sex: Transgressive Bodies, Governmentality, and the Limits of Trans Rights*. Albany: State University of New York Press, 2020.

Davis, Angela Y. *Abolition Democracy: Beyond Empire, Prisons, and Torture*. New York: Seven Stories Press, 2011.

Davis, Angela Y. *Freedom Is a Constant Struggle: Ferguson, Palestine, and the Foundations of a Movement*. Chicago: Haymarket Books, 2016.

Davis, Heath Fogg. *Beyond Trans: Does Gender Matter?* New York: NYU Press, 2017.

Davis, Madeline, and Elizabeth Lapovsky Kennedy. *Boots of Leather, Slippers of Gold: The History of a Lesbian Community*. New York: Routledge, 1993.

Delany, Samuel R. *Times Square Red, Times Square Blue*. 20th anniversary edition. New York: NYU Press, 2019.

D'Emilio, John. *Sexual Politics, Sexual Communities: The Making of a Homosexual Minority in the United States, 1940–1970*. Chicago: University of Chicago Press, 1983.

Desmoines, Harriet. "Notes for a Magazine." *Sinister Wisdom* 1, no. 1 (July 1976).

Dhamoon, Rita Kaur. "Considerations on Mainstreaming Intersectionality." *Political Research Quarterly* 64, no. 1 (March 1, 2011): 230–43. https://doi.org/10.1177/10659 12910379227.

"DHS Releases End of Fiscal Year 2015 Statistics," U.S. Immigration and Customs Enforcement, December 22, 2015, https://www.ice.gov/news/releases/dhs-releases-end-fiscal-year-2015-statistics.

Disch, Lisa. "The Impurity of Representation and the Vitality of Democracy." *Cultural Studies* 26, nos. 2–3 (2012): 207–22.

Donaldson, Stephen, Perry Brass, and John Knobel, eds. *The Come Out!* Reader. New York: Christopher Street Press, 2012.

Duberman, Martin Bauml. *Stonewall*. New York: Plume, 1994.

Duggan, Lisa. *The Twilight of Equality? Neoliberalism, Cultural Politics, and the Attack on Democracy*. Boston: Beacon Press, 2004.

Echols, Alice. *Daring to Be Bad*. Minneapolis: University of Minnesota Press, 1989. https://www.upress.umn.edu/book-division/books/daring-to-be-bad.

Eng, David. *The Feeling of Kinship: Queer Liberalism and the Racialization of Intimacy*. Durham, NC: Duke University Press, 2010.

Engel, Stephen M. *Fragmented Citizens: The Changing Landscape of Gay and Lesbian Lives*. New York: NYU Press, 2019.

Engel, Steven M., and Timothy S. Lyle. *Disrupting Dignity: Rethinking Power and Progress in LGBTQ Lives*. New York: NYU Press, 2021.

Enke, Finn. "Collective Memory and the Transfeminist 1970s." *TSQ: Transgender Studies Quarterly* 5, no. 1 (February 1, 2018): 9–29.

Ennis, Dawn. "Booking Jennicet Was Wrong, but Was What She Did Worse?," *Advocate*, July 1, 2015.

Enke, A. Finn. "The Education of Little Cis." In *Transfeminist Perspectives In and Beyond Transgender or Gender Studies, edited by A Finn. Enke*, 60-77. Philadelphia: Temple University Press, 2012.

Ewing, Eve L. "I'm a Black Scholar Who Studies Race. Here's Why I Capitalize White." *Medium*. July 2, 2020. https://zora.medium.com/im-a-black-scholar-who-studies-race-here-s-why-i-capitalize-white-f94883aa2dd3.

Faderman, Lillian. *Odd Girls and Twilight Lovers*. New York: Columbia University Press, 1991.

Feinberg, Leslie. "Transgender Liberation: A Movement Whose Time Has Come." In *The Transgender Studies Reader*, edited by Susan Stryker and Stephen Whittle, 205–20. New York: Routledge, 2006.

Fernandes, Leela. "Unsettling 'Third Wave Feminism.'" In *No Permanent Waves*, edited by Nancy A. Hewitt, 98–118. New Brunswick, NJ: Rutgers University Press, 2010.

Fetner, Tina. *How the Religious Right Shaped Lesbian and Gay Activism*. Minneapolis: University of Minnesota Press, 2008.

Flores, Andrew R., Donald P. Haider-Markel, Daniel C. Lewis, Patrick R. Miller, Barry L. Tadlock, and Jami K. Taylor. "Transgender Prejudice Reduction and Opinions on Transgender Rights: Results from a Mediation Analysis on Experimental Data." *Research & Politics* 5, no. 1 (January 2018). https://doi.org/10.1177/2053168018764945.

Foucault, Michel. "The Subject and Power." *Critical Inquiry* 8, no. 4 (1982): 777–95.

Fraser, Nancy. "Recognition or Redistribution? A Critical Reading of Iris Young's Justice and the Politics of Difference." *Journal of Political Philosophy* 3 (1995): 166–80.

Gallagher, John. "The Transgender Revolution." *The Advocate*, December 10, 1996.

Gambino, Elena. "Politics as 'Sinister Wisdom': Reparation and Responsibility in Lesbian Feminism." *Contemporary Political Theory* 20, no. 3 (September 2021): 524–46. https://doi.org/10.1057/s41296-020-00457-7.

Gamson, Joshua. "Must Identity Movements Self-Destruct? A Queer Dilemma." *Social Problems* 42, no. 3 (1995): 390–407.

Gamson, William A. *The Strategy of Social Protest*. Homewood, IL: The Dorsey Press, 1975.

Gash, Alison L. *Below the Radar: How Silence Can Save Civil Rights*. New York: Oxford University Press, 2015.

Gill-Peterson, Julian. *Histories of the Transgender Child*. Minneapolis: University of Minnesota Press, 2018.

Goffman, Erving. *Frame Analysis: An Essay on the Organization of Experience*. Cambridge, MA: Harvard University Press, 1974.

Gould, Deborah B. *Moving Politics: Emotion and ACT UP's Fight against AIDS*. Chicago: University of Chicago Press, 2009.

Greer, Germaine. *The Female Eunuch*. London: MacGibbon and Kee, 1970.

Gutiérrez, Jennicet. "No Pride in Detention of Transgender, Queer Communities," *Washington Blade,* June 15, 2022, https://www.washingtonblade.com/2022/06/15/to-biden-no-pride-in-detention-of-transgender-queer-communities/.

Halberstam, Jack. *Trans: A Quick and Quirky Account of Gender Variability*. Vol. 3. Berkeley: University of California Press, 2017.

Hancock, Ange-Marie. "Empirical Intersectionality: A Tale of Two Approaches." *University of California Irvine Law Review* 312 (October 2013): 259–94.

Hancock, Ange-Marie. *Intersectionality: An Intellectual History*. New York: Oxford University Press, 2016.

Hancock, Ange-Marie. "Intersectionality as a Normative and Empirical Paradigm." *Politics & Gender* 3, no. 2 (2007): 248–53.

Hancock, Ange-Marie. *The Politics of Disgust: The Public Identity of the Welfare Queen*. New York: NYU Press, 2004.

Hanhardt, Christina. *Safe Space: Gay Neighborhood History and the Politics of Violence*. Durham, NC: Duke University Press, 2013.

Harris Perry, Melissa V. *Sister Citizen: Shame, Stereotypes, and Black Women in America.* New Haven, CT: Yale University Press, 2011.

Harrison, Brian F., and Melissa R. Michelson. *Listen, We Need to Talk: How to Change Attitudes about LGBT Rights.* New York: Oxford University Press, 2017.

Heaney, Michael T., and Geoffrey M. Lorenz. "Coalition Portfolios and Interest Group Influence over the Policy Process." *Interest Groups & Advocacy* 2, no. 3 (2013): 251–77. https://doi.org/10.1057/iga.2013.7.

Higginbotham, Evelyn Brooks. *Righteous Discontent: The Women's Movement in the Black Baptist Church, 1880–1920.* Cambridge, MA: Harvard University Press, 1993.

Hillman, Betty Luther. "'The Most Revolutionary Act a Homosexual Can Engage In': Drag and the Politics of Gender Presentation in the San Francisco Gay Liberation Movement, 1964–1972." *Journal of the History of Sexuality* 20, no. 1 (2011): 153–81.

Hindman, Matthew Dean. *Political Advocacy and Its Interested Citizens: Neoliberalism, Postpluralism, and LGBT Organizations.* Philadelphia: University of Pennsylvania Press, 2018.

Hinojosa, Maria. "Obama Leaves Office as 'Deporter in Chief.'" *NPR,* January 20, 2017, https://www.npr.org/2017/01/20/510799842/obama-leaves-office-as-deporter-in-chief.

Hobson, Emily K. *Lavender and Red: Liberation and Solidarity in the Gay and Lesbian Left.* Vol. 44. Berkeley: University of California Press, 2016.

Hojnacki, Marie. "Organized Interests' Advocacy Behavior in Alliances." *Political Research Quarterly* 51, no. 2 (1998): 437–59.

Hollibaugh, Amber, and Cherrie Moraga. "What We're Rollin' Around in Bed With: Sexual Silences in Feminism." *Heresies* 12 (1981): 58–62.

Jagose, Annamarie, and Don Kulick. "Thinking Sex/Thinking Gender: Introduction." *GLQ: A Journal of Lesbian and Gay Studies* 10, no. 2 (2004): 211–12.

"Jim Obergefell Responds to Supreme Court Decision on Same-Sex Marriage." *PBS Newshour,* June 26, 2015, https://www.youtube.com/watch?v=qMxWLJGuPJk&t=226s.

Johnston, Laurie. "Mrs. Friedan's Essay Irks Feminists," *New York Times,* March 8, 1973.

Jones, Alexi. "Visualizing the Unequal Treatment of LGBTQ People in the Criminal Justice System," *Prison Policy Initiative,* March 2, 2021, https://www.prisonpolicy.org/blog/2021/03/02/lgbtq/

Julien, Isaac, and Kobena Mercer. "True Confessions: A Discourse on Images of Black Male Sexuality." In *Brother to Brother: New Writings by Black Gay Men,* edited by Essex Hemphill, 167–73. Boston: Alyson Publications, 1991.

Junn, Jane. "The Trump Majority: White Womanhood and the Making of Female Voters in the US." *Politics, Groups, and Identities* 5, no. 2 (2017): 343–52.

Keating, Cricket. "Building Coalitional Consciousness." *NWSA Journal* 17, no. 2 (2005): 86–103.

Kissack, Terrance. "Freaking Fag Revolutionaries: New York's Gay Liberation Front, 1969–1971." *Radical History Review,* no. 62 (1995): 104–34.

Klandermans, Bert. "New Social Movements and Resource Mobilization: The European and American Approach Revisited." *Politics & the Individual* 1, no. 2 (1986): 13–37.

Klandermans, P. G. "Identity Politics and Politicized Identities: Identity Processes and the Dynamics of Protest." *Political Psychology* 35, no. 1 (2014): 1–22.

Kornegger, Peggy. "Peggy Kornegger." *Sinister Wisdom* 1, no. 4 (Fall 1977).

Kramer, Sina. *Excluded Within: The (Un)Intelligibility of Radical Political Actors.* New York: Oxford University Press, 2017.

Kunzel, Regina. *Criminal Intimacy: Prison and the Uneven History of Modern American Sexuality.* Chicago: University of Chicago Press, 2008.

"Latine vs Latinx: How and Why They're Used." Dictionary.com. September 26, 2023. https://www.dictionary.com/e/latine-vs-latinx/.

Lee, Trymaine. "A Vast Wealth Gap, Driven by Segregation, Redlining, Evictions and Exclusion, Separates Black and While America." *New York Times*, August 14, 2019. https://www.nytimes.com/interactive/2019/08/14/magazine/racial-wealth-gap.html.

Lorde, Audrey. "The Master's Tools Will Never Dismantle the Master's House." In *This Bridge Called My Back*, edited by Cherríe L. Moraga and Gloria E. Anzaldúa, 94–103. Berkeley, CA: Third Woman Press, 2002.

Lowe, Lisa. *Immigrant Acts: On Asian American Cultural Politics.* Durham, NC: Duke University Press, 1996.

Luibheid, Eithne. "Introduction: Queering Migration and Citizenship." In *Queer Migrations: Sexuality, U.S. Citizenship, and Border Crossings*, edited by Eithne Luibheid and Lionel Cantú, ix–xlvi. Minneapolis: University of Minnesota Press, 2005.

Magni, Gabriele, and Andrew Reynolds. "Voter Preferences and the Political Underrepresentation of Minority Groups: Lesbian, Gay, and Transgender Candidates in Advanced Democracies." *The Journal of Politics* 84, no. 4 (October 2021).

Malatino, Hil. *Side Affects: On Being Trans and Feeling Bad.* Minneapolis: University Of Minnesota Press, 2022.

Mantler, Gordon K. *Power to the Poor: Black-Brown Coalition and the Fight for Economic Justice, 1960–1974.* Chapel Hill: University of North Carolina Press, 2013.

Marcus, Eric. *Making Gay History: The Half Century Fight for Lesbian and Gay Equal Rights.* Reprint edition. New York: Harper Perennial, 2002.

Marshall, T. H. *Class, Citizenship, and Social Development: Essays by T. H. Marshall.* New York: Doubleday, 1965.

Martin, Del. "If That's All There Is." *The Ladder* 15, nos. 3–4 (December–January 1970–71).

Martin, Del, and Phyllis Lyon. *Lesbian/Woman.* 4th edition. New York: Bantam Books, 1977.

Matsuda, Mari J. *Where Is Your Body? And Other Essays on Race, Gender, and the Law.* Boston: Beacon Press, 1997.

Mayo-Adam, Erin. *Queer Alliances: How Power Shapes Political Movement Formation.* Palo Alto, CA: Stanford University Press, 2020.

McAdam, Doug. *Political Process and the Development of Black Insurgency.* Chicago: University of Chicago Press, 1982.

McAdam, Doug, John D. McCarthy, and Mayer N. Zald, eds. *Comparative Perspectives on Social Movements: Political Opportunities, Mobilizing Structures, and Cultural Framings.* Cambridge: Cambridge University Press, 1996.

McCall, Leslie. "The Complexity of Intersectionality." *Signs: Journal of Women in Culture and Society* 30, no. 3 (2005): 1771–800.

Mello, Joseph. *The Courts, the Ballot Box, and Gay Rights: How Our Governing Institutions Shape the Same-Sex Marriage Debate.* Lawrence: University Press of Kansas, 2016.

Melucci, Alberto. *Nomads of the Present.* Philadelphia, PA: Temple University Press, 1989.

Meyer, David S., and Suzanne Staggenborg. "Movements, Countermovements, and the Structure of Political Opportunity." *American Journal of Sociology* 101, no. 6 (1996): 1628–60.

Meyerowitz, Joanne J. *How Sex Changed: A History of Transsexuality in the United States*. Cambridge, MA: Harvard University Press, 2002.

Miller, Neil. *Out of the Past: Gay and Lesbian History from 1869 to the Present*. New York: Alyson Books, 2006.

Minero, Laura P., Sergio Domínguez Jr., Stephanie L. Budge, and Bamby Salcedo. "Latinx Trans Immigrants' Survival of Torture in U.S. Detention: A Qualitative Investigation of the psychological abuse and mistreatment." *International Journal of Transgender Health* 23, nos. 1–2 (2022): 36–59.

Mock, Janet. *Redefining Realness: My Path to Womanhood, Identity, Love and So Much More*. Reprint edition. New York: Atria Books, 2014.

Moraga, Cherríe L. "Catching Fire: Preface to the Fourth Edition." In *This Bridge Called My Back*, edited by Cherríe L. Moraga and Gloria E. Anzaldúa, xv–xxvi. 4th edition. Albany: State University of New York Press, 2015.

Moraga, Cherríe L. "La Jornada." In *This Bridge Called My Back*, edited by Cherríe L. Moraga and Gloria E. Anzaldúa, xxxv–xxxviii. 4th edition. Albany: State University of New York Press, 2015.

Morgan, Robin. *Going Too Far: The Personal Chronicle of a Feminist*. New York: Random House, 1977.

Morgensen, Scott Lauria. *Spaces between Us: Queer Settler Colonialism and Indigenous Decolonization*. Minneapolis: University of Minnesota Press, 2011.

Moyer, Justin Wm. "Transgender Obama Heckler Jennicet Gutierrez Hailed by Some LGBT Activists." *Washington Post*, June 26, 2015.

Murdoch, Joyce, and Deb Price. *Courting Justice: Gay Men and Lesbians v. the Supreme Court*. New York: Basic Books, 2002.

National Gay and Lesbian Task Force, "General Information." February 4, 1999, http://web.archive.org/web/19990202042554/http://www.ngltf.org/gi.html.

Nestle, Joan. "Butch-Femme Relationships: Sexual Courage in the 1950's." *Heresies* 12 (1981): 21–25.

Newton, Huey P. "A Letter to Revolutionary Brothers and Sisters about the Women's Liberation and Gay Liberation Movements." In *Traps: African American Men on Gender and Sexuality*, edited by Rudolph P. Byrd and Beverly Guy-Sheftall, 281–83. Indianapolis: University of Indiana Press, 2001.

"NGLTF Convenes Third National Policy Roundtable." *Oasis Magazine*, 1998. Accessed using The Internet Archive: www.waybackmachine.org.

Norton, Anne. *Reflections on Political Identity*. Baltimore, MD: Johns Hopkins University Press, 1988.

Novkov, Julie. "Sacrifice and Civic Membership: The War on Terror (2010)." Paper presented at APSA 2010 Annual Meeting. Available at https://ssrn.com/abstract=1643175.

Panizza, Francisco, and Romina Miorelli. "Taking Discourse Seriously: Discursive Institutionalism and Post-Structuralist Discourse Theory." *Political Studies* 61, no. 2 (2013): 301–18. https://doi.org/10.1111/j.1467-9248.2012.00967.x.

Perez, Laura M. "Go Ahead: Make My Movement." In *Bisexual Politics: Theories, Queries, and Visions*, edited by Naomi S. Tucker, Liz Highleyman, and Rebecca Kaplan, 109–14. New York: Haworth Press, 1995.

Phelan, Shane. "(Be)Coming Out: Lesbian Identity and Politics." *Signs: Journal of Women in Culture and Society* 18, no. 4 (1993): 765–90.

Pierceson, Jason. *Before Bostock: The Accidental Precedent of Price Waterhouse v. Hopkins*. Lawrence: University Press of Kansas, 2022.

Polletta, Francesca, and James M. Jasper. "Collective Identity and Social Movements." *Annual Review of Sociology* 27 (2001): 282–305.

Raymond, Janice G. *The Transsexual Empire: The Making of the She-Male.* New York: Teachers College Press, 1979.

Reagon, Bernice Johnson. "Coalition Politics: Turning the Century." In *Home Girls: A Black Feminist Anthology,* edited by Barbara Smith, 356–68. New York: Kitchen Table/ Women of Color, 1981.

Reddy, Chandan. *Freedom with Violence: Race, Sexuality, and the U.S. State.* Durham, NC: Duke University Press, 2011.

Reger, Jo. "Identity Work, Sameness, and Difference in Social Movements." In *Identity Work in Social Movements,* edited by Jo Reger, Daniel J. Myers, and Rachel L. Einwohner, 1–17. Minneapolis: University of Minnesota Press, 2008.

Reger, Jo. "Organizational Dynamics and Construction of Multiple Feminist Identities in the National Organization for Women." *Gender and Society* 16, no. 5 (October 2002): 710–27.

Reger, Jo, Daniel J. Myers, and Rachel L. Einwohner, eds. *Identity Work in Social Movements.* Minneapolis: University of Minnesota Press, 2008.

Ridinger, Robert B., ed. *Speaking for Our Lives: Historic Speeches and Rhetoric for Gay and Lesbian Rights (1892–2000).* New York: Harrington Park Press, 2004.

Robinson, Cedric J. *Black Marxism: The Making of the Black Radical Tradition.* Chapel Hill: University of North Carolina Press, 2020.

Rodriguez, Matthew. "I Stand with Obama Heckler Jennicet Gutierrez." *Advocate,* June 26, 2015.

Rogin, Michael. *Blackface, White Noise: Jewish Immigrants in the Hollywood Melting Pot.* Berkeley: University of California Press, 1996.

Rosales, Steven. "Fighting the Peace at Home: Mexican American Veterans and the 1944 GI Bill of Rights." *Pacific Historical Review* 80, no. 4 (November 1, 2011): 597–627. https://doi.org/10.1525/phr.2011.80.4.597.

Rubin, Gayle. "Of Catamites and Kings: Reflections on Butch, Gender, and Boundaries." In *The Persistent Desire: A Femme-Butch Reader,* edited by Joan Nestle, 466–82. Boston: Alyson, 1992.

Salsa Soul Sisters. "A Lesbian Show," *Azalea* 1, no. 2 (Spring 1978).

Sathanson, Jessica. "Pride and Politics: Revisiting the Northampton Pride March, 1989– 1993." *Journal of Bisexuality* 2, nos. 2–3 (October 17, 2001): 143–61. https://doi.org/ 10.1300/J159v02n02_10.

Schattschneider, Eric E. *The Semisovereign People: A Realist's View of Democracy in America.* Revised edition. Hinsdale, IL: Wadsworth, 1975.

Schwartz-Shea, Peregrine, and Dvora Yanow. *Interpretive Research Design: Concepts and Processes.* New York: Routledge, 2013.

Shelley, Martha. "Martha Shelley." *Sinister Wisdom* 1, no. 3 (Spring 1977).

Shelley, Martha. "Stepin Fetchit Woman." *Come Out!* 1, no. 1 (November 1969).

Shklar, Judith N. *American Citizenship: The Quest for Inclusion.* Cambridge, MA: Harvard University Press, 1991.

Simien, Evelyn M. "Doing Intersectionality Research: From Conceptual Issues to Practical Examples." *Politics & Gender* 3, no. 2 (June 2007): 264–71. https://doi.org/ 10.1017/S1743923X07000086.

Smith, Charles Anthony, Shawn Schulenberg, and Eric A. Baldwin. 2017. "The 'B' Isn't Silent." In *LGBTQ Politics: A Critical Reader,* edited by Marla Brettschneider, Susan Burgess, and Christine Keating, 89–109. New York: NYU Press.

Smith, Barbara. "Toward a Black Feminist Criticism." *Radical Teacher*, no. 7 (March 1978): 20–27.

Smith, Christian, and Michael Emerson. *American Evangelicalism: Embattled and Thriving*. Chicago: University of Chicago Press, 1998.

Smith, Rogers M. *Stories of Peoplehood: The Politics and Morals of Political Membership*. Cambridge: Cambridge University Press, 2003.

Snorton, C. Riley. *Black on Both Sides: A Racial History of Trans Identity*. Minneapolis: University of Minnesota Press, 2017.

Somerville, Siobhan. "Sexual Aliens and the Racialized State: A Queer Reading of the 1952 U.S. Immigration and Nationality Act." In *Queer Migrations: Sexuality, U.S. Citizenship, and Border Crossings*, edited by Eithne Luibheid and Lionel Cantú, 75–91. Minneapolis: University of Minnesota Press, 2005.

Soss, Joe. *Unwanted Claims: The Politics of Participation in the U.S. Welfare System*. Ann Arbor: University of Michigan Press, 2002.

Spade, Dean. "Fighting to Win." In *That's Revolting! Queer Strategies for Resisting Assimilation*, edited by Matilda Bernstein Sycamore, 47–53. Berkeley, CA: Soft Skull, 2004.

Spade, Dean. "Mutilating Gender." In *Transgender Studies Reader*, edited by Susan Stryker and Stephen Whittle, 315–32. New York: Routledge, 2006.

Spade, Dean. *Normal Life: Administrative Violence, Critical Trans Politics and the Limits of Law*. Boston: South End Press, 2011.

Spivak, Gayatri Chakravorty. *Outside in the Teaching Machine*. New York: Routledge, 2012.

Springvine, Leslie. "Out from under the Rocks with Guns!," *The Ladder* 14, nos. 3–4 (December 1969–January 1970).

Stack, Liam. "Activist Removed after Heckling Obama at L.G.B.T. Event." *New York Times*, June 24, 2015.

Stoller, Robert J. *Sex and Gender: The Development of Masculinity and Femininity*. London: Karmac Books, 1994.

Stone, Amy L. *Gay Rights at the Ballot Box*. Minneapolis: University of Minnesota Press, 2012. https://www.upress.umn.edu/book-division/books/gay-rights-at-the-ballot-box.

Strolovitch, Dara Z. *Affirmative Advocacy: Race, Class, and Gender in Interest Group Politics*. Chicago: University of Chicago Press, 2007.

Strolovitch, Dara Z., and Chaya Y. Crowder. "Respectability, Anti-Respectability, and Intersectionally Responsible Representation." *PS: Political Science & Politics* 51, no. 2 (April 2018): 340–44. https://doi.org/10.1017/S1049096517002487.

Strolovitch, Dara Z., Janelle S. Wong, and Andrew Proctor. "A Possessive Investment in White Heteropatriarchy? The 2016 Election and the Politics of Race, Gender, and Sexuality." *Politics, Groups, and Identities* 5, no. 2 (2017): 353–63.

Stryker, Sheldon. "Identity Competition: Key to Differential Social Movement Participation." In *Self, Identity, and Social Movement*, edited by Sheldon Stryker, Timothy J. Owens, and Robert W. White, 21–40. Minneapolis: University of Minnesota Press, 2000.

Stryker, Sheldon, Timothy Joseph Owens, and Robert W. White, eds. *Self, Identity, and Social Movements*. Minneapolis: University of Minnesota Press, 2000.

Stryker, Susan. "Introduction." *TSQ: Transgender Studies Quarterly* 7, no. 3 (August 1, 2020): 299–305. https://doi.org/10.1215/23289252-8552908.

Stryker, Susan. "My Words to Victor Frankenstein Above the Village of Chamounix, *GLQ* 1, no. 3 (1994): 237–54.

Stryker, Susan. *Transgender History*. Berkeley, CA: Seal Press, 2008.

Stryker, Susan. "Transgender History, Homonormativity, and Disciplinarity." *Radical History Review* 2008, no. 100 (December 21, 2008): 145–57. https://doi.org/10.1215/01636545-2007-026.

Suran, Justin. "Coming Out against the War: Antimilitarism and the Politicization of Homosexuality in the Era of Vietnam." *American Quarterly* 53, no. 3 (2001): 452–88.

Tajfel, Henri, and J. C. Turner. "The Social Identity Theory of Inter-Group Behavior." In *Psychology of Intergroup Relations*, edited by Stephen Worchel and William G. Austin, 7–24. Chicago: Nelson Hall, 1986.

Tarrow, Sidney. *Power in Movement: Social Movements and Contentious Politics*. 2nd edition. Cambridge: Cambridge University Press, 1998.

Taylor, Keeanga-Yamahtta. *From #BlackLivesMatter to Black Liberation*. Chicago: Haymarket Books, 2016.

Taylor, Keeanga-Yamahtta. *How We Get Free: Black Feminism and the Combahee River Collective*. Chicago: Haymarket Books, 2017.

"Taylor Swift Calls Out Trump in VMAs Speech," *ET Canada*, August 27, 2019, https://www.youtube.com/watch?v=YtYTKSHQVBQ.

Taylor, Verta, and Nancy Whittier. "Collective Identity in Social Movement Communities: Lesbian Feminist Mobilization." In *Frontiers in Social Movement Theory*, edited by Carol McClurg Mueller and Aldon D. Morris, 104–29. New Haven, CT: Yale University Press, 1992.

Teal, Donn. *The Gay Militants*. New York: Stein and Day, 1971.

Tilly, Charles. *From Mobilization to Revolution*. New York: McGraw Hill, 1978.

Tobin, Kay, and Randy Wicker. *Gay Crusaders*. Reprint edition. New York: Arno Press, 1975.

Truman, David Bicknell. *The Governmental Process: Political Interests and Public Opinion*. New York: Knopf, 1951.

Urbinati, Nadia. "Representation as Advocacy: A Study of Democratic Deliberation." *Political Theory* 28, no. 6 (December 2000): 758–86.

Valentine, David. *Imagining Transgender: An Ethnography of a Category*. Durham, NC: Duke University Press Books, 2007.

Walsh, Katherine Cramer. *Talking about Politics: Informal Groups and Social Identity in American Life*. Chicago: University of Chicago Press, 2004.

Ward, Jane. *Not Gay: Sex between Straight White Men*. Vol. 19. New York: NYU Press, 2015.

Ward, Jane. *Respectably Queer: Diversity Culture in LGBT Activist Organizations*. Nashville, TN: Vanderbilt University Press, 2008.

Warner, Michael. *Fear of a Queer Planet: Queer Politics and Social Theory*. Minneapolis: University of Minnesota Press, 1993.

Weber, Cynthia. *Queer International Relations: Sovereignty, Sexuality and the Will to Knowledge*. New York: Oxford University Press, 2016.

White House, "Fact Sheet: President Biden to Sign Historic Executive Order Advancing LGBTQI+ Equality During Pride Month," June 15, 2022, https://www.whitehouse.gov/briefing-room/statements-releases/2022/06/15/fact-sheet-president-biden-to-sign-historic-executive-order-advancing-lgbtqi-equality-during-pride-month/

White House, "Opening the People's House," September 24, 2014, https://obamawhitehouse.archives.gov/blog/2014/09/15/opening-peoples-house.

Wilchins, Riki Anne. *Read My Lips: Sexual Subversion and the End of Gender*. Ithaca, NY: Firebrand Books, 1997.

Williams, Melissa S. *Voice, Trust, and Memory: Marginalized Groups and the Failings of Liberal Representation*. Princeton, NJ: Princeton University Press, 1998.

Wittig, Monique. *The Straight Mind and Other Essays*. Boston: Beacon Press, 1992.

Wodak, Ruth. *Methods of Critical Discourse Analysis*. London: Sage, 2009.

Wolf, Deborah Goleman. *Lesbian Community*. Berkeley: University of California Press, 1979.

Wuest, Joanna. "The Scientific Gaze in American Transgender Politics: Contesting the Meanings of Sex, Gender, and Gender Identity in the Bathroom." *Politics & Gender* 15, no. 2 (2019): 336–60.

Wuest, Joanna. "'From Pathology to Born Perfect': Science, Law, and Citizenship in American LGBTQ + Advocacy." *Perspective on Politics* 19, no. 3 (2021): 838–53.

Yamada, Mitsuye. "Asian Pacific Women and Feminism." In *This Bridge Called My Back*, edited by Cherríe L. Moraga and Gloria E., 68–72. Anzaldúa. Berkeley, CA: Third Woman Press, 2002.

Yanow, Dvora, and Peregrine Schwartz-Shea. *Interpretation and Method: Empirical Research Methods and the Interpretive Turn*. New York: Routledge, 2015.

Young, Iris Marion. *Justice and the Politics of Difference*. Princeton, NJ: Princeton University Press, 1990.

Zivi, Karen. *Making Rights Claims: A Practice of Democratic Citizenship*. New York: Oxford University Press, 2011.

Index

Students for a Democratic Society, 41–42
Supreme Court, 1–3, 6, 137–38, 166–68,
    179, 191, 199, 225–28, 233, 236
Sweet Honey in the Rock, 101–2
Swift, Taylor, "You Need to Calm Down,"
    231–33

Tafel, Rich, 169–70, 216
Taylor, Keeanga-Yamahtta, 89–91
Taylor, Verta, 19–20, 77–78
Teena, Brandon, 162, 171–73
This Bridge Called My Back (ed. Moraga
    and Anzaldúa), 96–99
Transexual Menace (activist group), 156–
    59, 162
Transgender Nation (activist group),
    156–58
Transgender Officers Protect and Serve,
    184–85
transgender people, 144–45, 262n.20,
    262n.23, 262n.33, 263n.40
  access to healthcare, 265n.28
  anti-trans bills in US, 6–7
  criminalization of, 263n.43
  discrimination against, 11, 156–57
  identity and, 144–77
  inclusion in LGBT politics, 5, 7, 81–84,
    122–23, 125–30, 138–42, 144–45,
    161–66, 180, 185, 192–95, 199–200,
    202–3, 214–18, 221–24, 235–36,
    264n.65
  inclusion in Women's movement, 95,
    103–4, 233–35
  medicalization of, 152, 193–94, 223
  murder of transgender women of color,
    6–7
  representation and, 145–46,
    153–55, 156–57, 159–61, 162–63,
    176–77
  rights and, 145, 154–61, 162–63, 168–73,
    174–75, 233–35
  sexual assault and, 1–3, 225–26
  state documents and, 225–27
  stigma transformation and, 153–55,
    156–57, 171–73
  as umbrella category, 165–66,
    173–77
  violence against, 1–3, 156–57, 169–73
  See also gender identity *under* gender

Tucker, Naomi, *Bisexual Politics: Theories,
    Queries, and Visions*, 36–37

United Nations Declaration on Human
    Rights, 122, 144–45
universalizing, 17, 68, 80–81, 83, 85–86,
    95–97, 103–4, 152, 160–61, 187–89
University of Minnesota Tretter
    Collection, 36–37

Vaid, Urvashi, 178, 181–82, 191–92, 199–
    200, 201–2, 204, 205–6, 207–8
Valentine, David, 170–71
Vietnam War, 41–42, 46
visibility, 60–64, 105–6, 111, 230–31
voting, 6, 62–63, 137–38, 157–58, 169,
    210, 214–15, 232–33. *See also*
    electoral politics
Voting Rights Act, 6, 17–18, 27–28

War on Terror, 180–81
Warner, Michael, 163–65
Wayback Machine (www.waybackmach
    ine.com), 36–37
Weise, Beth Reba, 126–27, 129
West Coast Lesbian Feminist Conference,
    81–82
West Coast Women's Music Festival, 101–
    2, 234–35
White supremacy, 9, 17–18, 22–23, 41–42,
    68–69, 98–99, 187, 188–89, 193, 232–
    33, 236–38
Whittier, Nancy, 19–20, 77–78
Wilchins, Riki, 162–66, 169, 170–71, 176, 194
Williams, Melissa, 34
Wilson, Phil, 196, 197–99, 200–1
Wittig, Monique, 83
Wolf, Deborah Goleman, 79
"Woman-Identified Woman, The"
    (manifesto), 75–77
Women's Liberation movement, 40–42
  inclusion of lesbians, 67, 73–84
  inclusion of Black and Third World
    feminists, 88–100
  inclusion of transgender women, 81–84,
    95–96
  See also Black and Third World
    feminism; feminism; lesbians;
    transgender people